D1346248

Rider Haggard

Edited by the same author

The Private Diaries of Sir Henry Rider Haggard

Rider Haggard:
The Great Storyteller

D.S. Higgins

CASSELL
LONDON

CASSELL LTD.
35 Red Lion Square, London WC1R 4SG
and at Sydney, Auckland, Toronto, Johannesburg
an affiliate of
Macmillan Publishing Co., Inc.,
New York.

First published 1981

ISBN 0 304 30827 7

Typeset by Inforum Ltd, Portsmouth
Printed and bound in Great Britain by
Richard Clay (The Chaucer Press) Ltd
Bungay, Suffolk

*To
Antoinette*

Acknowledgements

I should like to thank the many people who have helped me with this work, especially Professor Angus Wilson, Professor Richard Shannon, Professor Malcolm Bradbury, Mr John Ridgard, Mr D.H. Simpson, Mr Michael Horniman, Mr P.H. Muir, Dr Brian Goodge, and Mr Robert Lambourne. I am also grateful to the indexer, Ann Edwards.

For access to holographs and other material I am indebted to the staffs of the Norfolk Record Office; the University of East Anglia; the Henry E. Huntingdon Library, San Marino, California; Columbia University Library; the Royal Commonwealth Society; A.P. Watt & Son; Cassell Ltd.; and Suffolk County Council Library.

I thankfully acknowledge assistance from the Arts Council of Great Britain which allowed me to dedicate far more time to the research for this book than would have otherwise been possible.

Finally, for their hospitality, kindness and encouragement, I gratefully thank Commander and Mrs Mark Cheyne of Ditchingham House.

Contents

Illustrations

All photographs not otherwise acknowledged are reproduced by kind permission of Commander M.E. Cheyne, DSC, RN, DL.

Haggard's Published Works

This list of Haggard's publications is divided into three
sections. Titles of non-fiction works are given in capitals.

Year Written		First British Book Publication
	1882-1889 *'A deep but ill-comprehended need to write'*	
1882	CETYWAYO AND HIS WHITE NEIGHBOURS	22.6.1882
1883	Dawn	21.2.1884
1884	The Witch's Head	18.12.1884
1885	King Solomon's Mines	30.9.1885
1885	Allan Quatermain	1.7.1887
1885	Jess	3.1887
1886	She	1.1.1887
1886	Colonel Quaritch, V.C.	3.12.1888
1887	Cleopatra	24.6.1889
1887	Maiwa's Revenge	3.8.1888
1887/8	Beatrice	12.5.1890
1888	Mr Meeson's Will	10.1888
1888	Eric Brighteyes	13.5.1891
1888/9	The World's Desire (with Andrew Lang)	5.11.1890
1889	Allan's Wife	12.1889
1889/90	Nada the Lily	9.5.1892
	1890–1912 *'Pursuing interests in agriculture and ancient civilizations'*	
1891	Montezuma's Daughter	13.10.1893
1893	The People of the Mist	15.10.1894
1893/4	Heart of the World	27.3.1896
1894	Joan Haste	12.8.1895

Year Written		First British Book Publication
1895-7	Black Heart and White Heart and Other Stories	29.5.1900
1896	The Wizard	29.10.1896
1896	Swallow	1.3.1899
1898	A FARMER'S YEAR	2.10.1899
1898	Dr Therne	28.11.1898
1899	Lysbeth	11.4.1901
1899	Stella Fregelius	3.2.1904
1899	THE LAST BOER WAR (most material written in 1882)	20.10.1899
1900	A WINTER PILGRIMAGE	7.10.1901
1900/1	Pearl-Maiden	2.3.1903
1901/2	RURAL ENGLAND	28.11.1902
1903	The Brethren	30.9.1904
1903	A GARDENER'S YEAR	13.1.1905
1903	Ayesha	6.10.1905
1904	The Way of the Spirit	3.1906
1905	THE POOR AND THE LAND	18.8.1905
1905	Benita	7.9.1906
1905/6	Fair Margaret	9.9.1907
1906/7	The Ghost Kings	25.9.1908
1907	The Yellow God	5.3.1909
1907	The Lady of Blossholme	15.12.1909
1907/8	Morning Star	11.3.1910
1908	Queen Sheba's Ring	9.1910
1908/9	Red Eve	28.8.1911
1909	Child of Storm	21.1.1913
1909	Marie	25.1.1912
1910	REGENERATION	16.12.1910
1910/11	RURAL DENMARK	6.4.1911
1911	The Mahatma and the Hare	16.10.1911
1911/12	THE DAYS OF MY LIFE	7.10.1926

1912–1925
'Written while striving to serve his country'

1912	The Holy Flower	31.3.1915
1912	Smith and the Pharaohs and other stories (written in 1883 and 1905)	4.11.1920
1913	The Wanderer's Necklace	29.1.1914
1914	The Ivory Child	6.1.1916

Year Written		First British Book Publication
1915	*The Ancient Allan*	12.2.1920
1915	*Finished*	10.8.1917
1916	*Love Eternal*	4.4.1918
1916/7	*When the World Shook*	20.3.1919
1917	*Moon of Israel*	31.10.1918
1918	*She and Allan*	17.2.1921
1919/20	*The Virgin of the Sun*	26.1.1922
1920/21	*Wisdom's Daughter*	9.3.1923
1921/22	*Queen of the Dawn*	21.4.1925
1922/23	*Heu-Heu, or The Monster*	29.1.1924
1923	*The Treasure of the Lake*	9.1926
1923	*Allan and the Ice-Gods*	20.5.1927
1924	*Mary of Marion Isle*	4.1.1929
1924	*Belshazzar*	16.9.1930

Preface

On a cold winter's day in 1968, my wife, her father and I called at a junk-yard in Long Sutton, Lincolnshire, to buy a coal-scuttle. While my wife was searching through the ramshackle sheds I wandered with my father-in-law among the old furniture that was stacked outside. On top of a battered chest-of-drawers I found an old leather-bound album and with difficulty prised apart the rain-soaked pages. As I was peering at one of what was apparently a large collection of letters, my father-in-law said, 'Ditchingham House. That's where Rider Haggard used to live.' Peeling open the letter, I discovered that it was indeed signed by the man I knew only as the author of *King Solomon's Mines* and *She*. It was obvious that I could not inspect the letters further without damaging the wet pages, and so I asked the owner of the junk-yard how much she wanted for the album. She asked, in those pre-decimal days, five shillings. Although I tried to get her to take less, she adamantly refused. Eventually I borrowed the money from my father-in-law (for in those days, and on occasions since, I was exceptionally hard-up) and paid the woman what she had asked.

That evening, after the album had been carefully dried, I started to examine, with mounting excitement, the many letters it contained. Those written by and to Haggard were all but ignored, for I discovered that the collection, which I was later informed had been outside in the junk-yard for over three years and had been examined by hundreds of people, included several letters written by William and Dorothy Wordsworth. It appeared that, although over the years there had been several owners of the collection, it had been started by Christopher Wordsworth, the poet's nephew and literary executor, who became the Head of Harrow and later Bishop of Salisbury.

For years the Haggard letters, like those in the album from eminent Victorian churchmen and politicians, remained in my study virtually ignored. Then in 1974, while searching through an Ipswich second-hand bookshop for old children's books, I was asked if I was interested in purchasing some Rider Haggard first editions. Well aware of the good fortune he had brought me in the past, I said that I was and so I returned home with five books written by someone whose fiction I had not read since I was a young boy.

To my surprise I discovered that Haggard had written sixty-eight books and several Government reports. Even the titles of many of his publications were unknown to me. Fascinated, I decided to complete my collection of his works, and over the next eighteen months I was fortunately able to purchase first editions of all but the first three of Haggard's books. As I read them, I was most impressed by the range of his subjects and settings; but it was very clear that there was a most puzzling variation in the standard of his writing. I also found it difficult to understand why he was so obsessed by death and his quest for some form of immortality.

Determined to understand more, I began my investigations into Haggard's life. There was some essential introductory reading. *The Days of My Life*, Haggard's autobiography, is interesting but uneven and does not cover the last fifteen years of his life. Lilias Haggard, his youngest daughter, in *The Cloak That I Left*, provides a most readable and at times illuminating tribute to her father. Morton Cohen's *Rider Haggard — His Life and Works*, although published in 1960, is the only biography hitherto produced of any merit. These books, however, still left some mysteries unsolved.

Having decided to pursue my study of a man whose life and work fascinated me, I endeavoured to find collections of unpublished material apart from my own. From the Henry E. Huntington Library in San Marino, California, and from Columbia University Library I obtained microfilm of their Haggard material. I was also kindly permitted to examine and photocopy material owned by Commander Cheyne (Haggard's grandson), A.P. Watt and Sons, and Cassell Ltd. The major collection of Haggard documents, however, is held by the Norfolk Record Office, where in addition to the manuscripts of his early novels there are his note-books and many letters (including some donated by Lilias Haggard that were not available for inspection until 1978). Among the unpublished material I examined there were the diaries Haggard kept almost daily from just before the start of the First World War almost until his death. My edition of these, *The Private Diaries of Sir Henry Rider Haggard* was published by Cassell in 1980.

While working on the Haggard papers, I was fortunate enough to acquire an important addition to my own ever-growing collection of Haggard memorabilia. A friend of mine was dining in a Suffolk restaurant and chanced to overhear a conversation at the next table about a chair that had been owned by Rider Haggard. Rightly assuming that I would be interested in any story concerning Haggard, he politely inquired if it could be repeated. It emerged that one of the diners, some twenty years earlier, had successfully bid for a desk at a sale. The auctioneer then said, 'As you've bought the desk, you'd better have a chair to go with it. Take the previous lot which was unsold.' From then on, the purchaser of the desk kept the swivel-chair he had been given in his garden shed until, just a week before, the back had broken. Deciding to throw it out, he picked up the chair and for the first time noticed that underneath it was signed 'H. Rider Haggard' with the date 1886. My friend took the man's telephone number and a few days later I bought the chair, which from several photographs I know is the one on which Haggard sat at his desk while writing most of his books. It has been the chair on which I too have sat, while writing this, his biography.

D.S. Higgins
Framlingham

1

The Formative Years

I

'Rider,' his youngest daughter states, 'did not talk very much of his childhood to his family.'[1] Nor did he often write about it. In his sixty-eight published books Haggard makes only an occasional passing reference either to his own or anyone else's childhood. Even in his autobiography he only hints at the unhappiness and loneliness he so transparently experienced during his early years, but which he was reluctant to acknowledge then or later.

Rider Haggard was the eighth of ten children born to William Haggard, a flamboyant, irascible Norfolk squire, and his wife Ella. From the moment of his birth, circumstances separated Rider from his brothers and sisters. Alone of all the boys, he was not born in Bradenham Hall, the square Georgian house that for three generations had been the family seat of the Haggards. Because his father, being forced to economise, had temporarily let the Hall, Ella was confined at Wood Farm, a small thatched house on the Bradenham estate. It was there, on 22 June 1856, that Rider was born, weak and jaundiced. To most people the actual place of birth is unimportant, but to a dynastic traditionalist like William Haggard the birth of a son in a humble farmhouse rather than in the family home was most probably an event of ill omen. Certainly, from then on, Rider was treated differently from his six brothers, and he was encouraged to believe that there did exist some mystical link between himself and his birth-place. His daughter writes, 'In after years his mother used to say that Rider's passionate attachment to the land and agriculture must have sprung from the circumstances of his birth, as he alone of her ten children possessed it.'[2]

Against all expectations he recovered from the jaundice and on 30 July his mother registered his birth, giving his name as Henry Constantine Haggard. In early August, after the Haggards had resumed their occupation of the Hall, the seven-week-old infant was again taken ill — this time with severe inflammation of the lungs. Dr Clouting, the family physician, declared that there was no hope of recovery: there was no time for the baptism to be conducted in church and so the clergyman was hurriedly called to the Hall. From a large Lowestoft china bowl the baby, held anxiously by the distressed mother, was christened Henry Rider. Left alone with her sick child, Ella Haggard refused to accept that he was going to die. She dosed him with brandy and wrapped him in boiling flannels. He began to recover and, not surprisingly, this experience forged the bonds of the special relationship that always existed between Rider and his mother. A few weeks later he was in good health and on 22 September he was, according to the register for the West Bradenham parish, 'received into the Church'.

In his early years Rider was not looked after by his mother for long. The Haggard family was large and the responsibilities of organising the household were time-consuming and onerous. By September 1857 Ella Haggard was pregnant yet again and, as was the custom in the homes of the Victorian landed class, the infant Rider was exiled to the nursery, there to be brought up by a succession of nursemaids. He did, however, also have the company of the other children in the family during the day. Ella, his eldest sister, who was eleven when Rider was born, took a special interest in him. Much later he acknowledged his debt to his sister when in dedicating to her *The Brethren*, which was first published in 1904, he wrote:

> Let us for a little time think as we thought while we were young: when faith knew no fears for anything and death had not knocked upon our doors; when you opened to my childish eyes that gate of ivory and pearl which leads to the blessed kingdom of Romance.

So, apparently none the worse for his early ailments, Rider grew healthy and strong. It was not long, however, before he showed signs of developing the characteristic that more than anything else separated him from his family and especially from his pedestrian father — a vivid and inventive imagination. His flights of fancy went mainly unobserved by those around him, for they were usually experienced at night when alone in the darkness of the nursery. At least one person, however, became aware that secret fears haunted Rider's mind and used this knowledge to her own advantage. A nurse discovered that at night she could reduce the child in her care to a silent immobility born of terror. After Rider had been put to bed she opened the door of a cupboard close by, revealing 'a disreputable rag doll of particularly hideous aspect, with boot-button eyes, hair of black wool and a sinister leer upon its painted face'.[3] Then with a hissed warning that he was being left in charge of 'She-who-must-be-obeyed' she left the impressionable, sensitive child in the darkened room. There in the eerie moonlight it was difficult to determine whether the blurred figure was living or dead. Out of this nightmare, *She* was born:

> 'Why art thou so frightened, stranger?' asked the sweet voice . . . 'Thou wast afraid because mine eyes were searching out thine heart, therefore wast thou afraid . . . How is it that ye hold your lives so cheap as to place them in the hollow of the hand of *Hiya*, into the hand of She-who-must-be-obeyed?'

(From *She*)

It was Rider's mother, however, rather than his brothers and sisters or the variety of servants who most influenced him in childhood. She passed on to him a simple but devout religious faith and encouraged him to adopt the habit of regular church attendance that he retained all his life. After his last visit to Bradenham Church, on 21 August 1922, he wrote in his diary: 'I was glad to see this church again which I have known from infancy and to occupy the pew where I have often sat with my mother.' Apart from worshipping there, Haggard also loved visiting different churches, and on the weathered tombstones he found the names, and even biographical details, of some of his characters.

Rider's mother influenced him in other ways. Unlike his brothers and sisters, Rider shared his mother's devotion to gardening and her interest in ancient Egypt and Palestine. More important, he always believed that it was she who passed on to him much of his literary ability. The year after Rider was born, his mother's narrative poem of the Afghan War appeared, *Myra; or the Rose of the East,* and in 1890, Rider arranged for the posthumous publication of her poem *Life and its Author.* Such literary efforts point to her being unlike many of the county ladies with whom she mixed socially. Indeed she did come from a very different background, having been born and brought up in India, the daughter of a civil servant whose co-heiress she became. She may have been dissatisfied with her lot as Rider revealingly states that, 'She never complained, but I cannot think that the life she was called upon to lead was very congenial to her.' Although her large family and many responsibilities prevented Rider's mother from being with him as often as he wished, his love for her was profound and long-lasting. In his autobiography, written almost twenty-five years after her death, he writes, 'No night goes by that I do not think of her and pray that we may meet again to part no more.'

Rider had a very different relationship with and attitude to his father. While Ella Haggard was soft-spoken, refined and devout, her husband had a booming voice, a belligerent manner and a violent temper. He early concluded that Rider, alone of all his children, was incorrigibly stupid. Lacking as he was in sensitivity, it was impossible for Haggard to recognise the characteristic in his son, and even if he had been able to do so, it is likely that he would have considered it an unmasculine weakness. Haggard wrote: 'Nobody could be more absolutely delightful than my father when he chose, and, *per contra*, I am bound to add that nobody could be more disagreeable. His rows with his children were many, and often on his part unjust.' It is hardly surprising then that Haggard was unable to discuss his childish flights of fancy and the vividness of his dreams with his father. 'Certainly I was very imaginative,' Haggard writes, 'although I kept my thoughts to myself, which I dare say had a good deal to do with my reputation for stupidity.'

Nevertheless Haggard grew to envy the high regard in which his father, the archetypal country squire, was apparently held by the whole community.[4]

Despite his family's social position in Norfolk, Rider's childhood was not a settled one. William Haggard suffered from 'the vile exigencies of a narrow purse' and as a result the family had to endure 'frequent excursions abroad and certain

3

years that we spent at Leamington and in London when economy was the order of the day'. The family's 'excursions abroad' included periods of temporary residence in Dunkirk, Tréport, Coblenz, and Cologne. It was while staying at Coblenz that the Haggard family went for a trip up the Rhine to observe the scenery. Rider, however, stayed in a cabin reading. When his father realised that Rider was not on deck, he marched down to the cabin, dragged his son out by the scruff of the neck and, much to the amusement of the other passengers, thundered, 'I have paid five thalers for you to improve your mind by absorbing the beauties of nature, and absorb them you shall!'

At other times, when it was not let, the family moved back into Bradenham Hall. It was there that the family most enjoyed themselves and then 'the noise, of course, was tremendous', but Rider was still an outsider: 'I think that on the whole I was rather a quiet youth, at any rate by comparison.' Like his brothers, Rider spent many hours at Bradenham fighting, shooting and hunting, but even in these pursuits, he was considered, with some justification, not to be as proficient as his brothers. Having overridden and lamed a mare belonging to his elder brother Bazett, his father's favourite son, Rider was condemned to ride an old grey with a convulsive movement of the hind leg so pronounced that the animal was called Body-Snatcher. He loved guns and was given a single-barrelled muzzle-loader with which, after almost killing himself, he narrowly missed shooting his brother Andrew while out rabbit-hunting.

There was little intellectual stimulation at Bradenham and in 1887 when asked to comment on the books that had influenced him Rider admitted, 'Now to be frank, I have never been a very great reader.'[5] He did, however, recall that when he was eight or nine he had been once so enthralled by *Robinson Crusoe* that when it was time to go to church he hid under the bed so that he could continue reading. An elder sister and a governess discovered him and when he refused to come out they attempted to drag him by the legs. Rider, grabbing hold of the bed and his beloved book, put up a fierce struggle, and eventually the ladies admitted defeat and left him where he was. Later, in his autobiography, Haggard recalls that when he was young he had difficulty with his letters and it was clearly upsetting for him to recall 'when I was about seven my dear mother declaring that I was as heavy as lead in body and mind'.

Rider's formal education began when he was about nine years old. The family was living at 24 Leinster Square, London, and he was sent to a local day school. Shortly afterwards he was taken away because he had been bullied by an usher with a violent temper. He was then sent to another day school to receive 'a sound business education', but he did not stay there long either, for a test set by his future brother-in-law, the Reverend Charles Maddison Green who in 1869 married Ella, revealed that the boy had learned very little. Rider's father was incensed and roared that he was 'only fit to be a greengrocer'. After the row was over, Rider went for a walk with his elder brother, Andrew, who said, 'I say, old fellow, when you become a greengrocer, I hope you'll let me have oranges cheap!' Over forty years later

Haggard wrote, 'To this day I have never quite forgiven Andrew for that most heartless remark.'

As a result of the test, Rider, who was then ten, was sent away with two or three other young boys to be instructed by the Reverend H.J. Graham at Garsington Rectory, near Oxford. The three idyllic years that Rider spent in that peaceful village were always remembered with great affection. The details remained vivid — the low grey rectory, the seventeenth-century dovecote, the hollow trunk of the ancient pollard elm, the meadow path down which he used to bowl an iron hoop. Twenty years later Mrs Graham recalled that Rider was 'the little quiet gentle boy who used to drive with me about the Garsington lanes'.[6] He also made other friends there, one of whom was 'a fine handsome man of about fifty, with grey hair and aristocratic features'. This farmer was called Quatermain, and Rider gave his name to the hunter who was the hero of so many of his books.

At Garsington Rider was also told a story that greatly appealed to his still developing imagination. He wrote about it in his diary on 15 November 1920, fifty-five years later: 'Mr Graham wore a thick gold ring engraved in a curious, but rather conventional frieze or pattern, with symbols in it that may have been meant to represent the sun. He told me that an old friend of his who had business in Peru had opened some burial place and in it found a chamber wherein, round a stone table, sat a dead and mummified man at the head and about a dozen other persons ranged round the table — whether male or female or both, I do not remember — if indeed Mr Graham knew. All that I can recollect of the rest of the story is that the man at the head of the table wore this ring upon his hand and that the discoverer of the tomb took it thence and gave it to Mr Graham in after years . . . The tale made a deep impression on my youthful mind and, in fact, turned it towards Romance. I used it in *King Solomon's Mines* when I depicted the White Dead sitting round the Stone Board under the presidency of the White Death':

> At the first glance all I could discern was a massive stone table running down its length, with a colossal white figure at its head, and life-sized white figures all round it . . .
>
> It *was* a ghastly sight. There at the end of the long stone table, holding in his skeleton fingers a great white spear, sat *Death* himself, shaped in the form of a colossal human skeleton, fifteen feet or more in height . . .
>
> Anything more awe-inspiring than the spectacle of this long line of departed royalties . . . wrapped, each of them, in a shroud of ice-like spar, through which the features could be dimly made out, and seated round the inhospitable board, with Death himself for a host, it is impossible to imagine.
>
> (From *King Solomon's Mines*)

It is evident that Rider grew very fond of Mr Graham and this kindly rector greatly influenced him.[7] While at Garsington, Rider often played with 'a child of my own age, Mrs Graham's little sister Blanche, who was as fair in colouring as one of her name should be.' With her he learned 'the rudiments of flirtation'. Blanche was almost certainly the model for Stella Carson, the girl whom the young Allan Quatermain loves and marries in *Allan's Wife*. In this book, Garsington Rectory, 'the long grey house' that had once served as a refuge in times of plague, becomes Garsingham Rectory, the home of the boy Allan Quatermain, whom Haggard later said was 'only myself, set in a variety of imagined situations, thinking my thoughts, and looking at life through my eyes.'

In the first chapter of *Allan's Wife* a strange incident at a children's Christmas party is described:

> After that I hid myself as well as I could behind a chair, for I was shy, and watched little Stella Carson, who was the squire's only child, giving the children presents off the tree. She was dressed as Father Christmas, with some soft white stuff round her lovely little face, and she had large dark eyes, which I thought more beautiful than anything I had ever seen. At last it came to my turn to receive a present — oddly enough, considered in the light of future events, it was a large monkey. Stella reached it down from one of the lower boughs of the tree and handed it to me, saying: 'Dat is my Christmas present to you, little Allan Quatermain.'
>
> As she did so her sleeve, which was covered with cotton-wool, spangled over with something that shone, touched one of the tapers and caught fire — how I do not know — and the flame ran up her arm towards her throat. She stood quite still. I suppose that she was paralysed with fear; and the ladies who were near screamed very loud, but did nothing. Then some impulse seized me — perhaps instinct would be a better word to use, considering my age. I threw myself upon the child, and, beating at the fire with my hands, mercifully succeeded in extinguishing it before it really got hold. My wrists were so badly scorched that they had to be wrapped up in wool for a long time afterwards, but with the exception of a single burn upon her throat, little Stella Carson was not much hurt.
>
> (From *Allan's Wife*)

There is no evidence that such an incident actually occurred, although as there are several autobiographical references in the first part of the book it is a possibility. But even if Rider did not rescue Blanche from the flames and the incident is no more than a morbid, childish fear, it is still clearly important because involved in its remembrance are the three elements of the image used so powerfully by Haggard in several of his books — the monkey and the beautiful woman separated by fire recurs in more than one novel. It becomes the transformation scene in *She* in which the bewitchingly beautiful Ayesha, having bathed in the fire that brings eternal life, rapidly ages:

> 'Oh, *look*! — *look*! — *look*!' shrieked Job. . . . '*Look*! — *look*! — *look*!' she's shrivelling up! she's turning into a monkey!' and down he fell.
>
> True enough . . . she *was* shrivelling up; the golden snake that had encircled her gracious form slipped over her hips and to the ground; smaller and smaller

she grew; her skin changed colour, and in place of the perfect whiteness of its lustre it turned dirty brown and yellow, like an old piece of withered parchment . . . Smaller she grew, and smaller yet, till she was no larger than a baboon.

(From *She*)

For Haggard fire symbolized sexual desire that turns beauty into an object evoking guilt and disgust, and it seems likely that the incident in which Stella Carson is burnt at the Christmas party is an account of Rider's sudden awareness of his sexual desires which announced that the days of his childhood innocence were ended.

During these years, Rider also became aware of death. The resulting understanding of its meaning haunted his childhood and remained an obsession all his life. The discovery came first: the understanding later. In one of his notebooks Haggard records seeing a corpse when he was a young boy: 'An old man died in the village and I persuaded the carpenter to show me the body. I can see it now, pale and stern and beautiful, dressed in white with a pillow stuffed with shavings behind the head. I do not remember that the sight frightened me at all but it made me think.'[8]

A terrifying understanding of the reality of death came to him during the summer vacation before he left Garsington. It was on 21 July 1869, the day of his sister Ella's wedding. Because the house was crowded, Rider had been moved out of his usual bedroom to the Sandwich, a stuffy annexe to the library which was lined with books from floor to ceiling. Once again he was lying in the gloom unable to sleep. His mind was full of a sermon he had heard about the terrors of hell. Fear of the unknown made him hysterical. 'I shivered, I prayed, I wept. I thought I saw Death waiting for me by the library door.' His experience was 'the most terrifying remembrance of my childhood . . . as I lay there I realized — for the first time — that I myself must die — must cease to play and eat and sleep, and pass away into the dark of nothingness.' At last he did fall asleep, only to dream 'that I was already in this hell and that the peculiar form of punishment allotted to me was to be continually eaten alive by rats!'

Later, in the Sandwich Room, Rider had another, but different, revelation of an aspect of death. His daughter, Lilias, describes what happened: 'He woke up. The moon was shining through the window so brilliantly that he could see every detail in the room. A little breeze rattled the stiff magnolia branches outside, and the shifting shadow of the leaves danced over the bed. He put out his hand and let them flicker over it — how odd it looked in the moonlight, dead — dead.'[9]

The strange workings of Rider's vivid and macabre imagination enabled him to see a part of his own body as being separate and dead, but, like the old man's corpse, it was not frightening and hideous, it was pale and beautiful. This experience is reminiscent of a habit he had adopted earlier. In one of the few references to his early childhood in his autobiography he writes: 'Nothing would induce me to go to sleep unless a clean napkin folded in a certain way was placed under my head, which napkin I called *an ear*. To this day I have dim recollections of crying bitterly

7

until this *ear* was brought to me.' In this case the young Haggard was able, when once again alone at night, to identify an inanimate object with a part of the human body, and the white, clean 'ear', placed next to his face, gave comfort and security.

Haggard, still seeing the dead body as 'pale, stern and beautiful', became deeply interested in the methods used by the Egyptians for preserving their dead. Jottings in his notebooks testify that he frequently referred to *The Book of the Dead* by E.W. Budge, who in time became a close friend. His own stories too are often littered with the well-preserved dead. Such bodies are not intended by Haggard to be distressing or to cause offence; on the contrary, those of females, their beauty untarnished by sorrow or death, are often the recipients of men's love. Sometimes too parts of the body are separated from the whole without either their beauty or the man's desire being affected. A remarkable example of this occurs in *She* when Billali, the old man who guided Holly and Vincey to the Land of the Amahagger, talks about his youthful passion:

> I remember when I was a boy I found the body of a fair woman lying where thou liest now, yes, on that very bench. She was so beautiful that I was wont to creep in hither with a lamp and gaze upon her. . . . I learned to love that dead form, that shell which once had held a life that no more is. I would creep up to her and kiss her cold face, and wonder how many men had lived and died since she was, and who had loved her and embraced her in the days that long had passed away. . . . One day my mother, a watchful woman, but hasty-minded, seeing I was changed, followed me, and saw the beautiful white one, and feared that I was bewitched, as, indeed, I was. So half in dread, and half in anger, she took the lamp, and standing the dead woman up against the wall there, set fire to her hair, and she burnt fiercely, even down to the feet, for those who are thus kept burn excellently well. . . . She burnt even to the feet, but the feet I came back and saved, cutting the burnt bone from them, and hid them under the stone bench there, wrapped up in a piece of linen.
>
> (From *She*)

This extract is more than an illustration of Haggard's interest in death. The passage, charged as it is with sexuality, strongly suggests the experience of adolescent, masturbatory fantasies brought to an abrupt, frustrating halt by a mother's unexpected intervention and then recommenced in guilt-laden secrecy.

Living as he did in a rural household where shooting and animal killing were commonplace, Haggard's obsession with death must have been exceptionally intense even for a child brought up in the period when Queen Victoria and her subjects were mourning the death of Prince Albert. It is possible, however, that, as with many other things, his mother's attitudes influenced him. In his autobiography he mentions that his mother had a stillborn child, and adds, 'Although she had ten children living, my mother never ceased to regret this boy, and I remember her crying when she pointed out to me where he was buried in Bradenham churchyard.' The last words Ella Haggard is believed to have written show a calm acceptance of her own impending death:

Lo! in the shadowy valley there He stands:
  My soul pale down Earth's icy slope
Descends to meet Him, with beseeching hands
  Trembling with Fear — and yet upraised in Hope.

After the three years spent at Garsington, Rider was removed from the Reverend Graham's care and a decision had to be made as to which school he should then attend. Apart from Jack who entered the Navy, all of Rider's brothers went to public school — William and Bazett went to Winchester, Alfred to Haileybury, Andrew to Westminster, and subsequently Arthur to Shrewsbury. Once again, however, Rider was treated differently: it was decided that he would not be sent to a public school. Rider must have been close to the reason for this when he wrote: 'I dare say it was thought that to send me to a public school would be to waste money.' It was, therefore, decided to send him to Ipswich Grammar School, 'which had the advantages of being cheap and near at hand.'

Rider's father escorted him to his new school, buying for him when they passed through Norwich a black felt clerical hat. This peculiar and most inappropriate headgear was much mocked by the other boys and as a result Rider soon became involved in a playground brawl. After this inauspicious start, he spent three unsuccessful and somewhat unhappy years at the school. He remembered the vicious bullying, an unjust accusation of cheating, being elected captain of the second football team, and winning an essay competition for which he never received the prize. In his autobiography he states, 'I did not distinguish myself in any way at Ipswich — I imagine for the old reason that I was generally engaged in thinking of other things than the lesson in hand.' This daydreaming was perhaps a better preparation for a prolific writer than academic success. Certainly this has been true of many other writers, including Herbert Spencer, who claimed that because in his youth he 'was much given to castle-building' he was in his later years capable of intense concentration.[10]

During the summer holidays of 1872 Rider was sent by his father to stay with a family in Switzerland so that he could improve his French. In *Love Eternal* Godfrey Knight, a thinly veiled portrait of Haggard, is sent by his father on a similar holiday. At the time Godfrey, like Rider, was about sixteen:

In the course of these years of adolescence, Godfrey Knight had developed into a rather unusual stamp of youth. In some ways he was clever, for instance at the classics and history which he always liked; in others, and especially where figures were concerned, he was stupid, or as his father called him, idle. In company he was apt to be shy and dull, unless some subject interested him, when to the astonishment of those present, he would hold forth and show knowledge and powers of reflection beyond his years. By nature he was intensely proud; the one thing he never forgot was a rebuff, or forgave, was an insult.

(From *Love Eternal*)

After Mr Knight had bought the tickets for Godfrey's journey, he took him to the Charing Cross Hotel. The farewell speech he delivered might well have been also given to Rider. Certainly it is couched in the kind of language his father used and Rider's developing liking for women must by then have been well known to his family:

> 'Woman,' said Mr Knight, 'is the great danger of man. She is the Devil's favourite bait, at least to some natures of which I fear yours is one, though that is strange, as I may say that on the whole I have always disliked the sex, and I married for other reasons than those which are supposed to be common. Woman,' he went on, warming to his topic, 'although allowed upon the world as a necessary evil, is a painted snare, full of guile. . . . I have watched you closely and I am sure that your weakness lies this way. Woman is and always will be the sin that doth so easily beset you.'
>
> (From *Love Eternal*)

Rider did, however, have female company in Switzerland, later recalling, 'With the able assistance of the young ladies of the house I acquired a good colloquial knowledge of that language in quite a short time. I never saw any of them again.' Having had an enjoyable holiday, during which it can be assumed that he further practised the arts of flirtation first acquired at Garsington, Rider joined his family at Fluellen on Lake Lucerne. While on the way to say good bye at the St Gotthard Pass to his brother Alfred, who was setting off to start his career in the Indian Civil Service, Rider and his brother Andrew spent a night at a wayside inn. 'On the following morning,' he records, 'the pretty Swiss chambermaid, with whom we had made friends, took us to a mortuary near by and, among a number of other such gruesome relics, showed us the skull of her own father, which she polished up affectionately with her apron.' This incident made a deep impression on Rider, for a human skull plays an important part in several of his novels, including *The Witch's Head* where a skull found on a beach provides the book's title.

On his return to Ipswich School, Rider entered for the Army entrance examination, not, he later claimed, because he wished to become a soldier, but because he wanted to keep a friend company. He was, in his words, 'duly floored by my old enemy, Euclid,' and failed to pass. It was perhaps because of this and the realisation that if Rider could not pass the Army examination there was very little possibility of his following his elder brothers to university that Rider's father 'with characteristic suddenness' decided that his son should leave school and prepare for a career.

So, although he had not yet escaped his father's eccentric interference in his life, Rider's childhood came to an end. Subsequently the period seems to have been rarely referred to or remembered. There were perhaps two main reasons for this: firstly, that Rider stored away, unforgiven and unforgotten, the insults, reversals and criticisms he considered too painful to discuss with others; and, secondly, that in the next few years he achieved successes that even his domineering father was forced to recognise and which, in contrast to earlier memories, could be pleasurably recalled. Certainly the incidents of his childhood, unlike much of what happened later, were rarely used by Haggard in his books, but his childish dreams and fantasies, palatable realities, did provide the inspiration for much that is original in his fiction.

II

Rider's father decided that his son should pursue a career in the Foreign Office and so that he could prepare for the entrance examination he was sent to live in London with an elderly French professor whose wife had taught one of Rider's sisters. Although the professor and his wife individually were charming people, they were an ill-matched couple and the arguments Rider was forced to overhear were heated and numerous for it seemed that on almost all matters their opinions conflicted. She, for example, was a member of the Plymouth Brethren, an extremely strict religious sect, whereas he had much more liberal views. In the less than satisfactory year that Rider stayed with them he acquired little learning apart from some knowledge of French literature and the tenets of the Plymouth Brethren. It became obvious that his chances of passing the Foreign Office examination had not improved and so his father once again made an impetuous decision. This time it was to send Rider to Scoones', a crammer famed for getting the less than brilliant sons of the affluent middle class through such entrance tests.

Godfrey Knight's adolescent experiences in *Love Eternal* again mirror Rider's own. He too was sent to Scoones':

> Godfrey inquired his way to Garrick Street, where he was informed that Mr Scoones had his establishment. He found the place and, by good luck, found Mr Scoones also, a kindly, keen, white-haired man, who made a few inquiries and put him through a brief examination.

Becoming a student at Scoones' radically altered Rider's way of life. At just eighteen he was, for the first time in his life, free from the constant supervision of either family or friends. Later, recalling the period, he wrote: 'At this age I was thrown upon the world, as I remember when I was a little lad my elder brothers threw me into the Rhine to teach me to swim. After nearly drowning I learned to swim, and in a sense the same may be said of my London life.' Rider clearly relished his new-found freedom to savour the many pleasures London provided.

His first lodgings, near Westbourne Grove, were kept by a young widow, but his ever-watchful father quickly removed him 'as they did not turn out respectable'. He went then to lodgings in Davies Street, which he considered to be 'an excellent situation for a young gentleman about town', and that is soon what he became, for at Scoones' there were 'many charming but idle young men, often with a certain amount of means,' with whom he was delighted to make friends. One of these fellow-revellers, Justin Sheil, writing to Rider in 1879, after deciding to become a monk, refers to 'the idle, aimless, useless life I led when you knew me: my only object was pleasure and happiness, and I was unscrupulous in trying to get them.' It is more than likely that this object was also Rider's.

Another friend at Scoones', who lived in a lavishly furnished house in St James's Place, was called Norris and it appears that through him Rider was introduced to spiritualism and some of its more fashionable devotees. Among these was Lady Caithness (who had just become vice-president of the newly formed British National Association of Spiritualists) and Lady Poulett, at whose house, 20 Hanover Square, Rider frequently attended séances. Although he was later to conclude that 'never would I allow any young person over whom I had control to attend a séance', at the time Rider was extremely interested in and excited by the phenomena he observed and experienced. There is a possibility that the wealthy lady spiritualists whom Rider met, being aware of his sensitive and imaginative nature, thought that he might become a medium for their circle. This did happen to Godfrey Knight in *Love Eternal* where one of the followers states, 'I guess that either our young friend here has got the vision, or that he will make a first-class novelist.'

Among the many séances Rider attended was one at a private house in Green Street:

Two young women of great beauty — or perhaps I should say young spirits — one dark and the other fair, appeared in the lighted room. I conversed with and touched them both, and noted that their flesh seemed to be firm but cold. I remember that, being a forward youth of inquiring mind, I even asked the prettier of the two to allow me to give her a kiss. . . . She was draped in a kind of white garment which covered her head, and I asked her to allow me to see her hair. She pushed up the white drapery from her forehead, remarking sweetly that if I would look I should see that she had no hair, and in fact she appeared to be quite bald. A minute or two later, however, she had long and beautiful hair which flowed all about her.

(From *The Days of My Life*)

Experiences such as this, combined with his morbid interest in death whose ghost-like figure he had seen as a young boy in the Sandwich Room, clearly helped to create his vision of She, whom, on her first appearance, he describes in these words:

A tall figure stood before us. I say a figure, for not only the body, but also the face was wrapped up in soft white, gauzy material in such a way as at first sight to remind me most forcibly of a corpse in its grave-clothes. . . . I could, however clearly distinguish that the swathed mummy-like form before me was that of a tall and lovely woman, instinct with beauty in every part, and also with a certain snake-like grace which I had never seen anything to equal before. When she moved a hand or foot her entire frame seemed to undulate, and the neck did not bend, it curved.

'Why art thou so frightened, stranger?' asked the sweet voice. And with a little coquettish movement she turned herself, and held up one arm, so as to show all her loveliness and the rich hair of raven blackness that streamed in soft ripples down her snowy robes, almost to her sandalled feet.

(From *She*)

It may be that Rider's interest in Egyptology, already aroused by his mother, was further developed by the spiritualists he met, for mummies and ancient artefacts seem to have been part of their paraphernalia; but, however interesting his experiences may have been, they ceased to be important to him for, while still at Scoones', a far more momentous thing happened. He fell, as he put it, 'truly and earnestly in love'. In *The Days of My Life* he records that a friend took him to a ball at Richmond where he met 'a very beautiful young lady a few years older than myself to whom I was instantly and overwhelmingly attracted'. Her beauty so impressed him that, although he was writing nearly thirty-five years after the event, he could describe her as 'one of the three lovely women whom I have seen in my life'. In *The Witch's Head*, Haggard's second novel, Ernest Kershaw similarly first meets the beautiful Eva Ceswick, his ill-fated love, at a private ball:

Eva Ceswick was dressed in white *soie de chine*, in the bosom of which was fixed a single rose. The dress was cut low, and her splendid neck and arms were entirely without ornament. In the masses of dark hair, which was coiled like a coronet round her head, there glistened a diamond star. Simple as was her costume, there was a grandeur about it that struck the whole room; but in truth it sprang from the almost perfect beauty of the woman who wore it. . . .

It took but a few seconds, ten perhaps, for her to walk up the room, and yet to Ernest it seemed long before her eyes met his own, and something passed from them into his heart that remained there all his life.

(From *The Witch's Head*)

When the ball at Richmond ended, Rider escorted his belle to her carriage, hoping to learn where she lived. In this, however, he failed, either because in his excitement he did not hear what she said or because through coyness her reply was too vague. Not deterred, Rider, realising 'that even a goddess must eat', later successfully discovered her address by inquiring at a butcher's shop in her neighbourhood.

This girl whom Rider pursued was to remain throughout his life his only true love. Because of what subsequently happened, Haggard does not reveal the girl's name in his autobiography, in any other of his publications, or in his private diaries. Although her identity was known by Lilias Haggard, in her biography of her father, *The Cloak that I Left*, she refers to her only as 'Lilith'. After Lilias's death it would seem that there were few if any, including Haggard's descendants now living, who knew much of this 'girl with the golden hair and violets in her hand'. There are, however, several reasons why this most effective wall of secrecy was so deliberately erected — the enduring intensity of Rider's passion, the scandal of the events in which his loved one was later involved, and the most distressing circumstances of her death. It was exceptionally difficult to discover who she was, and it was only after this had been done that I realised the tragedy of her story and understood how intense and prolonged an impact its gradual unfolding must have had on Haggard. As his daughter pointed out, 'it was to be his fate that the deep emotional experiences, his loves and his tragedies, were not as with most men and women, if not forgotten, overlaid so deeply by the years that they became mere remembrances. They remained active, insistent, his daily companions until the hour of his death, no less present because jealously hidden, nor unspeaking, because of them he never spoke.'[11]

The lady with whom Rider fell so completely in love was Mary Elizabeth Jackson, called Lilly by all her friends and relatives. Her father, John Jackson, came from a long line of successful Yorkshire farmers. 'Jack of Oran', as he was known, became an expert on blood-stock and amassed a considerable fortune on the turf. He married twice. His first wife, Charlotte Goodricke, had four daughters: Eliza, Alice, Laura and Lilly, who was born on 19 October 1854. His second wife, Jane Outhwaite, whom he married against the wishes of her well-connected family, gave birth to a son, Frederick, on 17 February 1860. In 1869, at the age of forty-one, John Jackson died. The estate in Yorkshire then appears to have been sold and his vast wealth placed in trust. Lilly, with her stepmother and the other four children, moved south, eventually taking up residence at Aston Lodge, Leamington, in Warwickshire.

It is possible that one or other of the Haggards met the Jacksons first at Leamington, for that was one of the places to which Rider's father took his family during a period of economic difficulty. Certainly Edward Arthur Haggard, Rider's younger brother, and Frederick Jackson were at school together at Shrewsbury from 1873 to 1878, after which they both went up to Cambridge. So, although Rider may never have met Lilly before the fateful ball at Richmond, other members of their families did know each other.

After the ball, Rider saw a good deal of Lilly, who was at the time presumably staying with a relative, perhaps her stepmother's brother, Thomas Price Outhwaite, Honorary Chaplain to the Queen. Her family apparently did not object to the attentions paid to her by the impecunious younger son of an obscure Norfolk squire. He was obviously not the first, nor would he be the last, to succumb to her startling beauty and obvious charms. The reaction of Lilly to her suitor, like that of Eva, her fictional counterpart, seems to have changed from initial amusement to a conviction that she was in love:

After a while Eva's coquettishness began to be less and less marked. When they met she no longer greeted him with a smile of mischief, but with serious eyes that once or twice, he thought, bore traces of tears. . . .

The secret of all this change of conduct was not far to seek. Eva had toyed with edged tools till she cut her fingers to the bone. The dark-eyed boy, who danced so well and had such a handsome, happy face, had become very dear to her. She had begun by playing with him, and now, alas! she loved him better than anybody in the world. That was the sting of the thing; she had fallen in love with a *boy* as young as herself — a boy, too, who, as far as she was aware, had no particular prospects in life.

Given time Rider and Lilly might have been happy together, but time was something they were not given. That summer, his father once again intervened in Rider's life. Perhaps because he feared the seriousness of his son's romantic intentions, William Haggard, who had taken his wife and younger children on one of his Continental expeditions, ordered Rider to join the family at Tours. With many regrets Rider was obliged to say good-bye to Lilly, expecting he would be away for only a few weeks. In fact he was not to see her again for several years and by then her circumstances had radically changed. When in the summer of 1875 the couple parted, Rider, like Ernest when similarly he had to leave Eva, had agreed, reluctantly, that the engagement he believed had been made should not be publicly announced:

> 'O Ernest, Ernest, do be reasonable, there's a dear. . . . There is not the slightest possibility, so far as I can see, of our getting married at present; so the question is, if it is of any use to trumpet out an engagement that will only make us the object of a great deal of gossip.'
>
> (From *The Witch's Head*)

At Tours, Rider did not live with his family, but was sent to stay with an old French professor and his wife, so that he could continue his language studies. In arranging this, his father must have been all too aware that Rider's stay at Scoones had been spent more in the acquisition of worldly knowledge than academic learning and that, therefore, without further concentrated study, there would be little chance of his entering the Foreign Office.

Rider had been at Tours for only a few weeks, when his father saw an opportunity of solving all the problems his son was creating. In one move he could find work for his apparently feckless son and end his inappropriate desire to marry. Discovering that his Norfolk neighbour and friend, Sir Henry Bulwer, nephew of the novelist Bulwer-Lytton, was about to take up his appointment as Lieutenant-Governor of Natal, William Haggard wrote to Sir Henry asking if he would take Rider to Africa as part of his staff. Surprisingly, Sir Henry agreed, for he had never met the boy, and Rider was hustled back to England to meet his new chief. In London he was immediately set to work ordering wine and other stores that were to be taken to Natal. His mother, revealing her loving but fussy concern for her son, who, unlike his brothers, had shown no possibility of being successful, wrote to Rider from Tours: 'I hope you have managed the wine well. Your father begs me to tell you, for your consolation, that you will get into nice trouble if you have not! Be careful always to get a very clear understanding of Sir Henry's direction so as to make no mistake which might reflect on you. Make him repeat anything you are in doubt about — if you can! This I give you as a general hint only, which may be useful, and do not forget what I said about order and punctuality.'

The few farewells Rider was able to make were hurried. There was apparently not even time to visit Lilly. His father's intervention had unexpectedly brought to an end the formative adolescent period that Rider later would recall and reinterpret in his novels, a period during which he had tentatively sought new experiences, successfully made new friends, achieved some degree of independence and, by falling so desperately in love, laid the foundations for much unhappiness. But, whatever his motives might have been, William Haggard, by acting as he did, provided for Rider the opportunity he most needed — to be free of his father's limiting and intolerable control. It was an opportunity that Rider did not squander. In Africa he found the essential elements hitherto absent in his life — responsibility, respect, justified praise, much adventure, and the companionship of influential men. His education was completed, his ambitions fired, and an inadequate, uncertain boy was to turn into a man of passion and determination who would become one of the outstanding successes of his generation.

2

African Experiences

Settling down to enjoy the remainder of his stay at Tours after Rider's departure, William Haggard must have felt well pleased to have dealt so successfully with his troublesome son. It seemed as though he would have few problems with his children. William, the eldest son, was in the Diplomatic Service. Bazett, a barrister, and Alfred, an Indian Civil Servant, had both made most acceptable marriages. Andrew had just left university and was about to enter the Army. Edward, the youngest son, was an exemplary scholar at Shrewsbury. As Ella had been married for six years, only Cissie and Mary were left at home. So, although Rider had been accepted only as an unpaid member of Sir Henry Bulwer's staff and would still need some financial support, it appeared that the considerable demands his children's education and upkeep had for so long imposed upon William Haggard were all but over. For that he must have been extremely grateful, especially as he had been investing heavily, and, as it transpired, unwisely, in land, the value of which had already begun to fall.

Rider left with Sir Henry Bulwer and his party in July, 1875. He wrote: 'Of our voyage to Africa there is little to be said except that in those days it was long.' Yet it must have been a time of great mental and emotional turmoil: not only was he leaving behind both the woman he loved and all his friends; he was also heading for a continent about which he knew little, with men very much older than himself, whom he had but recently met. He must have listened eagerly to their tales with alternating excitement and apprehension, but characteristically he did not show his inner feelings. His elder sister, Ella, has said that at the time he appeared conceited, and so he may have done, but his conceit was the public face masking a naturally sensitive young man thrust into an unknown environment. He must, however, have felt quickly at ease in the company of Sir Henry and the rest of his party. Despite the difference in age and rank, Rider shared a common background with them, for it was the country squires of Britain and their sons who were the administrators of Victoria's expanding empire. Their attitudes, born of their inherited position as benevolent rural despots, determined the methodology of colonial government; their simple patriotism encouraged the xenophobia that in South Africa exacerbated the Anglo-Boer conflict; their traditionally paternal treatment of their labourers and servants was easily extended to subjugated races; their enthusiastic interest in their own rural traditions and heritage was transferred to the indigenous cultures of the lands they colonised; their unswerving belief in the natural justice of the legal system they administered at home as magistrates, barristers and judges allowed them to enforce it unquestioningly on the people they governed; and the moral superiority derived from their privileged position in the Established Church encouraged their disdain of the infidel and heathen savage, while making them suspicious of the excessive zeal of evangelical missionaries. These attitudes, which Rider absorbed and retained, made him the enthusiastic advocate of Imperialism that he was to remain throughout his life.

Aboard ship Rider was set to work extracting information on affairs concerned with the colony from the mass of official reports that Sir Henry was taking out with him. The party also produced a magazine to which Rider wrote the prologue. By the time the ship arrived at Cape Town on 17 August, Rider was integrated into the team of the new Lieutenant-Governor of Natal, and, although looking forward to his somewhat ill-defined duties as a social aide-de-camp, he had hopes of being made Sir Henry's private secretary. In *The Days of My Life* he describes himself as he was when, at the age of nineteen, he arrived in Africa: 'I was a tall young fellow, quite six feet, and slight; blue-eyed, brown-haired, fresh-complexioned, and not at all bad-looking. . . . Mentally I was impressionable, quick to observe and learn whatever interested me, and could hold my own in conversation. I was however, subject to fits of depression and liable to take views of things too serious and gloomy for my age — failings, I may add, that I have never been able to shake off.'

In Cape Town Sir Henry's party stayed for a week at Government House with Lady Barkly. Rider there received his first taste of the hectic social life he was going to experience. There was a ball given by the merchants, dinners, meetings with important citizens, and drives through the beautiful countryside in the Barklys' 'first-rate four-in-hand'. Then, after four or five days steaming around the Cape, Rider and his companions reached Durban where, having been met by a reception committee, they stayed for a few days at the Royal Hotel. On 28 August Bulwer, accompanied by Rider, went to see Sir Garnet Wolseley, the acting Governor of Natal who, not impressed by Rider, wrote in his diary: 'Sir H. Bulwer called upon me in the afternoon. . . . His only staff consists of a leggy-looking youth not long I should say from school who seems the picture of weakness and dulness.'[1] After a few days the party set off for Maritzburg, the administrative capital of Natal. Rider travelled in a four-horse wagonette with Sir Henry Bulwer, Theophilus Shepstone (Secretary for Native Affairs), Napier Broome (Colonial Secretary) and W.H. Beaumont (the secretary to the previous Governor of Natal) whom Rider, in a letter home, stated 'puts me up to a lot of things; he is an excessively nice fellow and we are great allies'. As the horses went at full gallop and they were accompanied by a mounted guard of honour, the occupants of the wagonette were choked by dust and so, despite the fine scenery, did not enjoy the five-hour journey.

At Maritzburg Rider settled into Government House where he was given a large bedroom and an office in the Executive Council chamber. The swearing-in ceremony was a great strain on Rider because, 'It was a very swell ceremony indeed, and I had to go through an extraordinary amount of scraping and bowing, presenting and pocketing, or trying to pocket, enormous addresses, commissions, etc., etc.' He was disappointed to discover that he was not to become Bulwer's private secretary. This meant that he would still have to be an unpaid member of the staff and he wrote to his mother, 'I am sorry, very sorry, still to be dependent on my father, but you may be sure, my dear mother, that I will be as moderate as I can. At any rate I shall cost less than if I had been at home.'

As Rider rapidly became familiar with his duties — copying dispatches and making the arrangements for the interminable round of dinner parties — he had time to study the country and its people. The scenery so impressed him that he always believed Natal was the most beautiful country in the world, but it was the indigenous people who most interested him. Around him lived the Zulus 'living in their kraals filled with round beehive-like huts, bronze-coloured, noble-looking men and women clad only in their *moochas*'. To discover more about the Zulus and their history, Rider carefully perused the voluminous official reports, or bluebooks, and listened attentively to 'men who, for thirty or forty years, had been intimately acquainted with the Zulu people, with their history, their heroes, and their customs'. In March 1876 he saw a witch-dance and in a letter home records that F.B. Fynney, the Chief Interpreter of Natal, had told him about a witch-finding he had seen some years previously in Zululand: ' "There," he said, "were collected some five thousand armed warriors in a circle, in the midst of which the witches [I should have said the witch-doctors] danced. Everyone was livid with fear, and with reason, for now and again one of these creatures would come crooning up to one of them and touch him, whereupon he was promptly put out of the world by a regiment of the king's guard." ' This scene was elaborated on by Haggard in Chapter Ten, 'The Witch-Hunt', of *King Solomon's Mines*:

> Quicker and quicker she danced, till she lashed herself into such a frenzy of excitement that the foam flew in flecks from her gnashing jaws, her eyes seemed to start from her head, and her flesh to quiver visibly. Suddenly she stopped dead and stiffened all over, like a pointer dog when he scents game, and then with outstretched wand began to creep stealthily towards the soldiers before her. It seemed to us that as she came their stoicism gave way, and that they shrank from her. . . .
>
> Suddenly the end came. With a shriek she sprang in and touched a tall warrior with the forked wand. Instantly two of his comrades, those standing immediately next to him, seized the doomed man, each by one arm, and advanced with him towards the king. . . .
>
> (From *King Solomon's Mines*)

Fynney obviously told Rider many such stories because in the preface to *Nada the Lily* he is thanked for 'much information given . . . in bygone years by word of mouth.'

Rider saw a good deal of the area around Maritzburg while he participated in the country pursuits that the expatriate country squires adapted to the even greater opportunities provided in the African bush. Riding, hunting and shooting were considered to be as much the worthy occupation of a gentleman in Africa as in the rural counties of Britain. Rider quickly purchased a horse, declaring in a letter home dated 14 February, 'I am getting on all right and have quite got over all signs of liver since I got a horse. This place, if only you take exercise, is as healthy as England.' He also announces that he has been hunting with hounds and describes a day's buck-shooting during which 'I never had a more exciting ride in my life.'

Rider also spent some time reading although admittedly, as an extension of his duties, he concentrated upon books dealing with the exploration and history of Africa. He occasionally turned to fictional works however, and it seems likely that among these were novels written by his chief's uncle, Bulwer Lytton. Certainly in 1887 he claimed that, 'My two favourite novels are Dickens's *Tale of Two Cities* and Lytton's *Coming Race*. Both these books I can read again and again, and with an added pleasure.'[2] It can be assumed that among the stories to which Rider listened so attentively were Sir Henry's accounts of the financial rewards obtained from writing by his famous uncle who successfully combined the careers of popular novelist and respected diplomat. This example may have prompted Rider to consider writing for publication.

It was part of Rider's duties to accompany Sir Henry on his official tours of Natal. In May 1876, while camped outside Chief Pagáté's kraal, Rider saw a war dance arranged in honour of the Governor. It so impressed him that two days later, on 13 May, he included a detailed description of what he had seen in a letter to his mother. A little later he expanded this description into an article, 'A Zulu War-Dance', that was published above the initials H.R.H. in *The Gentleman's Magazine* of July, 1877.

After his return from this tour, during which he once lost his way while riding alone in the bush, Rider went briefly to Durban with Sir Henry Bulwer who cut the first turf on the railway line to Maritzburg. Afterwards at the banquet in the market building, Rider made a speech which so impressed Sir Alfred Page that he wrote saying he would keep a copy of it, and when Rider became famous he would remind him of it. 'I need hardly say,' Haggard recalled when he revisited Durban in 1914, 'he forgot all about it.'[3]

About this time, Rider became more concerned about and interested in politics. Public attention at home was being increasingly concentrated on the Transvaal, an independent territory to the north of Natal, which had been founded by the Boers after the Great Trek of 1835, the story of which later inspired Haggard's novels *Marie* and *Swallow*. The Boers' rule over the Transvaal was an uneasy one and for years the native chiefs systematically harassed the European settlers. In the summer of 1876 Chief Secocoeni began gathering his armies, apparently intending to attack the Boers, and it was feared that any war would also involve Cetywayo, the Zulu king to whom Secocoeni owed allegience. In October, Lord Carnarvon, the

Colonial Secretary in Disraeli's imperialistic cabinet, appointed Theophilus Shepstone, who had been summoned back to England and awarded the K.C.M.G., to be the British Government's special commissioner to investigate the causes of friction in the Transvaal. Amid the growing rumours of war, Rider Haggard wrote a second article, 'The Transvaal', which appeared, once again over the initials H.R.H., in *Macmillan's Magazine* for May 1877. After a somewhat biased account of the territory's history, he makes a case for annexation that concludes: 'Decidedly, the day when the British flag — a flag that has always brought blessings in its train — is first unfurled there should be a glad day for the Transvaal, Republic no more — for the South African colonies, who will welcome a new and beautiful sister, and for England, who will add another lusty child to her splendid progeny.'[4] His comments on the Boers, considering the difficulties of the time, were unfortunate. The picture he paints, although accurately reflecting the attitudes of his superiors, seems almost calculated to damage Anglo–Boer relationships: 'Take the average Dutch Boer. . . . you see an awkward-looking man, of large stature, and somewhat heavy, obstinate face, which is lit with a broad and kindly smile of greeting. His home, it is true, is not over-clean, nor are his habits over-nice, but his hospitality is most hearty.' Rider must have been aware that his comments were likely to upset the Boers, for in a letter home on 6 October 1876, he stated: 'Don't say anything to anybody about my having written things in magazines.'

His interest in writing was clearly growing. In addition to the reports and regular letters home that he was obliged to compose, he had begun to make detailed notes of stories he had been told and descriptions of places he had visited. There were, of course, many tales to be told and many to tell them. It was, however, Sir Theophilus Shepstone to whom Rider listened most. With his missionary father, Shepstone had arrived at the Cape in 1820 when he was three, and in his youth learned the vernacular language of several tribes. From 1856 he had been Secretary of Native Affairs in Natal. Despite the considerable difference in their ages, he and Rider became very close friends. Rider learned much from him: 'He had the power of silence, but he observed everything and forgot little. To me, however, when the mood was on him, he would talk a great deal — the stories I have heard from him would fill half a volume — and sometimes even unfold to me the secret springs of his actions.' Haggard later gave to Allan Quatermain some of Shepstone's earlier biographical details:

I was always a keen observer of the ways of men and nature. By the time that I was twenty I could speak Dutch and three or four Kaffir dialects perfectly, and I doubt if there was anybody in South Africa who understood native ways of thought and action more completely than I did. Also I was really a very good shot and horseman.

(From *Allan's Wife*)

Shepstone's influence on Rider and his novels is clearly considerable. *Nada the Lily* was dedicated to him and he appears as himself in *The Witch's Head*.

In view of the close friendship between the two men, it is not surprising that, when in late November Sir Theophilus Shepstone arrived back in Maritzburg to make preparations for his journey to the Transvaal, he wished to include Haggard in his party. On 2 December 1876, Rider wrote home to inform them that he would be going. He also said that Shepstone had included him in the party for two reasons: 'First, we are very good friends and he was kind enough to say he wished to have me as a companion. Second, I imagine there will be a good deal of what is called the champagne and sherry policy up at Pretoria and he wants somebody to look after the entertaining. It will be a most interesting business.'

Accompanied by an escort of twenty-five Natal Mounted Police, Shepstone with his officials and the servants set off for the Transvaal on 15 December. In addition to Rider and his friend Fynney, the interpreter, the officials included Melmoth Osborn and Marshal Clarke, both of whom were later knighted. The trek from Maritzburg to Pretoria took thirty-five days, during which Rider kept a detailed diary. A prophetic extract from this was included, over twenty years later, in Haggard's *A Farmer's Year*: 'Those wastes, now so dismal and desolate, are at no distant date destined to support and enrich a large population. . . . This vast land will one day be the garden of Africa, the land of gems and gold, of oil and corn, of steam-ploughs and railways.'

The enforced leisurely pace of the party meant that much time was spent each evening round a roaring camp-fire. Years later Haggard remembered the 'moonlit nights of surpassing brilliancy which we watched from beside the fires of our camp. Those camps were very pleasant, and in them, as we smoked and drank our 'square-face' after the day's trek, I heard many a story of savage Africa from Sir Theophilus himself, from Osborn and from Fynney.' In his autobiography Haggard recalls: 'There were never any quarrels among us of Shepstone's staff during that long journey or afterwards. Indeed we were a band of brothers — as brothers ought to be. Personally I formed friendships then, especially with Osborn and Clarke, that endured till their deaths.' Captain Marshal Clarke, like Captain Good in *King Solomon's Mines*, wore an eyeglass. To him, after he had become a Lieutenant-Colonel, Haggard dedicated *Swallow*. On Melmoth Osborn, Haggard based his character Mr Alston in *The Witch's Head*, even using in the novel some of their actual conversations. In *The Days of My Life*, writing about Osborn, Haggard states: 'I never quite fathomed his religious views, but I remember that one night, when I was talking to him on such matters, he stretched out his arm and clasped a handful from the swarm of white ants that were flying past us. "What is the difference between us and these?" he asked with a little laugh, and let them go again.'

'Why should you suppose that for you is reserved a bright destiny among the stars more than for these?' and he put out his hand and clasped several of a swarm of flying-ants which were passing at the time. 'Just think how small must be the difference between these ants and us in the eyes of a Power who can produce both . . . We are bigger, walk on two legs, have a larger capacity for suffering, and, we believe, a soul. Is it so great that we should suppose that for us is reserved a heaven, or all the glorious worlds which people pace — for these, annihilation? Perhaps we are at the top of the tree of development, and for them may be the future, for us the annihilation. Who knows? There, fly away, and make the most of the present, for nothing else is certain.'

(From *The Witch's Head*)

Among the stories that Rider heard from Osborn was his account of the battle he had witnessed at Tugela in 1856 between the two rival sons of Chief Panda, Umbelazi and Cetywayo. This battle Haggard describes in *Child of Storm*, stating in his Author's Note: 'My friend, Sir Melmoth Osborn, who died in or about the year 1897, was present at this battle, although not as a combatant. Well do I remember his thrilling story, told to me over thirty years ago, of the events of that awful day.'

Accompanying Rider on the treck from Maritzburg was his Zulu servant, Mazooku, who appears in *The Witch's Head*:

He was not a very tall man; but, standing there nude except for the *moocha* round his centre, his proportions, especially those of the chest and the lower limbs, looked gigantic. He had been a soldier in one of Cetywayo's regiments, but having been so indiscreet as to break through some of the Zulu marriage laws, had been forced to fly for refuge to Natal, where he had become a groom, and picked up a peculiar language which he called English. Even among a people where all the men are fearless he bore a reputation for bravery.

(From *The Witch's Head*)

Another person, whom Haggard was later to make even more famous, also travelled with the party, as the head attendant to Sir Theophilus. He was Umslopogaas, the son of Mswazi, King of Swaziland, and was then about sixty. Haggard describes him in *The Days of My Life*: 'He was a tall, thin, fierce-faced fellow with a great hole above the left temple over which the skin pulsated, that he had come by in some battle. He said that he had killed ten men in single combat, of whom the first was a chief called Shive, always making use of a battle-axe. However this may be, he was an interesting old fellow from whom I heard many stories that Fynney used to interpret.' This battle-scarred warrior and his tales of battles long ago clearly made a deep impression on Rider:

He was a very tall, broad man, quite six feet three, I should say, but gaunt, with lean, wiry-looking limbs. . . . He came out with his thin aristocratic-looking hand placed before his face to hide a yawn, so I could only see that he was a Keshla, or ringed man, and that he had a great three-cornered hole in his forehead. In another second he removed his hand, revealing a powerful-looking Zulu face, with a humorous mouth, a short woolly beard, tinged with grey, and a pair of brown eyes keen as hawk's. I knew the man at once. . . . 'How do you do, Umslopogaas?' I said quietly in Zulu.

(From *Allan Quatermain*)

In *Nada the Lily* Haggard tells of Umslopogaas's early life and how in fair combat he won possession of his famous battle-axe.

There was much to excite and enthral Rider on the long trek. For the first time he was taking part in a dangerous mission that was important enough to be of interest even at home. It was an experience that he would often attempt to re-create. Only one thing marred his pleasure — he was travelling even farther from contact with Lilly whom, despite the enforced irregularity of their correspondence and his uncertainty about the future, he loved with a constantly deepening intensity. On the hot Christmas day spent trekking to Ladysmith his thoughts turned to his loved ones left at home. In his travel diary he wrote: 'It seemed queer, riding along in the heat over those desolate African plains, gun in hand, to think of the people at home, and the holly-decked rooms, the warm fire and the church bells. We never realize what it means until we become wanderers on the face of the earth — the old home, the old faces, and the Christmas Days of our childhood.'[5]

On 27 January 1877, Shepstone and his party arrived in Pretoria and were given an unexpectedly enthusiastic welcome. The public affirmation that the Transvaal's independence would be respected seemed to have been accepted by most people, as was the belief that the British presence would prevent the anticipated attack from Secocoeni's armies. Dinners, balls and receptions were given on such a lavish scale that Rider pondered over where the money to pay for them was found in a country that was almost bankrupt and so mismanaged that taxes were no longer being collected.

It became obvious in the following weeks that the real purpose of Shepstone's mission was to achieve the annexation of the Transvaal by the British. President Burgers protested weakly, but, having lost the support of the more traditionalistic, recalcitrant Boers, he was unable to act effectively. Opposition to the British, led by Paul Kruger, began to grow. Yet, despite the vitriolic public debate and proliferating intrigue, Shepstone appeared to be doing nothing. On 1 March Shepstone informed the Executive Council of the Transvaal that annexation was the best solution to the country's problems. Although the Volksraad (people's parliament) angrily rejected the proposal and appointed Paul Kruger the Vice-President, it was prorogued until October 1881 and its members rode back home to their farms. It was clear that annexation was inevitable and that there would be no organised, armed resistance to it.

During these two months of inactivity coupled with noticeably increasing hostility, Rider grew restless. The excitement, adventures, and paid employment for which he had hoped were not forthcoming. With time to brood, Rider could think only of Lilly. As his anxiety about the possible outcome of their continued separation grew, he decided that he must return home, make public their engagement and speedily marry. He wrote first to his mother and his sister Mary to tell them of his intention. Then he informed Shepstone, who, because of his affection and concern for Rider, tried to dissuade him from acting rashly. Rider, however, was adamant and so, perhaps to delay his departure, Shepstone said that he wanted

24

his protégé to take some dispatches to England on the situation in the Transvaal and promised him a job when he returned. While he waited for the documents to be prepared, Rider packed his belongings and sent them down to the Cape. On 13 March he wrote a long letter to his father to inform him of the high honour Shepstone had bestowed on him, claiming 'it is indirectly a great compliment to myself. Any young fellow can carry despatches, but it is not everybody of my age and short experience who would be trusted to give private information on so important a subject as the unexpected annexation of a splendid territory as large as Great Britain, information which may probably be made use of in Parliament.' He did not, however, mention his marriage plans.

At this time rumours were circulating in Pretoria that Chief Secocoeni had signed a peace treaty with the Boers, thus removing the threat of war that was the main justification for the British presence in the Transvaal. Shepstone, however, received a letter denying the existence of such a treaty from the Rev. A. Merensky, a German missionary at Botsabelo, close to Secocoeni's country. Shepstone and President Burgers agreed that the rumour should be investigated by a commission consisting of two representatives of the Transvaal Government and, from Shepstone's staff, Osborn and Clarke, to whom Haggard would act as secretary. His appointment to this important and dangerous mission thus postponed Rider's return home.

The journey to Secocoeni's encampment took the commissioners through spectacular scenery and fever-infested valleys. On the second day they stayed with the Rev. Merensky at Botsabelo. This cultured agent of the Berlin Missionary Society was famed for his armed defence of the mission station that Rider later described: 'On a hill-top overshadowing the station, are placed the fortifications, consisting of thick walls running in a circle with upstanding towers, in which stand one or two cannon; but it all reminds one more of an old Norman keep, with its village clustered in its protecting shadow, than of a modern mission establishment.'

After many difficulties, including the death of one of their horses, the commissioners on 27 March entered the Basuto chief's camp. 'It was an uncanny kind of place. If you got up at night, if you moved anywhere, you became aware that dozens or hundreds of eyes were watching you. Privacy was impossible.' Discussions with Secocoeni lasted throughout most of the next day, and Rider faithfully made notes of the conversation as translated from Sesutu and Dutch into English. Eventually it was clear that the Chief had not signed a treaty with the Boers. The three members of Shepstone's staff were asked to meet Secocoeni privately. After the meeting they returned to their hut and discovered that the Boer members of the commission had already departed, leaving the three without guides. After a considerable time two young men were produced, called Sekouil and Nojoiani, whose names Rider and his companions corrupted into Scowl and No-joke.

They set off on their return journey at about 3.30 p.m. Travelling through the night, they found the scenery even more impressive by moonlight. Later Rider recorded: 'It was solemn, weird. Every valley became a mysterious deep, and every hill, stone and tree shone with that cold pale lustre which the moon alone can throw. Silence reigned, the silence of the dead, broken only once or twice by the wild whistling challenge of one of Secocoeni's warriors as he came bounding down the rocks, to see who we were that passed.'[6] In time Rider embroidered upon this incident, exaggerating the danger and the role he played in securing the party's safe return. It was to become one of his favourite stories. In the version retold in his autobiography the party reached a place in the mountains where the path forks, one branch going upwards, the other running down into the deep valley. In the discussion as to which path should be taken the guides, supported by Osborn and Clarke, strongly advocated the upper path, but Rider, convinced that the view would be better in the moonlit valley, disagreed. At last Osborn said, 'Oh! let the young donkey have his way. Who knows, perhaps he is right!' Rider's choice of path saved the party from an ambush and almost certain death for, after travelling some distance, they heard war-horns and saw armed Basuto warriors on the mountain path. Rider was later informed that Secocoeni had indeed planned to kill them, and, being forewarned, the Boer commissioners had gone on ahead. Haggard also tells the story of the party's narrow escape in *The Witch's Head*. In this case, however, Ernest's choice is the upper path:

On they rode steadily through the moonlight and the silence, little guessing how near death was to them. The faint beauty of the scene sank deep into Ernest's heart, and presently, when they came to a spot where a track ran out loopwise from the main pass, returning to it a couple of miles farther on, he half insisted on their taking it, because it passed over yet higher ground, and would give them a better view of the moon-bathed valley. Mr Alston grumbled at 'his nonsense' and complied, and meanwhile a party of murderers half a mile farther on played with their assegais, and wondered why they did not hear the sound of the white men's feet. But the white men had already passed along the higher path three-quarters of a mile to their right. Ernest's love of moonlight effects had saved them all from a certain and perhaps from a lingering death.

(From *The Witch's Head*)

On the way back, all the horses, including Rider's, died of horse-fever. Having reached Pretoria, Scowl refused to return home and was employed by Rider 'until he took to wearing a black coat, and turned Christian, when he shortly afterwards developed into a drunkard and a thief'. He appears, as Allan Quatermain's servant, in *Child of Storm*.

During Rider's absence from Pretoria, rumours proliferated and it was widely believed that Cetywayo was about to attack the capital. The return of the commission allowed Shepstone to act and on 9 April he informed the Government that he was about to declare the Transvaal British territory. Three days later, at about eleven o'clock in the morning, while Shepstone remained in his residence, several members of his staff, including Rider, marched into the Market Place. Osborn started to read the proclamation but, as the trembling of his hands made it difficult,

Rider stepped forward and completed the reading.

An account of the events leading up to the annexation form a substantial part of Haggard's first book *Cetywayo and his White Neighbours*. He also uses the period in *The Witch's Head*. But the most surprising reference to the annexation in Haggard's writing occurs in his novel *Finished* where the part he played is related by Alan Quatermain:

> In the middle appeared an elderly gentleman with whiskers and a stoop, in whom I recognized Mr Osborn, known by the Kaffirs as Malimati, the Chief of the Staff. By his side was a tall young fellow, yourself, my friend, scarcely more than a lad then, carrying papers. The rest stood to right and left in a formal line. *You* gave a printed document to Mr Osborn who put on his glasses and began to read in a low voice which few could hear, and I noticed that his hand trembled. Presently he grew confused, lost his place, found it, lost it again and came to a full stop. . . .
>
> There followed a very awkward pause such as occurs when a man breaks down in a speech. The members of the Staff looked at him and at each other, then behold! you, my friend, grabbed the paper from his hand and went on reading it in a loud clear voice. . . .

The annexation accomplished, Rider prepared to leave Pretoria for Cape Town, but the day before his departure he received a letter from his father, written on 27 March, the same day the commission had entered Secocoeni's camp. Although it had been posted before Rider's letter giving the reasons for returning had arrived, his father had obviously been informed of Rider's plan. He forbade his son to return home and chastised him for abandoning a good career with the intention of again becoming financially dependent on his family. To rub salt into the wound he further pointed out that Rider had overdrawn his annual allowance of £100 by £25. Rider was deeply upset and at once destroyed 'this most painful letter'. His father's words, he recalled some thirty-four years later, 'hurt me so much that immediately after reading them I withdrew my formal resignation and cancelled the passage I had taken in the post-cart to Kimberley *en route* for the Cape and England.' A few days later another letter from his father arrived, presumably in response to his own. The message, however, had not changed. So at yet another important juncture in Rider's life, his impatient, autocratic father had dictated the course his over-sensitive son was to take.

II

The days following the annexation were anxious ones for Shepstone and his staff as they waited to hear how it had been received throughout the country, but it was soon obvious that the announcement was not going to be met by any troublesome resistance. At the beginning of April a British army battalion entered Pretoria and a superficial tranquillity settled on the Transvaal. Business began to recover and on 24 May, the Queen's birthday, it was thought acceptable to hoist the Union Jack for the first time. As the army band played the National Anthem and the artillery fired a salute, Colonel Brooke, Shepstone's secretary, and Haggard ran up the flag. 'Twenty years hence,' he wrote to his mother at the time, 'it will be a great thing to have hoisted the Union Jack over the Transvaal for the first time.' Throughout his life this act remained a source of great pride and it was included in many of the potted versions of his life that later appeared so frequently in newspapers and magazines.

Shortly after the annexation, the British Government sent William Sergeaunt, a Crown Agent for the Colonies, to the Transvaal to report on the country's financial condition. Among the people who accompanied him were three young men: Mr J. Sergeaunt, his son, Captain Patterson and Arthur Cochrane, who stayed on in the Transvaal and with whom Rider struck up a close friendship. For the first time since arriving in Africa, Rider had young men of his own age as friends.

As the British Government established control over the Transvaal, the administrative structure was revised and many new appointments made. Because of his friendship with and allegiance to Shepstone, Rider obviously expected to be given a permanent and salaried post in the new Government. While he waited, perhaps spurred on by the appearance in May of his article 'The Transvaal', he wrote for the *Gentleman's Magazine* his account of 'A Visit to the Chief Secocoeni'. Feeling bitter at the continuing hostile attitude to the British of many Boers, Rider included an outspoken description of a Boer family: 'In the corner, on a chair, made twice as large as any of the others, reposed the mother of the family, a woman of large size. The whole house was pervaded by a sickly odour, like that of a vault, whilst the grime and filth of it baffle description.' The article appeared, above the initials H.R.H., in September 1877.

At last Rider's hopes of a post in the new administration were realised. On 1 June he was appointed English Clerk to the Colonial Secretary's Office with an annual salary of £250. He was also made Clerk to the Executive Council with an additional £50 a year. Obtaining the two jobs meant that he would work for both Osborn, the Colonial Secretary, and Shepstone, the Governor. Delighted at the news, he wrote to his father for the first time since receiving the order not to return home. His letter began: 'My dear father — I have to acknowledge your two letters dated respectively 27 March and the 4 April. I do not think it will be of any good to dwell any more on what is to me, in some ways at least, a rather painful subject.' Having given the details of his appointment, he continued, 'I think that I shall always do pretty well here. However, my aim is of course to rise to the position of a Colonial Governor, and to do that I must trust to good fortune and my interest.'

Haggard concluded by apologising for having overdrawn by £25 the allowance of £200 that his father had given him to last for his first two years in Africa, but he pointed out that his expenses involved in the Secocoeni mission had been considerable. Unless he was paid for the work he had done, he would have to borrow a further £20 to meet the cost of transporting his baggage to and from Cape Town. Rider obviously discussed his financial difficulties with Shepstone, for he was given a gratuity of £25, 'an acknowledgment of your services to the mission for which you received no pay', and £20 as compensation for the horse that had died.

Unfortunately this payment did not solve all Rider's problems and four days later, on 5 June, he wrote again to his father, pointing out that he would have to find somewhere to live in Pretoria. He had decided that his most sensible course of action would be to build a house and so, as in a few days he would come of age, he inquired if the trustees would consent to his obtaining a legacy of £500 that had been left to him by a godparent. Even though his father wrote giving consent, it was over a year before Rider went ahead with his plan. During that period he first stayed in Shepstone's residence, the new Government House, before moving into Obsorn's house.

Having accepted his appointment, Rider was committed to staying in the Transvaal much longer than he had at first anticipated. Although pleased to be on the way to achieving financial independence, he was distressed that it prolonged his separation from Lilly. This must have been much in his mind when, on 17 June, he wrote to his mother: 'My absence, which I remember we set down at five years at the most, is likely to be a long one now, my dearest mother. The break from all home and family ties and the sense of isolation are very painful, more painful than those who have never tried them know.' It is unlikely that his separation from his family upset him most. It was Lilly he missed. Unfortunately we do not know what he wrote to her — his letters are no longer extant — but his feelings must have been similar to those he later attributed to Ernest in *The Witch's Head*:

> Already Ernest began to find it something of a labour to indite epistles to people in England, and yet he had the pen of a ready writer. The links that bound them together were fast breaking loose. Eva, and Eva alone, remained clear and real to the vision of his mind. She was always with him; and to her, at any period of his life, he never found difficulty in writing.
>
> (From *The Witch's Head*)

In August Rider was given an unexpected opportunity to further his career. The Master and Registrar of the new High Court, which had been ceremonially opened on 22 May, suddenly died. As he had been the chief assistant to John G. Kotzé, the newly appointed and only judge for the entire Transvaal, the post was important in the uncertain and acrimonious post-annexation period. Shepstone, looking for an honest, reliable man, asked Rider to act as a replacement. This was a great honour for someone who was only just twenty-one and who had not had legal training or experience.

As there was only one judge, the high court was peripatetic and shortly after Rider was armed with a Martini-Henry carbine rifle and a shotgun and the Judge circuit through the Transvaal. They travelled in a comfortable spring-wagon drawn by eight oxen. Inside they carried an ample store of provisions. The High Sheriff and the Acting Attorney-General accompanied them in a similar wagon. As Rider was armed with a Martini-Henry carbine rifle and a shotgun and the Judge also carried a rifle, the party was kept well supplied with fresh meat.

Rider also took with him his servant, Mazooku, and Moresco, the hunter he had purchased to replace Metal, the pony that had died during the Secocoeni mission. On the third day of the circuit, Rider went hunting alone on Moresco. He rode into a herd of wildebeest. 'When once he began to gallop game, Moresco was a horse that could not be held; the only thing to do was to let him have his head. Into that herd he plunged.' At length, having killed a crazed bull he had previously wounded, Rider realised that he was lost. Despite riding around for hours, he could not find his camp. In the gloom Moresco stumbled and Rider took a terrible fall, but he remounted and rode on until it was dark. In his autobiography he recalls: 'Then I dismounted, slipped the horse's reins over my arm, and, lying down on the fire-swept veld, placed the saddle-cloth over me to try to protect myself against the cold, which at that season of the year was very bitter on this high land. Wet through, exhausted, shaken, and starved as I was — for I had eaten nothing since the previous night — my position was what might be called precarious. Game trekked past me; I could see their outlines by the light of such stars as there were. Then hyenas came and howled about me.' This experience, like so many others, was used by Haggard in his fiction:

> Then he got off his horse and took off the saddle, which he put down on the bare, black veld, for a fire had recently swept off the dry grass, and wrapping the saddle-cloth round his feet, laid his aching head upon the saddle. The reins he hitched round his arm, lest the horse should stray away from him to look for food. The wind was bitterly cold, and he was wet through; the hyenas came and howled round him.

(From *The Witch's Head*)

Before Rider went to sleep, he discharged his last three cartridges. Eventually he awoke to hear shots in the distance. It was Mazooku who, when his master did not return to the camp, had set off on foot to find him. At last he saw the flashes from the rifle and walked for several miles towards their source, shouting all the way. Mazooku then led Rider safely back to camp. This incident created the special relationship Rider had with both Mazooku and Moresco.

As they travelled through the Transvaal, Rider and the Judge enjoyed each other's company and the freedom of life in the open. Rider shot a good deal of game and, as Kotzé records in his *Memoirs and Reminiscences*, revealed an unexpected talent: 'To our pleasant surprise, I may say astonishment and admiration, this genial, high-spirited and romantic young man, bred and educated as befits a gentleman's son, proved himself to be an excellent cook! He prepared for our evening meal dishes which would have done credit to a first-class chef.'[4] Rider also profited from being on circuit. He not only quickly acquired an understanding of his duties, he also met many influential citizens and visited most of the important settlements. The notes he kept were later invaluable in providing scenes and characters for his novels, especially *Jess*.

One of the places the two men visted was a cave at Wonderfontein. Kotzé records the visit in his memoirs: 'We had each provided ourselves with a packet of candles, and by the light of these the moist and glistening stalactite formations presented an unusual and pretty sight. The dripping water from above, charged with lime, had formed numerous pillars of varying thickness. . . . In the centre, about eight feet from the floor, there was an opening in a very thick pillar resembling a pulpit':[8]

> Its stupendous size was the least of the wonders of the place, for running in rows adown its length were gigantic pillars of what looked like ice, but were, in reality, huge stalagmites . . .

> Sometimes the stalagmites took strange forms, presumably where the dropping of the water had not always been on the same spot. Thus, one huge mass, which must have weighed a hundred tons or so, was in the form of a pulpit, beautifully fretted over outside with what looked like lace.

> (From *King Solomon's Mines*)

After returning to Pretoria towards the end of October, Rider wrote to his mother about his travels: 'Do you know one quite gets to like this sort of life. It is a savage kind of existence but it certainly has attractions, shooting your own dinner and cooking it — I can hardly sleep in a house now, it seems to stifle one.' He also reports that he had met Anthony Trollope during his visit to the Transvaal: 'I talked with him a good deal. He has the most peculiar ideas and is as obstinate as a pig.'[9] Rider's first encounter with the novelist was amusing. Having returned to Government House late at night, Rider went into his bedroom and began to look for some matches. To his surprise a gruff voice asked who he was. Rider identified himself and demanded to know who was in his bed. 'Anthony Trollope,' was the reply.

In Pretoria the social life of the British was pleasant, for there was much entertaining. The presence of the military with its band meant that there were balls given either by the officers or the townsfolk. There were also riding parties, games of croquet, whist evenings and musical 'At Homes'. At Government House, Shepstone presided with a paternal kindness. Kotzé states, 'His after-dinner anecdotes of frontier life on the Cape Border and of his numerous other native experiences were related with a clearness and impressiveness that made it a real pleasure to listen to him. To young Rider Haggard they were indeed a revelation and delight.'[10]

Yet, despite the pleasant social whirl, there were problems. Opposition from the Boers to British rule was being more effectively organised. Kruger went to England as part of a deputation to demand the repeal of the annexation. The native tribes were also growing restive. The British were able to deal with the early attacks, repelling the Galekas who invaded across the Bashee in September, 1877. Rider was indirectly involved on his return to Pretoria in an apparently unimportant situation, which had tragic consequences. A succession dispute arose among the Matabele, whose territory was near the Zambesi. Lobengula had usurped the rightful heir, Kuruman. Sir Bartle Frere, the High Commissioner for South Africa, decided to send a friendly mission to Lobengula. It was suggested that Captain Patterson and Mr Sergeaunt should go, because they were keen to visit the Zambesi Falls and do some hunting. Rider wanted to accompany his friends, but he was informed that he could not be released from his duties. He did, however, lend Patterson and Sergeaunt two of his servants — Khiva and Ventvogel — and on the day they set off he rode with them for a few miles. He never saw them again. The whole party was murdered by soldiers of Lobengula.

Rider was deeply upset by the tragic loss of his friends. It is possible that the Matabele succession dispute provided the idea for the fictional struggle between Ignosi and Tuala in *King Solomon's Mines*. Certainly Rider must have heard much about the conflict because, as he states in *Cetywayo and His White Neighbours*, K(u)ruman 'for a time acted as gardener to Sir T. Shepstone in Natal' and when the murders took place was living in the Transvaal. Haggard's two servants, Khiva and Ventvogel, appear in *King Solomon's Mines* and he stated in 1907, 'In life they were such men as are there described.'[11]

In November the high court opened in Pretoria. As the Boers were extremely litigious, Rider had much work to do. Among the lawyers Rider met in the high court was G.H. Buskes. According to Lilias Haggard, 'He was an extraordinarily handsome man with a golden beard, intelligent, highly educated, musical, but black-hearted and cruel beyond belief.'[12] Later in the Anglo-Boer War of 1880, Buskes was secretary of the Boer Committee at Potchefstrom, where, according to the British, he was responsible for a number of atrocities which Haggard describes in an appendix to *Cetywayo and His White Neighbours*. Buskes was the original of Frank Muller in *Jess*:

> He was a large and exceedingly handsome man, apparently about forty years old, with clear-cut features, cold, light-blue eyes, and a remarkable golden beard that hung over his chest. For a Boer he was rather smartly dressed in English-made tweed clothes, and tall riding boots.
>
> (From *Jess*)

As 1878 approached, fear of a Zulu uprising grew, and on 10 December Rider enlisted as a cavalry volunteer, although, because of the importance of his duties, he was not called on to serve with the force that under Major Clarke was dispatched to keep Secocoeni's army in check. Shepstone too left Pretoria to arbitrate in a contentious Zulu border dispute. The Boers were also increasing their agitation against the British. Rider, because of his position as acting Registrar (which many of the Boers hoped would not be made permanent), was an object of attack and suitable mud to sling was soon found. The comments on the Boers that Rider had made in his articles were traced back to him and then, as he wrote to his mother in a letter on 4 March, 'Some spiteful brute translated it into Dutch with comments and published it in the local papers. The Boers are furious; there are two things they cannot bear — the truth and ridicule. . . . It is precious little I care about them and their threats.'

As a footnote to this letter Rider adds, 'I have a pleasing duty to peform early to-morrow — go and see a man executed.' The man who was executed was the Swazi chief Ubekana who had been found guilty in the high court of responsibility for the murder of Mr Bell, the Special Justice of the Peace for New Scotland. In his autobiography Haggard declares: 'The executioner proved to be hopelessly drunk. . . . The High Sheriff, Juta, overcome by the spectacle, retired into a corner of the yard, where he was violently ill. The thing had to be done, and between a drunken executioner and an overcome High Sheriff it devolved upon me. So I stood over that executioner and forced him to perform his office.'

According to the Judge Kotzé, whose accurate memory Haggard praised, the actual events were very different. In his memoirs he calls Haggard's version 'pure romance, and not in keeping with fact'. He continues, 'It was not Mr Juta, the High Sheriff, as stated by him, that was overcome that morning and retired sick into the corner of the gaol yard, but Sir Rider himself; nor was the hangman intoxicated; and the statement that Haggard was consequently left alone to force the unfortunate hangman to do his duty is wholly imaginary.' To this Kotzé adds a most illuminating footnote: 'Those who knew Haggard recognized in him a man of honour and truth. But his was an extraordinary mind. He was emotional and much given to romancing. His imagination impelled him into a world of fancy which for the time had complete hold of his sense, and hence he described as fact what was mere fiction.'[13]

During the first three months of 1878 Rider was still somewhat unsettled. He had been separated from Lilly for over two and a half years and yet he was still not in a secure enough position to marry her. Again his father cautioned against acting rashly and on 31 March Rider replied, 'Very many thanks for your long and kind letter of 20 February 1878 and all the advice it contained. With what you say I to a very great extent agree. I had some idea of shifting, but recent events have considerably altered my plans.' The reason for the changed plans was that Rider had heard that he was almost certain to be appointed Master and Registrar. Seven days later he again writes home, gleefully announcing the confirmation of the appointment at an annual salary of £400 per annum.

Rider had every reason to be pleased; at twenty-one he had become the youngest head of a government department in South Africa. His future seemed assured and he was able to inform Lilly that he was at last in a position to marry her.

Impatiently he waited for her reply. 'Then one day,' he records in *The Days of My Life*, 'the mail cart arrived and all was over. It was a crushing blow, so crushing that at the time I should not have been sorry if I could have departed from the world.' Lilias Haggard in her biography adds a little more information, although, as has been pointed out, she does not identify the woman she calls Lilith who jilted her father: 'It was an ordinary enough tale. Africa was a long way from England and the impecunious young man was a long time coming home. The rich and desirable match meanwhile dwelt persistently on the doorstep, persistently reminding her how desirable he was. . . . So she wrote a sad little letter and married the other man.'[14]

We do not now know what Lilly Jackson wrote. It is possible that her brief note was enclosed in a letter from Mary, Rider's sister and confidante. Certainly the Haggard family were aware of Lilly's decision and the pressures that had been placed upon her before Haggard received the news, because Lilias gives us this surprising information: 'William Haggard, evidently now fully aware of the state of affairs . . . wrote and offered [her] a home at Bradenham until Rider could get back from Africa. She refused it and went her way.'

The actual news that Rider received from England was that on 4 June 1878, Lilly Jackson was going to marry at St James's Church, Westminster, Francis Bradley Archer, banker and stockbroker, the sole trustee of the Jackson fortune. The information arrived too late for Rider to do anything about it. He could not even send a letter that would arrive before the wedding ceremony took place. The match was ill-fated for, as Lilias Haggard comments, 'that marriage brought disaster and sorrow to her and her relatives'.

Rider was heartbroken by the news and says, 'Its effects on me also were very bad indeed, for it left me utterly reckless and unsettled.' He did, however, decide to stay in the Transvaal, and on 2 June — two days before the wedding — he wrote to his father asking for the £500 that a year earlier his trustees had agreed to advance. With this, he announced that he intended 'to build a nice house with Cochrane. In a place of this sort it is a great thing to have a pleasant home, and it will also be a very sound investment. I have bought two acres at the top end of the town, where land will soon become very valuable.' When the money arrived, the house was built for a total cost of £300, including the land. Because it had only two rooms and a kitchen, Cochrane and Rider called their house 'The Palatial'. Years after Rider had left the Transvaal it became known as 'Jess's Cottage':

> About a quarter of a mile from the outskirts of the camp stood a little house known, probably on account of its diminutive size, as 'The Palatial'. . . . It consisted of two rooms — a bedroom and a good-sized sitting-room, in which still stood a table and a few chairs, with a stable and a kitchen at the back.
>
> (from *Jess*)

In August, Rider set off on another circuit tour with Judge Kotzé. The places visited were much the same as before, but, unlike the first trip, all the men were armed, because of the growing fear of a Zulu attack. Rider wrote to a friend in England, on 23 August, 'We had rather a lively time of it. . . . The road was dangerous, and there was a chance of our being attacked at night. It is a great nuisance as one has to keep a sharp look out. . . . We had to sleep with a perfect armful of loaded guns and rifles of which I was more afraid than of the Kaffirs.'[15] When the party was travelling through the horse-breeding area of New Scotland, Moresco, Rider's hunter, broke away from the wagons to join a troop of mares. After a fruitless search, the party had to continue without Rider's favourite horse. Three days later, on climbing out of the wagon first thing in the morning, he discovered Moresco standing untied among the other horses. In *A Farmer's Year*, published eleven years later, Haggard concludes, 'I can only suppose that this horse, when he was tired of the company of the mares, had deliberately taken up our spoor and followed it till he found us forty or fifty miles away.'

Back in Pretoria, Rider and Cochrane moved into 'The Palatial'. How these two carefree young men, living apart from their elders, spent the last six months of 1878 is difficult now to reconstruct for, unlike the remainder of Rider's sojourn in Africa, it is almost completely unrecorded. Rider hints at what happened when he says a setback in love affects a young man: 'It unsteadies him, makes him reckless, and perhaps throws him in the way of undesirable adventures.' His daughter is a little more specific, thereby suggesting that the matter was at least a subject of family speculation. About Cochrane and her father she writes, 'They were, however, both young, healthy and more than a little wild, and in Rider's case the shock and bitterness of his disastrous love affair had left him utterly reckless and unsettled, without any anchor or particular goal on which to fix his ambitions. . . . There is no doubt . . . the inevitable feminine complications ensued.'[16]

The references to 'undesirable adventures' and 'feminine complications', suggest that Rider had more than emotional entanglements with women. The remorse and moral censure with which Haggard later described his peccadilloes after Lilly's marriage strongly suggest that they had been sexual ones. Living as he did in a country where there were few single British women, Rider's 'feminine complications' could have arisen from a relationship with either a married British woman or a foreigner. That Rider would have made advances to married women is unlikely for, as a child of his age, he regarded them as sacrosanct. It is impossible that Rider had any relationship with a Boer woman. His hostility to the Boers at that time was well-known. Judge Kotzé, writing about the circuit completed in August 1878, states, 'Haggard could not, however, be persuaded into visiting the homes of the Boers. He was strongly prejudiced against them, and so avoided them, although they had never offended him in any way.'[17] There is some evidence in his fiction to suggest that he may have found female companions who came to Africa from other European countries: in *Marie*, for example, Allan Quatermain marries Marie Leblanc, who came from France. It is, however, much more likely that, if Rider had his first sexual relationship at this time, the girl was black.

It was, of course, not uncommon for the white colonialist to find African women sexually attractive. As they were considered to be godless and therefore incorruptible, they were legitimate sexual prey to Victorian young men, deprived of the company of young unmarried women, who had been brought up in a country where the prevailing sexual *mores* tolerated prostitution as a necessary evil. Characters in Haggard's novels are often advised to take a native mistress:

Take my advice, Ernest: . . . go in for an Intombi. It is not too late yet, and there is no mistake about the sort of clay of which a Kafir girl is made.

(From *The Witch's Head*)

The possibility that Rider followed such advice and had an illicit relationship with a black woman seems to be strongly supported by the frequency with which he deals in his fiction with a love affair between a white adventurer and a coloured girl. He also frequently describes the physical beauty of African women with an enthusiasm that must have seemed strange to many of his Victorian readers:

> There, standing in a beam of golden light that, passing through the smoke-hole, pierced the soft gloom of the hut, stood the most beautiful creature that I have ever seen — that is, if it be admitted that a person who is black, or rather copper-coloured, can be beautiful.
>
> She was a little above the medium height, not more, with a figure that, so far as I am a judge of such matters, was absolutely perfect — that of a Greek statue indeed. On this point I had an opportunity of forming an opinion, since, except for her little bead apron and a single string of large blue beads about her throat, her costume was — well, that of a Greek statue.

(From Child of Storm)

Most of the native women described as being beautiful by Haggard have some European facial features, and so it is possible to accuse him, as some modern critics have done, of merely describing white women with black faces. It seems far more probable that he was in fact recalling the beautiful 'copper-coloured' girl with whom he had once, however fleetingly, had an affair and whose image, like all those other matters of importance to him, he could never forget.

By the end of 1878, circumstances had brought Rider's period of wild, irresponsible adventures to an end. On 11 December Sir Bartle Frere, concerned at the mounting threat of a Zulu invasion, issued an ultimatum to Chief Cetywayo. The demands, including the disbandment of the army and the payment of reparations, were not met within the stipulated thirty days and so on 11 January, 1879, Frere sent a large contingent of British troops into Zululand. Eleven days later 10,000 Zulu warriors attacked a carelessly unprotected camp of 772 European and 851 native soldiers at Isandhlwana. Within hours all but fifty-five of the British soldiers had been killed, including several of Rider's friends, for many of the men were volunteers. It took about four days for news of the massacre to reach Pretoria. Rider, however, heard of it the day after the battle, for an old Hottentot woman, washing clothes in his garden, told him that the redcoats lay upon the plain 'like leaves under the trees in winter'. When the full horror of the story was confirmed, there was panic throughout South Africa and bemused anger in Britain at the proved incompetence of the army commanders.

Deeply upset by the tragedy, Rider collected all the information he could about the tragic battle, and was able to talk with some of the survivors. Fourteen years later he wrote a detailed account of the events at Isandhlwana for inclusion in Andrew Lang's *The True Story Book*. The battle is also described in *The Witch's Head*, *Finished* and, more briefly, in *Black Heart and White Heart*.

After Isandhlwana, it seemed likely that Cetywayo's army would sweep through the Transvaal and Natal. Shepstone was recalled to the Colonial Office to discuss the situation in the Transvaal, where the stunned, demoralised British residents, no longer able to rely upon the protection of their army, were forced to organise their own defence.

Rider wrote to his father: 'You and my mother must not be alarmed my dear father when I tell you that I shall very likely go down to the border with a volunteer troop shortly. The emergency is too great, and mounted men are too urgently needed for us to hang back now, especially when one's example may bring others.' The men of Pretoria, including Rider and Cochrane, formed a mounted troop they called 'The Pretoria Horse' and to his lasting pleasure Rider was elected adjutant and one of the corps' two lieutenants.

It was intended that the volunteers would ride out to attack the Zulu enemy, but events changed the plan. The Boers, realising the vulnerability of the British, determined to press their demands for the independence of the Transvaal. About three thousand of them gathered in and around a laager some thirty miles from Pretoria. Haggard was sent with a few men to keep watch on the camp. He took his responsibilities seriously, relishing the possibility of being at war either with Boers or Zulus. In the early weeks there were a few dangerous moments, but in time the pleasurable feeling of expectancy gave way to the tedium of military routine. The Zulus did not advance and eventually it became clear that the Boers, although still threatening, would not attack. Rider was, therefore, denied the adventures he had so keenly anticipated.

In April Sir Bartle Frere arrived in Pretoria to conduct negotiations with the Boer leaders. Rider commanded the guard of honour that escorted Frere into the town, and met him several times. At one of these meetings Frere reprimanded Rider for having been critical of the Boers in the articles he had written. When Rider replied that he had written only the truth, Frere said, 'Haggard, do you not know that there are occasions on which the truth is the last thing that should be uttered? I beg you in future to keep it to yourself.'

The incident led Rider to believe that he was likely to lose his position as Master and Registrar. In a letter, sent to his mother in April, he writes: 'Sir Bartle was very civil to me. . . . They say, however, that he intends to get rid of us all — the Annexationists — to please the Boers. I am perfectly indifferent, as I can do much better in other ways.'[18]

There were other factors exacerbating Rider's feeling of uncertainty about his future. The close comradeship he had at first found with the team of administrators in the Transvaal no longer existed. It is also clear that, perhaps because of the 'feminine complications' that had arisen, he had decided to return home for a spell, perhaps in the hope of finding a suitable wife.

Presumably Rider discussed his future with Osborn who, while Shepstone was in Britain, was his superior. Osborn, however, was also disillusioned with the British Government's obvious failure either to recognise the significance of the annexation or to provide determined support. Rider wished to leave both the Transvaal and government service in order to take up farming on his return from

England, and Osborn offered to sell Rider some three thousand acres of land at Newcastle in Natal, together with Hilldrop, the house that Osborn had built when he was the Resident Magistrate there. Rider and Arthur Cochrane accepted Osborn's offer and his advice to breed ostriches on the land which neither of them had ever seen.

Having previously informed Judge Kotzé of his intention, Rider, on 29 May 1879, tendered his resignation to Osborn, stating, 'I also wish to state that I resign my appointment for private reasons only, since it is one that had circumstances permitted I should have been proud to continue to fill.[19] His resignation was accepted. 'The Palatial' was sold for £650, thus making a handsome profit, and the two young men rode off to buy ostriches in the area that is now Johannesburg. Cochrane drove the ostriches to Hilldrop; Mazooku followed with Moresco, his master's favourite horse; and Haggard, accompanied by John Osborn, the sixteen-year old son of Sir Melmoth, rode to the coast, the first stage of the journey back to England.

Haggard had been away from home for four years. During that time the boy had become a man. He had been forced by the extreme demands of the uncertain life in Africa to acknowledge his weaknesses and glory in his strengths and after sampling many pleasures, he was adjusted to accepting readily the comfortable security of matrimony. He had not, however, survived unscathed. Throughout the rest of his life he suffered silently from the ineradicable scars of Lilly's rejection and the remorse-inducing sins he believed he had committed. Most important, he carried back with him a mind full of incidents, people and places that, if in years to come he had not re-created in the pages of his early fiction, would have been forgotten.

3

The Marriage Settlement

I

By not announcing his intention to return home, Rider had pre-empted his father's irascible interference. Although during his years in Africa he had grown in confidence, he knew that he could not predict his father's reaction when they met. When Rider's ship called at Ascension Island, his brother Jack, who was based there as a First Lieutenant on H.M.S. *Flora*, gave him a gigantic live turtle to take back home in the hold as a present for their father. This unusual gift was a source of great amusement to the other passengers, one of whom composed this not inappropriate rhyme:

> 'Tis true, O my Father, from distant lands
> I've come, a bad penny, back on your hands;
> But when once you have tasted this nice green fat,
> You won't care, O my Parent, one kipper for that.

Unfortunately when Rider arrived at London Docks in August, 1879, the turtle had mysteriously disappeared.

No doubt concerned by this inauspicious start to his return as the prodigal son, Rider decided not to travel straight to the family home at Bradenham, but went instead to see his brother Andrew, who was with his regiment at Devonport. On 11 August, Andrew wrote as a harbinger to their father: 'Rider has been stopping with me two or three days. He expects to be able to get home to Bradenham at the end of the week. I have talked over his plans with him carefully and am of the opinion his step has been a very wise one . . . I do not think he will ever return to Pretoria in an official capacity, and I think it will make his stay at home a much pleasanter one to him and you all if he is not pressed to do so'[1] Perhaps to emphasise the merit of his brother's plans, Andrew added that he was considering investing in the ostrich farm.

Rider arrived home to a great welcome, especially from his mother. His father, however, did not receive him with any enthusiasm. The turtle's disappearance started an almighty row, during which, Rider recalled, his father 'remarked with great candour that I should probably become "a waif and a stray", or possibly — my taste for writing being already known — "a miserable penny-a-liner".' Rider, attempting to defend his actions, was grateful when a few days later a letter arrived from Sir Melmoth Osborn who reported that, according to Cochrane, the ostriches were doing well and added, 'Depend upon it ostriches alone will secure you a very handsome and certain return. Cochrane is thoroughly alive to the importance of the main branch of the enterprise and will do all he can to push it.'[2]

William Haggard could not, however, be persuaded that his son had been right to resign from his official post and on 23 August in a letter Rider sent to Osborn he stated that his father wished him to return to the Colonial Service.

By accepting his father's wishes, Rider appears to have mollified him and was, therefore, able to enjoy the pleasant summer days and country pursuits at Bradenham. Mary, Rider's sister to whom he had confided all the details of his love for Lilly, was living at home and seems to have invited eligible friends she had made at school to stay with her a week or so at a time. Rider immediately became close friends with one of these young ladies who in the next few years was to have an important influence on him and his writing. She was Agnes Marion Barber, whose sister Marjorie, under the pseudonym 'Michael Fairless', was to write the best-seller *The Road Mender*.

Among the Haggard papers that have survived is one headed 'Character of Agnes Marion Barber as told under the influence of paint and worry — 16 Sept., 1879'.[3] It begins, 'The above mentioned young lady is one of the most peculiar individuals that I ever came across in my long and varied experience. All her passions are strong, especially her love and hate.' Rider concludes, 'She has a most insane desire to take care of all she loves whatever the consequence may be to herself. She will never marry till she finds her master and then will make a devoted but not jealous wife.' Rider later described Agnes Barber as 'a woman with a fine literary sense and all-round ability'. Because of her interest in literature and in writing poetry, Rider was for the first time able to discuss with an informed friend his own writing and his hopes of becoming an author.

Agnes was not, however, to become Rider's wife. Her family, although genteel, were impoverished and from his observation of family and friends Rider knew that the most sensible prerequisite for the wife of a landed gentleman's younger son was to be the owner of or heiress to a profitable estate. In this way the Haggard fortune had been built up and consolidated. His mother had been the co-heiress of Bazett Doveton, his grandmother a rich Russian Jewess, and his great-grandmother a member of the Amyand banking family.

It was not going to be easy for Rider to make such an advantageous match. Despite his bronzed good looks, worldly experience and considerable charm, he believed himself incapable of ever loving any other woman with the intense passion he still felt for Lilly. He was also penniless and without any obvious prospects. He did not even have access to the funds necessary to purchase the equipment needed for the ostrich farm. His father had forbidden Andrew to invest in Rider's agricultural enterprise and had refused further to subsidise a son who he considered at twenty-three ought to be pursuing a worthwhile career.

Apart from the Colonial Service, the only career to which Rider was attracted was writing, but since being jilted by Lilly he had written nothing for publication.

Inspired perhaps by his conversation with Agnes Barber, Rider considered writing another article. On 3 November he wrote to Chatto and Windus, the publishers of the *Gentleman's Magazine*, inquiring if they would care to take an article on 'Volunteering in the Transvaal', 'giving my experiences as officer of a corps raised in Pretoria on receipt of the news of the Isandhlwana disaster, and afterwards employed against the Boers'.[4] The article was not required. Isandhlwana was no longer of public interest, its horror having been erased by the British conquest in August of the Zulus and the capture of Cetywayo. Attention had shifted to the Boers whose determination to overthrow the British was hardening. Rider's renewed, but half-hearted, interest in writing was not pursued.

It seemed, therefore, that he was left with no alternative but to follow father's wishes and rejoin the Colonial Service. Osborn, writing from Pretoria, gave Rider this advice: 'With regard to your returning to the Colonial Service your father is quite right, and I think you should return. The business between you and Cochrane could be easily arranged, although I dare say to you there seems a difficulty about it. If you start again fairly in any other colony but this you are sure to succeed, and I strongly advise you to do so — it would simply be following a pursuit for which you are eminently suited and abandoning one for which you are not.' This remarkable *volte-face* of Osborn's shows just how strongly Rider's father was pressing his opinion. The problems with the ostrich farm could not easily be solved. By almost every mail, letters arrived from Cochrane demanding to know when Rider was returning and giving details of heavy debts, disasters with ostriches, and difficulties with labour and equipment.

Then Rider found an admirable solution to all his problems. One of Mary's friends who came to stay at Bradenham was Louisa Margitson, the only surviving child of Major Margitson of Ditchingham House, Norfolk, who had died when she was nine. The previous year, on 28 September 1878, her mother also had died, leaving Louie an orphan in sole possession of a modest but worthwhile estate that until her twenty-first birthday on 6 October, 1880, was managed by her uncle and trustee, William Hartcup. At the end of her week's stay, Rider announced his engagement to Louisa. His wily father saw the sense of this move and from then on did all he could to help the couple's marriage plans.

Louie Margitson was a determined, strong-willed girl, described by Rider at the time as being 'good and sensible and true-hearted'. She was, however, like the women Haggard's heroes so often married, no beauty:

> Maria Lee was not very pretty . . . but she was a perfect specimen of a young English country girl; fresh as a rose, and sound as a bell, and endowed besides with a quick wit and a ready sympathy. She was essentially one of that class of Englishwomen who make the English upper class what it is — one of the finest and soundest in the world.
>
> (From *Dawn*)

Louie was clearly swept off her feet by Rider. Coming as she did from a sleepy, secluded parish in south Norfolk with a dearth of suitable, single young men, she can never have met his like. Although she accepted Rider's proposal, she knew so little about him that in the announcement to her trustees of her engagement she spelt his name Ryder.

The couple anticipated that their marriage plans might not be readily accepted by Louie's trustees, her uncles William Hartcup and Dr Frank Hamilton. Immediately after she had left Bradenham, Rider wrote, 'Certainly getting engaged has its drawbacks — I can only hope that your other Uncle will follow Mr Hartcup's lead and that there will be no difficulties thrown in our way. Now the great thing is to get me asked down to Ditchingham with as little delay as possible.'[5] It was, however, Hartcup who objected to the marriage, announcing that it could not take place until Louie had come of age. Rider wrote almost daily to reassure Louie. In a letter sent early in December he writes, 'Giving up one's whole life into the hands of another is a solemn thing, and dear, I have now done so to you and you to me. All I ask is always to trust me entirely. If you do so and keep your share of the compact, from the day you put your hand in mine and told me that you loved me, till the day, which may be far off or near, that death separates us, will I be your true and faithful lover and husband.'[6]

A few days later he wrote in response to Hartcup's threat to make Louie a ward of court, 'I am so very glad to see, love, that you are prepared to take a line of your own, and to back me up if it should come to any difference of opinion. Two things are very clear. 1. That I do not see my way clear to stopping in England until next October. 2. That I will not leave England without you. So the sooner that your respected Uncle makes up his mind to treat the matter on that basis the more comfortable we shall get on together.'[7]

In order to help Rider combat this threat, William Haggard on 11 December wrote to a London acquaintance, Fred John Blake, of Wordsworth, Blake and Co., asking him to act as solicitor for his son who, he explained, was 'to be married to a lady of some considerable landed property'. Two days later, Blake presented to the Chancery Court terms of settlement of Louie's property which gave the gross annual rental as 'about £1,700'.[8]

Rider was invited to spend Christmas with Louie and for the first time he was able to inspect Ditchingham House and the rest of her estate. His presence there can have done nothing to pacify Hartcup or endear him to the local population. He was considered by many to be a fortune-hunter, a supposition which was difficult for him to contradict as his own fortune was at such a low ebb. His presence at Ditchingham seems to have completed the rift between Louie and the Hartcups. On 21 December Rider wrote to his brother William, then at the British Embassy at Teheran, informing him of his difficulties: 'She is willing to come to Africa, so we propose returning there shortly, i.e. as soon as we can get satisfactorily married. There is property concerned, and trustees, who, as I dare say you know, are gentry difficult to deal with. They want us to postpone the marriage till she comes of age next October, but we don't see the force of it in any way.'

Any delay in his plans did not suit Rider. Cochrane seemed to be getting desperate and Rider, living solely off his father, had no funds of his own. He wanted to return to Africa as soon as possible. Aware of Rider's position, Hartcup made his niece a Ward in Chancery, thus enforcing a postponement of the wedding. The anxiety and depression this act caused were further aggravated by the advice Rider received from friends in Africa whom he had informed of his engagement. Napier Broome, a colonial secretary on Bulwer's staff, wrote, 'I hope you will have many happy years before you, but they cannot begin, take my word for it, until you get rid of your farm, your mill, your ostriches, and your Cochrane! No gentleman ever did any good in Natal.'[9] Colonel Brooke, a member of Shepstone's staff, was equally insistent that Rider should not take up farming: 'For *you* to take up such a calling is to my mind simply wicked. You are capable, and you know it, of making a name for yourself either at the Bar, or in official life. Go to South Africa if you like — but go in some position in which you will be able to stamp the name of Rider Haggard on the history of future generations. This you only require the will to do.'[10] Persuaded by such advice, in January 1880 Rider wrote to Sir Garnet Wolseley, who the previous August had become the Governor of the Transvaal, asking if he could be reappointed to the post he had held. In the reply he was informed 'that arrangements are in contemplation which prevent your reinstatement in the office of Master of the High Court in the Transvaal'.

There was little time for Rider to do much more about his career for, having decided to contest the court's ruling, he and Louie became involved in litigation that was to prove both expensive and time-consuming. In mid-February the couple appeared before Vice-Chancellor Malins. A letter from Sir Theophilus Shepstone concerning Rider's character and prospects seems to have persuaded the Vice-Chancellor that it was 'a very suitable match'. The complaint of Hartcup's lawyer that Rider and Louie had become engaged after knowing each other for only four days was dismissed by Malins with, 'Have you never heard of love at first sight before?' It was, however, decided that guardians should be appointed for Louie and that until that was done the couple should not see each other more than two days a week. At first Louie refused to accept the proposal that Hartcup and his wife Jane should be her guardians, but at a later meeting with Malins it was agreed that Mrs Hildyard, her mother's sister, and Hartcup should share the guardianship. On 27 February Louie wrote to Hartcup: 'Your lawyer will have told you the result of this interview with the V.C. on Wednesday last, and also that I opposed the appointment of my Aunt Jane and yourself. The fact is you have made things so unpleasant for me lately and caused me so much anxiety of mind, that I do not think you can have been surprised at the course I took. I have only to say now (although the breach made between your family and myself can never be completely healed), you and my Aunt will find me perfectly amenable to all reasonable restrictions as long as I am under your control.'[11]

Hartcup, was not amenable and insisted that there should be no wedding before October. Informed of his decision by Louie, Rider replied: 'Dearest, let me give you a word of council. Do not let these things worry you, I beg of you. Your position is doubtless a bad one, but it is not hopeless. Let the worst come to the worst there are but seven short months between you and your majority, and you are not the woman I take you for if you cannot put up with annoyance for that time.'[12] The squabbles between Louie and the Hartcups, whom previously she had treated almost as parents, were well known in the area. In early April William Haggard wrote that his son was staying at the King's Head, Bungay, in order to see his 'Lady Love' and that 'he (& she) have had all sorts of botherings, all sorts of unpleasant remarks being made in that gossiping neighbourhood with regard to her.'[13]

As Rider had no money of his own Louie had to pay the considerable legal expenses. As these amounted to £3000, or the total income from the estate for two years, it was impossible for the couple to live at Ditchingham without an additional income. Rider was unable to obtain any suitable employment, for despite his experience he had neither professional nor academic qualifications, and returning to Africa to take up farming was the only possible course of action; but, being certain that the marriage would eventually take place, he started to make arrangements for the necessary marriage settlement. As he had no wealth of his own Rider arranged with the Legal and General a life insurance for £5000, with an annual payment of £110 4s 2d, coming into effect on 23 April. The initial premium was advanced by his father.

The marriage settlement had to be approved by the Chancery Court before the wedding could take place and once it had been submitted the couple could do nothing but wait. In an effort to speed up the proceedings, William Haggard wrote on 14 June to a friend, E. Borton, Vice-Chancellor Malin's secretary, asking him to give the judge 'a hint that it would be a great obligation if he would "polish them off" quick. The wedding was provisionally arranged for 13 July, but because the acceptance of the settlement was delayed the date had to be postponed to 11 August. Hartcup, who fought every item of expenditure including the £115 for Louie's wedding dress, made a final effort to delay the marriage further by demanding that William Scudamore, the Rector of Ditchingham, should refuse to read the banns as Louie was under age. The ensuing difficulty was sorted out only after William Haggard had been to see the Bishop of Norwich. Scudamore did request, however, that Louie should repair the breach with the Hartcups and invite them to the wedding. Louie adamantly refused.

On 9 August Rider wrote to Louie from Bradenham the last letter before they married: 'I will do my honest best to make you a good husband. Year after year as our wedding day comes round may we, if we live, be able to look back on it as the happiest step we ever took.'[14] Two days later Rider and Louie were married at Ditchingham Church. The Hartcups did not attend. Aware that the reasons for their absence were well known in the village, Louie, as a small gesture of defiance, arranged for her new husband and herself to travel the thirteen miles from the church to Norwich in a carriage drawn by four grey horses with two postilions.

After a honeymoon in the Lake District, the couple moved to London, staying at

29 Downs Road, Clapton, from where Rider wrote letters to friends and business contacts on his new monographed notepaper. There was much to be done: the trustees of the marriage settlement — Hartcup, Hamilton and Charles Maddison Green, Rider's brother-in-law — had to be contacted; furniture and equipment had to be purchased and packed; and new relatives had to be visited. On 14 September, Rider and Louie went to Bradenham where, for the first time as man and wife, they were warmly welcomed and entertained. After Louie's birthday, on 6 October, their wills were made and at last, a year after first meeting her, Rider was ready to take his bride out to a house he had never seen, close to the borders of the Transvaal where it seemed increasingly likely an Anglo-Boer war would soon break out. In November, 1880, the Haggards sailed for Durban. Rider's anticipated short stay at home had lasted eighteen months.

By marrying Rider and being prepared to leave her home and friends Louie was willingly accepting difficulties and a hazardous future. Most remarkably, from the start she accepted that whatever Rider felt for her, it was Lilly, as his daughter states, 'whom . . . he still loved, with an affection that transcends all earthly passion and stretches out hands beyond the grave'.[15] Haggard always believed that his love for Lilly was eternal and that in an after-life they would, in some way or other, be united. This belief in eternal love is a theme to which he constantly returns in his fiction. In *Dawn*, his first novel, it is clearly stated:

> Yes, the fiat has gone forth; for good or for evil, for comfort or for scorn, for the world and for eternity, he loves her! Henceforth that love, so lightly and yet so irredeemably given, will become the guiding spirit of his inner life, rough-hewing his destinies, directing his ends, and shooting its memories and hopes through the whole fabric of his being like an interwoven thread of gold. He may sin against it, but he can never forget it; other interests and ties may overlay it, but they cannot extinguish it; he may drown its fragrance in voluptuous scents, but, when these have satiated and become hateful, it will re-arise, pure and sweet as ever. Time or separation cannot destroy it — for it is immortal; use cannot stale it, pain can only sanctify it.
>
> (From *Dawn*)

Although his opinions were later modified, Rider at the time of his marriage appears to have had little more than a perfunctory belief in Christianity. His obsession in his youth with death had, even before he met Lilly, encouraged him tentatively to explore various possibilities of life beyond the grave, including spiritualism and Egyptian methods of mummification; but his conviction that his love for Lilly was eternal demanded a more acceptable version of life after death. Both reincarnation and a traditional Christian heaven were acceptable, and throughout his life Rider weighed their respective merits and sought to make their disparate natures compatible. His early religious training prevented him for wishing for death but, as he was confident that he would then be reunited with Lilly, he saw the rest of his life as merely a waiting, a period of trial and tribulation which had to be endured: his marriage did not mean that he would 'live happily ever after'. It would, he was convinced, be only death that provided the happy ending. This from the start he had tried to make clear to Louie. He was her husband only until death. In a letter to her he states 'till the day, which may be far off or near, that death separates us, will I be your true and faithful lover and husband'.

Perhaps Louie had neither the imagination nor the experience to understand the significance and strength of Rider's beliefs. Perhaps she hoped that as she and Rider grew to know each other better, his love for Lilly would fade. If this was her hope, she was to be disappointed.

II

When they sailed for Africa, Rider and his wife took with them a spider carriage that had been specially made for them in Norwich, a considerable stock of furniture and provisions, three dogs, and two servants — Lucy Gibbs, a middle-aged maid of Louie's, and Stephen Lanham, a young groom from Bradenham. The Norfolk wit and country manners of Stephen and Gibbs provided Rider with a constant source of amusement even in the most trying situations. (Stephen appears in *She* as Job, the servant Holly hired to help look after the young Leo Vincey.)

On their arrival in Natal, the Haggards were informed that the Boers had declared the Transvaal a republic on 16 December and that four days later at Bronker's Spruit a party of Boers had in an ambush either killed or taken prisoner a column of 264 British soldiers. They also heard the story of Captain Elliot, a survivor of Bronker's Spruit, and Captain Lambart who were released from capture on condition they left the country. They were taken by their Boer escort in a storm to the Vaal river and ordered to cross. It was dark and the river was swollen with the heavy rain. Despite their entreaties, Elliot and Lambart were refused permission to wait till the next morning. A few yards from the bank their cart struck a rock and the Boers opened fire. Elliot was killed but, although the cart was riddled with bullet-holes, Lambart was not touched and he succeeded in swimming to the opposite bank. The Boers continued to fire at him each time the lightning showed his whereabouts. The story deeply upset Haggard, and he gives a full account of it in *Cetywayo and His White Neighbours*.

As the Haggards' new home in Newcastle lay close to the border of the Transvaal where open rebellion had broken out, Rider was uncertain as to whether it was wise to travel there. For the time being, therefore, they stayed at Maritzburg, first with the Shepstones, and then in an hotel, which proved to be extremely expensive. Unfortunately, at a cost of £155, all their belongings had been sent to Newcastle immediately on arrival and so they were left with little more than the clothes they were wearing. On 2 January 1881 Louie wrote to her London solicitor: 'We've got this far OK, but we're detained by the Boer outbreak which began as we were about to start up country. We hope it will be safe to venture forth this week.'[16] She adds that, as the war had caused a great increase in prices, more money should be sent by the next post. She also asked how much the annual income from the Ditchingham estate was likely to be after insurance and legal expenses had been paid.

After over three weeks of inactivity in Maritzburg, Louie, even though she was several months' pregnant, announced that she would have no more of it, and so on 14 January, riding in the spider carriage, the strange party, augmented by two parrots bought when the ship called at Madeira, set off on the two-hundred-mile trek to Newcastle. As it was the wet season, the roads were little more than interconnected mud-holes scored out by the passage of guns and heavily-laden ox-wagons. The new carriage proved less than ideal transport for the conditions. On the first day Gibbs, still hanging on to one of the dogs, was thrown out under one of the back wheels which ground her deep into the mire. Her piercing yells assured the others that she had survived, albeit badly shocked and mud-soaked.

After this they all had to walk much of the way. The journey was uncomfortable and full of incidents. Late one evening, they had a flooded river to cross before reaching the inn where they were to spend the night. Although warned against making the crossing, with two Zulus hanging on to the carriage to prevent it overturning, Rider drove the horses into the rapidly rising mill-race. 'Soon the horses were off their legs, but they were plucky beasts and struck out for the farther shore of the drift. The water ran through the bottom of the carriage, which began to float, but the brave Kaffirs hung on, although they were up to their arm-pits and could scarcely stand. . . . There were a few fearful moments of doubt, then, thank God! the horses got their feet again, and we dragged through, damp but safe, and slept that night in comfort in the inn.' This experience no doubt reminded Rider of Elliot and Lambart's attempted crossing of a similarly swollen river under Boer fire. In *Jess* Haggard combined the experience and the story to create the exciting escape of John Neil and Jess from the Boers:

> Jess turned herself on the seat to look, and just then a blaze of lightning flamed which revealed Muller and his two companions standing dismounted on the bank, the muzzles of their rifles pointing straight at the cart.
> 'O God!' she screamed, 'they are going to shoot us.'
> Even as the words passed her lips three tongues of fire flared from the rifles' mouths, and the Zulu Mouti, sitting by her side, pitched heavily forward on to his head into the bottom of the cart, while one of the wheelers reared straight up into the air with a shriek of agony, and fell with a splash into the river. . . .
>
> (From *Jess*)

At last, after a nine-day journey the Haggards arrived at Newcastle. The little town was very different to what it had been when Rider had last seen it. The hotels were overflowing with refugees from the Transvaal and on every spare patch of land tents, mud huts and canvas shacks had been erected to help accommodate them. The Haggards did not stay in Newcastle, but drove on the mile and a half to Hilldrop, their house at Rooipoint. Backed by a steep rocky hill and ringed with orange trees and a plantation of black wattle, it was in a beautiful setting. Both

Louie and Rider were delighted with their first home. It was spacious and had been made most comfortable with their furniture that Cochrane had painstakingly unpacked and arranged. The house, renamed Mooifontein, and the surrounding area was used as the setting for the early part of *Jess*:

> It was a delightful spot. At the back of the stead was the steep boulder-strewn face of the flat-topped hill that curved round on each side, embosoming a great slope of green, in the lap of which the house was placed. It was very solidly built of brown stone, and . . . was covered with rich brown thatch. All along its front ran a wide verandah, up the trellis-work of which green vines and blooming creepers trailed pleasantly, and beyond was the broad carriage-drive of red soil, bordered with bushy orange-trees laden with odorous flowers and green and golden fruit.

(From *Jess*)

After the Haggards had inspected their new home, Cochrane told them all the latest news. Cheeringly, it seemed likely that the farm would yield a profit of two thousand pounds for the year. Even more amazing was the story of Moresco. While Rider was in England his favourite hunter had been stolen by horse-thieves. Cochrane offered a reward and searched desperately, eventually discovering that the horse had been ridden the twelve hundred miles to the Cape. Six months later Cochrane discovered Moresco in the farm's horse-pound. He was indescribably thin, with a dreadfully neglected sore back. Cochrane did what he could, but when Rider saw him it was obvious that, although much improved, the stallion's stamina had gone.

The Haggards were not destined to enjoy a peaceful life at Hilldrop. A few days after their arrival, on 28 January, Rider in his garden heard the distant boom of heavy guns. It was the Battle of Lang's Nek at which the British troops, who had set out from Newcastle under Sir George Colley, attacked a strongly defended Boer encampment over the border in the Transvaal. It was a decisive battle. The British were outnumbered, outmanoeuvred, and heavily defeated. On 30 January, Rider wrote to his father, 'We have got all our things up here safely and have made the place quite pretty, but somehow one can take no pleasure in anything just now with blood being shed like water all round. Every time one sees a Kaffir runner coming to the house one feels anxious lest he should be the announcer of some fresh evil.'

For a few days after the battle everything seemed quiet, but then on 8 February, about midday, heavy fighting was again heard, this time coming from Scheins Hoogte, a hill about eleven miles away from Hilldrop. As he listened, Rider wrote to his mother, 'Last night we slept in our clothes ready to make a bolt for it, as there was a report the Boers were coming in to Newcastle.'[17] The guns continued until dusk, shortly after which a messenger arrived with the news that a force of British soldiers were surrounded on the hill by the Ingogo River. The inhabitants of Hilldrop had a sleepless night, and in the morning they heard of yet another British defeat at the hands of the Boers.

As this meant that the border areas of Natal were left without an effective army to defend the inhabitants, Rider posted servants, led by Mazooku, on the surrounding hills so that a warning could be given if a Boer attack on the homestead appeared imminent. All the men in the house slept with loaded rifles to hand and horses saddled in the stables. Nor were the fears groundless. A party of Boers did swoop down on the neighbouring property and steal all the stock. After a few days the Haggards were advised that the Boers intended to occupy their house as a base from which to attack the expected British army reinforcements. It was decided to evacuate Hilldrop, and so all the occupants, taking with them a few valuables, moved to Newcastle. There was little enough protection there, however, and an attack was expected at any time.

But the Boers did not invade and on 17 February the army reinforcements arrived. Rider and his household returned to Hilldrop where to their relief they found everything safe. Ten days later the thunder of guns was again heard. This time it came from Majuiba Hill where the British suffered another heavy defeat in what turned out to be the final, decisive battle of the first Boer War. As at Isandhlwana, many of Rider's friends and acquaintances were among the dead and wounded.

Despite the alarums, incursions, and bloody battles going on around them, Rider and Cochrane had work to do on the farm. On 7 March, Louie wrote to her mother-in-law: 'The farm is pretty flourishing. We are now in the middle of haymaking, and the lazy Rider is routed out about 6 a.m. every fine morning to go and cut. He looks all the better for it, in fact I think we are both in better health than when we left England.' The hay-cutting was not an easy task. While Cochrane led the four oxen, Rider sat on the machine to which they were yoked, operating the levers controlling the blades. As the land was very uneven, with stones, deep holes and solid ant-hills, Rider had to take great care neither to smash the valuable machine nor throw himself into the thrashing blades. The two men cut a considerable amount of hay and the product of three weeks' work was sold as fodder to the army for £240. Rider was always justifiably pleased with this achievement: 'This proved to be the most profitable bit of farming that ever I did, and I am always proud to remember that I once earned £240, or the half of it, by the labour of my own hands.'

Large quantities of bricks were also made on the farm for sale in Newcastle. Rider claimed that he worked so hard at this that people used to ride some distance to see the unusual spectacle of a white farmer working with his hands. The steam-driven grinding mill that Rider had sent out from England was installed, but it was scarcely a profitable venture for to keep it running they had to employ an engineer. It was, however, the ostriches that created the greatest problems. In his autobiography Haggard recalls: 'In my experience the ostrich is an extremely troublesome bird. To begin with he hunts you and knocks you down. One of ours gave Cochrane a frightful drubbing, and through a pair of opera glasses I saw an unfortunate Kaffir barely escape with his life from its attentions by going to earth in an ant-bear hole like a hunted jackal'.

Rider was extremely concerned about the outcome of the negotiations taking place between the British and the Boers. These concluded on 23 March with the signing of an armistice that made certain the retrocession of the Transvaal. When the news became known in Newcastle there were angry scenes: the refugees and soldiers crowding the hotels and bars made and burnt an effigy of Gladstone, the British Prime Minister, for the decision to hand back the Transvaal to the Boers was seen by most of the British in South Africa as an ignoble surrender and defeat. Haggard remained bitterly upset by this action: 'I would not have believed it possible that I could feel any public event so keenly as I did this; indeed, I quickly made up my mind that if the peace was confirmed, the neighbourhood of the Transvaal would be no fit or comfortable residence for an Englishman, and that I would, at any cost, leave the country.'

Rider's decision to leave Natal was made considerably easier by another helpful act of his shrewd father. About this time there arrived at Hilldrop George Blomefield, for whom, with £1000 from the boy's own inheritance, William Haggard, as his executor, had purchased a partnership in the farm with Rider and Cochrane, taking as security a part-mortgage on the estate. Considering the difficulties of the times, this was a most generous payment for a one-third partnership and, if nothing else, allowed all outstanding debts to be repaid. The peace negotiations also brought an unexpected but welcome boost to the now healthy finances of the estate. Sir Hercules Robinson, leader of the Royal Commission appointed to consider the terms of peace, decided to make Hilldrop the Commission's headquarters. Rider signed an agreement on 6 April renting the property at £50 a week. As the staff of the Commission were not to arrive until the beginning of May and would stay for about five weeks, Rider stipulated in the agreement that her bedroom should be retained by Louie, whose baby was due in June.

Unfortunately at this time there was an epidemic of horse-sickness. In a single week, Rider lost two hundred pounds' worth of horses. At last Moresco, who having once had the disease was considered to be immune, fell ill. Naturally Rider did what he could for his favourite horse, but it was clear there was little chance of recovery. About midnight the Haggards were awoken by a knocking on the back door. On going to inspect, Rider found that it was Moresco who, knowing that he was dying, had made his way over a four-foot wall to call for assistance. Sadly there was nothing that could be done, and in the morning Moresco was dead.

Towards the end of April Rider wrote to his father, informing him that he intended to leave Natal. On 3 May, in a letter to his mother, he said: 'Every day that passes has only strengthened my conviction that we can look for no peace or security in South Africa. . . . We have more or less fixed on Vancouver Island for our next Colonial venture.'

At the same time, Rider received a telegram from his brother Jack, who had just resigned from the Royal Navy, announcing that he had arrived at the Cape and was on the way to stay with them. He apparently hoped to obtain employment in Natal.

As Louie pointed out in a letter to her mother-in-law on 4 May, he would not be able to stay in the house, because the Commission had taken up residence: 'We shall have to live in a kind of picnic fashion, I expect for about a fortnight, as our house-room will consist of a bedroom and two tents! — one of which we shall convert into a kitchen and the other into a room for Jack.' When Jack arrived, he was made most welcome. With his fund of amazing stories he was, as always, excellent company.

Jack and all the members of the Commission were staying at Hilldrop when at 17.45 on 23 May — three weeks earlier than expected — Louie gave birth to a boy. A native woman was hastily summoned to help with the delivery, because Gibbs proved incapable of doing much more than sit moaning to herself. Rider was overjoyed and the next day wrote to his father, 'I hope by now you will have received the telegram I despatched yesterday telling you of the safe birth of a son. . . . On the whole I think Louie had a good time of it. The child is a very perfect and fine boy, he weighed nine pounds just after birth, and is a very well nourished child. He has dark blue eyes and is a fair child with a good forehead.' The boy was christened Arthur John Rider Haggard, but to Rider he was always known as Jock.

Having decided to leave Africa, Rider had to make plans for his family's future. Jack's tales of Vancouver Island had persuaded him to drop the idea of going there. At this time of uncertainty, in the middle of July, Rider received a letter from his father, and Blake, his solicitor, advising him to return to England. One of the major tenants at Ditchingham had been made bankrupt and thus the estate was likely to lose several hundred pounds. It also meant that instead of having to relet the land at a substantially reduced rent, Rider could, if he wished, farm the 195 acres thus made available. On 30 July, Rider wrote to his father, 'I must now tell you that after thoroughly thinking the matter over I have made up my mind to return to England next month. . . . First I have given due weight to what you and Mr Blake write to me, and admit that there is a great deal in what you say. What brings me back in such a hurry however is the state of the country. I can only trust that I have arrived at a wise decision.'

It was decided that Cochrane, who was suffering from a prolonged attack of dysentery, would return home with the Haggards. The farm would be left in the charge of George Blomefield and North, the engineer. All the preparations for departure had then to be made. An auction of the furniture, imported at such great expense, was held. Fortunately, because of the war and the rarity of many of the items, the goods were sold for high prices: thus a piano, bought second-hand in England for £40, fetched £200.

At last it was time to depart. As they drove away from the house for the last time, Rider felt extremely sad: 'There my son had been born; there I had undergone many emotions of a kind that help to make a man; there I had suffered the highest sort of shame, shame for my country; there, as I felt, one chapter in my eventful life had opened and had closed. It was sad to part with the place, and also to bid good-bye to my Zulu servant Mazooku.'

On 31 August, 1881, the family group sailed for England aboard the *Dunkeld*. On the way back home the Haggards and their servants stayed for a fortnight in Madeira. Far away from the work and tribulations of Natal, they enjoyed the pleasant climate of the semi-tropical island. The abundance of flowers and the old town with its cobbled streets and shuttered houses appealed especially to Rider. Later in life he often expressed the desire to have a summer house there and in *Dawn* he sets much of the action on the island he loved and knew so well.

In October, 1881, the Haggards arrived back in England, less than a year after they had departed. Although he would still have to work to help provide for his wife and family, now that he was receiving a reasonable income from the estates in Norfolk and Natal, Rider could look forward to becoming in England an active member of the upper middle class to whose ranks, driven by the desire both to appease and copy his father, he had so desperately aspired. For one who, on his previous return two years earlier, had been dismissed as 'a waif and a stray', he now came back almost in triumph, a man of substance and the founder of a new dynasty to carry the ancient Haggard name.

4

In Search of Success

Because Ditchingham House had been let when they went to Africa, the Haggards had to stay at Bradenham on their return to England. As usual the family house was full of relatives and friends, all of whom welcomed and pampered the young couple and their infant son. Among the old friends Rider met was Lilly's younger brother, Frederick Jackson, who had just come down from Cambridge where he had been studying with Edward Arthur Haggard. Jackson was planning to hunt big game in Kashmir and so he had much to discuss with Rider. Thus flowered the deep affection that existed between the two men throughout their lives.

After the exciting but troubled time in Africa, the late autumn days spent in the Norfolk countryside were happy and relaxed. Rider thoroughly enjoyed the partridge shoots, the Sunday services in the parish church, dinner parties, and the occasional ball, including one at Sandringham, after which Louie noted in her diary that Princess Alexandra 'looked lovely in pearl grey satin and was the prettiest woman in the room with the exception of Lady Lonsdale'. Rider, however, did not wish to slip into the comfortable but undemanding life as a minion in his father's household: 'I was determined,' he later recalled, 'to make a success in the world in one way or another, and that of a sort which would cause my name to be remembered for long after I had departed therefrom, and my difficulty was to discover in which way this could best be done.' At first he was anxious to farm the land on the Ditchingham estate previously occupied by the recently bankrupted tenant. The matter was discussed at considerable length with William Simpson, the Norfolk auctioneer who was the agent for the estate. He pointed out that about £2000 would be needed to take the farm in hand. Rider was at first prepared to spend this amount, but at last he was dissuaded from setting up as a gentleman farmer by Simpson who was frightened by the outlook for farming, pointing out that since 1879 there had been poor crops and estimating that he would certainly lose £1000 on the venture. Having accepted Simpson's judgement, but unwilling to sell any land, Rider arranged for the farm of 195 acres to be relet for £50 a year, the highest amount that could be obtained. As the annual rent at the beginning of 1881 had been fixed at £200 (and in 1868 had been £252), this immense decline not only made Rider aware of the appalling agricultural depression from which the country was suffering, but also forced him to abandon all hopes of becoming a practising farmer. Even worse, a continued decline presented the real possibility that the

Ditchingham estates would cease to produce an income sufficient to support him and his family adequately.

It became imperative, therefore, for Rider to pursue a socially acceptable and potentially lucrative career. His father encouraged him to follow his own example and read for the Bar. This was a course of action Judge Kotzé had already recommended, and one for which his Transvaal experiences had prepared him; but Rider was reluctant. There would be three years' study, which his previous lack of academic success suggested would be neither easy nor enjoyable. Until he qualified it would be unlikely that he would have any income other than the declining one derived from the Ditchingham estate. This was likely to create some difficulties, for while studying Rider would either have to live in or frequently travel to London so that he could satisfy the requirement of eating his dinners at his chosen Inn of Court. The main cause of Rider's reluctance was, however, that the long period of study would be one of enforced inactivity and boredom. Having already sampled and enjoyed the experience of participating in important events, he could not bear the prospect of standing on the sidelines and watching the world pass by. His doubts and uncertainties were discussed with his elder brother Andrew, with whom he had much in common, for both were restless and over-active, able to charm women but reluctant to accept adverse criticism. Andrew, who had some hopes of becoming an author, advised Rider to fill up his time while studying law by writing books.

As winter approached, Rider applied to enter Lincoln's Inn, like his father before him. To his disgust, he was informed that to be accepted he must first pass an examination in Latin and English History. He argued that his experiences as Master of the High Court in the Transvaal should qualify him for exemption, but to no avail. There was then no alternative for him, if he wished to pass the entrance examination, but at the age of twenty-five to enrol with another crammer. Just before Christmas, Rider and his family moved into a furnished house in Norwood, south London, and he began his studies in earnest. In just over a month he had learned enough to pass the examination.

This hurdle successfully surmounted, Rider was left with plenty of time on his hands. He was living apart from his friends, among strangers in a London suburb. Louie had a young baby to occupy her and a household to organise. Her strength of will and her independence meant that she could cope efficiently with her new life. Rider was not so fortunate. He desperately needed some intellectual stimulation and that his wife could not provide. The companionship he had hoped for in marriage had not developed. In a letter written to a friend a couple of years later he states revealingly, 'Marriage is generally speaking very good fun for about three months, *mais* after . . .'[1] Also Rider had been away from city life for too long to feel at ease in London. Increasingly, Africa, so far away, came uppermost in his mind. He had discovered, like many other returned colonists, that the public was ignorant of African affairs and indifferent to his own exploits. To remedy this, when he decided to accept Andrew's advice, Rider chose the South African situation as a subject for a book. He was convinced that with the retrocession of the Transvaal the British Government's policy had gone badly awry, creating an impasse that would lead inevitably to Boer supremacy throughout the whole area. The subject had some topicality because Cetywayo's fate had remained undecided since his capture and there was some debate about his future and that of his country, Zululand.

Before commencing his writing, Rider bought all the government blue-books dealing with affairs in the Transvaal, Natal and Zululand and made summaries of them. From these notes, he first compiled a study of 'Cetywayo and the Zulu Settlement' in which, contrary to the romantic picture then being painted of the noble, dethroned monarch, he asserted that Cetywayo was a bloodthirsty tyrant who should not be restored to his kingdom. Zululand, he argued, must be annexed and ruled by Britain for the benefit of the Zulus. He next dealt with the proposed grant of a constitutional government to Natal. Then, as a warning of the dire results of a weak, liberal administration, he moved on to his major topic, 'The Transvaal'. In six detailed chapters he covered the events before, during and after the annexation. His bitterness at the retrocession led him to continue his opinionated attacks on the Boers: 'Personally Boers are fine men, but as a rule ugly. Their women-folk are good-looking in early life, but get very stout as they grow older. . . . None of the refinements of civilization enter into the life of an ordinary Transvaal Boer. He lives in a way that would shock an English labourer at twenty-five shillings the week, although he is very probably worth fifteen or twenty thousand pounds. His home is but too frequently squalid and filthy to an extraordinary degree. He himself has no education, and does not care that his children should receive any.' To these three sections he added an appendix which included two of his previously published articles, 'A Visit to the Chief Secocoeni' and 'A Zulu War Dance'.

As he worked Haggard became obsessed by his subject. In March and April six letters were published in journals such as *The Standard* on such topics as 'Constitutional Government for Natal', 'Cetywayo', and 'Should We Abandon South Africa?'. To his bitter disappointment, however, a letter he submitted to *The Times* was not included.

By the end of April the book — a pot-pourri of facts, opinions, and memories — was finished. It was only then that Haggard realised he had no idea of how he could find someone to publish it. Having purchased a copy of *The Athenaeum*, he selected several firms at random and wrote to them offering to submit his manuscript. In his letter he gave the reasons why he believed there would be interest in his book: 'The parts of the book, however, which would, I think, ensure the sale at the present moment, both here and in the Colonies, are the chapters dealing with the proposed grant of responsible government to Natal and the question of the reinstatement of Cetywayo. As you are no doubt aware, the ex-king will visit England very shortly, when I think an opportunely published work on the subject would find a ready sale. The book is written in as interesting a style as I can command and would be published under my own name.'

While we waited for replies, Haggard decided it was no longer necessary to accept the tedium of life at Norwood. As he had become a member of the Windham Club, he had a place to stay while in London for his dinners at Lincoln's Inn. His law studies could be continued in the country just as well as in the town. More important, from mid-May there would be no tenants occupying Ditchingham House, in which, although now married for over eighteen months, the Haggards had never lived. It was an opportunity, however brief, that was too good to miss.

Early in May, as the first of the letters arrived from publishers rejecting his book, Haggard took his family to Bradenham for a couple of weeks before moving on to Ditchingham. It was while staying with his parents that he heard from Trubner & Co. that they would be interested in publishing his manuscript at his own cost. A sample of their books was enclosed with the letter. On 14 May Haggard, who had received no encouragement from any other source, replied to Trübner & Co.: 'I am forwarding the manuscript to you by rail together with the book you sent me. Kindly advise me of its arrival. . . . The book has mostly been rewritten with the exception of the Transvaal portion, which though not very neat in appearance I trust there will be no difficulty in reading.'[2] In a letter dated 18 May, the publishers stated that the manuscript would make a volume of three hundred and twenty pages and 'if you will send us a cheque for the sum of £50 sterling we will undertake to produce an edition of seven hundred and fifty copies'.[3] Haggard sent the cheque by return.

With his book at the publishers, Haggard with his wife and son moved for the first time into Ditchingham House. Built in the eighteenth century close to the main Bungay–Norwich road, it was known locally as 'The Mustard Pot' because of its unusually shaped chimneys. Outside there was a tennis court, a flower garden, a range of out-buildings including a vinery, and at the back a lawn stretching to the top of a steep slope falling down to the River Waveney.

Soon after arriving at Ditchingham Haggard did find companionship when a young lady who had been at school with Louie arrived to help look after Jock. She was Agnes Barber, with whom Haggard had flirted at Bradenham before he met Louie. She had recently moved to Bungay with her sisters and mother. Agnes was then twenty-two. Her interests in literature, especially poetry, had continued to develop. She had many attributes that Louie lacked. She was sensitive, creative, intellectual and had become a sympathetic conversationalist. Haggard, starved of stimulating and feminine company, renewed the friendship with enthusiasm. In mid-June, when he went to stay in London for a few days, she wrote telling him of his son's progress and Louie's ill-health. On 17 June Haggard replied, 'My dear Miss Barber: Many thanks for your kind note telling me of the little pilgrim's progress. I expect that by the time we get back again he will look upon you as his sole surviving parent . . .'[4] Their relationship was soon to develop from this still formal level.

While still in London Haggard also wrote on 20 June to Trübner & Co., giving for the first time the title of his forthcoming book: 'You will see in *The Times* today that fighting has begun in Zululand. As it is probable that this will attach some interest to S. African affairs do you not think it might be advisable to announce the book without further delay. Of course this is a matter of which you are the best judges — but when you do advertise please call the book *Cetywayo and His White Neighbours*, or Remarks on Recent Events in Zululand, Natal and the Transvaal. You see the first is a mere catchpenny title, whereas the second heading is more likely to appeal to persons really interested in South Africa.'[5] The next day Haggard returned to Ditchingham, and during the following couple of weeks he and Agnes spent many hours talking about books and the art of writing. She gave him some of her poems and short stories to read and together they discussed them at great length.

Early in July Agnes left Ditchingham, for the Haggards were packing before moving once more to Bradenham. Shortly afterwards,[6] to his great delight, Haggard received his copies of *Cetywayo and His White Neighbours*, bound in green cloth and lettered in gold. Leaving the packing to Louie, he sent copies of his book to famous men he thought would be interested, such as Lord Carnarvon, Sir Marshal Clarke, Lord Randolph Churchill, and Lord Lytton. He also, bubbling with excitement, on 7 July sent the book and a chatty, flirtatious letter to Agnes: 'I have been wanting to write to you all the morning to tell you that I have by this mail sent you a copy of the great work. It was my intention to inflict a long letter upon you, full of various uninteresting details, but Louisa under pretext of packing has been driving me to and fro all the morning in a manner that precluded the possibility of calling my soul my own . . . I have written your name in the book. I wished to add, in words as happy as I could command, a slight but forcible tribute of my admiration — something in this style: To Miss Barber, from one who having for a short while basked in the full effulgence of intellectual light is now left in all his primitive darkness but who etc. etc. But the wicked Louisa who had just then ceased from troubling and was (temporarily) at rest from her packing, prevented me from expressing my feelings. I hope however that you will understand them.'[7]

At Bradenham, Haggard eagerly searched through the newspapers and journals for the few reviews of his book that appeared, some of which, he was pleased to discover, were favourable. He also received letters of thanks from those to whom the book had been sent, including one from Carnarvon that concluded, 'I hope I may have the opportunity of talking about this to you.' Keen to further his claim to be an expert on African affairs, Haggard wrote more letters to *The Standard* on Natal and Zululand. He was also asked by *The South African* to write six articles. These appeared weekly from 28 September to 9 November, and included 'The Restoration of Cetywayo' and 'Some Aspects of the Native Question in the Transvaal'. Despite his efforts, however, his African expertise attracted little interest and his book did not sell well. Even his family did not seem very impressed by it. His sisters, Cissie and Mary, did not read beyond the first chapter. Louie had seen enough of it in the proof stages and, as she was again pregnant, had her own thoughts and worries. Andrew told him that a book on African affairs was not of interest to the public: 'No one wants to hear about that, old chap, the whole thing has raised stink enough as it is; write a novel.'[8]

On 6 September, Haggard, still at Bradenham, received the comments on his book for which he had been waiting most eagerly. It came from Agnes. Immediately he wrote to thank her: 'The criticism for which I have been thirsting like — like a turnip field in very dry weather for the bursting of a thunder storm, has arrived in perfect safety and a fine state of preservation.' He thanks her for spotting some minor mistakes and continues: 'I have had a good many very fair reviews of it in the principal literary papers and it seems to have been generally accepted as more or less of a standard work, so I ought to be satisfied I suppose. Of course one can hardly expect to make much of a financial success of such a work'. After commenting on some stories she had sent, Haggard concludes: 'I have begun my novel. I read Louisa a bit the other day and she incontinently wept. Louis is my lactometer. I use her to test the literary milk and register her feeling. . . . I should like to have your opinion on a good many things in connection with it, but I cannot enter into them in a letter. I must wait till you come to see us again which I hope you will do soon, when if I do not bore you out of your literary existence believe me to be very sincerely yours.'[9] This novel was to be, despite his legal studies, Haggard's major preoccupation throughout the next twelve months.

In many ways, the decision to begin a novel was a strange one. Haggard had previously shown little interest in either reading or writing fiction. Perhaps he began because of Andrew's comments on his non-fiction. Perhaps it was because of Agnes's encouragement and enthusiasm. Perhaps he was merely trying to recover the financial loss he had made on his first book. Haggard himself seems not to have known why he first attempted to write fiction. Years later he claimed, 'Whilst we were at Norwood a little incident occurred which resulted in my becoming a writer of fiction. At the church which my wife and I attended we saw sitting near to us one Sunday a singularly beautiful and pure-faced young lady. Afterwards we agreed that this semi-devine creature — on whom to the best of my knowledge I have never set eyes again from that day to this — ought to become the heroine of a novel. So then and there we took paper, and each of us began to write the said novel. I think that after she had completed two or three folio sheets my wife ceased from her fictional labours. But, growing interested, I continued mine.'

Yet this is a most unsatisfactory explanation. The novel was begun at Bradenham and not at Norwood. It is not in character for the eminently practical but unimaginative Louie to be inspired by a young lady's beauty — whatever its effect on her husband — to start writing a novel. Such a joint venture as Haggard describes might have been undertaken by him and Agnes, but she was not with him when he began. The story of the girl in a Norwood church first appeared in an article Haggard contributed in April 1893 to the series 'My First Book' running in *The Idler*. In the following year he added to a new edition of his first novel a dedication to 'That Unknown Lady, once seen, but unforgotten . . . the magic of whose face turned my mind to the making of books.' It seems more than likely then that the whole story arose because Haggard had been forced to find a glib but acceptable answer to the question he was in later years most frequently asked: 'How did you start to write fiction?' It was a question that Haggard was unable to answer. His career as a novelist began because of a deep but ill-comprehended need to write: there was something within him that demanded expression.

After returning with his family to Norwood in mid-September, Haggard spent the following three months completing the novel, which he had now called *Angela*. He did not find the task easy. The technicalities of writing kept getting in his way. Although he had a story he wished to tell, the number of words used had to be calculated, characters he had invented kept merging into people he knew, and the chapter divisions broke up his narrative.

Early in December, Haggard and his wife decided that they would leave Norwood and return to Ditchingham House which was standing empty and would provide a more sensible place for Louie's confinement. So he put aside his incomplete and unsatisfactory novel and by Christmas 1882 the Haggards were ensconced in Ditchingham, prepared to play their roles as gentry of the parish.

At 10.45 on 6 January 1883, Louie gave birth to a girl. Haggard immediately wrote to Agnes: 'They say that she is a very fine and healthy child, but as I have not seen her I can express no opinion. Louisa was only bad for about an hour and seems quite well now. . . . The infant is evidently not deficient in lung power, as I can hear it hallowing through the wall.'[10] The baby was called Angela after the heroine of Haggard's incomplete novel. The other two names she was given were Agnes and Rider.

Shortly after the birth, Agnes came to live at Ditchingham House, where she was to stay for the next six months. Together Haggard and Aggie, as he now called her, read and discussed his manuscript. Her encouragement having helped to clarify his thoughts, he began to rewrite it, this time with the title *There Remaineth a Rest*. Although the first section had to be completely rewritten, he found that some chapters from his original version could be used without alteration. In just three months he had finished the manuscript of 493 foolscap pages. Despite having a complex substructure of violent incidents and the machinations of evil characters, the main story was a simple one that reflected Haggard's unhappy love affair with Lilly. Arthur Preston Hyam falls in love at first sight with Angela Caresfoot, but her scheming father forbids their marriage until they have first been separated for a year. Arthur travels to Madeira where he has a casual affair with an older woman, Muriel Carr. On discovering that Angela has married another man, Arthur sails for South Africa. There he hears that Angela's husband has died and Muriel is expecting his baby. Just as he is about to return to England so that he can marry Angela he is killed in a native uprising and the broken-hearted Angela falls dead into an open grave.

Despite the melodrama, it is at times a moving story. It suffers, however, from an uncertain touch that as much as anything arises from Haggard's difficulty in fictionalising his own experiences which he most frequently attempts to do by amalgamating two places or people he has known to make one in his novel. Thus

Angela Caresfoot lives in an area that owes much to the countryside around Bradenham, but Abbey House, where she lives, is derived from Garsington Rectory where Haggard went to school. Angela, who appears both as a young girl and as a mature woman, is an amalgam of Blanche, the Rector of Garsington's orphaned niece with whom Haggard had first learned 'the rudiments of flirtation', and Lilly Jackson, the woman he loved. His unpublished dedication to *There Remaineth a Rest* strongly supports this factual basis for the character, rather than the fanciful one he subsequently claimed. It begins:

> Little maiden with the tearful face, when first I met you, tottering to your Mother's grave, my heart went out towards you; when I found you wandering in the glade of your shadowed home, or gliding like some white bird through the waters of its lake, I thought you very sweet; but when I knew you, proud and beautiful and gracious, with the light of knowledge in your grey eyes and heaven's own soul upon your lips, I learnt to love you. Oh Angela! creature of my mind, what are you?

(From the unpublished *There Remaineth a Rest*)

Many of the other characters are limited, two dimensional copies of the country gentlemen and their ladies who made up the Bradenham social circle. Muriel Carr is one of the exceptions. It is possible that, in creating her, Haggard was recalling the mystery and sensuality that had appealed to him in the affluent older women, such as Lady Poulett and Lady Caithness, he had met among the spiritualists when he was a student at Scoones. Mrs Carr is, however, a strange, original creation of whom, thirty-three years later, he states in his diary: ' [She] has become quite as real to me as many persons whom once I knew in the flesh. She has joined the company of my dead, that is all.'[11] Yet much of what was in the story, Haggard drew from real life. This we know because when Andrew read the manuscript he said, 'There is a little too much of your own personal experience in the book, and when you write another I would, if I were you, draw a little more upon your own imagination.'[12]

The manuscript was sent to a number of publishers but was speedily rejected. James Payn of Smith and Elder stated that, although the opening chapters had an abundance of action, there was no dramatic interest in them for they lacked any exhibition of characters influencing each other. Haggard refused to be discouraged. He consulted Mr Trübner who suggested that the manuscript should be sent for his opinion to Cordy Jeaffreson, the then well-known biographer and critic. This practical, kindly man sent Haggard a detailed, sympathetic critique. He stated that although the story was better than two-thirds of those published, Haggard, whom he assumed was a young man, must rewrite it: 'You have written it with your *left hand* without strenuous pains; you must rewrite it with your *right hand*, throwing all your force into it. If you produce it in its present crude state you will do so only to regret in a few weeks you did not burn it. If you rewrite it slowly with your right hand — suppressing much, expanding much, making every chapter a picture by itself, and polishing up every sentence so that each page bears a testimony to the power of its producer — the story will be the beginning of such a literary career as I conceive you to be desirous of running.'

The only one of the detailed recommendations Haggard did not feel happy about was that the ending should be changed; but impressed by the attention Jeaffreson had given him, he immediately sent his thanks. After giving some information about himself, he asked if Jeaffreson thought he could succeed as well as writers like Payn and Blackmore. To this Jeaffreson replied: 'Could you succeed in literature? Certainly up to a certain point: unquestionably up to the point you indicate, though you might never earn as much money as the two novelists you mention; for in that respect they have been singularly fortunate. But you may not hope to succeed in a day. You might become famous in a morning; but you may not entertain the hope of doing so'. He also invited Haggard to dine, so that they could 'talk all around the literary question over a cigar'.

Haggard then wrote to Aggie, who was away from Ditchingham, inquiring if she thought the ending should be changed. She did not and so Haggard went to dinner with Jeaffreson hoping to show that the change was unnecessary. Jeaffreson, however, was adamant. An unhappy and melodramatic ending was unsatisfactory.

Having accepted all Jeaffreson's suggestions Haggard was faced, on his return home, with the awesome task of rewriting the complete novel. There was, however, little else for him to do that could break the monotony of his solitary legal studies. At Ditchingham, apart from Aggie, there was nobody whose company he enjoyed. The local people regarded him with coldness or open suspicion. All his old friends were in Africa and he had made no new ones. His trips to London for the dinners at Lincoln's Inn were his only break. Later he recalled, 'Outside members of my own family our visitors were few, and in the main we had to rely on ourselves and out little children for company.' Also his financial situation was not improving. The ostrich farm in Natal failed to produce an income and on 29 April the partnership between Haggard, Cochrane and Blomefield was dissolved. Assets, after liabilities, amounted to £350. 16s. 7d. and this was divided between the three men.

Haggard started rewriting his novel, under the original title *Angela*, on 15 May. Changing the ending meant that if the manuscript was to be long enough for the usual three-volume publication of novels he had to write several new chapters at its beginning. Helped considerably by Aggie, he worked steadily through the summer months. Unfortunately Haggard had little notion of how he could polish his prose. He tinkered about with the story, making many minor alterations. The spelling of the hero's name was changed to Heigham, and as the ending had been altered, he no longer went to Africa and was not informed by Mrs Carr that she was pregnant. Many of the other changes appear almost as if they were accomplished with scissors and paste.

At the end of July, Aggie Barber left Ditchingham House. On 5 August, Haggard wrote to her, suggesting an idea for a long poem he wanted her to write:

'Farewell is a big subject, the whole world is one long farewell. . . . Let us suppose a man and a woman, young since it is in youth that the passions strike deepest, beautiful if you will, and let these two love one another. Then let circumstances separate them with or without a mutual engagement, better without perhaps. Then make the woman weak and let her in spite of the written remonstrance of her absent lover let herself be forced or frightened with her eyes open into a marriage with some other man, and do not make her an injured angel as it is the fashion to do when a woman plays false with herself and her lover. Let the blow fall upon him as heavily as you will, but in the end let him also marry. . . .'

So far the story is an accurate summary of both Haggard's own experience and the plots of the novel on which he was working and the next one he would write. But he continues, 'After a time, ten years or so, let these two meet again whilst still in the flush of their beauty and in the June tide of their lives. Then follows the struggle that will ensue when their sleeping or rather imprisoned love rises again in all its strength and takes possession of them when they find that time has only rendered each more thoroughly the perfect counterpart of the other.'[13]

This ending may have been suggested because Haggard was struggling with an alternative conclusion to his own story; it may have arisen from wishful thinking; or it may be that he had actually met Lilly again and that fleetingly their love had been reaffirmed. Certainly Haggard did meet the other Jackson sisters both at Ditchingham and in London and, after his return from Kashmir, Frederick Jackson renewed his close friendship with Haggard. 'At his instigation,' Jackson recalls in his memoirs, 'I had taken a little house some two miles or so from his house in Norfolk.'[14] As he saw so much of the Jackson family, it is unlikely that Haggard avoided Lilly.

Later in August, Louie, who was again pregnant, and the two children, left Ditchingham to stay with relatives in London. Haggard remained to work on his manuscript. When the rewriting was nearly complete, he wrote again to Jeaffreson, who sent him a letter of introduction to Arthur Blackett of the publishers Hurst and Blackett. Having said that he advised Haggard to rewrite the novel when first it was sent to him, Jeaffreson continues: 'He has acted on my advice, and if the result of his renewed labour answers my anticipation, he has produced a work that will make your reader rub his hands and say "This will do."' Haggard was jubilant when he received the publisher's reply: 'We shall be very happy to undertake the publication of your novel on the following terms. To produce the work at our own expense and risk. To pay you the sum of £40 on the sale of four hundred copies and £30 on the sale of every hundred copies after. The title *Angela* has been used before.' The offer was gratefully accepted and three days later Haggard received the agreement by which he sold the copyright for one year from the date of publication. As Hurst and Blackett planned to publish only four hundred copies of the three volume novel, Haggard was informed that he could make what arrangements he wished for a cheap edition.

Inspired by this success, Haggard worked long hours until he completed the handwritten manuscript of four hundred and ninety-three foolscap pages. On the title page and as a preface he added two poems by 'Edmund Ollier', which almost certainly is a pseudonym for Aggie, to whom he wrote on 10 September: 'Since Louie has been away I have been able to work later and often have not knocked off till about twelve or till my eyes gave out. You would be amused if you could see me now writing with closed shutters and in a pair of green glasses. However there is nothing serious the matter with my eyes and now that I can give them a rest they will get perfectly right. I brought the trouble on myself by working by a paraffin lamp and with the sunlight on my paper and at one time thought that I should have to put my book by. However yesterday having rewritten the last sheet three times and corrected it at least six I dispatched the manuscript to the address of Messrs Hurst and Blackett.'[15]

The trouble with his eyes became so severe that Haggard went to London to see an oculist who informed him that he was suffering from overwork and ordered him to take a complete rest. Haggard, following the doctor's advice took his family to stay for a month in lodgings at Southwold in Suffolk. There he walked a little and exercised by throwing a ball against the wall of a room. While they were at Southwold, Haggard's brother Jack came to visit before setting off for Lamu, on the East African coast, where he was to take up his new appointment as Vice-Consul. Haggard read him sections from earlier versions of his manuscript and, although generally complimentary, Jack objected to Mrs Carr's forename, claiming that 'every shop girl he had ever met was called Muriel'. To please him, Haggard changed the name to Mildred Carr.

Late in October, Haggard, fully recovered and full of his normal energy, returned to Ditchingham. Once again he quickly became bored and on 12 November he started a second novel which he called *Eva, or A Tale of Love and War*. Soon, however, the printer's proofs of *Dawn*, as it had been decided to call his first fictional work, began to arrive. He went through them carefully, and then walked over to Frederick Jackson's cottage to discuss them with his young friend. Then he sent them off in batches to Aggie.

On 23 January, 1884, he wrote to her: 'I send you two bits more. They have brought the second vol. to a somewhat abrupt conclusion and have added two lines per page to the third which will work it out about 826 pages long. The book is to come out in the beginning of March under my own name. They say it is much better to bring it out thus, though I confess to a certain nervousness in the matter.' Five days later, he wrote again: 'I send you two more bits of proof. I suppose that we shall come to an end of it at last.' In another letter written to her, on 21 February, he says: 'I must thank you for your kindness in going through the proof of *Dawn* for me, and for the many valuable suggestions you made.' Having thanked her for correcting some errors, he continues: 'I have ideas of writing a one volume sequel to *Dawn*, on purpose to further develop the character of Angela, which is now only taking form. I should shew her after a spell of ordinary married life and becoming the mother of a charming family falling again under the fascination of her love of knowledge and power and unable to any longer keep in check the mighty intellect now only beginning to touch its possibilities.'[16]

His thoughts on this subject may well have been prompted by his knowledge of Lilly's circumstances. She was at the time living in affluence with her banker husband at 10 Somers Place, near Hyde Park. She also had three charming young sons, the youngest of whom, Geoffrey Francis Archer, had been born on 4 July, 1882. Haggard did not write the sequel, but this is not surprising. He had already adopted the habit he retained throughout his life of jotting down into a pocket-book many ideas for stories, and most of these were never used. About this time he did note two interesting ideas: the first was 'Witch story. Woman in cave w(ith) fire w(ith) eye out. Curse Him. Is it well to put out an eye . . . Fetish dance of all the people dressed like animals. Raising the dead.' The second was alarmingly pro-phetic: 'Character for book. Worn out old novelist who has been a g(rea)t man in his day & is forced to continue writing f(or) his living. (Nay pathetic & may happen to any of us.)'[17]

Early in 1884 Haggard received from his brother Jack in Lamu a letter that he immediately took to Frederick Jackson, who later recalled: 'In that letter it was suggested that Rider, his wife, and I should go out there for a year, and have the time of our lives. Between us, he and I were to pay all expenses from the proceeds of elephant-hunting; and during the intervals between such trips, he was to write his books, while I was to amuse myself with smaller game. . . . It was altogether most alluring, and after reading the letter, the question he put to me was: "Will you go, if we do?" '[18] It was agreed that in about a year's time, after the baby had been born and Haggard had taken his law examinations, they would all go. The prospect of returning to Africa excited Haggard and, as a result, he decided to include African adventures and locations in the novel he was writing.

First, however, was the excitement caused by the publication, on 21 February, of *Dawn*. Haggard was impressed for 'it appeared in charming type, such as we do not get in novels nowadays, and three nice volumes bound in green'. He was, though, still worried about the alterations he had made. In his autobiography he states, 'To this day I often wonder whether Jeaffreson was right in making me turn my story inside out and give it a happy ending.' Jeaffreson, I am sure, was right to suggest that Haggard's story would benefit from rewriting, but, because of his inexperience, what Haggard did was to break up the tale he wished to tell. With all its obvious defects *There Remaineth a Rest* is a superior story to the published version, *Dawn*, about which Haggard rightly said 'that it ought to have been cut up into several stories'.

About his heroine, Angela, Haggard makes the significant comment: ' [In *Dawn*] the final fires through which the heroine had to pass were those of marriage to a not very interesting young man. I have always found young men . . . somewhat difficult to draw. Young men, at any rate to the male eye, have a painful similarity to each other, whereas woman is of an infinite variety and therefore easier to depict.' Throughout his life Haggard remained impressed by the 'infinite variety' of women. In 1950 his nephew, Godfrey Haggard, recalled: 'Rider's manner and appearance were distinctly formidable to a number of people, especially women without much power of self-assertion. The fact is that he was not very good with the sex as a whole. And yet how well he understood women! Not one of his heroines but is a warm, living human being, the beautiful, adorable mate, full of tantrums and intelligence such as he would himself have chosen . . . for himself.'[19] Women too had an immense impact on his own character, emotions and attitudes. As a child he felt drawn to his mother and was close to his sisters. After his love affair with Lilly, there were the 'feminine complications' in Africa. Then there was Louie and the intellectually stimulating Aggie. They all affected him, although it was in his fiction that Haggard proved best able to explore the women who fascinated him.

After *Dawn*'s publication Haggard eagerly read the reviews, which ranged from scathing condemnation to unqualified praise. George Saintsbury in *The Academy* asserted, 'It covers too great a stretch of time. There are too many heroines, and they are too beautiful. There are too many minor characters, and they have too much to do. The wicked people (of whom there are several) are too elaborately wicked.[20]

The review in *The Times* was much more enthusiastic: '*Dawn* is a novel of merit far above the average. From the first page the story arrests the mind and arouses the expectation.' This provided all the encouragement Haggard needed to continue with his second novel which, far more than *Dawn*, was based upon his own experiences. Ernest Beyton Kershaw meets and falls in love with Eva Ceswick at a ball. After they have become unofficially engaged, Ernest goes abroad temporarily, but is prevented from returning and so travels to Africa where he has many adventures similar to Haggard's. Eva is pressurised by her elder sister into marrying an older man. Ernest, when he is informed by letter, reacts wildly. Then, just after the battle of Isandhlwana, he is shot and blinded. Later he returns to England where he marries Dorothy Jones, the ward of his uncle and heiress to his estate. Later, by arrangement, Ernest once more meets Eva in a churchyard overlooking the sea:

> Slowly he turned towards her, and looked into her sweet face till he could feel their eyes meet and their influence which had overpowered him overpowering her too and her words died on her lips which now uttered nothing but sighs. Together, close together, they sway and presently his arms closed round her and his lips were on her own.
>
> (From the unpublished *Eva, or a Tale of Love and War*)

Recognising their folly, they pull apart, but consoling themselves with the belief that they will be reunited in heaven. Unfortunately Eva's husband has followed them and he tries to push Ernest over the cliff. To prevent him, Eva grabs her husband and, locked together in a tight embrace, they plunge to their deaths.

As in *Dawn*, Rider sets the action in a combination of places he knew. Dorothy's home, Dum's Ness, is very like Ditchingham House, but the area around, called

Kesterwick, is really Dunwich, a spot on the east coast just south of Southwold. He makes much less effort to fictionalise the characters. Ernest is a self-portrait; Alston is drawn from Sir Melmoth Osborn; Dorothy has some of Louie's characteristics; Eva owes much to Lilly; and Mazooku, Haggard's African servant, appears as himself.

On 25 March, 1884, Louie gave birth to her third child, a girl. She was called Dorothy after the character in the novel her father was writing. Her full name was Sybil Dorothy Rider Haggard. After the child's birth, Aggie Barber once more moved into Ditchingham House and once more she spent much time discussing Haggard's writing with him. The way they worked together is described by Admiral Vernon H. Haggard, another of Rider's nephews: 'When, as a young boy of about ten, he spent the summer at Ditchingham, he was permitted on rainy days to sit in his uncle's study while Rider worked on his stories with Miss Barber. The author either dictated or read aloud what he had already written. "And then he said to her," Rider would read from his foolscap and on occasion turn to Miss Barber to ask, "What did he say to her anyway?" '[21]

It was fortunate that he had Aggie's encouragement, for the news he received about the sales of his two previous books was depressing. On 17 April 1884, Trubner wrote to say that only one hundred and fifty-four copies of *Cetywayo and His White Neighbours* had been sold. The letter continued: 'You will no doubt consider the account a most unsatisfactory one, as we do, seeing that we are out of pocket to the extent of £82 15s. 5d. Against this, of course, we hold the £50 advanced by you, but we fear that we are never likely to recover the balance, £32 15s. 5d.' The sales of *Dawn* were also poor. Nor was his work on the new novel a complete success, and as soon as he had finished he set about rewriting it. Conscious of Jeaffreson's criticism of *Dawn* he decided that the unhappy and melodramatic ending should be changed. In time, therefore, the reunion of Ernest and Eva with its fatal consequences was removed. The title was also changed to *Found Wanting*.

In August, when the rewriting was nearly complete, Aggie again left Ditchingham and the Haggards went to stay at Marvin House in Criccieth, Wales. With them went Frederick Jackson and his two unmarried sisters. Surrounded by Lilly's relations, Haggard was as near as he could get to being with the woman he loved. While at Criccieth, he decided that he would not visit his brother Jack in Lamu after all. He gave the reasons for his decision in a letter dated 28 August: 'First there are the children to be considered, then the money question, then the question of the desirability of my, after being called, getting a practical knowledge of law by reading with a barrister. Beyond these there is another matter. There is some chance — rather a faint one I think — but still a chance of my being asked to contest a seat at the next election, and I do not think that I should at present be justified in throwing the opportunity away should it arise. Of course it could not arise in my absence at Lamu. Still I ardently hope to be able to see you out there some time.'[22]

Haggard's desire to enter Parliament was retained for much of his life, but it was never realised; nor did he ever visit Jack at Lamu.

Fred Jackson, however, decided to make the planned journey to East Africa on his own. After their return to Ditchingham, Haggard took a great interest in all Jackson's preparations and purchases. Together they tested the .500 Express rifle Jackson had taken to Kashmir, blasting a huge hole in the brick wall of a cowshed. Jack, who was a prolific writer of letters crammed with romantic anecdotes, sent a message urging Jackson to take with him a boat, recommending as most suitable a Dundee 30-foot whaleboat. To support spending so much money, Jack gave a hair-raising account of how, because of an unexpected bore rushing up a creek, he had spent a night in his ancient six-oared cutter marooned on a sandbank, expecting at any moment to be thrown with his crew into the raging seas. Eventually the tide rose sufficiently to refloat the leaking boat. Jackson took the request seriously and, with Haggard's advice, ordered from Messrs John Brown of Dundee a miniature lifeboat. It 'was 30 feet long, carvel built, with block tin air-tight compartments all round and at both ends, with lockers also all round long enough to take guns, rifles and such-like, and with lids almost flush with the gunwale, a central board, six water-beakers, and set of seven oars, anchor and chain, and yawl-rigged'.[23] Haggard used the boat in *She*:

> The whale-boat, I may explain, was one specially built for us at Dundee, in Scotland. We had brought it with us, as we knew that this coast was a network of creeks, and that we might require something to navigate them with. She was a beautiful boat, thirty feet in length, with a centre-board for sailing, copper-bottomed to keep the worm out of her, and full of water-tight compartments.
>
> (From *She*)

There were many other things, apart from helping Jackson, to keep Haggard busy in the autumn of 1884. Having completely revised his second novel he sent it to Hurst and Blackett, who agreed to publish it on the same terms as for *Dawn*, even though it had sold only four hundred and fifty copies, earning for Haggard the princely sum of £10. In mid-September he had to stay in London for a couple of weeks so that he could concentrate on his legal studies before taking his final examination. He found the written papers difficult, but he enjoyed the *viva voce*. When one old gentleman on the panel asked him if he was a relative of a certain Dr Haggard, he replied, quite untruthfully, that the physician was his uncle. Much of the time was then spent talking about this fictitious relative. Although he was awarded his certificate on 3 October Haggard decided to wait until the new term before being called to the Bar.

On 5 November, Haggard wrote to Aggie about his new novel: 'They won't have any of my titles for the new book — want more. The only thing I could think of was *The Witch's Head* which I don't like much. Have you got such a thing as a title about you? There has been a book called *Found Wanting*, or something like it.' His suggestion for the title was accepted, as he states in another letter to Aggie a few days later: 'The title which Hurst and Blackett have chosen for my book is *The*

Witch's Head. I suggested it among others and they jumped at it and said it was striking. Louisa suggests your poem beginning "Swell out sad harmonies" should be placed at commencement of the book and I think it a good idea. Have you any objection? Please let me know by return. I should suggest putting it with your name after it. What do you say? I get my first proofs today. I am afraid that I cannot send them to you as the book is to be published next month and the printing is to be . . . without revises.

Aggie gave her consent and the twelve-line poem appeared in the book when it was published. In the same letter Haggard states: 'I have nearly finished my little story about the two brothers, but I don't know if I can get a magazine to bring it out. There is a rather good article on Egyptian affairs in *Blackwoods* (October) by my brother Andrew. They gave him £20 for it.'[24]

The story which was at first called 'Bottles' was yet another attempt to rationalise in fiction the way he had been jilted by Lilly. It tells how John George Peritt, a soldier in Natal, is informed by his sweetheart, Madeline Spenser, that she is to marry Sir Alfred Croston. When he returns to England, Peritt finds that Lady Croston is a widow. He visits her and seems to win back her love, but his eldest brother, Sir Eustace Peritt, assures him that the lady would give her affections to anybody else who had more money. To prove his point Sir Eustace proposes and is accepted. John, deeply distressed, commits suicide.

As soon as he had finished the story Haggard sent it to a magazine, hoping to duplicate the success of his brother Andrew, who from his one article had earned twice as much as Haggard's total income from writing.

Hurst and Blackett refused, as they had with *Dawn*, to publish *The Witch's Head* in a cheap edition, and Haggard was well aware that there was little possibility of his finding another publisher to do so. He had to accept that he would probably be unable to earn a living from writing. 'I came to the conclusion,' he later recalled, 'that I would abandon the making of books. The work was very hard, and when put to the test of experience the glamour that surrounds this occupation vanished.' He decided, therefore, that as he had qualified for the Bar, he would pursue a career as a barrister. Arrangements were made for him to work in the chambers of Henry Bargrave Deane, a relative by marriage, and to attend the Probate and Divorce Courts. Ditchingham House was let, although unfortunately the tenant died before he could take possession. Louie rented 1 Fairholme Road, West Kensington, and it was agreed that Aggie would move in with them to help look after the children. On 26 December, Haggard set off from Ditchingham for his new home, which he had not previously seen. With two nurses and his three children, he travelled by train to Liverpool Street, where a four-wheeled cab, pulled by two men, carried their many pieces of baggage to the destination, while the three adults, each holding a child, took a railway bus. Jock knelt on a seat next to his father and, in a letter to Aggie written on the day of arrival, Haggard reported: 'The Thames Embankment struck him greatly and he informed me several times that he never did see such a fine road as that before, did he?'[25] They were greeted at the house by Louie, a very dirty cook, an even dirtier dog, and a French maid. As the plumbing was not working, it was fortunate that they had arranged to dine that night with the Jacksons.

In a letter Haggard wrote to Aggie on 30 December, just before her arrival, he stated: 'By the way 'Bottles' is *de retour*. I wonder how people ever get things into magazines. I suppose it must be through being regularly connected with them. I am sure 'Bottles' is better than most things that appear in these magazines and behold they will have none of him.'[26]

This rejection was the final blow to Haggard's writing ambitions. He was determined, as 1885 began, to make his way in life as a hard-working lawyer. He could not afford to wait any longer for the success that Jeaffreson had stated could be his. At twenty-eight he was still, in his own eyes as well as his family's, what he had been all his life — 'a waif and a stray'. The only successful thing he had apparently managed to do was to marry a less than perfect wife whose dwindling, inherited fortune had so far subsidised his fruitless attempts to obtain a satisfactory income of his own.

5

The Golden Years

I

While he was waiting to be called to the Bar, Haggard settled into the new routine of life at 1 Fairholme Road. It was not long, however, before his determination to concentrate on his legal career was weakened by the favourable reviews of *The Witch's Head* that began appearing in mid-January, 1885. As Haggard later commented in his autobiography, his second novel was extremely well received: 'Indeed, after the lapse of more than a quarter of a century they [the reviews] still make pleasant reading.' Almost all the reviewers selected the African sections of the novel for special praise. The *Pall Mall Budget* of 16 January contained a glowing review: 'Only one book is said to have got Dr. Johnson out of bed before he wanted to rise. Only one novel, for a very long time, has kept us out of bed when we were anxious to go thither. That novel is *The Witch's Head* . . . . Here is a novelist of Kingsley's school, not so much a poet as Charles Kingsley, not so reckless a humourist as the author of *Ravenshoe*, but still a succesor in the art of truly patriotic and adventurous fiction.'[1] The following day *The Saturday Review* praised the African adventures and concluded that Haggard 'exhibits a great deal of power and originality and knowledge of his subject'.[2]

Despite such favourable reviews Haggard was aware that, as Hurst and Blackett had refused to publish more than the first edition of five hundred copies, he would earn little from the book. This lack of financial reward and popular acclaim was in marked contrast to the current successes achieved by another work 'of truly patriotic and adventurous fiction' that since its publication as a book in late 1883 had become 'a widely read and nationally hailed best-seller'.[3] This was Robert Louis Stevenson's *Treasure Island*, which was first published as a serial by 'Captain George North' in *Young Folks* between October 1881 and January 1885. In *The Days of My Life* Haggard claims that 'I read in one of the weekly papers a notice of Stevenson's *Treasure Island* so laudatory that I procured and studied that work, and was impelled by its perusal to try to write a book for boys.'

Haggard's daughter, Lilias, gives a different account of how her father was influenced by Stevenson's success to start work on the novel that was to become the most talked-about story of the decade: 'Travelling up to London with one of his brothers they started discussing *Treasure Island*, just then making a great success. Rider said he didn't think it was so very remarkable, whereupon his brother replied, rather indignantly: "Well, I'd like to see you write anything half as good —

bet you a bob you can't." "Done," said Rider.'[4]

When he was called to the Bar on 26 January, Haggard had already started writing *King Solomon's Mines*. The first entry in his 1885 notebook is 'Solomon's Mines 77,400 words (about). Begun January. Finished 21 April 1885'.[5] and so, although subsequently he claimed 'the task occupied me about six weeks', Haggard spent thirteen weeks writing his 'book for boys'. He worked on the task with single-minded enthusiasm, for there was very little else to occupy him. At the chambers of Bargrave Deane there was the tedious inactivity all newly called barristers were expected to endure. At home, his wife was busy with her children, servants, friends, and growing love of croquet. Only with Aggie Barber, who was again living with the family, could Haggard share his enthusiasm for his story of adventure that linked him, however tentatively, with his fond remembrances of Africa that seemed increasingly distant but so desirable. As he wrote, Aggie discussed the manuscript with him and provided much help and assistance, most notably creating the map, written in blood on a piece of dirty linen allegedly torn from the shirt-tail of Don José Silvestra, that was the starting-point for the adventure. Also encouraged by her and the continuing complimentary reviews of *The Witch's Head*, Haggard, who rejection normally reduced to sullen inactivity, endeavoured to find a publisher for 'Bottles', his short story. This time he sent it to *Harper's*. On 28 March, the editor, Andrew Lang, wrote to Haggard: 'Your paper "Bottles" has reached me as London editor of *Harper's*. I am much pleased by it, but I am unable to accept anything except by permission of the American editor. . . . I am glad to take this opportunity of thanking you for the great pleasure *The Witch's Head* has given me. I have not read anything so good for a long while.' Haggard was rightly delighted to receive such praise from a critic as influential and knowledgeable as Lang, and he continued writing with even greater dedication.

Writing to the editor of *The Book Buyer* (New York) on 20 March 1887, Haggard states: '*King Solomon's Mines* was written as an experiment in boys' books. It would be impossible for me to define where fact ends and fiction begins in the work, as the two are very much mixed up together.'[6] The story is indeed a most complex amalgam of fact with fantasy, of people and places recalled with the imaginative retelling of other men's stories. The book's narrator is Allan Quatermain, named after the pig-farmer with whom Haggard spent so much time as a schoolboy at Garsington. The character and the method of narration proved to be so successful that Allan Quatermain reappeared in seventeen further books and short stories by Haggard, who in his autobiography claims that the character was 'only myself set in a variety of imagined situations, thinking my thoughts and looking at life through my eyes'.

This may well be true of later books in which the freshness had faded of the African hunter who was 'not a literary man, though very devoted to the Old Testament and also to the *Ingoldsby Legends*', but the earlier Quatermain is similar in many ways to F.C. Selous who, according to *The Dictionary of National Biography* possessed 'indomitable courage, enduring energy and great tenacity . . . a man of high and simple character'. Selous's *A Hunter's Wanderings in Africa*, published in 1881, had attracted much attention. It is unlikely that the book was unknown to Haggard, whose interest in Africa was constantly refreshed by the purchase and thorough study of a large number of non-fiction books about it. Haggard always denied any link between Selous and Quatermain, stating in his diary: 'Although he was not the original of Allan Quatermain as everybody says, I have known him for many years and once he stopped with us at Ditchingham.'[7]

Most of Haggard's contemporaries, however, assumed that Quatermain owed much to Selous, and on 9 January, 1917, Charles Longman wrote to Haggard: 'My dear Rider, Of course you have seen the announcement of Selous' death. . . . The public will have it that he was the original of Allan Quatermain. I do not know whether you consciously based the character of A.Q. on Selous. There is of course some resemblance in their careers and modes of life.'[8] The most obvious influence Selous had on *King Solomon's Mines* was not supplying accounts of adventures that could be translated to Quatermain, but suggesting to Haggard an acceptable and appropriate style, the simple but forceful anecdotes of a non-literary sportsman. The character of Allan Quatermain, who according to the first line of *King Solomon's Mines* was fifty-five, is a successful amalgamation of the elderly men he had served in Africa, hunters like Selous about whom Haggard had read, and an imaginative projection of himself as a late-middle-aged ex-colonial.

The story begins aboard a ship steaming down the east coast of Africa. It is the *Dunkeld*, in which the Haggards actually sailed home from the Cape. Quatermain meets two fellow-passengers, Sir Henry Curtis and Captain John Good. Curtis is a fair-haired, tall man of about thirty 'with large grey eyes set deep into his head'. Like Haggard, he claims to be 'of Danish blood'. Good, a retired naval officer, is the more interesting of the pair:

> He was broad, of medium height, dark, stout, and rather a curious man to look at. He was so very neat and so very clean shaved, and he always wore an eye-glass in his right eye. It seemed to grow there, for it had no string, and he never took it out except to wipe it. At first I thought he used to sleep in it, but I afterwards found that this was a mistake. He put it in his trousers pocket when he went to bed, together with his false teeth, of which he had two beautiful sets.
>
> (From *King Solomon's Mines*)

There is a wealth of claimants to be the original of Captain Good. J.E. Scott states, 'The character of Captain Good is really a study of the author's brother, John G. Haggard.'[9] J. Stanley Little, who first met Haggard in Natal in 1876, claimed that he contributed the eye-glass and personal neatness, but there is no proof that this is so. The attributes belonged to several other friends of Haggard's, including Captain Marshal Clarke, who was in the party that went to Secocoeni's encampment, and Frederick Jackson, Lilly's brother. Lord Cransworth in *The Field* of 14 February 1929 emphatically states that Jackson was the original of Good. It may be so, although it is more than likely that in creating this entertaining character,

72

Haggard was thinking of both his brother Jack and his friend Fred Jackson, who together were at the time on the hunting expedition in East Africa in which, but for his family responsibilities and shortage of money, Haggard would have participated. He does join in his imagination for the fictional adventures that befall Quatermain and his party. It is even possible that the hunting episodes in *King Solomon's Mines* owe something to the letters the two men sent to Haggard. Certainly Jack was a voluminous and inventive correspondent. In 1884 Haggard wrote to him: 'Your letters are delightful. I keep them and so they will always be available for reference.'[10]

The nature of these letters, which do not seem to have survived, can be gathered from this extract from Fred Jackson's autobiography: 'One of the letters received by Rider just before I left home described how a herd of buffalo "could be seen," as he wrote, "grazing on the island opposite". The island in question, Manda, about three-quarters of a mile away from Lamu, was covered with the densest bush, and was so flat that the top of an odd baobab tree here and there stood out boldly against the skyline. It was, furthermore, so completely screened from view by a fringe of tall mangroves that a herd of elephants would have been invisible; and there were, of course, no buffaloes on it. Nevertheless, such letters made good reading, and beyond being misleading and very disappointing when it came down to the bedrock of toilsome investigation, they did no harm.'[11]

After they had disembarked, Quatermain and his two companions prepare for their journey in search of Curtis's younger brother and, aided by the Silvestra map, the treasures of Solomon's mines. Among the five servants hired by the party is Umpoba, a huge native who suspiciously is willing to work without payment. Also included are Khiva and Ventvogel, the two men Haggard, in real life, had lent to Captain Patterson and J. Sergeaunt when they went on their ill-fated mission to the Matabele. Their journey, and his own experiences when with Osborn and Clarke he travelled to Secocoeni's camp, seem to have been very much in Haggard's mind while he was writing *King Solomon's Mines*.

The first adventure is an exciting elephant hunt during which Khiva is killed. Then the party barely survives a long trek across a sunburnt desert towards the twin mountain peaks known as Sheba's Breasts:

> There, straight before us, were two enormous mountains, the like of which are not, I believe, to be seen in Africa, if indeed there are other such in the world, measuring each at least fifteen thousand feet in height, standing not more than a dozen miles apart, connected by a precipitous cliff of rock, and towering up in awful white solemnity straight into the sky. These mountains standing thus, like the pillars of a gigantic gateway, are shaped exactly like a woman's breasts. Their bases swelled gently up from the plain, looking at that distance perfectly round and smooth; and on the top of each was a vast round hillock covered with snow, exactly corresponding to the nipple on the female breast.
>
> (From *King Solomon's Mines*)

While climbing Sheba's left breast, the party shelters in a cave where Ventvogel is frozen to death and the preserved corpse of Don Silvestra, dead for three hundred years, is found. The pattern of the narrative is set. Exciting discoveries and escapes from danger follow each other in quick succession.

Having crossed the mountain peaks, the explorers travel along Solomon's Road. While resting on their journey, they are captured by hostile natives, who are apparently intent on killing them, but they escape death when Good plays tricks with his false teeth and Quatermain shoots an antelope with his 'magic tube'. Their captors agree to take the white men to meet their king.

These natives are called Kukuanas in *King Solomon's Mines*, but in an article written in 1906 Haggard states: 'Of the Matabele, who in the tale are named the Kukuanas, I did know something in those days.'[12] It has already been pointed out that Haggard also knew a great deal about the conflict among the Matabele that his friends, Patterson and Sergeaunt, were sent to investigate. It was caused by a succession dispute between two claimants to the throne and there is a similar dispute in *King Solomon's Mines*. As soon as the adventurers meet Twala, the one-eyed king of the Kukuanas, Umpoba announces that he is really Ignosi, the rightful king. The witch-finding that follows is based on the description given to Haggard in 1876 by F.B. Fynney. Gagool, the hideously ugly, vulture-headed woman who is in charge of the grim ceremony is, as Norman Ellington has pointed out in *Notes and Queries*,[13] strikingly similar to the haggish old wife of the Amatoga chief in *The Ruined Cities of Zululand*, an all but forgotten novel by Hugh Mulleneux Walmsley, first published in 1869. It is probable that this book was known to Haggard, for its author was the brother of Shepstone's Natal border agent. In Walmsley's novel a German missionary named Wyzinski is a thinly disguised portrait of Merensky, with whom Haggard stayed on his journey to Secocoeni and who inspired the armed missionary Mackenzie in *Allan Quatermain*.

At the witch-finding, Ignosi is saved from death only after Quatermain intervenes, threatening to shoot Twala. As a proof that Ignosi's claim to the throne is just, Good, who has fortunately brought with him an almanac and knows that there will be an eclipse, promises that the next day the sun will be temporarily extinguished. While waiting for the eclipse, Quatermain and his companions watch the annual 'dance of girls', during which the most beautiful maiden is selected to be a human sacrifice. Foulata is chosen, but once again the white men intervene and as the eclipse occurs they escape with the girl through the darkness. (After the publication of *King Solomon's Mines* it was pointed out to Haggard that an eclipse of the sun at the time of the full moon, as he had described it, was an impossibility. He changed the passage and all editions after 1887 have an eclipse of the moon.)

On the next day a battle between the two rival armies is fought, called by Haggard 'The Last Stand of the Greys'. It owes much to the description he had heard from Melmoth Osborn of the battle at Tugela between the two rival sons of Chief Panda. The relish with which Haggard described the defeat of the usurpers' armies may have owed something to his desire to expunge from his consciousness the horror of the Zulu victory over the British, using almost identical tactics, at Isandhlwana. In *King Solomon's Mines* it is Sir Henry Curtis who finally dispatches the false king, Twala. In describing the incident, Haggard indulges in the fascination of his youth for severed limbs and decapitations:

> Once more Twala came on, and as he came our great Englishman gathered himself together, and, swinging the heavy axe round his head, hit at him with all his force. There was a shriek of excitement from a thousand throats, and, behold! Twala's head seemed to spring from his shoulders, and then fell and came rolling and bounding along the ground towards Ignosi, stopping just at his feet. For a second the corpse stood upright, the blood spouting in fountains from the severed arteries; then with a dull crash it fell to the earth, and the gold torque from the neck went rolling away across the pavement.
>
> (From *King Solomon's Mines*)

After the battle, Ignosi assumes the throne. Good, who is ill, is nursed by the grateful Foulata. As Good recovers, Quatermain nervously realises that the patient and his nurse are falling in love. As a reward to the white men for their assistance, Ignosi orders Gagool to conduct them to the caves of Solomon, set high in the mountains. After another long journey along Solomon's Road the party, including Foulata, reach three giant stone colossi, erected by a long-dead civilisation.

Some people assumed that Haggard owed his idea of a deserted city to the recently discovered ruins of Zimbabwe but he always denied this. In his autobiography he states: 'Since that day . . . Rhodesia has been discovered, which is a land full of gems and gold, the same land, I believe, as that whence King Solomon did actually draw his wealth. Also Queen Sheba's Breasts have been found, or something very like to them, and traces of the great road that I describe. Doubtless I heard faint rumours of these things during my sojourn in Africa, having made it my habit through life to keep my ears open; but at the best they were *very* faint.' In an article 'The Real *King Solomon's Mines*', written in 1907, he asserts: 'When I wrote of Solomon's Road I never guessed that the old-world Road of God, as I think that it is called, would be discovered in the Matoppos. When I imagined Sheba's Breasts, I was ignorant that so named and shaped they stand — *vide* the latest maps — not far from the Tokwe River, guarding the gate to the Great Zimbabwe.'

Haggard does, however, also say: 'Although I think that Mr Baines, one of the first wanderers in much of the country which is now Rhodesia, died shortly after I reached Natal, and I do not recall ever having spoken to him, I knew his family, and doubtless heard something of that country from them and others, with the result that it must have been ingrained in my mind that it had once been occupied by an ancient people.'[14] It is most unlikely that Haggard had not heard of Zimbabwe when he wrote *King Solomon's Mines*. He kept up-to-date with his readings about Africa and, even when he first arrived in Natal, Zimbabwe had been discovered. Thomas Baines's 'Map of the Gold Fields of South Eastern Africa', published in 1873, shows 'Simbaby, ruined cities C. Mauch, Sept. 1871'. J.R. Jeppe's 'Map of the South African Republic', which in 1877 was published in Pretoria while Haggard was living there, includes a two-inch square view of the ruins. Such maps as these must have been consulted by Haggard while he was in the Transvaal or, even if they were not, men like Shepstone and Osborn would have been well aware of the new, important discoveries.

The mine which Quatermain and his party entered was, as Haggard points out, similar to the diamond mines at Kimberley with which he was very familiar:

> 'Can't you guess what this is?' I said to Sir Henry and Good, who were staring in astonishment down into the awful pit before us.
>
> They shook their heads.
>
> 'Then it is clear that you have never seen the diamond mines at Kimberley. You may depend on it that this is Solomon's Diamond Mine.'
>
> (From *King Solomon's Mines*)

Passing through a narrow opening in the cliff, the party enter the Place of Death whose description owes much to the cave at Wonderfontein Haggard had visited with Judge Kotzé and the story of the mummified man told to him by Mr Graham at Garsington.

After the three white men have entered the inner treasure chamber, Gagool treacherously pulls the lever that closes the massive door of solid rock that would leave them entombed within. Foulata tries to stop her, but she is stabbed by Gagool who is then crushed to death beneath the descending rock door. As Foulata dies, she asks Quatermain to translate for Good her final words:

> 'Even now, though I cannot lift my hand, and my brain grows cold, I do not feel as though my heart were dying; it is so full of love that could live a thousand years, and yet be young. Say that if I live again, mayhap I shall see him in the stars, and that — I will search them all.'
>
> (From *King Solomon's Mines*)

It is perhaps in Foulata's moving promise of everlasting love and suggestion of rebirth that Haggard found the germ of the idea he was to develop into the everlasting love of the ageless She.

Eventually the explorers manage to escape from the treasure chamber, although they have to leave behind the hoard of diamonds, apart from the handful of gems Quatermain has sensibly pocketed. On their long journey back to Durban they discover Curtis's younger brother living in a native hut where, because his leg had been crushed, he has been forced to stay. At the end of the story, the Quatermain diamonds prove to be worth a vast fortune and he returns to England so that he can 'see my boy Harry and look after the printing of this history, which is a task I do not like to trust to anybody else'.

Still lacking any contacts with the literary establishment, Haggard first submitted his completed manuscript to Hurst and Blackett, the publishers of his first two novels. The tale, dedicated as it was by Haggard 'to all the big and little boys who read', was clearly unsuitable for inclusion in the list of a publisher whose métier was the three-volume novel largely purchased by the circulating libraries. The manuscript was speedily rejected.

Early in May, Haggard never one not to take advantage of a contact, on the strength of the letter he had received from him, took his manuscript to Andrew Lang. He could not have made a better choice. Lang, who the previous year had written the first of what was to become an immensely successful series of books for children, was already established as the doyen of literary reviewers. His opinion could create or destroy a book's popular reputation, and in the debate then being conducted as to the course literature should take he was the enthusiastic advocate of adventurous romance and the scourge of the everyday realism of the American novelists Henry James and W.D. Howells. He was to declare: 'If the battle between the crocodile of Realism and the catawampus of Romance is to be fought out to the bitter end — why, in that Ragnarok, I am on the side of the Catawampus.' His perennial demand for 'more claymores' was to be well satisfied by Haggard.

Not surprisingly, Andrew Lang was overjoyed when he read *King Solomon's Mines*. Before he had finished reading it, he wrote to Haggard: 'I have got as far as Sir Henry's duel with the king. Seldom have I read a book with so much pleasure: I think it perfectly delightful. The question is, what is the best, whereby I mean the coiniest, way to publish it? As soon as possible I will find out what Harper's *Boys' Magazine* is able to do. I believe that all boys' magazines pay hopelessly badly. There is so much invention and imaginative power and knowledge of African character in your book that I almost prefer it to *Treasure Island*.' Almost certainly Lang decided that the manuscript should be sent to his friend William Ernest Henley, who at the time was the editor of Cassell's *Magazine of Art*. It was Henley who had encouraged Cassell's to publish *Treasure Island*. Sir Newman Flower, who became the publisher's managing director, describes what happened next: 'A colleague of mine at Cassell's . . . told me that he was in the office of John Williams — the chief editor of the firm — when Henley came hobbling through the door with the manuscript of *King Solomon's Mines* under his arm. He threw it across William's desk and exclaimed: "There's a fine thing for you!" '[15]

With Henley and Lang combined in their admiration for the book, Cassell's enthusiastically accepted the manuscript. Haggard was invited to visit Williams at La Belle Sauvage, their office in the City, and there the chief editor offered him an alternative. Cassell's would either puchase the copyright for £100, or pay Haggard £50 on account of a royalty of ten per cent. As up to that time Haggard had earned so little from his writing, the offer of £100 was most attractive and he announced that he would sell the copyright. Williams then left to fetch the agreement. What then took place was recalled by Haggard: 'As it chanced, however, there sat in the corner of the room a quiet clerk, whom I had never even noticed. When the editor had departed this unobtrusive gentleman addressed me. "Mr Haggard," he said in a warning voice, "if I were you I would take the other agreement." Then, hearing some noise, once more he became absorbed in his work, and I understood that the conversation was not to be continued.' Haggard accepted his advice, and, when Williams returned, announced that he had changed his mind.

The agreement was prepared and on 29 May 1885, signed by Haggard, whose last minute change of mind had secured the considerable fortune that would be paid in royalties during the ensuing ninety years that the book remained in copyright. The agreement stipulated that the royalty would be 10 per cent of the published price (reckoning 13 copies as 12). It was to be some time, however, before Haggard realised that, although he earned royalties, the copyright was not his. The second clause of the agreement Haggard signed reads: 'The said story is to be the sole and exclusive copyright of Cassell & Company for publication in any form subject to the royalty hereinafter mentioned . . .'[16] As a result of this clause, Cassell's over the years were to receive considerable sums from the vast number of editions and translations of *King Solomon's Mines* published by other firms.

Perhaps it was his realisation that he had not been treated as generously by Cassell's as he might have been that drove Haggard to include a description of the publishers, which he named Meeson's, in his *Mr Meeson's Will*, first published in the 1888 summer number of *The Illustrated London News*:

> The firm employed more than two thousand hands; and its works, lit throughout with the electric light, cover two acres and a quarter of land. One hundred commercial travellers, at three pounds a week and a commission, went forth east and west, and north and south, to sell the books of Meeson (which were largely religious in their nature) in all lands; and five-and-twenty tame authors (who were illustrated by thirteen tame artists) sat — at salaries ranging from one to five hundred a year — in vault-like hutches in the basement, and week by week poured out that hat-work (i.e. work with no head in it) for which Meeson's was justly famous.
>
> (From *Mr Meeson's Will*)

When the story was published, nobody at Cassell's had any doubt that it was their firm that Haggard was describing. The board contemplated taking legal action, but the idea was rejected. A complaint must, however, have been made, for when *Mr Meeson's Will* was published in book-form, Haggard began his preface: 'A letter received from a member of an eminent publishing firm who seems to take Mr Meeson very solemnly, suggests that it may be well to preface this story with a few explanatory words. I cannot begin them better than by saying that Mr Meeson and his vast establishment exist, so far as I am aware, in the regions of romance alone'. By 1888 this was Haggard's standard, glib reply to any suggestion that his material was anything other than original.

Immediately after the acceptance of his manuscript Haggard's annoyance with Cassell's lay in the future, and, while waiting for the publication of *King Solomon's Mines*, he spent his idle moments at home and in the Probate and Divorce Courts jotting down in his notebooks ideas for other stories, including 'Tale of the young authoress & the Company — marries the Head of the Firm'; 'Story of the man w[ith] the will tattooed on his back' (both of which were used in *Mr Meeson's*

Will); 'Paper on novels & novel writing' (written in 1886); and 'Incident for book of adventure — People floating about in a boat bottom upwards'[17] (a *Poseidon Adventure* that was never written). Spurred on by the acceptance of *King Solomon's Mines*, Haggard attempted to find a publisher willing to bring out his first two novels, *Dawn* and *The Witch's Head*, in a cheap edition. J. & R. Maxwell agreed to do this and Haggard happily signed the contract with them which gave him one-third of the profits but bound him to allow them to publish on the same terms the cheap editions of any other books he might write within the next five years.

Early in July Haggard's brother Jack arrived to stay, having been invalided home from East Africa where Frederick Jackson had remained to continue his hunting expedition. The two brothers were delighted to be reunited and Haggard spent many hours listening to Jack's imaginative tales of African adventures. In mid-July, just as Cassell's announced the forthcoming publication of *King Solomon's Mines* 'by Allan Quatermain', the Haggards left 1 Fairholme Road to spend the summer holidays at a Denton farm, not far from the Ditchingham estate. Agnes Barber returned home, but it was obvious that, before they parted, she and Jack Haggard had struck up a very close friendship.

On 17 July, Haggard started writing a sequel to *King Solomon's Mines* which he provisionally entitled *The Frowning City*. During the pleasant summer weeks spent with his family around him, Haggard worked busily on his new boys' book. He seemed determined to complete it before 30 September, the publication date of *King Solomon's Mines*. On 28 September he finished the book, later retitled *Allan Quatermain*. It had taken exactly ten weeks.

The story, which is a continuation of *King Solomon's Mines*, is also narrated by Allan Quatermain. It begins with his lament for the death of his son, Harry. As Quatermain, at the end of *King Solomon's Mines*, had returned to England so that he could see his son, Haggard presumably felt it was advisable to dispose of Harry, who had not appeared in the book, to allow his father the freedom to set off on another adventure. Haggard, writing while spending his holidays in a lonely part of rural Norfolk and recalling the African tales he had just heard from his brother Jack, gives Quatermain another reason, apart from his son's death, for wanting to leave England:

> No man who has for forty years lived the life I have, can with impunity go coop himself in this prim English country, with its trim hedgerows and cultivated fields, its stiff formal manners, and its well-dressed crowds. He begins to long — ah, how he longs! — for the keen breath of the desert air; he dreams of the sight of Zulu impis breaking on their foes like surf upon the rocks, and his heart rises up in rebellion against the strict limits of the civilised life.
>
> (From *Allan Quatermain*)

This *cri de coeur* was clearly Haggard's own and, reacting to his passionless marriage and money worries, he continues in his nostalgia to compare the Zulu women of his memories with the English ladies of his acquaintance:

79

I say that as the savage is, so is the white man, only the latter is more inventive, and possesses the faculty of combination; save and except also that the savage, as I have known him, is to a large extent free from the greed of money, which eats like a cancer into the heart of the white man. It is a depressing conclusion, but in all essentials the savage and the child of civilisation are identical.

(From *Allan Quatermain*)

Allan Quatermain, Sir Henry Curtis and Captain John Good decide to set off on a further African adventure, selecting as their first port of call, Lamu, the East African settlement where Jack Haggard for nearly two years had been the Vice-Consul. From there they plan to make their way 'about 250 miles inland to Mt Kenia' and then on into the unknown interior to investigate 'rumours of a great white race' supposed to be living in the area. After a long sea journey, the explorers arrive at Lamu, whose description draws heavily upon Jack Haggard's stories:

Lamu is a very curious place, but the things which stand out most clearly in my memory in connection with it are its exceeding dirtiness and its smells. These last are simply awful. Just below the Consulate is the beach, or rather a mud bank that is called a beach. It is left quite bare at low tide, and serves as a repository for all the filth, offal, and refuse of the town. Here it is, too, that the women come to bury coconuts in the mud, leaving them there till the outer husk is quite rotten, when they dig them up again and use the fibres to make mats with, and for various other purposes. As this process has been going on for generations, the conditions of the shore can be better imagined than described. I have smelt many evil odours in the course of my life, but the concentrated stench which arose from that beach at Lamu as we sat in the moonlit night — not under, but *on* our friend the Consul's hospitable roof — and sniffed it, makes the remembrance of them very poor and faint. No wonder people get fever at Lamu.

(From *Allan Quatermain*)

At Lamu, Quatermain engages bearers and servants, including Umslopogaas, who in life had been Shepstone's steward. The party then sets off by canoe up the Tara River, as Jack Haggard must have done many times. On the way, Masai warriors attack the explorers, and Haggard describes with relish the severing of yet another limb:

Snatching at the first weapon that came to hand, which happened to be Umslopogaas's battle-axe, I struck with all my force in the direction in which I had seen the flash of the knife. The blow fell upon a man's arm, and, catching it against the thick wooden gunwale of the canoe, completely severed it from the body just above the wrist. As for its owner, he uttered no sound or cry. Like a ghost he came, and like a ghost he went, leaving behind him a bloody hand still gripping a great knife, or rather a short sword, that was buried in the heart of our poor servant.

(From *Allan Quatermain*)

Rider Haggard about 1902, unusually formally dressed

(*Left*) 'I have just heard on the telephone . . that my nephew, Mark Haggard, "died of wounds" on the 15th.' 18 September 1914

(*Opposite*) Chief Telélekn

(*Right*) Umslopogaas, when he was in Government service about 1875. The hole in his forehead can be clearly seen

Haggard with four of his six brothers about 1882. Left to right: Alfred, Andrew, Rider, William and Jack. Bazett and Arthur are missing

Family group at Ditchingham, 1884. Mrs Haggard with baby Dorothy, Rider, his son Jock, daughter Angela, and his mother Ella Haggard. Also Haggard's faithful and intelligent bulldog Caesar

Haggard's three daughters: Angela, Lilias and Dorothy.
About 1894

Lilias, Rider's youngest daughter, about 1906. She
was born after the death of his son

The court presentation of Haggard's two eldest daughters, Agnes Angela and
Sybil Dorothy

(*Opposite*) 'Jock', Haggard's only son. A boy with 'a nature of singular
sweetness'. He died of peritonitis in 1891 while his parents were in Mexico

Lady Haggard in the garden at Ditchingham

At last they safely reach their destination — the Reverend Mackenzie's mission station, which Haggard based on the fortified home of Merensky which he had visited on the way to Secocoeni's camp.

Mackenzie's cook, a comic Frenchman called Alphonse, upsets Umslopogaas who takes his revenge by swinging his axe round his tormentor's head in a scene that is strongly reminiscent of Troy's sword-play in Thomas Hardy's *Far From the Madding Crowd*, which had been published the previous year:

> Then followed the most extraordinary display of sword, or rather of axemanship, that I ever saw. First of all the axe went flying round and round the top of Alphonse's head, with an angry whirl and such extraordinary swiftness that it looked like a continuous band of steel, ever getting nearer and yet nearer to that unhappy individual's skull, till at last it grazed it as it flew. Then suddenly the motion was changed, and it seemed to literally flow up and down his body and limbs, never more than an eighth of an inch from them, and yet never striking them. It was a wonderful sight to see the little man fixed there, having apparently realised that to move would be to run the risk of sudden death, while his black tormentor towered over him, and wrapped him round with the quick flashes of the axe.
>
> (From *Allan Quatermain*)

Flossie, Mackenzie's daughter, is captured by the Masai while out in the bush searching for a lily to give Quatermain, who after a sad meal sits alone on the veranda. In the dark an object lands close by. Having picked it up, Quatermain discovers that 'It was a newly severed human head!' The Masai had killed one of the servants sent to search for Flossie. The white hunters rescue the girl from a Masai kraal and then set off into the interior. After several narrow escapes, their canoe is dragged through underground caverns by the current. At last they reach a deep gorge where they camp and eat some food:

> It was a curious meal. The gloom was so intense that we could scarcely see the way to cut our food and convey it to our mouths. Still we got on pretty well . . . till I happened to look behind me — my attention being attracted by a noise of something crawling over the stones, and perceived sitting upon a rock in my immediate rear a huge species of black freshwater crab, only it was five times the size of any crab I ever saw. This hideous and loathsome-looking animal had projecting eyes that seemed to glare at one, very long and flexible antennae or feelers, and gigantic claws. Nor was I especially favoured with its company. From every quarter dozens of these horrid brutes were creeping up, drawn, I suppose, by the smell of the food, from between the round stones and out of holes in the precipice. Some were already quite close to us . . . Seizing whatever weapons were handy, such as stones or paddles, we commenced a war upon the monsters . . . When they could they nipped hold of us — and awful nips they were — or tried to steal the meat. One enormous fellow got hold of the swan we had skinned and began to drag it off. Instantly a score of others flung themselves

upon the prey, and then began a ghastly and disgusting scene . . . The whole scene might have furnished material for another canto of Dante's *Inferno*.

(From *Allan Quatermain*)

An almost identical incident occurs in E.F. Knight's *The Cruise of the 'Falcon'*, which was first published in 1884. Knight and his two companions are exploring the interior of Trinidad:

More weird than even in the morning was the appearance of this ravine, now that the shades of night were falling. . . . The land crabs certainly . . . were fearful as the firelight fell on their yellow cynical faces, fixed as that of the sphinx, but fixed in a horrid grin. . . . Smelling the fish we were cooking, they came down the mountains in thousands upon us. We threw them lumps of fish, which they devoured with crab-like slowness, yet perseverance.

It is a ghastly sight, a land crab at his dinner. A huge beast was standing a yard from me; I gave him a portion of fish, and watched him. He looked at me straight in the face with his outstarting eyes, and proceeded with his two front claws to tear up his food. . . . And when I looked around, lo! there were half a dozen others all steadily feeding. . . . It was indeed horrible, and the effect was nightmarish in the extreme. While we slept that night they attacked us, and would certainly have devoured us, had we not awoke, and did eat holes in our clothes. One of us had to keep watch, so as to drive them from the other two, otherwise we should have had no sleep.

Imagine sailor cast alone on this coast, weary, yet unable to sleep a moment on account of these ferocious creatures. After a few days of an existence full of horror, he would die raving mad, and then be consumed in an hour by his foes. In all Dante's *Inferno* there is no more horrible a suggestion of punishment than this.

(From *The Cruise of the 'Falcon'* by E.F. Knight)[18]

When *Allan Quatermain* was published the similarity between the two passages did not go unnoticed.

Continuing their canoe journey, the travellers eventually arrive at the Frowning City, the capital of Zu-Vendis or the Country of Gold that was occupied by the people for whom they searched who were 'as white, for instance, as Spaniards or Italians'. What follows is a story not dissimilar to that in *King Solomon's Mines*. In *Allan Quatermain*, however the struggle for the throne is between two beautiful sister queens, the fair Nyleptha and the raven-haired Sorais and in the battle that inevitably follows, Quatermain's party, having taken Nyleptha's side, help to defeat her sister's army. Umslopogaas is fatally wounded in his defence of the stairs leading to the palace. Afterwards Sorais commits suicide, Sir Henry Curtis marries Nyleptha and becomes king, and some months later Allan Quatermain dies.

The story, although even more violent than *King Solomon's Mines*, is told in a similar style, the apparently authentic, but nevertheless fictional travelogue, based upon material gathered from a wide range of sources and told by Quatermain, a man not unlike Haggard who, in the introduction to *King Solomon's Mines*, states he 'cannot make any pretence to the grand literary flights and flourishes'. Haggard, however, used few of his own experiences in the book, and, in his desire to write it as quickly as possible, appears to have been too willing to rely upon other people's ideas. He also appears to have written the book without the help and encouragement of Agnes Barber, although, after he had returned to London, she did supply important supplementary material, including two plans and a poem entitled 'Sorais' Song' that begins:

> As a desolate bird that through darkness its lost way is winging,
> As a hand that is helplessly raised when death's sickle is swinging,
> So is life! ay, the life that lends passion and breath to my singing.

Immediately after it had been finished, *Allan Quatermain* was put aside, because Haggard became preoccupied with the public sensation caused by the publication, on 30 September, of *King Solomon's Mines*. Because the manuscript had received lavish praise from eminent critics, Cassell's decided the book should be launched with a publicity campaign that appears to have been unprecedented. Sir Newman Flower describes how this was done: ' [The firm] prepared long narrow posters — each as long as a hoarding — on which was printed in big type: KING SOLOMON'S MINES — THE MOST AMAZING BOOK EVER WRITTEN. Some nights after the publication of *King Solomon's Mines* the firm put up these posters, *after dark*, all over London. People went to their work on horse-buses in the morning to find the message at every turning. They could not get away from it. They went to their lunches — rich men and poor — with the same statement staring them in the face: KING SOLOMON'S MINES — THE MOST AMAZING BOOK EVER WRITTEN. People began to believe it. What was this book? They must know. Cassell's had put Haggard on the literary map in one night.'[19]

Even the reviewers were unanimous in their praise of 'the most amazing book ever written'. Naturally Lang led the way. His enthusiastic essay appeared unsigned in *The Saturday Review* on 10 October: 'We have only praise for the very remarkable and uncommon powers of invention and gift of *vision* which Mr Haggard displays. . . . In this narrative Mr Haggard seems, as the French say, to have 'found himself'. He has added a new book to a scanty list, the list of good, manly, and stirring fictions of pure adventure. . . . To tell the truth, we should give many novels, say eight hundred (that is about the yearly harvest), for such a book as *King Solomon's Mines*.'[20]

A week later *The Spectator* devoted an editorial article to the book which, it asserted, was one of the most exciting ever published in a modern language. This so delighted Lang that he sent Haggard a note: '*The Spectator* in a "middle" gives you more praise than *I* did, and is neither known personally to you, I fancy, nor an amateur of savages, like me. I hope they will give a review also. . . . I never read anything in *The Spectator* before with such pleasure.'

A fortnight later *The Spectator* did review the book, calling it 'as effective a piece of writing as we have seen for a long time' and declaring that Haggard was 'a story-teller of no common power'.[21] The other journals concurred. *The Athenaeum* called it 'one of the best books for boys — old and young — which we remember to have read', adding that 'there is some fighting hardly to be beaten outside Homer and the great Dumas'.[22] *Vanity Fair* unreservedly recommended 'this clever and highly exciting story'[23] to all its readers. *Public Opinion* declared that 'nothing of the kind has ever been better conceived. It stands foremost as a work of art.'[24]

The public agreed with the reviewers and *King Solomon's Mines* instantly became not just a literary success but a runaway best-seller. It did so because it clearly expressed the spirit and interests of the age. Haggard's knowledge of Africa and the realism of his writing appealed to a country deeply involved in 'the scramble for Africa'. Earlier in 1885, people's attention had been caught by the Berlin Conference during which fourteen major countries divided the spoils of Africa. Imperialism was so much the doctrine of the day that, in his inaugural lecture as Slade Professor of Art at Oxford, Ruskin spoke not of art but of the need for Britain to expand its empire: 'This is what England must do or perish. She must found colonies as fast and as far as she is able, formed of the most energetic and worthiest of men; seizing any piece of fruitful waste ground she can set her foot on, and then teaching her colonists that their chief virtue is to be fidelity to their country, and that their first aim is to advance the power of England by land and sea.'[25]

Middle-class young men were, as Haggard had been, more than willing to respond to such calls and their ever-increasing involvement in imperial affairs created an apparently insatiable desire for books about Africa, India and other far-away places. Although many soldiers, travellers and hunters wrote about their experiences in Africa there were surprisingly few novels set there. The only one of merit to appear before *King Solomon's Mines* was Olive Schreiner's *The Story of an African Farm*, first published under her pseudonym Ralph Iron in 1883; but, as it was, despite its portrait of upcountry Boer life, a domestic rather than an adventure novel, it did not at first make much of an impact. *King Solomon's Mines* was the first African story to find a wide readership. Its subject, the hazardous quest and ultimate triumph of a group of English gentlemen, was a fictional version of what the public assumed was actually happening in the new African colonies. Quatermain's cult of manliness, the virtues of which were so closely linked to the muscular Christianity then the vogue, had immense appeal both for the bourgeoisie, softened by affluence, and for the proletariat, emasculated by monotonous labour. Both Haggard, the writer, and Quatermain, his character, provided, for people who had not been involved in a major war for over fifty years, the manly heroes they desired. Both had travelled in uncharted parts of the Dark Continent, where the strangely different cultures were of such interest to so many Victorians that the study of them became an obsession. In any atlas, Haggard's readers could find the blank, unexplored area where Quatermain had discovered Solomon's treasure. So successfully did Haggard imbue *King Solomon's Mines* with a feeling of realism that many people were convinced that the story was true and more than one party planned to set off in search of the remaining horde of diamonds.

The instantaneous success of *King Solomon's Mines* arose not just from Haggard's ability to express the interests of his age. He was fortunate that the book appeared not only at a time when there was a considerable interest in Africa but also when a revolution in book publishing was taking place. Prior to that time the popularity of books was usually determined by the circulating libraries, which had effectively controlled the sale of novels in book-form since the beginning of the century. Publishing, although benefiting from the increased mechanisation of the printing industry, remained geared to providing the three-volume novels for these libraries, which not only monopolised the market, but dictated that publishers could only issue books thought suitable by circulating libraries like Mudie or W.H. Smith for 'family reading'. In the mid-eighties, however, there was a growing number of middle-class readers willing to purchase books and yet unprepared to pay the 30/- demanded for a three-volume novel. Haggard was, therefore, extremely fortunate that Cassell's chose to publish *King Solomon's Mines* as one of the first 6/- one-volume novels. (Books for boys and girls were usually published only in cheap editions. None of these, however, had the wide appeal of *King Solomon's Mines*.) Even more fortunately, 1885 was the year in which both typesetting processes, Linotype and Monotype, were developed, and Cassell's, one of the few publishers to own a printing works, took advantage of these new technological advances to produce four printings of the book, all of 2,000 copies, between 30 September 1885 and the end of the year. (So rapidly was the book printed that the binders seem to have had difficulty in keeping pace, and even copies of the first edition were bound in September, October and November.) So in three months 8,000 copies of the book were printed, whereas the total printing of each of Haggard's first two novels had been 500.

The book's success ensured that Haggard was the talk of the literary world. Lang and Walter Besant, the littérateur, were among those who sought his company. On 27 October he visited Olive Schreiner with Philip Marston, the poet. He was asked to contribute a short story to *In a Good Cause*, a volume being compiled for charity that was also to include 'African Moonshine' by Olive Schreiner. He wrote 'Hunter Quatermain's Story', an after-dinner hunting tale delivered by Allan Quatermain on his return to England immediately after the adventures recorded in *King Solomon's Mines*.

Despite his new-found and unexpected fame, Haggard was still uncertain about his literary future, for his income was still negligible. Realising that immediate financial success lay in the publication by journals of either his short stories or serialisations of his novels, Haggard wrote to Walter Besant asking for his work to be recommended to *The Graphic*. On 28 October, Besant replied, refusing to do so because 'recommendations are unfortunately regarded with suspicion'; but he continued: 'Now I believe your best plan would be to do what Payn, Wilkie Collins and I myself do — put yourself in the hands of Watt, the literary agent. It pays me pecuniarily well to give him 10% on the price he gets for my novels. . . . I think there can be no doubt that you may follow up a now certain success profitably.'[26]

It is obvious from this letter that Haggard was still seriously hoping to pursue a career as a Member of Parliament, for Besant concludes, 'It is unlucky for you that the din of politics drowns everything else.' Similar disapproval of Haggard's ambition had been expressed a few weeks earlier by Lang, who wrote: 'Abstain from politics; let civilisation die decently as die it must, and as we have no fight in us. I don't belong to the Voting classes. *Ni Elettori ni Eletti.*'

It appears that Haggard did not immediately contact A.P. Watt, the literary agent, as Besant had advised. Instead, perhaps inspired by his contact with Olive Schreiner, he started work on another novel, *Jess*, a story of life and love among the Boers at the time of the Retrocession of the Transvaal. At the time he was sharing chambers at 1 Elm Court with Commissioner Kerr's son and much of the writing was completed there when he was not engaged in his legal duties which included, for a spell, reporting Divorce and Probate cases for *The Times* while the regular reporter was on holiday. He wrote with intense concentration, even though, as he subsequently recalled: 'Sometimes this was no easy task, since young barristers of my acquaintance, with time upon their hands, would enter and scoff at my literary labours.' Each evening he placed what he had written in 'a kind of American cloth music-roll', made for him by Agnes Barber, and took it home so that he could continue writing after dinner. On one occasion the roll with about a dozen pages of manuscript was lost, and Haggard had to rewrite the passage from memory.

While he was writing *Jess*, Haggard's successes continued. To his delight, on 3 November *The Times* published the first of his letters. Even more important, on 9 December Cassell's wrote: 'Our actual sales [of *King Solomon's Mines*] up to the present time may be taken as about 5000 copies more or less and we have much pleasure in enclosing you a cheque for £75 on account of royalty on these sales.'[27] During his lifetime Cassell's alone were to sell a further 650,000 copies of the book.

On 31 December 1885 Haggard completed *Jess*. It had taken him nine weeks. In *The Days of My Life* he gives his reasons for writing the book: 'Being somewhat piqued by the frequent descriptions of myself as "a mere writer of romances and boys' books", I determined to try my hand at another novel.' This statement reveals much about Haggard's nature. As *King Solomon's Mines* had been published less than a month when he started *Jess* and as all its reviews had been full of praise, such dismissive statements can hardly have been 'frequent'. Yet Haggard was so goaded that he was prepared to spend nine weeks writing what he must have anticipated would not prove to be a commercial success. Ironically, even though *Jess* is one of Haggard's most satisfactory novels, a mistake he made in writing it was to unleash a storm of critical condemnation that permanently undermined his literary standing and was to be largely responsible for his becoming, quite incorrectly, little more than a footnote in even current histories of literature. Haggard states that *Jess* is 'a gloomy story . . . so gloomy and painful indeed that Lang could scarcely read it, having a nature susceptible as a sensitive plant.' It begins:

THE GOLDEN YEARS

The day had been very hot even for the Transvaal, where the days still know how to be hot in the autumn, although the neck of the summer is broken — especially when the thunderstorms hold off for a week or two, as they do occasionally. Even the succulent blue lilies — a variety of the agapanthus which is so familiar to us in English greenhouses — hung their long trumpet-shaped flowers and looked oppressed and miserable, beneath the burning breath of the hot wind which had been blowing for hours like the draught from a volcano. The grass, too, near the wide roadway that stretched in a feeble and indeterminate fashion across the veldt, forking, branching, and reuniting like the veins on a lady's arm, was completely coated over with a thick layer of red dust.

(From *Jess*)

The atmosphere of foreboding, so successfully introduced, pervades the story of Captain John Neil, the ex-British Army officer, and the two Croft sisters who fell in love with him, the beautiful Bessie and the intellectual Jess. Satisfactorily distanced from them in time, Haggard deftly re-creates in the novel people and places he had known well in South Africa, including Hilldrop, the Haggards' first home (the Crofts' farmhouse), 'The Palatial' which Cochrane and Haggard built outside Pretoria (Jess's Cottage), and the lawyer G.H. Buskes (the evil Frank Muller, Bessie's unwanted suitor). The relationships between the main characters develop against the background of the Transvaal's Retrocession, an event which Haggard continued to recall with acrimony and regret.

Jess tells the moving story of the sacrifices made by a young woman who refuses to come between her younger sister and the man they both love. Forced by the Boers' rebellion to spend much time alone with Captain Neil, Jess at last confesses her hitherto secret love for him when she believes they are both about to die. Surviving, the couple are separated by their Boer captives. When she returns home, Jess finds that her sister and uncle are held captive by Frank Muller, whom, with the assistance of a Hottentot servant, she determines to kill. First, however, she writes her farewell letter to Captain Neil, adding 'almost without correction' three verses which begin:

> If I should die to-night,
> Then wouldst thou look upon my quiet face,
> Before they laid me in my resting-place,
> And deem that death had made it almost fair;
> And laying snow-white flowers against my hair,
> Wouldst on my cold cheek tender kisses press,
> And fold my hand with lingering caress —
> Poor hands, so empty and so cold to-night!

(From *Jess*)

Later, after stabbing Muller, Jess runs off into the mountains. Eventually, knowing that she will shortly die, she enters a cave and finds there Captain Neil who, having escaped, has collapsed in exhaustion. Deciding not to waken him, Jess pushes her letter into his clasped fingers, kisses him, and then lies down by his side where she dies. Neil, when he at last awakes, in horror carries Jess's body back to her home which the Boers, deprived of their evil leader Muller, have left. In time Bessie and Neil return to England where they marry. There John Neil, though content, patiently awaits his own death so that he can find 'Jess waiting to greet him at its gates'.

Surprisingly, although the reaffirmation of Haggard's belief in eternal love shows that Lilly Jackson was still very much in his mind, Jess is not a portrait of Lilly, being a very different type of person:

> She was small and rather thin, with quantities of curling brown hair; not by any means a lovely woman . . . but possessing two remarkable characteristics — a complexion of extraordinary and uniform pallor, and a pair of the most beautiful dark eyes he had ever looked on.
>
> (From *Jess*)

It was not then her beauty that attracted John Neil. It was her other qualities which endeared her to him when circumstances forced them together:

> He reflected what a charming companion she was, and how thoughtful and kind, and breathed a secret hope that she would continue to live with them after they were married. Unconsciously they had arrived at that point of intimacy, innocent in itself, when two people become absolutely necessary to each other's daily life . . . He only knew that she had the knack of making him feel thoroughly happy in her company. When he was talking to her, or even sitting silently by her, he became aware of a sensation of restfulness and reliance that he had never before experienced in the society of a woman.
>
> (From *Jess*)

Only one woman Haggard knew matches the description of Jess's appearance and characteristics. She was Aggie Barber, on whom Haggard had relied so much during the previous couple of years. Such a vital part of his life and household had she become that he must often have 'breathed a secret hope that she would continue to live' with him and his wife. Even when he started writing *Jess*, however, Haggard knew that soon Aggie Barber would be leaving for good. She and his brother Jack had announced their engagement and their plans to marry early in the New Year. Knowing that he would be deprived of her company, Haggard seems in *Jess* to have included, in passages like the one quoted above, a touching tribute and valediction to the woman who, more than any other individual, had by her encouragement and stimulating advice helped him become a writer.

The completion of *Jess* marked the close of a remarkable year, during which Haggard had written three novels destined to become best-sellers and had seen the publication of *King Solomon's Mines*, the greatest literary sensation produced for years. Yet his rewards from writing had been small. Even including his unexpected supplementary payment from Cassell's because of *King Solomon's Mines'* success, his total income from three and a half years of writing was only £135.

II

There were several problems disturbing Haggard at the beginning of 1886. Having at last placed his literary affairs in the hands of the literary agent A.P. Watt, he had discovered that the clause in the agreement he had signed with J. & R. Maxwell giving them the right to bring out cheap editions of all his books written within five years meant there would be difficulties in obtaining acceptable terms for the publication of *Allan Quatermain* and *Jess*. Eventually A.P. Watt, an extremely astute negotiator, persuaded J. & R. Maxwell, who were threatening legal action, to accept as a compromise the sole rights to publish in book form two novels that Haggard would write within three years. Watt also placed *Allan Quatermain*, still called *The Frowning City*, with Longmans, Green & Co. who, in the contract signed on 12 January 1886, agreed to pay £225 for the serial rights and a 10 per cent royalty on book sales. This was the first of Haggard's novels accepted for serialisation. There were other successes. Another Quatermain hunting anecdote, called 'Long Odds' was sold to *Macmillan's Magazine*, in which, almost nine years earlier, Haggard's first published article had appeared. The Haggards also moved to a larger house at 69 Gunterstone Road, West Kensington.

Nevertheless Haggard was unsettled. He discussed his uncertainties about his future with Andrew Lang, who gave a dinner at the Oxford and Cambridge Club so that his protégé could meet Arthur James Balfour, who was then president of the Local Government Board, because, as Haggard recalls in his autobiography, 'he knew that already I wished to escape from novel-writing and re-enter the public service, a matter in which he thought Mr Balfour might be of assistance'.

On 25 January, Haggard applied to join the Colonial Service, stating: 'I am a practising barrister (Lincoln's Inn) and am possessed of moderate independent means, which were considerably larger before the fall in the nature of landed properties. Also I may state that my name is not unknown as a writer. I began active life in the Colonial Service and though circumstances have for a few years turned me from that career it is my desire and ambition, if opportunity offers, to devote my time and such abilities as I possess to the branch of the public service.'[28] Nothing, however, came of his approaches.

But perhaps the major reason why Haggard was unsettled in January 1886 was the considerable change in his domestic life and personal relationships that he knew would result from the marriage of Aggie Barber to his brother Jack. During the three years he had been writing fiction she had almost permanently been his charming, stimulating companion. She was one of the three women who throughout this period occupied his thoughts and compositely provided what he needed in a relationship with a woman. The other two were, of course, Lilly Jackson (Mrs Archer) and his wife, Louie. For Lilly he felt a deep romantic love which, as time passed, became even more intense and important. He depended on his wife for economic and domestic security, and their three children prove that a sexual life existed, at least in the early years.

Aggie Barber's departure brought an end to this female triumvirate that had provided him with wife, lover, and companion. Taking stock of his position, Haggard was all too aware that the situation in which he was left was unsatisfactory and unsatisfying. His relationship with his wife, which had never been a passionate one, had continued to deteriorate. Although she remained a loyal and supportive wife, as Lilias Haggard states, 'In later years the faults which sprang from the virtues sometimes troubled the relationship of their married life. Thus her common sense temperament lacked, almost entirely, imagination in the sense that Rider possessed it. Also she had tremendous strength of will. Her sense of duty made her always give in to her husband — if only to him — but its suppression bred an irritability which grew on her with the years.'[29] She was not interested in literature and had no understanding of what her husband was writing or, even more important, thinking. It is also apparent that, after the birth of Dorothy in March 1884, Haggard and his wife ceased to have a sexual relationship. Clearly this led not just to repression but also to disappointment, for Haggard, a child of his class and environment, longed for a large family. Much later, on 15 July 1917, he writes scathingly in his diary of the Victorian ideal: 'And what a sham it was! That no lady of consideration could possibly spoil her figure by extensive child-bearing which also prevented her from dancing and other delights. That the one thing to be discouraged, indeed, was the growth of population, since it meant a decrease in the amount to be divided.'

After Aggie's marriage, the only constant in Haggard's relationships with women, was the romantic, non-sexual love he felt for Lilly. It was to remain so for the rest of his life. Yet, although, as Lilias Haggard states, 'Louie well knew, he still loved [Lilly] with an affection which transcends all earthly passion and stretches out hands beyond the grave,'[30] it was a secret love that he discussed neither with his family nor with his new-found literary friends. The nature of this love and his unsatisfactory marriage combined to provide him with both motive and motif for his writing. This was recognised by his nephew, Godfrey Haggard, who states: 'His marriage went as far with him as it needed to go, and for the rest of the time he was with his own thoughts. He was thrown in upon himself, and his novels were his principal outlet. He gave expression in his writings to the thoughts that overflowed his mind, confiding vicariously to his readers a great many things he would not have said otherwise, even in his private letters.'[31] For Haggard, writing was a substitute for sexual passion and a means of escaping from the commitment required in a sexual relationship.

In January 1886, when Aggie's marriage destroyed Haggard's platonic ménage à trois, his romance with Lilly had been over for nearly nine years, a sufficient period for his continuing but sublimated love to inspire a creative work which could be an unconscious substitute for the sexual passion missing from his marriage. On 25 January, three days before Aggie's wedding, Haggard started writing a new novel, but almost immediately, after only five pages had been completed, it was put aside. A week later, however, he returned to his story and in a little over six weeks had completed his most creative work, in which were integrated his nightmares, suppressed desires and fantasies. The novel was called *She*.

Haggard later claimed: 'I remember that when I sat down to the task my ideas as to its development were of the vaguest. The only clear notion that I had in my head was that of an immortal woman inspired by an immortal love. All the rest shaped itself round this figure.' This is transparently an over-simplification, for he must have been thinking about his story for some time. In 1892 an interviewer reported in *The Strand Magazine*: 'A story which a lady once wrote and told him — the story of a woman and a cave — helped him in writing *She*.'[32] This idea was recorded in his notebook for 1884: 'Woman in cave w(ith) fire w(ith) eye out'. (Although, of course, it cannot now be proved, it is surely worth surmising that the lady story-teller was Agnes Barber.) In any case, before Haggard started writing, he had sought the help of Andrew Lang, who on 1 February wrote explaining how the ancient Greeks named their children, but adding, 'My Greek prose has 20 years of rust on it.'[33] He also suggested how the name of the hero, Vincey, could be connected with Latin names: 'Vindex, Vindici, Vincey would knit.' (Vindex and Vindicis appear on the Sherd of Amenartas which starts Leo Vincey and his companions on their quest.)

Once he had started, however, it was as though flood waters had been released. Later he stated: 'And it came — it came faster than my poor aching head could set it down. . . . The fact is that it was written at white heat, almost without rest.' Early in March he wrote to Dr H.A. Holden, who had been his headmaster at Ipswich, asking for help with the Greek inscription for the sherd. Holden replied: 'Your task is not quite so big as one of the labours of Hercules, but by no means easy without further data. Do you want the Greek to be such as to deceive the learned world into thinking that it is no forgery, but a genuine bit of antiquity? If so, the *style* will have to be taken into account: it won't do to imitate Herodotus, though it is just the bit suitable for his style, because of the date 200 B.C.' After Holden had provided the Greek passage, Haggard obtained from his friend, Dr Raven (an authority on early languages), the medieval inscription for the sherd and its old English translation. Aggie, as her final contribution to any of his books, then made for him the elaborate sherd, complete with its inscriptions. So meticulous was her workmanship that when the sherd was shown as a genuine antique to Sir John Evans he declared, 'All I can say is that it might *possibly* have been forged.'

A.P. Watt continued to deal with Haggard's increasingly complex literary affairs. On 24 February, the copyright of *Jess*, a novel incorrectly assumed to have little popular appeal, was sold to Messrs Smith, Elder & Co. for £450. The same day Haggard sent a letter of thanks to his agent: 'In acknowledging the receipt of your letter of to-day, announcing the satisfactory conclusion of the agreement with Messrs Smith, Elder & Co. for the sale of my novel *Jess*, I wish to take the opportunity of thanking you very heartily for your services in connection with it, and also with the disposal to Messrs. Longmans of my boys' book *The Frowning City*. Without entering further into the matter, I may say that those services have included a very delicate negotiation which has been, to my great advantage, most admirably and successfully conducted by you.'[34] On one of his visits to his agent, Haggard found that Watt was not in the office. 'As the business was urgent,' he records in *The Days of My Life*, 'and I did not wish to have to return, I sat down at his table, asked for some foolscap, and in the hour or two I had to wait wrote the scene of the destruction of She in the Fire of Life.' After completing *She* on 18 March, Haggard took the manuscript to Watt and handed it over with the prophetic comment, 'There is what I shall be remembered by.'

She is narrated by Ludwig Horace Holly, an ugly man: 'Short, thick-set, and deep-chested almost to deformity, with long sinewy arms, heavy features, deep-set grey eyes, a low brow half overgrown with a mop of thick black hair.' Late one night Holly is studying in his rooms at Cambridge when Vincey, his only friend, arrives carrying a massive iron box. He announces that he is dying and asks Holly to be the sole guardian of his five-year old son, Leo, the sole descendant of a most ancient family. The next morning Vincey dies and a few days later Leo arrives to stay with his guardian, who has taken new lodgings and hired a manservant, called Job (in real life the Norfolk groom who accompanied the Haggards to Africa).

In time Leo grows into a handsome young man. On his twenty-fifth birthday the iron box is opened, revealing a broken potsherd covered with writing, from which is learned the strange story of Leo's ancient forefather, Killikrates, a priest of Isis in Egypt who fled his country with Amenartas, a young princess. The couple found shelter in a remote part of Africa ruled by a strangely beautiful white queen who was thought by her savage people to be a goddess and who had access to 'the rolling Pillar of Life that dies not'. When Killikrates rejected the queen's offer of immortality she killed him, but Amenartas escaped, giving birth in Athens to their son, Tisisthenes, or the Mighty Avenger from whom Leo's descent can be traced. The inscription includes Amenartas's plea that a descendant should 'seek out the woman, and learn the secret of Life'. A letter in the iron box from Leo's father states that he had travelled to Africa on this quest and had heard of a people that 'speak a dialect of Arabic, and are ruled over by a *beautiful white woman* who is seldom seen by them, but who is reported to have power over all things living and dead'; but illness prevented him from travelling farther into the interior.

Three months later Leo, Holly and Job set sail for Africa. On their arrival they sail down the coast in a dhow that is towing their whaleboat (identical to that actually taken to Lamu by Frederick Jackson). A sudden squall blows up:

Then I remember no more; till suddenly — a frightful roar of wind, a shriek of terror from the awakening crew, and a whip-like sting of water in our faces. . . . A huge white-topped breaker, twenty feet high or more, was rushing on to us. It was on the break — the moon shone on its crest and tipped its foam with light. . . . Then — a shock of water, a wild rush of boiling foam, and I was clinging for my life to the shroud. . . .

The wave passed. It seemed to me that I was under water for minutes — really it was seconds. . . . Then for a moment there was comparative calm, and in it I heard Job's voice yelling wildly, 'Come here to the boat.'

Bewildered and half drowned as I was, I had the sense to rush aft. I felt the dhow sinking under me — she was full of water. Under her counter the whaleboat was tossing furiously, and I saw the Arab Mahomed, who had been steering, leap into her. I gave one desperate pull at the tow-rope to bring the boat alongside. Wildly I sprang also, and Job caught me by one arm and I rolled into the bottom of the boat. Down went the dhow bodily, and as she did so Mahomed drew his curved knife and severed the fibre-rope by which we were fast to her, and in another second we were driving before the storm over the place where the dhow had been. . . .

(From *She*)

An almost identical incident is described by Frederick Jackson in his autobiography *Early Days in East Africa*, when off the African coast his whaleboat was also being towed by a dhow:

Before we could realize what had happened, a great black bank of water came surging towards us, and when within a few yards began to curl over and show its white crest. To lean forward, grasp the tow-rope with one hand, jam my cap on with the other, and duck my head was a matter of seconds, before the wave curled over and completely engulfed us. How I managed to retain my grip on the rope, against such a weight and onrush of water, I don't know. . . . The first thing I saw on the water clearing away was the captain jumping overboard, the boat lying astern, and the dhow, all but the poop on which Horton, Isaac and myself were left, had completely vanished. . . . The boat was our only hope, and it was again a matter of seconds to sit down with feet against the stern-post, seize the tow-rope, and give three desperate heaves until she came up close astern; then shouting to Horton and Isaac to follow, I took a header, and landed on my chest on a thwart. . . .

Horton and the captain were then hauled aboard, and in the meantime Maktubu promptly carried out an order to cut the tow-rope. . . . The last thing I saw of the dhow on looking round was some ten or twelve feet of the narrow peak of the lateen sail standing erect in the midst of a seething and merciless upheaval of white wave-crests.

(From *Early Days in East Africa* by Frederick Jackson)[35]

The passages are so similar that it seems unlikely that Jackson, whose autobiography was edited from his notebooks by his wife and first published in 1930 after his death, had not described his experience, which occurred in the spring of 1885, in one of his many letters to Haggard.

Having landed safely by a river's mouth, the three adventurers and Mahomed explore an ancient wharf that reminds them of 'those buried Persian cities that the consul showed us at Kilwa' (suggesting Haggard was again making use of stories told by his brother, Jack). The party sails up the river, shoots game and witnesses a

fight between a lion and a crocodile. Entering an ancient canal, the men are forced
to tow their boat. Eventually they are surrounded by Arabic-speaking natives who
are about to kill them until an old man among the tribesmen states that She-
who-must-be-obeyed had ordered that the white men should be taken to her. So the
travellers are ushered into litters and carried into the interior by bearers. On the
way they rest in a village where, from the old man whose name is Billali and a
beautiful young girl called Ustane who attaches herself to Leo, they learn something about the customs of the Amahagger people and their white Queen. They
witness a ritualistic meal during which the villagers plot to eat Mahomed, after
thrusting a red-hot cooking-pot on his head. Attempting to stop this, Holly fires his
revolver at Mahomed's female attacker:

> She sank down dead, and as she did so, to my terror and dismay, Mahomed, by a
> superhuman effort, burst from his tormentors, and, springing high into the air,
> fell dying upon her corpse. The heavy bullet from my pistol had driven through
> the bodies of both.
>
> (From She)

In the mêlée that follows, Leo is wounded and all three white men are saved only by
the intervention of Billali.

Up to this point, the adventures described are little different from those in *King
Solomon's Mines* and *Allan Quatermain*, but as the three men lie recovering from the
skirmish a new note is struck — one resounding with overt sexuality. Billali tells
Holly the story of how after his mother had set fire to the corpse of the young
woman with whom he had fallen in love, the feet survived and were cherished by
him. This seemingly adolescent sexual fantasy is a prelude to the appearance of
She, whose ominous but unseen presence dominates the narrative as the travellers
are carried across volcanic plains, through fever-infested marshes and, blind-
folded, along tunnels leading to She's kingdom of Kôr. The caves there inhabited
by the Amahagger were 'nothing more or less than vast catacombs, in which for
tens of ages the mortal remains of the great race whose monuments surrounded us
had been first preserved'.

After having washed, Holly is led into an embalming chamber, in describing
which Haggard displays his adolescent obsession with death and the results of his
later research into the burial customs of ancient races. On the walls of the chamber
were pictures of bodies being embalmed.

In this macabre setting, Holly and Job eat an excellent meal, after which they
visit Leo, who is extremely ill with fever and is being nursed by Ustane. Holly is
then summoned to meet She. He is led by Billali down corridors into her sumptu-
ous chambers. A curtain opens, eventually revealing the veiled Queen, called
Ayesha, whose appearance re-echoes Haggard's memories of shrouded corpses, the
ghost seen as a child, and the beautiful female manifestations witnessed at séances
during his adolescence. She is the child of his fertile imagination. From her the
astounded Holly discovers that she has been alive for two thousand years, separated

from the outside world, waiting for the rebirth and return of the man she loved. When Holly asks to see her face, Ayesha warns, 'Never may the man to whom my beauty hath been unveiled put it from his mind.' Then slowly, teasingly she unveils, revealing herself to be both beautiful and evil — the angelic whore:

> She lifted her white and rounded arms — never had I seen such arms before — and slowly, very slowly, withdrew some fastening beneath her hair. Then all of a sudden the long, corpse-like wrappings fell from her to the ground, and my eyes travelled up her form, now only robed in a garb of clinging white that did but serve to show its perfect and imperial shape, instinct with a life that was more than life, and with a certain serpent-like grace that was more than human. On her little feet were sandals, fastened with studs of gold. Then came ankles more perfect than ever sculptor dreamed of. About the waist her white kirtle was fastened by a double-headed snake of solid gold, above which her gracious form swelled up in lines as pure as they were lovely, till the kirtle ended on the snowy argent of her breast, whereon her arms were folded. I gazed above them at her face, and — I do not exaggerate — shrank back blinded and amazed. I have heard of the beauty of celestial beings, now I saw it; only this beauty, with all its awful loveliness and purity, was *evil*. . . . Though the face before me was that of a young woman of certainly not more than thirty years, in perfect health, and the first flush of ripened beauty, yet it had stamped upon it a look of unutterable experience, and of deep acquaintance with grief and passion.
>
> (From *She*)

Afterwards, alone in his chamber, Holly curses 'the fatal curiosity that is ever prompting man to draw the veil from woman'. Then, noticing an opening in the wall, he enters a passage that leads him eventually to a little cavern where, through a curtain he sees Ayesha leaning over a fire, her face full of vindictiveness:

> For a moment she stood still, her hands raised high above her head, and as she did so the white robe slipped from her down to her golden girdle, baring the blinding loveliness of her form. She stood there, her fingers clenched, and the awful look of malevolence gathered and deepened on her face.
>
> Suddenly, I thought of what would happen if she discovered me, and the reflection made me turn sick and faint. But even if I had known that I must die if I stopped, I do not believe that I could have moved, for I was absolutely fascinated.
>
> (From *She*)

Holly, the proficient voyeur, continues to observe unnoticed as Ayesha, still naked to the waist, lifts and drops her arms, making the fire rise and fall. Suddenly she stops and crosses to a corpse lying on a stone which, having identified as Kalli-krates, she appears determined to raise. The horrified Holly believes the body begins to quiver beneath the winding sheet, but then Ayesha stops and begins to weep. Holly's fascination with the scene turns suddenly to distress:

RIDER HAGGARD

I could no longer bear to look at it, and turning, began to creep, shaking as I was in every limb, slowly along the pitch-dark passage, feeling in my trembling heart that I had a vision of a Soul in Hell.

(From *She*)

Immediately he returns to his chamber and falls fast asleep.

The next morning, Holly is summoned again to meet Ayesha. Led by Billali, he enters a large cave where, surrounded by her followers, the Queen, heavily veiled, mounts a dais and dispatches to the caves of torture the villagers who at the hot-pot ritual had attacked the travellers. Ayesha then shows Holly round the caverns of Kôr, which he learned had first been inhabited by a people whom a pestilence had decimated, the few survivors fleeing north to become the first Egyptians. Before the sickness the dead had been embalmed and Holly is shown perfectly preserved bodies of people dead for thousands of years. In one of the tombs, there were but two bodies:

They lay together on a single shelf. I withdrew the grave-cloths, and there, clasped heart to heart, were a young man and a blooming girl. Her head rested on his arm, and his lips were pressed against her brow. I opened the man's linen robe, and there over his heart was a dagger-wound, and beneath the girl's fair breasts was a like cruel stab, through which her life had ebbed away. On the rock above was an inscription in three words. Ayesha translated it. It was *Wedded in Death*.

(From *She*)

This coupling in death is similar to the fate that befell Mahomed and his attacker earlier in the story.

After his conducted tour, Holly is once again taken by Ayesha into her chamber where she removes her white wrappings. Now the temptress, she orders Holly to admire her beauty 'feature by feature' and then says:

'But see, give me thy hands — so — press them round me, there, with but a little force, thy fingers touch, oh Holly.'

I could bear it no longer. I am but a man, and she was more than a woman. Heaven knows what she was — I do not! But then and there I fell upon my knees before her, and told her in a sad mixture of languages — for such moments confuse the thoughts — that I worshipped her as never woman was worshipped, and that I would give my immortal soul to marry her.

(From *She*)

Ayesha laughs, but as Holly kneels, she leans forward, daring him to kiss her:

Her fragrant breath played upon my face, and made me faint and weak. Then of a sudden, even as I stretched out my arms to clasp, she straightened herself, and a quick change passed over her. Reaching out her hand, she held it over my head, and it seemed to me that something flowed from it that chilled me back to common sense, and a knowledge of propriety and the domestic virtues.

(From *She*)

Her mood changed, she demands to be told something about 'the philosophy of the Hebrew Messiah'. Holly, 'feeling bitterly ashamed of the weakness into which I had been betrayed', talks to her about the teachings of Christ and Mohammed.

Later when Ayesha visits Leo Vincey, she is astonished to discover her lost love. After she has cured the fever from which he was dying, Ayesha kisses him tenderly on the brow, but the sight upsets Holly. He is jealous! Next she orders that Ustane must be killed for 'she stands between me and my desire', but Holly successfully pleads for the girl's life and so Ayesha sends her back to her village. When, in Ustane's stead, Ayesha has nursed Leo back to health, she organises a spectacular ball in honour of her three white guests. The illumination is provided by burning embalmed corpses. One of the dancers, dressed as a leopard, turns out to be Ustane, whom Ayesha kills with a mysterious force. Leo is angry and confused, but when Ayesha removes her veils, he is bewitched by her beauty:

> I saw him struggle — I saw him even turn to fly; but her eyes drew him more strongly than iron bonds, and the magic of her beauty and concentrated will and passion entered into him and overpowered him — ay, even there, in the presence of the body of the woman who had loved him well enough to die for him. . . . I looked up again, and now her perfect form lay in his arms, and her lips were pressed against his own; and thus, with the corpse of his dead love for an altar, did Leo Vincey plight his troth to her red-handed murderess — plight it for ever and a day.
>
> (From *She*)

Once again the novel's dominant motif of sexual passion occurring at the time of death is reiterated.

Next day Ayesha informs Leo:

> 'As yet I may not mate with thee, for thou and I are different, and the very brightness of my being would burn thee up, and perchance destroy thee. . . . No: listen, thou shalt not be tried beyond endurance, for this very evening, an hour before the sun goes down, shall we start hence, and by tomorrow's dark, if all goes well, and the road is not lost to me, which I pray it may not be, shall we stand in the place of Life, and thou shalt bathe in the fire, and come forth glorified, as no man ever was before thee, and then, Kallikrates, shalt thou call me wife, and I will call thee husband.'
>
> (From *She*)

The three white men accompany Ayesha across a vast plain, through the ruined city of Kôr, and scale a cliff, eventually entering the cave of the Pillar of Life. There the exhilarated men watch as Ayesha prepares to enter first the strange flame that will bring eternal life. What happens next is one of the most impressive scenes in all literature:

> At last, from far far away, came the first murmur of sound, that grew and grew till it began to crash and bellow in the distance. As she heard it, Ayesha swiftly threw off her gauzy wrapping, loosened the golden snake from her kirtle, and

then, shaking her lovely hair about her like a garment, beneath its cover slipped the kirtle off and replaced the snaky belt around her and outside the masses of falling hair. There she stood before us as Eve might have stood before Adam, clad in nothing but her abundant locks, held round her by the golden band; and no words of mine can tell how sweet she looked — and yet how divine. Nearer and nearer came the thunder wheels of fire, and as they came she pushed one ivory arm through the dark masses of her hair and flung it round Leo's neck.

'Oh, my love, my love!' she murmured, 'wilt thou ever know how I have loved thee?' and she kissed him on the forehead, and then went and stood in the pathway of the flame of Life. . . .

On came the crashing, rolling noise, and the sound thereof was as the sound of a forest being swept flat by a mighty wind, and then tossed up by it like so much grass, and thundered down a mountainside. Nearer and nearer it came; now flashes of light, forerunners of the revolving pillar of flame, were passing like arrows through the rosy air; and now the edge of the pillar itself appeared. Ayesha turned towards it, and stretched out her arms to greet it. On it came very slowly, and lapped her round with flame. I saw the fire run up her form. I saw her lift it with both hands as though it were water, and pour it over her head. I even saw her open her mouth and draw it down into her lungs, and a dread and wonderful sight it was.

Then she paused, and stretched out her arms, and stood there quite still, with a heavenly smile upon her face, as though she were the very Spirit of the Flame.

The mysterious fire played up and down her dark and rolling locks, twining and twisting itself through and around them like threads of golden lace; it gleamed upon her ivory breast and shoulder, from which the hair had slipped aside; it slid along her pillared throat and delicate features, and seemed to find a home in the glorious eyes that shone and shone, more brightly even than the spiritual essence.

Oh, how beautiful she looked there in the flame! No angel out of heaven could have worn a greater loveliness. Even now my heart faints before the recollection of it, as she stood and smiled at our awed faces, and I would give half my remaining time upon this earth to see her once like that again.

But suddenly — more suddenly than I can describe — a kind of change came over her face. . . . The flaming pillar slowly twisted and thundered off whithersoever it passes to in the bowels of the great earth, leaving Ayesha standing where it had been.

(From *She*)

Then, horrifically, before the love that had sustained her for two thousand years had been consummated, Ayesha rapidly ages, withers and dies. The fire with its disastrous effects symbolises for Haggard sexual lust that consumes all it touches. This he states explicitly in this passage from his later novel *Love Eternal*, which might well have been used as an explanatory footnote to the scene:

Although he did not altogether understand it, this was the eternal complication of sex which curses more than it blesses in the world; of sex, the eating fire that is so beautiful but burns. For when that fire has passed over the flowers of friendship, they are changed into some new growth, that however gorgeous it may be, yet always smells of flame.

(From *Love Eternal*)

It seems, therefore, that, disturbed by his own sexual repression and obsessed with his desire to retain untarnished his romantic love for Lilly with whom he believed he would be united only in death, Haggard in Ayesha's sudden transformation describes the nightmare of satiated lust instantly giving way to guilt and disgust.

The rest of the story is speedily concluded by Haggard. Shocked by the horror of the transformation, Job drops dead. Leaving his body in the cave, Leo and Holly escape with difficulty, make their way to the coast and then sail back to England. Finally Haggard paves the way for a sequel, for Holly states, 'A story that began more than two thousand years ago may stretch a long way into the dim and distant future.'

The story of *She* is so unusual, with its blend of anthropological, psychological and supernatural elements, that there has been much speculation about the sources of Haggard's ideas and inspiration. As has been shown, his own experiences, interests and reading provided some material. His method of writing at speed and his emotional state allowed him to draw upon his unconscious to produce what C.J. Jung termed an 'extroverted' work: 'These works positively force themselves upon the author; his hand is seized, his pen writes things that his mind contemplates with amazement. . . . He is overwhelmed by a flood of thoughts and images which he never intended to create and which his own will could never have brought into being.'[36] In another paper Jung contends that, in creating Ayesha, Haggard drew upon 'an inherited collective image of women' existing in his unconscious.[37] It is likely, however, that, while in Africa, Haggard obtained information that at least helped create the idea of a beautiful white queen ruling over a savage people. In his introduction to *Nada the Lily* Haggard quotes from a pamphlet by F.B. Fynney one such possible source: 'The natives have a spirit which they call *Nomkubulwana*, or the *Inkosazana-ye-Zulu* (the Princess of Heaven). She is said to be robed in white, and to take the form of a young maiden, in fact an angel.'

Morton Cohen points out in his biography[38] that when Haggard was in the Transvaal the Lovedu tribe, living in the north-east of the country, were ruled over by a fair-skinned woman called Mujaji who, like Ayesha, was thought to be immortal. She was by no means the only white woman rumoured to rule an African tribe. In South Africa throughout the nineteenth century stories were often told of three white women who survived the wreck of the *Grosvenor* on the Pondoland coast in the eighteen-nineties. They were taken as wives by native chiefs and, when found, refused to return to civilisation. Shortly after the rescue one of the women gave birth to a white girl who was later taken by Moziligazie when he broke away from Chaka to live in the northern mountains of the Transvaal, where she in time ruled that Zulu impi.[39]

An even more likely source of inspiration for the creation of Ayesha and her story is a novel written by Lord Lytton, one of Haggard's favourite writers and the uncle of Sir Henry Bulwer, with whom Haggard first went to Africa. It is *A Strange Story*, first published in 1862, which tells of the quest for an elixir giving eternal life. The novel's climax is a mystical ceremony that involves many ingredients found in *She* — there is a dismembered foot, a fire, and a disastrous conclusion to the ritual which is conducted by a veiled woman called Ayesha:

As I thus stood, right into the gap between the two dead lamps, strode a gigantic Foot. All the rest of the form was unseen; only, as volume after volume of smoke poured on from the burning land behind, it seemed as if one great column of vapour, eddying round, settled itself aloft from the circle, and that out from that column strode the giant Foot. And, as strode the Foot, so with it came, like the sound of its tread, a roll of muttered thunder.

I recoiled, with a cry that rang loud through the lurid air.

'Courage!' said the voice of Ayesha. 'Trembling soul, yield not an inch to the demon!'

At the charm, the wonderful charm, in the tone of the Veiled Woman's voice, my will seemed to take a force more sublime than its own.

(From *A Strange Story* by Lord Lytton)[40]

It would, however, be wrong to imply that, unlike some other books by Haggard, *She* is a patchwork of material collected from other sources. It is a work of both originality and brilliance in which Haggard, revealing his inner feelings, charts not as in *King Solomon's Mines* the adventures of men searching for treasure, but the sufferings and setbacks experienced in the elemental search for love and the achievement of ambition.

The manuscript of *She* greatly impressed A.P. Watt and he realised immediately it was destined to become a best-seller. On 15 April *The Graphic* purchased the serial rights for £200. Agreeing also to give Haggard one of the drawings, if produced, the paper's editor stated, 'We expect to illustrate the story, though possibly the lack of costume may prevent it.'[41] A few weeks later, Longmans, Green & Co. signed a contract agreeing to pay Haggard a royalty of 20 per cent of all book sales, which was double that paid by Cassell's on *King Solomon's Mines*. This delighted Haggard, for he was very disappointed by the income earned from *King Solomon's Mines*, a best-seller throughout the English-speaking world. Not only had the serial rights not been sold but, as no copyright agreement existed with the United States until July 1891, English books could be freely pirated there and within twelve months of *King Solomon's Mines'* first publication, at least thirteen different American editions had appeared. As a result Cassell's could sell few copies of the book in the United States and by 30 July Haggard had received only £3. 10s. 0d. from American sales.[42] Both he and Watt were, therefore, extremely keen to sell the American rights of *She* before its British publication. After protracted negotiations, Harper Brothers agreed to pay £100 for the serial rights and a 10 per cent royalty on sales over 1500 copies of a library edition.

During the summer of 1886, while *Jess* was being serialised in the *Cornhill Magazine*, growing interest in Haggard and the increasing popularity of *King Solomon's Mines* attracted comments in the popular press. The literary journals also began to search for possible sources of Haggard's story. On 29 May, *The Athenaeum* printed a letter from C. Welsh suggesting that Good's 'white legs' had been taken from Johnson's *Kilima-Njaro Expedition*. It was a silly charge, for the alleged source had been published in December 1885, six weeks after *King Solomon's Mines*. A more plausible case of Haggard's having used incidents from another book was made in a good-natured letter from F. Faithfull Begg published in *The Athenaeum* on 3 July. He points out several similarities between Haggard's book and Joseph Thomson's *Through Masai Land*, first published in February 1885. The letter concludes: 'What your former correspondent did not point out, however, seems to me to be clear, viz. that Haggard, who is writing in an exaggerated vein, has chosen this method of conveying a species of mild chaff or gentle badinage directed against travellers' tales in general.'[43]

Haggard, clearly incensed by the letter, wrote a long reply that was published in *The Athenaeum* on 10 July. He states that his tale of the false teeth owes nothing to Thomson's book. (This may be true, but Haggard had certainly read the book, for in a note included in the first edition of *Allan Quatermain* he states, 'I wish to acknowledge my indebtedness to Mr Thomson's admirable history of travel *Through Masai Land*.') After attacking all Begg's 'confidently published charges against me,' Haggard boldly states: 'But I would suggest, independently of the present case, that criticism of this nature, in whatever spirit it is offered, is somewhat beside the point, since the literary value of a work surely depends upon the quality of the execution and the finish of the style, and not on the question as to whether or no this or that incident has, with or without the author's knowledge, already done duty elsewhere.'[44] For a time Haggard's denial brought to an end the game of identifying sources, but it was to be resurrected with the most unfortunate consequences for his reputation.

The Haggards moved from London to The Red House, Mendham, so that they could spend the summer recess in the countryside near Ditchingham House, which was still let. There Haggard first dealt with the proofs for the serialisation of *She*. As he was no longer able to discuss them with Aggie he sent them instead to his mentor, Andrew Lang. On 22 July Lang wrote: 'I have pretty nearly finished *She*. I really must congratulate you; I think it is one of the most astonishing romances I ever read.' He points out, however a number of weaknesses: 'You really must look after the style more when it comes out as a book. I would also, if it is not impertinent, reduce the comic element a good deal — it is sometimes so sudden a drop as to be quite painful.' In another letter on 24 July he comments on the hot-potting episode: 'I thought the potting might be modified slightly in the *selling* interest of the book, as many people funk giving children or boys anything of that sort.' On the following day Lang writes again: 'I have just finished *She*, previously I skipped a bit to get to the end. I certainly still think it the most extraordinary romance I ever read, and that's why I want you to be very careful with the proofs, before it goes out in a volume. I will read them over again, and annotate.'

Haggard made many of the alterations suggested by Lang, but he was not prepared and was perhaps even incapable of, undertaking any major rewriting. The writing of *She* had been a purgation: once completed Haggard's mood changed. Also with publishers and the public clamouring for further works, his continuing successes boosted his confidence. Even his story 'Bottles', renamed 'The Blue Curtains', was sold by Watt to Smith, Elder & Co. (The story, written in 1884, was published in the September number of the *Cornhill Magazine*.) In any case Haggard had no time for rewriting. He was intent on writing another novel during his summer holidays.

Living again in the beautiful Waveney valley, Haggard had begun to relax. Relieved of the pressures and pace of London life, he quickly renewed his natural interest in the countryside and the social round of the rural upper class. Yet, although it was peaceful and pleasant, Haggard was all too aware of the depressed state of British agriculture. The competition from massive and mounting imports of grain and meat, so welcomed by consumers because food had become plentiful and cheap, ruined many farmers. Whole farms were abandoned and landlords found it impossible to let land. The wheatlands of East Anglia were the greatest sufferers. The income from the Ditchingham estate had slumped to less than a quarter of what it had been when the Haggards married. Although this was a cause for concern, Haggard's growing income from writing at least gave promise of a better future. He was, however, aware that this did not apply to his father who, having invested all his own and his wife's wealth in land when its price was high, had no other source of income. It seemed possible that, unless the financial rewards from farming improved dramatically or additional funds were obtained, the Bradenham estate, which had been owned by the Haggards for a hundred years, would have to be sold. All too conscious of his parents' unanticipated impoverishment, Haggard began on 29 July to write *Colonel Quaritch, V.C.: A Tale of Country Life*. Planned as a three-volume novel, it was another attempt by Haggard to establish his reputation as a novelist, for he was still resentful that some people dismissed him as merely a writer of boys' books.

The story of *Colonel Quaritch, V.C.* is simple: Quaritch, the hero, falls in love with Ida de la Molle, the only surviving child of an impoverished landowner. After many difficulties, Quaritch, using clues in an old document, discovers the de la Molle treasure, which had been hidden since the days of Cromwell. The estate is therefore saved, and Quaritch marries Ida. The supporting characters include a corrupt solicitor, a scheming banker, a lady of dubious virtue, and a wronged wife. Incidents in the sub-plot include bigamy, a marriage settlement, legal problems, and a murder. Events take place against a background of tennis parties, shoots, and country house dinners. It is, as Haggard himself described it in a letter to Aggie, 'a rather feeble novel',[45] but reveals much about Haggard's thoughts at the time and how his mood had changed since the writing of *She*.

In *Colonel Quaritch, V.C.* Haggard is immersed in his rural surroundings. The setting for the novel is a composite of places all within walking distance of Mendham, where Haggard was staying. Honham Castle, the seat of the de la Molles, with its two great towers and ancient drive, is Wingfield Castle. The Ell is the Waveney. Boisingham is Bungay. The Molehill, or 'Dead Man's Mound', thought to have been used as an early British settlement and the hiding-place of the treasure, is the dipped motte at Darrow Green, known locally as 'Hangman's Hill'.

The main characters too are based on people Haggard knew well. De la Molle is a most sympathetic portrait of his father. In his diary on 21 August 1922 Haggard states that George, de la Molle's factotum, is based on Samuel Adcock who similarly served his father: 'The churchyard [at Bradenham] is now full of the tombstones of those whom I knew in my youth, such as poor old Sam Adcock who is the original of George in my tale of country life *Colonel Quaritch, V.C.*' Ida appears to owe much to Louie, his wife, and Quaritch, the ex-colonialist who has retired to the country, is a revealing self-portrait:

> Plain as the countenance of Colonel Harold Quaritch undoubtedly was, people found something very taking about it, when once they became accustomed to its rugged air and stern regulated expression. . . . Any person of discernment looking on Colonel Quaritch must have felt that he was in the presence of a good man — not a prig or a milksop, but a man who had attained a virtue by thought and struggle that had left their marks upon him; a man whom it would not be well to tamper with, one to be respected by all, and feared of evildoers. Men felt this, and he was popular among those who knew him in his service, though not in any hail-fellow-well-met kind of way. But among women he was not popular. As a rule they both feared and disliked him.
>
> (From *Colonel Quaritch, V.C.*)

(Godfrey Haggard wrote about his uncle: 'Rider's manner and appearance were distinctly formidable to a number of people, especially women.'[46]) Although the similarity of appearance is interesting, far more important are the attitudes Haggard gives to Quaritch:

> He had made up his mind to come to reside at Molehill, and live the quiet, somewhat aimless, life of a small country gentleman. His reading, for he was a great reader, especially of scientific works, would, he thought, keep him employed. Moreover, he was a thorough sportsman, and an ardent, though owing to the smallness of his means necessarily not a very extensive, collector of curiosities, and more particularly of coins.
>
> At first, after he had come to his decision, a feeling of infinite rest and satisfaction had taken possession of him. The struggle of life was over for him.

No longer would he be obliged to think, and contrive, and toil; henceforth his days would slope gently towards the inevitable end. Trouble lay in the past, now rest and rest alone awaited him. . . .

Foolish man and vain imagining! Here, while we draw breath, there is no rest. We must go on continually, on from strength to strength, or weakness to weakness; we must always be troubled about this or that, and must ever have this to desire and that to regret.

(From *Colonel Quaritch, V.C.*)

This seems to accurately express Haggard's own position in the summer of 1886. Although he had gone to the country for a rest, he had so enjoyed the life that he had determined above all else to become what he had hoped to be for much of his life — a country squire like his father and squire de la Molle.

Because views such as this are expressed in *Colonel Quaritch, V.C.*, it is very different from Haggard's earlier country novels *Dawn* and *The Witch's Head*. It is as if, having in *King Solomon's Mines* and *She* turned his thoughts to the decline of great civilisations, Haggard, again living in the countryside he loved, became acutely aware that the social structure he held so dear and of which he was so typical a member was decaying. He became determined to do what he could in his own life to shore it up, just as, a wish fulfilled, he enabled his hero to do in *Colonel Quaritch, V.C.*

Haggard spent five months on the novel, completing it on 29 December. By that time he had returned to London and *She* was being serialised in *The Graphic*. It created considerable controversy, so that Haggard was concerned about how it would be received as a book. In December he wrote to W.H. Pollock: 'I am so glad that you like *She*. I am very nervous about the book myself, being doubtful as to its reception. It remains to be seen if the average reader — or for the matter of that the average reviewer — will see that the whole thing is an attempt to deal with the possible results of immortality informing the substance of the mortal, and that the surrounding atmosphere of gloom and terror is necessary to the picture. I fear lest like the gentleman who wrote to the *Graphic* they should set it down as "Bally Rot".'[47]

Partly because of his concern, but mainly because he was grateful for the help given with the proofs, Haggard wanted to dedicate *She* to Andrew Lang. When approached, Lang replied: 'It is awfully good of you to think of putting my name in *She* and I consider it a great distinction. The only thing is that, if you do, I shan't be able to review it, except with my name signed thereto and my honest confession. Probably I could do that in the *Academy*.' (*She* was dedicated to Andrew Lang, who did review it in the *Academcy*.)

Before *She* was published as a book, Haggard, in response to a request, quickly wrote, for *The Contemporary Review*, an article called 'About Fiction' about which he had already had some thoughts. As soon as *She* appeared on 1 January, 1887, it was obvious that the book was going to be a tremendous success. He was delighted, especially as he also received from Cassell's a statement showing that in 1886, 25,000 copies of *King Solomon's Mines* had been sold, making his royalties for the year £675. With the boost to his finances, he decided to give up all pretence of practising as a barrister and to concentrate on earn his living by writing. He also made up his mind to visit Egypt, the country in which he had become increasingly interested. While there he planned to gather material for a novel about Cleopatra.

Before leaving England towards the end of January, Haggard was showered with congratulations on *She*. On 8 January, Edmund Gosse, the distinguished man of letters, wrote: 'I feel constrained to write again to you about *She* before the impression the book has made upon my mind in any degree wears off. In construction I think you have been successful to a very marvellous degree. The quality of the invention increases as you go on.' Walter Besant added his words of praise: 'While I am under the spell of Ayesha, which I have only just finished, I must write to congratulate you upon a work which most certainly puts you at the head — a long way ahead — of all contemporary writers. . . . Whatever critics say the book is bound to be a magnificent success.'

The reviews of *She* that appeared in the literary journals were long and discursive, but there was not the unanimous praise that had been bestowed on *King Solomon's Mines*. Haggard was prepared for some misunderstanding by critics and so, when among the first adverse comments, *The Spectator* took exception to Ayesha's end, Haggard immediately wrote a long letter explaining what he saw to be the book's deeper meaning: '*She* was not intended to be a story of imaginative adventure only. In the first place, an attempt is made in it to follow the action of the probable effects of immortality working upon the known and ascertained substance of the mortal. . . . Secondly, the legend is built up upon the hypothesis that deep affection is in itself an immortal thing. . . . Lastly, it occurred to me that in She herself some readers might find a type of the spirit of intellectual Paganism, or perhaps even of our own modern Agnosticism; of the spirit, at any rate, which looks to earth, and earth alone, for its comfort and rewards.'[48]

With such verbosity, Haggard, even if he had not left for Egypt, would not have been able to stem the mounting flow of adverse criticism. *The Athenaeum* stated: 'Mr Haggard's language and dramatic force rarely rise to the level of a really great occasion; they often fall disappointingly below it. . . . The inequality of language is, perhaps, pardonable, but we do not find the thought and imagination are any better sustained. It is difficult to take *She* seriously as a philosophical allegory.[49]

The Pall Mall Budget claimed, 'It is as though a subject roughed out by Michael Angelo had been executed with an eye to New Bond Street popularity by Gustave Doré.[50] It seems that it was *She*'s 'New Bond Street popularity', rather than its style or story, that damned it in the eyes of at least some critics, for there appears in their comments a touch of envy that was soon to turn into malice.

Whatever the critics wrote, however, the public had no doubts. Within a few weeks the first edition of 10,000 copies had been sold. The London correspondent of *The Literary World* (Boston), obviously as upset as any of the critics by *She*'s popularity, peevishly informed his editor on 11 February: 'The extraordinary success of Mr Rider Haggard's *She* is somewhat disconcerting to the lover of literature. . . . Impossible in any house to attempt any conversation which is not interrupted by the abominable introduction of *She*. "By the way, have you read . . ." at that point it is generally safest to rise and flee. Artist, author, pedant, politician, man of science, man of the world, there is only *one* book that all of them just now are likely to ask if you have read.'[51]

To discover why *She* was so immediately successful it is necessary to consider the nature and *mores* of the contemporary society. In 1887, the year in which *She* was published, the people of the British Empire celebrated Queen Victoria's Golden Jubilee. During the fifty years Victoria had reigned, her people had prospered. For the previous thirty years there had been unbroken peace. Since Palmerston's death in 1865 the middle class had effectively governed with a benign authority over the working-class, whose conditions the trade unions strove to improve, albeit with an ever-increasing respect for the establishment. In return for this co-operation the establishment, as proof of its charity, made concessions to the trade unions. So there were Parliamentary acts improving factory conditions, educational provisions, sanitation, and the administration of the Poor Law. Their aspirations thus mollified and their revolutionary potential quelled, working-class people were led to believe that they owed their gradual improvement to their masters and betters whose outward respectability and way of life they were encouraged to ape. As Malcolm Elwin points out in *Old Gods Falling*, 'Respectability was the bulwark erected by the middle class to preserve its prestige against revolutionary irregularity.'[52] In the ever-expanding groves of suburbia sin-watching in others became a national pastime.

It was during this heyday of Victorian repression and moral censure that *She* was published and the vision of the most beautiful woman in the world standing naked, arms outstretched in the flames' embrace, was found acceptable. Why did this excessively prudish age welcome so warmly the exotic but destructive Ayesha — 'The femme fatale' as Henry Miller[53] calls her? Its strange double standards that condemned divorce but tolerated prostitution also allowed — while demanding that Anglo-Saxon women should expose no part of the body in public — detailed drawings of naked 'savages' to appear in the most reputable of magazines. If Haggard had deliberately intended to find an acceptable way of circumventing literary constraints so extreme that George Moore declared, ' "Naked" is using a word that nobody of taste would think of using,'[54] he could not have done better than to set the story in Africa, make the beautiful heroine both primeval and reginal (but, by a master-stroke, also white), and finally dispatch her, in case her eroticism had been too appealing, with punishing flames so like the fires of hell which each Sunday were vividly kindled in the imagination of church and chapel congregations throughout the country.

The underlying, though on Haggard's part unconscious, sexuality is not the sole reason for the success of the book, which has remained immensely popular throughout far more liberated and permissive eras. In *She* Haggard proves himself to be a master story-teller and the creator of a mystical character who ranks amongst the most powerful and original in English literature. As Samuel M. Clark wrote about Haggard shortly after the publication of *She*: 'He has freshened and quickened literature by showing in a distinctive and original way that the stories are not all told. . . . With all his patent defects, he seems to us to have the divine incommunicable gift of creation: that genius which survives transient faults and endures in its own right.'[55]

6

The Price of Fame

When Haggard left on his journey to Egypt he had every reason to be extremely pleased with his successes. Three of his novels were at the time appearing as serials (*She* in *The Graphic*, *Jess* in the *Cornhill Magazine*, and *Allan Quatermain* in *Longman's Magazine*), his books were selling exceptionally well, in the previous year he had received over £1,700 from writing (compared, for example, with £970 earned by the well-established Edmund Gosse[1]), and he was well on his way to becoming the most talked-about novelist in Great Britain. Even more amazingly, just before Haggard's departure Watt informed him that the serial rights of the unwritten novel about Cleopatra had been sold to *The Illustrated London News* for the staggeringly huge sum of £1,500.

Even the disasters of the rail journey through Europe, during which the train broke down and his luggage was lost, did not dampen Haggard's good spirits. After embarking at Brindisi he was delighted to discover that several of his friends were aboard, including Sir Henry Bulwer's sister, and that nearly everyone was reading either *King Solomon's Mines* or *She*. Haggard was met at Alexandria by his brother Arthur, who was stationed in Egypt with his regiment, and taken to Cairo, where for a while he was entertained; but he soon tired of the social round, writing to Louie: 'Notoriety has many drawbacks, I think.'[2] The ancient treasures of Egypt, on the other hand, fascinated him. 'It is impossible,' he wrote, 'to begin to tell you the impression that all this has made upon me.'

From Cairo Haggard proceeded up the Nile, inspecting the temples and tombs at Thebes. In one tomb he entered, lit only with dim torches, millions of bats had to be beaten away. In his autobiography he records: 'I can see them now, those bats, weaving endless figures in the torch-light, dancers in a ghostly dance. Indeed, afterwards I incarnated them all in the great bat that was a spirit which haunted the pyramid where Cleopatra and her lover, Harmachis, sought the treasure of the Pharaoh, Men-kau-ra':

> Lo! fixed to his chin, by its hinder claws, hung that grey and mighty bat, which flying forth when we entered the pyramid, vanished in the sky, but returning, had followed us to its depths. There it hung upon the dead man's chin slowly rocking itself to and fro, and we could see the fiery eyes shining in its head.
>
> Aghast, utterly aghast, we stood and stared at the hateful sight; till presently

the bat spread his huge wings and, loosing his hold, sailed to us. Now he hovered before Cleopatra's face, fanning her with his white wings. Then with a scream, like a woman's shriek of fury, the accursed Thing flittered on, seeking his violated tomb, and vanished down the well into the sepulchre.

(From *Cleopatra*)

At Aswan, Haggard watched a young man named Brownrigg successfully climb to the summit of the second pyramid, but when, in stockinged feet, he began his descent of the smooth granite cap he was unable to find a foothold, 'and then remained quite still upon the cap with outstretched arms like one crucified':

I remembered things. . . . Remembered how once in Egypt a foolhardy friend of mine had ascended the Second Pyramid alone, and become thus crucified upon its shining cap, where he remained for a whole half hour with four hundred feet of space beneath him. I could see him now stretching his stockinged foot downwards in a vain attempt to reach the next crack, and drawing it back again; could see his tortured face, a white blot upon the red granite.

(From *Ayesha*)

Early in March, Haggard returned to Cairo undecided about whether or not he should take up an invitation to visit his old chief, Sir Henry Bulwer, the High Commissioner of Cyprus. He wrote to his wife: 'I don't want to go at present, it would cost another fifty pounds, and it seems to me the trip would be better left to another year, when Will would be at Athens, and when you and I might, perhaps, manage it together. I seem to have seen enough for one go, and I want to get home now and get to work.'[3]

Haggard did, however, make the trip to the 'beautiful island of Venus'. When he arrived, wearied by travelling and suffering from the brooding loneliness that was to spoil many of his journeys overseas, he wrote again to Louie: 'I cannot tell you, dear old girl, how homesick I am — or how I want to see you and the kids again. I will never come on a trip of this kind again without you. I miss you very much and get quite low and lonely. Also I am very anxious to get to my work again, my head is full of Cleopatra, for which I have got a very strong plot. I think and hope it will make the British Public sit up! If it is feasible I shall go down to Ditchingham to write it. Kick that old Hampton out. I think we can afford to go there this summer. I forget when his lease ends, but when it does, dear, go down and see the place is put to rights. . . . We seem to be a good deal better off now, in fact, there must be a great deal of money due, though, of course, there are debts to pay. Still, I think we shall be justified. I cannot tell you, my dear, what a pleasure it will be to me if I find myself in a position to give you back the home again which in a way you lost by marrying me. I think that the best thing to me about such measure of success as I have won is that it has relieved my conscience of a great weight. I do not think I had any business to marry you when I did — it was pulling you down in the world. However, I think that I have now attained, in name if not in fortune, such a position you would not have been likely to exceed if I had not met you, and for that I am very thankful. I dare say that you think me a queer chap for writing like this, more especially as you have always been so gentle and considerate about things, but the matter taken in addition to my other weaknesses and failings, has always pressed upon me, though it is only now, after all these years, when I have fought and to some extent won the day, that I can speak of it.'[4]

This exceptionally honest letter, displaying the private front of modesty he continued to present to friends and relatives throughout his life, was no doubt prompted by the letter he received in Cyprus from Charles Longman: 'I am glad to tell you that *She* keeps on selling capitally. We have printed twenty-five thousand already, and have ordered another five thousand and do not think we shall have many left when the printers deliver them. Last week we sold over a thousand copies.'

But not all the news received from home was as pleasing. His article 'About Fiction', that had been published in February, aroused much hostility. Later he was to comment: 'It is almost needless for me to say that for a young writer who had suddenly come into some kind of fame to spring a dissertation of this kind upon the literary world over his own name was very little short of madness. Such views must necessarily make him enemies, secret or declared, by the hundred.' The article is superficial, poorly conceived and badly organised. It begins with a development of the comment made by Andrew Lang in his review of *King Solomon's Mines*: 'We should give many novels, say eight hundred (that is about the yearly harvest) for such a book as *King Solomon's Mines*)':

A writer in the *Saturday Review* computed not long ago that the yearly output of novels in this country is about eight hundred; and probably he was within the mark. It must be presumed that all this enormous mass of fiction finds a market of some sort, or it would not be produced. Of course a large quantity of it is brought into the world at the expense of the writer, who guarantees or deposits his thirty or sixty pounds, which in the former case he is certainly called upon to pay, and in the latter he never sees again. But this deducted, a large residue remains, out of which a profit must be made by the publisher, or he would not publish it. Now, most of this crude mass of fiction is worthless. If three-fourths of it were never put into print the world would scarcely lose a single valuable idea, aspiration, or amusement. Many people are of opinion in their secret hearts that they could, if they thought it worth while to try, write a novel that would be very good indeed, and a large number of people carry this opinion into practice without scruple or remorse. But as a matter of fact, with the exception of perfect sculpture, really good romance writing is perhaps the most difficult art practised by the sons of men . . .

(From 'About Fiction')

There is more of this bumptious regurgitation of the flattery Haggard had heard from his new-found literary friends before he changes tack and bewails the lack of a copyright agreement with America so that best-selling books, like his own, could be published there without the author receiving any royalties. This grievance dealt with, he attacks 'the laboured nothingness of this new American school of fiction' and 'the Naturalistic school, of which Zola is the high priest'. Finally, and somewhat incongruously, Haggard pleads that writers should be given greater freedom:

> The present writer is bound to admit that, speaking personally and with humility, he thinks it a little hard that all fiction should be judged by the test as to whether or no it is suitable reading for a girl of sixteen. There are plenty of people who write books for little girls in the school-room; let the little girls read them and leave the works written for men and women to their elders.

(From 'About Fiction')

Haggard was not to make the same mistake again. He never wrote another critical article. But by then the damage had been done, and an avalanche of attacks commenced. On 11 March 1887, the *Pall Mall Gazette* published 'Who is *She*, and Where Did *She* Come From?' in which the anonymous author (perhaps the editor W.T. Stead) accuses Haggard of copying ideas and incidents in *She* from Thomas Moore's *Epicurean*. Even though passages from both books are quoted, the article has no case to present and is clearly intended merely to be mischievous. It concludes: 'Not only does resemblance exist between the ideas of the two celebrated authors, but it extends to incidents, scenes, references, and words. Moore's conclusion is, however, commonplace; Mr Haggard's dénouement is so good that the public have already forgiven him much and may even forgive him more — or should we not say Moore?'[5]

Amost a fortnight later, on 24 March, in 'The Song of *Jess* and Who Wrote It' the *Pall Mall Gazette* published a far more serious and obviously more damaging charge which pointed out that verses almost identical to those written by Jess in her farewell letter to Captain Neil had previously appeared in the *Transatlantic* for March, 1874. They begin:

> If I should die, to-night,
> My friends would look upon my quiet face
> Before they laid it in its resting-place,
> And deem that death had left it almost fair;
> And, laying snow-white flowers against my hair,
> Would smooth it down with tearful tenderness,
> And fold my hands with lingering caress.
> Poor hands, so empty and so cold, to-night.

The article, having stated that the verses had also been previously published in the London *Guardian* (4 March, 1874), *The Anglo-American Times* (31 January, 1874), and the *Christian Union*, concludes: 'On this state of things, three hypotheses are

111

tenable. First, Mr Rider Haggard may himself have contributed the lines to the *Christian Union* — in which case he merely joins the company of authors who plagiarize from themselves. Or, secondly, he may have written the lines in *Jess* quite independently, without having the *Christian Union*, or the *Transatlantic*, or the *Guardian** before him. In this case the literary coincidence is a genuine wonder before which the imaginary wonders in the rest of his books sink into insignificance. Mr Haggard will doubtless lose no time in letting the public know which of these two hypotheses is the true one, in order that nobody may be tempted to adopt a third.'[6]

Unfortunately, as the editor of the *Pall Mall Gazette* was all too aware, for it had been mentioned several times in his columns, Haggard was abroad and could not immediately reply to the serious accusation of plagiarism that was widely repeated on both sides of the Atlantic. On 26 March, the *Pall Mall Gazette* published letters from three people who had rallied in Haggard's support. Louie wrote to say that her husband had never read Moore's *Epicurean* and that 'The poem in *Jess* was sent to Mr Haggard from South Africa in manuscript in a private letter about seven years ago, by a lady now dead, and he has always supposed it to be her own composition, and never to have been published';[7] Charles Longman wrote that when he had happened to mention Moore's *Epicurean* to Haggard before his departure for Egypt, 'He certainly told me that he had not read it, and I believe he said that he had never heard of it'; and James Stanley Little confirmed the story of the verses having been sent by a lady from South Africa.

The increasingly vitriolic criticism of Haggard was not stemmed by these letters, on which in the correspondence column of *Court and Society* on 30 March the novelist George Moore comments: 'I would ask if this asseveration and denial are necessary; for if we may regard anything as proven, if anything may be taken for granted, it is that no man ever did read, or even so much as heard of, any book which he is accused of borrowing from. . . . On the subject of Mr Haggard's reading, my difficulty lies, not in exoneration of him from having read this or that book, but in conceiving him to have read anything, saving, perhaps, the *London Journal*.'

Moore continues with an attack on 'About Fiction', stating that Haggard belongs not to the Realistic but to the illiterate school. He concludes: 'I predict for Mr Rider Haggard a brilliant future. As time goes on, he will sell innumerable editions of his books; he will sell as Holloway's pills and as Pears soap sell; he will become great and famous; he will buy a yacht, and a house in Grosvenor Square. He may be made a knight or a lord; but there is one thing he will never do — he will never obtain our

---

* The verses were published anonymously and their author appears never to have been identified. J. E. Scott, Haggard's bibliographer, states: 'To this day, however, their authorship is still wrapped in mystery.' (Scott, p. 42) After protracted investigations I have discovered that in 1873 the American *Christian Herald* (subsequently *The Outlook*) published the verses, crediting them to Miss Belle Smith. At the time she was a school teacher in Freemont county, Iowa, where she had been born. Later after attending Tabor Cottage, Newton, she became the city librarian and founded the Junior Endeavor Society. Several other people, however, have claimed to have written the verses.

literary esteem.'[8] On 30 March, under the heading 'The Ethics of Plagiarism', the *Pall Mall Gazette* published further letters on the verses in *Jess*, concluding: 'For our part, we hold our judgment in suspense until Mr Haggard's own answer is before us; for the "further explanation" for which we have asked may entirely change the aspect of the matter. The general question above discussed is indeed in any event of considerable literary interest; but in this particular case it is, of course, perfectly possible that inverted commas were omitted only in inadvertence, or even that a note acknowledging the author's obligation was by a printer's or publisher's oversight forgotten.'[9] The next day, 31 March, *The Whitehall Review* also commented on the letters sent in Haggard's defence and stated: 'But it will be interesting to have Mr Rider Haggard's own explanation, not as to how he came by the poetry, but how he came to use it as original work.'[10]

In Cyprus, Haggard heard first about the accusation that *She* was modelled on Moore's *Epicurean*. Distressed, he wrote to the *Pall Mall Gazette* on 30 March stating that he had never read a single line of Moore's book. When this letter was published, on 15 April, the editor added the barbed comment: 'We are sincerely glad to publish this explicit and straightforward letter. Cases of plagiarism are always unpleasant; cases of literary coincidence are always interesting.'[11]

Before Haggard's letter arrived, the *Pall Mall Gazette* published on 1 April 'Some More About *She*' which included parallel passages from *She* and the *Epicurean*. Two days later, a further article in the *Pall Mall Gazette*, again under the sensational heading 'The Ethics of Plagiarism', included a long letter from Andrew Lang in which he states: 'My confidence in Mr Haggard's honour is absolutely unshaken.'[12] Haggard's brother Alfred also wrote, giving reasons for concluding that there was no resemblance between *She* and the *Epicurean*.

On 5 April, Haggard, having received the most unwelcome news of furore caused by the *Jess* verses, wrote again from Cyprus to the editor of the *Pall Mall Gazette*: 'I have since I last had the honour of addressing you seen in your columns a comparison between the three verses that I have put into the mouth of Jess and some verses published in 1874 in the *Transatlantic Magazine*. It is obvious that the verses are identical. The history of these lines, so far as I am concerned, is as follows: They were, as I believed, an original composition, written and sent me as such some years ago by a friend who wrote some very beautiful poetry, and as that friend's work I have at different times read and shown them to various people. That friend is now dead, but I believe that I still have the original copy of verses, with alternative endings, among my papers in England. I put the lines, or rather some of them, into the mouth of Jess, because I knew that my dead friend would have been pleased at my doing so. I have, however, never claimed the authorship of them, and I should have acknowledged it in the book, only to do so would have been to spoil the *vraisemblance* of the scene. Whether or no my friend was the true author of these lines, I do not know. If not, I owe a most humble apology for my mistake to their unknown producer. Putting aside all higher considerations, it will be obvious even to those who are by nature, or from other causes, prone to put the worst interpretation on such matters, that I should not have resorted to so clumsy a device — for no object — as the bodily appropriation of lines which I knew to have been published elsewhere. To do so would have been to court certain detection.'[13]

Stead commented tartly: 'Mr Haggard's explanation does not strike us as satisfactory. His incorporation of some one else's verses in his novel without any acknowledgment, not in inadvertence but deliberately, seems to us a clear case of literary dishonesty.'

As he returned to England by sea, Haggard was most dispirited, feeling that his honour had been impugned. On arrival he found himself 'quite a celebrity, one whose name was in everybody's mouth'. Although he had clearly made important enemies, both his friends and some new acquaintances provided necessary support. Lang, on hearing Haggard was so depressed that he was thinking of giving up writing, wrote: 'If you jack up Literature, I shall jack up Reading. . . . Probably I think more highly of your books than you do, and I was infinitely more anxious for your success than for my own, which is not an excitement to me.'

The Hon. George Curzon (later Lord Curzon) wrote enclosing a letter that he had sent to the *Pall Mall Gazette*, but which the editor had not accepted for publication. After dismissing each of the examples Stead had provided of the *Epicurean*'s alleged influence on *She*, he concludes: 'I have no acquaintance with Mr Haggard beyond that which an admiring perusal of any author may give to every reader, but that holding the honour of our literary men to be not merely their private concern but the public property of the community at large, I have ventured to utter this protest against an attack upon him which I believe to be defamatory and untrue.'[14] During his absence, Haggard had been elected to the Savile Club, according to Lang, 'in a triumphant manner'. At this important meeting-place of literary men he joined an inner coterie that dined at a special table on Saturdays. Its members included Lang, Gosse, Besant, W.J. Loftie (the Egyptologist), R.A.M. Stevenson (the writer's cousin), and Eustace Balfour.

The attacks on Haggard still continued. In May, *Time* published Augustus M. Moore's article 'Rider Haggard and The New School of Romance', in which Haggard is accused of having stolen material from, among other books, Moore's *Epicurean*, Flaubert's *Salammbô*, Prescott's *The Conquest of Mexico*, Théophile Gautier's stories, Bishop Hall's *Mundus Alter ed Idem*, and Bacon's *New Atlantis*. Moore also quotes many stylistic and grammatical errors in *She*, claiming that he would not have troubled to do so 'if Mr Haggard had not gone out of his way in a recent article to denounce the writers of "realistic" novels'. He concludes: 'It is a sad thing to own that such a commonplace book as *She*, so full of other men's ideas, and so crammed with tawdry sentiment and bad English should have become the success it has undoubtedly been. It is a bad sign for English literature and English taste, and argues that the English Press which has trumpeted its success must be utterly corrupt, and the people who have listened and believed must be very ignorant and wholly devoid of judgement of any kind.'[15]

Following this intemperate and highly imaginative article, Lang wrote to Haggard: 'I've seen August Moore's [attack]! Splendid, not a rag left of *you*, and *I* am 'corrupt'. . . . The whole shindy is now explained: it was your *Contemporary* article and the blood of the Moore's thereby aroused. Of course you won't notice him in any way. You steal from Bishop Hall, Campanella, via Lord Bacon, and I don't remember who (or is it whom?) besides.'[16] Lang also derided Haggard's attackers in rhyme:

> The Critics, hating men who're Dabs
> At drawing in the dibs,
> Declare that Haggard cribs his crabs,
> And so they crab his cribs.[17]

Attacks on Haggard's work were also made in America. In May, *The Dial* published a wide-ranging critique of 'Mr Haggard's Romances', written by Samuel M. Clark, who states: 'Mr Haggard has entered the lists against the dullness of the American fashion in novels, and resolute to keep you awake as one of his prime purposes. . . . But our reading of his stories has not shown us that he has any marked quality of mind save imagination, or any noteworthiness as a writer save invention. He has no wit. He has not written one sentence sprightly enough to catch the reader's attention.'[18]

The reading public was unaffected by the bombastic outpourings of the literati. All Haggard's books, including the recently published single-volume editions of *Dawn* and *The Witch's Head* were selling in the thousands. Even Samuel M. Clark acknowledged 'the sudden and phenomenal eagerness with which Mr Haggard is now sought after'. There were other signs of recognition. In May *Vanity Fair*, confirming that Haggard had become a public figure, printed a Spy cartoon of him, standing erect with his hands behind his back. *Punch* published several parodies of his work, including '*Hee-Hee!* by Walker Weird, author of *Solomon's Ewers*'[19] Longman's published a one-hundred-and-twenty-page parody of *She* by Andrew Lang and W.H. Pollock entitled '*He*, by the author of *It*, *King Solomon's Wives*, *Bess*, *Much Darker Days*, *Mr. Morton's Subtler*, and Other Romances'.

Before he could start writing again, Haggard had to attend to several business matters concerning his books. Despite there being at least ten pirated editions of *She* on sale in America, Harper's sent Haggard a cheque for £30. 12s. 3d. as a royalty on the sales of their library edition and inquired if they could publish *Dawn* and *The Witch's Head* under a similar arrangement. Haggard gave his consent.[20] On 20 May he reached a new agreement with A.P. Watt by which he undertook to pay his agent 5 per cent on all moneys received for three years after the publication of each book placed. (This replaced the initial verbal agreement by which Haggard was to pay 10 per cent.) On the same date, Watt informed Haggard that the article 'Our Position in Cyprus' which he had received the previous day, had been placed with *The Contemporary Review*.[21] (It appeared in July.)

Towards the end of May, Haggard, intent on writing his novel about Cleopatra, 'fled from London to Ditchingham, because in town there were so many distractions and calls upon my time that I could not get on with my work'. He was bitterly disappointed to discover that an invitation to the special service in Westminster Abbey for the Jubilee of Queen Victoria was waiting for him at Ditchingham, but he could not use it because the event had already been held.

On 27 May, Haggard, living for the first time alone at Ditchingham House, began to write *Cleopatra: being an account of the fall and Vengeance of Harmachis, the Royal Egyptian, as set forth by his own hand*. Lang, in response to Haggard's request for background information, had already sent him Theocritus (good for a picture of Alexandria two hundred years before Cleopatra), Apuleius (good for one hundred and twenty years later), and a list of books on Cleopatra. Lang was to provide considerable help with the novel. He also continued to defend Haggard in public, in June, for example, contributing to *The Contemporary Review* a general article on 'Literary Plagiarism' which, although not mentioning Haggard by name, states: 'Probably no man or woman (apart from claiming a ready-made article not their own) ever consciously plagiarized in verse. The smallest poetaster has too much vanity to borrow on purpose.'[22]

While Haggard was working at Ditchingham, his wife found a much larger London house, suited to the new-found affluence and social position. During the summer she and her family moved into 24 Redcliffe Square, Earls Court, an elegant but comfortable home surrounded by several acres of garden. It was large enough to permit the Haggards, for the first time since living in London, to entertain a little during the winter months.

While working on *Cleopatra* Haggard had also to prepare *Allan Quatermain* for publication as a book. He decided to dedicate the novel to his son: 'I inscribe this book of adventure to my son Arthur John Rider Haggard in the hope that in days to come he, and many other boys whom I shall never know, may, in the acts and thoughts of Allan Quatermain, as herein recorded, find something to help him and them to reach to what, with Sir Henry Curtis, I hold to be the highest rank whereto we can attain — the state and dignity of English gentlemen.' Unfortunately for Haggard the similarity between his description of the attack by the giant crabs and that written by E.F. Knight had attracted attention while *Allan Quatermain* was being published as a serial. Surprisingly, as accusations of plagiarism against Haggard were then rampant, it was not Haggard but Knight who was accused of purloining another's material. The editor of *Cassell's Saturday Journal*, having been impressed by *The Cruise of the 'Falcon'*, asked Knight to submit a story. This he did, basing it on his own experiences in Trinidad. The following week this comment appeared in the press: 'Mr Rider Haggard is beginning to pay the penalties imposed on genius. Last week a story by E.F. Knight appeared in *Cassell's Saturday Journal*, which story is mainly abstracted from Mr Haggard's *Allan Quatermain*; that fascinating work we have all been reading. Anyone who looks at Chapter X of Mr Haggard's story will at once see that Mr Knight has transferred, without acknowledgment, a large portion of perhaps the most striking pages in Allan's adventures. This certainly shows some audacity, and an even stronger word might be used.'[23] When this was pointed out to Haggard, who was all too aware of the sensation likely to arise if another case of unacknowledged borrowing was proved against him, decided to add to the first edition of *Allan Quatermain* a note on 'Authorities'. In this he acknowledges an indebtedness to Thomson's *Through Masai Land*, John Haggard, Aggie, and 'also to an extract in a review from some book of travel of which I cannot recollect the name, to which I owe the idea of the great crabs in the valley of the subterranean river. But if I remember right, the crabs in the book when irritated projected their eyes quite out of their heads. I regret that I was not able to 'plagiarise' this effect, but I felt that, although crabs may, and doubtless do, behave thus in real life, in romance they "will not do so".'

In a footnote Haggard adds: "It is suggested to me that this book is *The Cruise of the 'Falcon'*, with which work I am personally unacquainted.' A further addition made to the serial version of *Allan Quatermain* was an epitaph for Umslopogaas, written in Greek and English verse by Andrew Lang, who, when he sent it to Haggard, stated, 'I am much grieved by the death of Umslopogaas.'

Haggard also had discussions with Messrs Smith, Elder & Co. about *Jess*, which had proved so successful that the third edition was already being printed. It was agreed that in the fourth and all subsequent editions the troublesome farewell song of Jess should be removed.[24] The publishers, delighted with the tremendous sales resulting from the unexpected publicity, most generously paid Haggard a further £450, the sum for which they had purchased the book's copyright.

On 20 June, Charles Longman wrote to Haggard: 'You have broken the record — at least so I am told. We have subscribed over 10,000 copies of *Quatermain* in London, which they say is more than has ever been subscribed of a 6/- novel before.' On 1 July, *Allan Quatermain* was published in an edition of 20,000 copies. Longmans also issued 112 copies of a large paper edition with mounted illustrations. (*Cleopatra* and *Allan's Wife* were the only other books by Haggard to have a large paper issue.) Once again it was obvious that Haggard had written another immediate best-seller. Among the many letters of congratulations Haggard received from admirers and cranks was one from a thirteen-year-old boy, who had been sent a copy of *Allan Quatermain* because Haggard knew his aunt, Lady Lisle: 'Thank you so much for sending me *Allan Quatermain*, it was so good of you. I like 'A.Q.' better than *King Solomon's Mines*; it is more amusing. I hope you will write a great many more books. I remain, Yours truly, Winston S. Churchill.'

As might be expected, however, not all the reviewers were enthusiastic about *Allan Quatermain*. J.M. Barrie, writing as 'Gavin Ogilvy', stridently declared in *The British Weekly*: '*Allan Quatermain* tells the adventures of three worthless old men, who go to Africa and slay their thousands of human beings. (They are responsible for the deaths of not less than 50,000.) It would have been a nobler part to stay at home and hire themselves out to butchers. . . . The popularity of our author need not be taken too seriously. A dozen years hence, *Allan Quatermain* will be as dead, rotten, and forgotten as this morning's newspaper.'[25] The popular press, responding to its readers' demands, continued to supply laudatory words about Haggard, his books, and his new successes, including *Devil Caresfoot*, a play adapted by C. Haddon Chambers and Haggard's friend J. Stanley Little from *Dawn*. It was first performed at the Vaudeville Theatre on Tuesday afternoon, 12 July. *The Theatre* described it as 'a play that will hold an audience for the length of a hot July afternoon not only interested, but that will at times bring tears to their eyes and a choking sensation in their throats'.[26] (A month later the play was transferred to the Strand Theatre.)

On 2 August, in just under ten weeks, Haggard completed *Cleopatra*. He then went to stay for a few days in Stirlingshire with Andrew Lang so that he could hand over his completed manuscript. Shortly after his return to Ditchingham, where he was joined by his wife and family, he wrote to Aggie, who was living in Madagascar where Jack was consul. The letter, while not re-establishing the playful intimacy of their correspondence before Aggie's marriage, is refreshingly honest: '*Allan Q.* had done very well, I believe, having sold about 20,000 up to the present. Of course I am now a great deal attacked, the *Pall Mall* business is a specimen but I jog along.. . . Jones and a friend of his dramatised *Dawn* and have made a very fair play of it. . . . Now *Jess* is being dramatised and there are negotiations about *She*. . . . I confess I am avaricious. I should like to make enough money to be able to stop writing at any rate for a time. But that can only be done out of a play or plays. As it is, I am doing pretty fairly and am glad to say that I am now able to keep Ditchingham going decently. I am going to build a new garden wall there and put an orchard [*sic*] house on it and also to put some split palings along the road and other small improvements.'[27]

For a few weeks Haggard pottered around Ditchingham. The day after a nostalgic return visit to Garsington he wrote a short article 'On Going Back'. He also completed two short stories, 'A Tale of Three Lions' (published in *Atlanta* between October and December 1887) and 'Nesta Amor' which, on Lang's recommendation, was never published. Lang also expressed some reservations about *Cleopatra*. He wrote: 'You will loathe me for the advice, but if I were you I'd put *Cleopatra* away for as long as possible, and then read it as a member of the public. . . . I would condense a good deal and it could be done. You'll find *that* when you come fresh to it again. . . . The style occasionally is not consistent. But the main thing is, at any expense, to hurry on more — to give the impression of solemnity, but at more speed, and with much fewer strokes. I know you hate altering, so it is *à prendre ou à laisser*, this long screed of opinion.'

As Lang suggested, Haggard delayed the publication of *Cleopatra*, its serialisation in *The Illustrated London News* not commencing until 5 January 1889. Although he happily corrected all the mistakes Lang found, Haggard neither rewrote nor condensed his novel. It seems from the letter Haggard sent Aggie in August that he had hoped that Lang would undertake the rewriting of *Cleopatra* for him, because he says: 'Possibly Lang and I shall collaborate in the final copy.'[28] When this idea came to nothing, he appears to have decided to leave well alone. In any case, yet again, he had no time to spend on revision: there was another novel he wanted to write.

In mid-September, Haggard started *Maiwa's Revenge*, another after-dinner hunting anecdote told by Allan Quatermain, although, like some of his earlier books, it did not preoccupy him. His mounting income meant that there were many other things to do — he and his wife spent weekends with friends, the proposed alterations at Ditchingham had to be put in hand, there were frequent trips to London, and business matters had to be discussed. Unfortunately Haggard's attempts to find lucrative investments were usually unsuccessful. Later he recalled: 'The investments suggested by kind friends connected with the City were apt to prove disappointing.' The main reason for this was that he was naturally inclined to speculate in risky mining ventures in remote parts of the world. On 21 September, he signed an agreement he hoped would provide him with the substantial sum from a play that in his letter to Aggie he had said he wished to obtain. Unfortunately, many years later, its existence resulted in a considerable loss of money. The agreement gave William Rose 'the sole and exclusive right to adapt the novel *She* for the stage for Great Britain'.[29] In return Haggard was to receive 50 per cent of the profits from the play, terms he felt to be most generous. The play was presented in 1888, and Haggard did earn a reasonable sum, but that was not the end of the matter. Amazingly, on 13 October 1925, five months after Haggard's death, the Rose Trustees successfully claimed, because of the agreement signed thirty-eight years earlier, 50 per cent of the royalties paid for the film version of *She* made that year in Great Britain by G.B. Samuelson, and starring Betty Blythe.

In the autumn of 1887, however, Haggard's income from writing was more than adequate to cover any losses from unwise investments. On 19 October he heard that Longmans had agreed to purchase the copyright of *Colonel Quaritch, V.C.* That day he wrote to A.P. Watt: 'I think £3000 a very fair price for Col. Q. I have had a letter from Longman, he seems to like it. . . . I am very glad to hear that you like *Cleopatra*. It is rather a favourite of mine also. I suppose Mr Longman read Col. Q. in the type.'[30] Perhaps as pleasing as Watt's news to Haggard, in view of all the harsh things that had been written about his work, was an article published in November on 'The Present State of the Novel' by George Saintsbury, in which he asserted: 'Mr Stevenson and Mr Rider Haggard . . . have done a great deal to further that return to the pure romance, as distinguished from the analytic novel, which was seen to be coming several years ago. . . . I shall not say whether I like *Treasure Island* better than *King Solomon's Mines*, or *King Solomon's Mines* better than *Treasure Island*. I only wish I had either drawn the personage of John Silver or written the fight between Twala and Sir Henry.'[31]

In October, Frederick Jackson, Lilly's brother, who had returned from his African hunting expedition, spent several weeks at Ditchingham. During his stay, Haggard started writing *Maiwa's Revenge*, a short, unpretentious Allan Quatermain tale, that he completed on 10 November. It includes the elements in his work beloved by the general public — several hunting adventures, a beautiful native girl, a missing white hunter, a battle between two African tribes, and, predictably, a severed limb. It tells, at least in part, how Maiwa revenges herself on her wicked husband, the murderer of her son, whose severed hand she keeps as a gruesome souvenir:

> The woman, who, as I have said, was quite young and very handsome, put her hand into a kind of little pouch made of antelope hide which she wore fastened round the waist, and to my horror drew from it the withered hand of a child, which had evidently been carefully dried in the smoke.
>
> (From *Maiwa's Revenge*)

Much of the novel is based on Frederick Jackson's hunting yarns. Early in the book, Good tells 'a most miraculous story of how he once went shooting ibex in Kashmir'. Jackson had been hunting in Kashmir, a part of the world not visited by Haggard, from 1881 to 1883. In his autobiography, Jackson gives a remarkable account of how he provided Haggard with information:

> Haggard used to ask me after dinner to tell him a few of my experiences with, say, the rhinoceros; and as one story would lead to another, I might tell him three or four.
>
> By the time his pipe had gone out, he would be lying back in his chair, with eyes shut, and apparently fast asleep, and only showed that he was awake by interjecting now and again a few such questions as:
>
> 'In a charge, would you be safe behind an ant-heap?' 'Could it knock it down?' 'Will it hunt you like a buffalo?' and so on.
>
> To such my reply would be that, generally speaking, an ant-heap would be safe, as it would probably be too large, and certainly much too solid and hard to knock down; and if the great blundering beast missed you, it would not turn, but go straight on.
>
> (From Frederick Jackson's *Early Days in East Africa*)[32]

In addition to the hunting yarns used in *Maiwa's Revenge*, the information about the lion trap used by Maiwa's husband to discipline her and his enemies was also provided by Jackson. He had given a similar trap to Chief Mandara who had likewise used it as a way of punishing his opponents.[33] In his preface to the book, Haggard says: 'It may be well to state that the incident of the "Thing that bites" recorded in this tale is not an effort of the imagination. On the contrary, it is "plagiarized". Mandara, a well-known chief on the east coast of Africa, has such an article, *and uses it*.' After its publication, *Maiwa's Revenge*, the first of the many pot-boilers Haggard wrote, was to prove one of his best-sellers.

Shortly after completing *Maiwa's Revenge*, Haggard took up residence in his new London home and began writing *Beatrice*, his third novel that year. Unlike all the other books he had written since *King Solomon's Mines*, it was to be a contemporary story set in England.

Although Haggard spent much time writing in his study at the rear of his

Redcliffe Square house, there were many other demands made upon him. In *The Days of My Life* he recalls: 'I became what is called famous, which in practice means that people are glad to ask you out to dinner, and when you enter a room everyone turns to look at you. Also it means that bores of the most appalling description write to you from all over the earth, and expect answers.' There were, however, compensations. He regularly dined at the Savile, a confrère of the most influential literary circle in the country; his letters to *The Times* on African affairs were readily published; and there was a continually increasing demand for his books. Early in December, Cassell's, after sales of fifty-three thousand, brought out the first illustrated edition of *King Solomon's Mines*. On 23 December, Longmans agreed to pay a 20 per cent royalty on sales of *Cleopatra*. His income from writing was astronomical. In 1887 he received:

From	
Cleopatra — serial rights	£1,500
Colonel Quaritch, V.C. — sale of copyright	£3,000
Jess — additional payment	£450
Allan Quatermain — 10% of 40,000 at 6/-	£1,200
She — 20% of 60,000 at 6/-	£3,600
— American sales	£30. 12s. 3d.
King Solomon's Mines — 10% of 30,000 at 6/-	£900
Total	£10,680. 12s. 3d.

He earned more from Tauchnitz editions, translations, the play 'Devil Caresfoot', cheap editions of *Dawn* and *The Witch's Head*, and his articles. He also received money from the Ditchingham estate and his investments. By the end of 1887, Haggard, aged thirty-one, was almost certainly the country's best-paid novelist.

The pattern of phenomenal public success combined with vicious critical attacks that had been established in 1887 was to continue. In January 1888 *The Church Quarterly Review* published an unsigned article of twenty-three pages entitled 'The Culture of the Horrible' that expressed disgust at the violence in five of Haggard's novels (*The Witch's Head*, *King Solomon's Mines*, *She*, *Allan Quatermain* and *Jess*): 'We have more weighty objections to these stories than that they are disfigured by many literary blemishes. We regard them as a serious offence against the reverence and delicacy with which horrible things ought to be treated in books whose object is pure amusement. We look upon the repeated introduction of scenes of slaughter, and of every detail of the charnel-house, interspersed as these scenes are with purposely ludicrous effects and comic allusions, as a violation of the decency we have a right to demand from all who handle such solemn themes.'[34] In the same month, Trubner & Co., conscious of Haggard's immense popularity, decided to publish a second edition of his first book, *Cetywayo and His White Neighbours*. To bring his story of the Transvaal up to date, Haggard wrote a new introduction, which interestingly contains this statement, that gives the lie to those who in modern times have labelled him as a jingoistic advocate of white supremacy:

> There is a party that does not hesitate to say that the true policy of this country is to let the Boers work their will upon the natives, and then, as they in turn fly from civilisation towards the far interior, to follow on their path and occupy the lands that they have swept. This plan is supported by arguments about the superiority of the white races and their obvious destiny of rule. It is, I confess, one that I look upon as little short of wicked. I could never discern a superiority so great in ourselves as to authorise us, by right divine as it were, to destroy the coloured man and take his lands. It is difficult to see why a Zulu, for instance, has not as much right to live in his own way as a Boer or an Englishman.
>
> (From *Cetywayo and His White Neighbours*, 2nd ed.)

On 28 February, Haggard completed his novel *Beatrice*, an account of the ill-fated and unconsummated love affair of Beatrice Granger, a free-thinking, independent but impoverished school-teacher, and Geoffrey Bingham, an unhappily married man of ability and social prominence who, reflecting Haggard's own frustrated ambition, was set to achieve political success.

After Bingham has confessed that he loves her, Beatrice, to save him from social disgrace, commits suicide, confident that their love will reunite them after death. *Beatrice* is, however, more than a reaffirmation of Haggard's belief in eternal love. Consideration of his own relationship with his wife had clearly encouraged Haggard to examine the problems of marriage, a matter of considerable interest to a public so concerned with respectability that had no socially accepted solutions, for few Victorians could accept divorce as a solution to the problem of failed marriages.

By Queen Victoria's Golden Jubilee, consideration of what had come to be known as 'the marriage question' was becoming a commonplace, especially in novels. Indeed the matter became so often considered that *The Athenaeum's* anonymous reviewer of *Jude the Obscure*, having called it 'a titanically bad book', went on to tax Thomas Hardy for writing about 'the marriage tie and its permanence': 'Not that the subject is in itself out of place in fiction . . . but lately so many of the inferior writers of novels have stirred up the mud with this controversy, that one would have been content if so great a writer as Mr Hardy had not touched it, if he was not going greatly to dignify it.'[35]

Haggard's contribution to the debate about marriage in *Beatrice* was not only to present sympathetically the love affair of a woman and a married man but to show that in a society that refused to countenance divorce a husband was as trapped by matrimony as a wife. Geoffrey Bingham is married to Lady Honoria who, 'although by far too cold and prudent a woman to do anything that could bring a breath of scandal on her name, was as fond of admiration as she was heartless'; but when she realises that her husband has fallen in love with Beatrice she issues this warning:

'If you go on with it, beware! I will not be made to look a fool. If you are going to be ruined you can be ruined by yourself. I warn you frankly, that at the first sight of it, I shall put myself in the right by commencing proceedings against you. Now, of course, I know this, that in the event of a smash, you would be glad enough to be rid of me in order that you might welcome your dear Beatrice in my place. But . . . remember: that you could not marry her, supposing you to be idiot enough to wish to do so, because I should only get a judicial separation, and you would still have to support me.'

(From *Beatrice*)

After Beatrice's suicide, Haggard dispatches Lady Honoria with his much-favoured device — she is burnt to death.

Haggard, as has become his custom, sent the completed manuscript of *Beatrice* to Andrew Lang, who commented: 'The thing I like least . . . is where Godfrey is rather schoolboyishly talky with her; it may be in nature, but it is not good manners. Perhaps, married men in love are unmannerly.' Lang was right to criticise Bingham — he is the weak, cardboard cut-out of a young man that Haggard so often created. But in Lady Honoria, Beatrice and her scheming sister Elizabeth, Haggard again revealed his awareness and affection for 'the infinite variety of women'. Even they, however, do not save the novel, despite its historical insights, from now appearing dated and unconvincing.

Shortly after completing *Beatrice*, Haggard started work on *Meeson v. Addison & Another*, a light-weight novel destined to be one of the two books he was contracted to write for Spencer Blackett, the successor to the publishers J. & R. Maxwell. It tells the story of Augusta Smithers, a young lady who writes a best-selling novel published by Meeson's. Unfortunately, unlike Haggard when he was placed in a similar position at Cassell's, she takes the fifty pounds paid for the copyright rather than a royalty of seven per cent. Her contract also includes a clause, as Haggard's had done with Maxwell's, binding her to offer Meeson's all books written during the next five years. When the publisher's nephew and heir, Eustace, supports the impoverished Augusta's request for more money, he is sacked and disinherited. Augusta emigrates to New Zealand on the R.M.S. *Kangaroo*, and on board she meets Mr Meeson, the publisher. The ship sinks, and the occupants of a lifeboat, including Augusta and Mr Meeson, land on Kerguelen Island. Before Meeson dies, his will, leaving everything to Eustace, is tattooed on to Augusta's back. After her rescue, the will is considered by Mr Fiddlestick, Q.C. in the Probate, Divorce and Admiralty Division of the High Court. Eustace inherits, marries Augusta, reforms Meeson's (giving vast royalties to all authors) and uses much of his fortune to found an institute for poor writers.

In the novel, subsequently renamed *Mr Meeson's Will*, Haggard both vents his ire on the publishers he felt had tricked him and uses some of his legal experiences. Fiddlestick is based upon Mr Inderwick, a judge he knew,[36] and Haggard later claimed that 'the story of the tattooed will had its origin in a trick which was played with some success upon a certain learned Q.C. by his own irreverent pupils'.

Interestingly, Haggard includes in the court scene a reference to himself:

'The short gentleman in the middle is Telly; he reports for the *Times*. You see, as this is an important case, he has got somebody to help him to take it — that long man with a big wig. He, by-the-bye, writes novels . . . romances, you know, mere romances! and mostly plagiarised from the Book of Genesis and the Egyptian Novelists of the Ancient Empire; at least so I'm told in minor literary circles.'

(From *Mr Meeson's Will*)

While working on *Mr Meeson's Will*, which he completed towards the end of April, Haggard was discussing with Andrew Lang ideas for a novel on which they would collaborate. It appears that at first they were undecided about their subject. On 8 March, Lang wrote from Paris: 'It occurs to me that you had better read the Helen of Euripides in a prose crib. . . . The name "The Wanderer" is already taken by one of Lord Lytton's poems. I had thought of "A Priestess of Isis".' On 25 March, Lang wrote from Florence: 'Just had your letter on the Jews. Do you think it worth while, if it won't run easily? You have so much on hand, and I am afraid you will tire out your invention. The idea of Odysseus and Helen is a good idea, but don't thrash a willing and perhaps weary Pegasus.'

It was, however, decided that the two men would write a novel about Odysseus, and, after his return to England, Lang wrote to Haggard: 'Odysseus calls himself *Eperitus*, as a by-name, in Od. 24. Or *Laertiades*. Helen should be a priestess in Egypt, say of Pasht. You won't want much help from *me*. All the colour is in the Odyssey.'

Late in April, Haggard began writing the Odysseus tale which, although at first entitled *The Song of the Bow*, was published as *The World's Desire*. While Haggard wrote, Lang was working on the proofs of *Beatrice*. On 8 May he wrote: 'I have read *Beatrice*, and if she interests the public as much as she does me, she'll do. But I have marked it a good deal, and would be glad to go through it with you, looking over the scribbled suggestions. It is too late, but what a good character some male Elizabeth would have been: nosing for dirt, scandal, spite, and lies. He might easily have been worked in, I think. . . . It is odd: usually you "reflect" too much, and yet in this tale, I think, a few extra reflections might have been in place. I feel a Thackerayan desire to moralise.'

Odysseus did not occupy all Haggard's thoughts for Meredith Townsend, a part-owner of *The Spectator*, had, in a letter, given him another idea. He wrote: 'It would be worth living to read your account of a Berserk, a white Umslopogaas, with a vein of pity in him for women only.' Accepting the idea, Haggard chose a white equivalent of the noble savage — an Icelandic warrior. He had already heard much about the traditional sagas from Lang and his admirer E.W. Gosse, who in 1879 had issued in *The Cornhill Magazine* a brief epitome of the Egils Saga. In order to collect material for his own book and see a country that fascinated him, Haggard decided to visit Iceland. First, to obtain advice and letters of introduction, he went to see William Morris, who had visited Iceland and written versions of several sagas including *The Story of the Volsungs and Niblungs* (1870) and *Three Northern Love Stories* (1875). Haggard, impressed by the beautiful oak furniture, priceless tapestries and fine china in Morris's house, afterwards stated: 'I remember that when I departed I rather wished that Fate had made me a Socialist also.'

At this time Haggard also patched up the fractured friendship with W.E. Henley who, having placed *King Solomon's Mines* with Cassell's, had reproached Haggard for letting other people handle his writing. On 8 June, Haggard sent Henley a letter saying how much he had enjoyed his recently published book of verse. Next day, Henley replied: 'I found yours at the Club last night. I *do* care for your approbation very much; for I do not think I should have it if my verses hadn't a kind of basis of life. Lang hates 'em, I believe; and I shall tell him of your note with pride and glee.'

Haggard sent Lang all of *The Song of the Bow* that he had written, before sailing from Leith to Iceland with his friend A.G. Ross on 14 June. Five days later they reached Reykjavik where, on the recommendation of Morris, they hired as a guide Thorgrimmer Gudmundson, a local schoolmaster. They stayed on the island for a month fishing and trekking around on thin, shaggy ponies to investigate the sights described in the Njal Saga. On 21 June he wrote home from Thingvellii: 'I only wish you were familiar with the Njal Saga, for then you would understand the interest, the more than interest, with which I look upon it. Every sod, every rock, every square foot of Axe River, is eloquent of the deeds and deaths of great men.'

As he travelled, Haggard became entranced by the land and its historical links with the Njal Saga. Later he stated: 'The account of the burning of Bergthorsknoll in the Njal Saga is not only a piece of descriptive writing that for vivid, simple force and insight is scarcely to be matched out of Homer and the Bible, it is also obviously true. We feel as we read, that no man could have invented that story. . . . That the tale is true, the writer can testify, for, saga in hand, he has followed every act of the drama on its very site.' It was while visiting the site of the burning at Bergthorsknoll and the nearby tomb of the slain warrior Gunnar that Haggard mapped out the plot of the saga he was to write.

On 20 July, Haggard and Ross sailed for home on the *Copeland*, which was laden with hundreds of ponies. Immediately they ran into bad weather, as Haggard's entries in his notebook tersely record: '20th: At Sea. Bad weather. 21st: Gale. 22nd: Worse gale. 23rd: Worse gale still. Lay to. 24th: Tried to go about four o'clock. Strained the ship so much that we had to lay to again.'

The ponies began to die and, as the captain tried desperately to reach port, the *Copeland* ran aground on the rocks of Stroma, the island just north of John o' Groats. Orders were given for the lifeboats to be launched, but in the chaos the crew did not manage to get one into the water. 'Understanding that the position was serious,' Haggard later recalled, 'I went to my cabin, packed what things I could, then called the steward and made him bring me a bottle of beer, as I did not know when I should get another. He, such is the force of habit, wanted me to sign a chit for the same, but I declined. Whilst I was drinking the beer I felt the vessel slip back several feet.'

Haggard joined his fellow-passengers and the crew on deck, from which, shortly afterwards, they were rescued by some islanders who, at no small risk to themselves, managed to get a boat alongside. When they landed on Stroma they were met by the local schoolmaster who, recognising Haggard, said, 'The author of *She* I believe? I am verra glad to meet you!' Some ten hours later the *Copeland*'s passengers and crew were taken in an open boat to the mainland and then on by carts to Wick, where they slept at an inn.

Haggard in his autobiography states: 'I did not sleep very well. During the shipwreck and its imminent dangers my nerves were not stirred, but afterwards of a sudden they gave out. I realised that I had been very near to death; also all that word means. For some days I did not recover my balance.' Immediately afterwards, Haggard wrote an article about his experiences, 'The Wreck of the *Copeland*', which appeared in *The Illustrated London News* on 18 August.

Relaxing at Ditchingham, Haggard received a letter dated 2 August from Charles Longman who had just been sent a typescript of *Beatrice*: 'I was very much interested in *Beatrice*. It is of course a terrible tragedy — unrelieved in its gloom which increases from start to finish. Still there is no denying its power.' On 3 August, *Maiwa's Revenge* was published in an edition of 30,000 at 2s 6d. The following day, Longman wrote again to inform Haggard that 20,000 copies of the book had been sold on the day of publication. He also said: 'I think, too, that *Beatrice* is your best piece of purely modern, nineteenth-century work. I believe I like you best among the caves of old Kôr, or looking back over King Solomon's great road to the old civilisations dead two thousand years ago. But it is a great thing to have several strings and not always harp on the same.'

Andrew Lang also contacted Haggard. Amazingly he had mislaid the manuscript of the first part of *The Song of the Bow*. Not having the heart to recommence the book, Haggard, on 29 August, started writing his saga, to which he gave the somewhat unsatisfactory title *Eric Brighteyes*.

Meanwhile the attacks on him continued. Following the publication of *Mr Meeson's Will* in *The Illustrated London News* towards the end of June, a further charge of plagiarism was brought against him, it being pointed out that 'Le Cas de Mademoiselle Suzanne', a tale in *Les Nouvelles Amoureuses* by M. Charles Aubert, concerns a young woman whose birthright was tattooed on her back in the form of a cryptogram. This led Haggard to declare: 'I never even heard of the very foreign story from which I am accused of borrowing an idea till long after *Mr Meeson's Will* was written, and to this hour I have not seen it.' A more incisive attack on Haggard was made by Frank Harris who, as recently appointed editor of *The Fortnightly Review*, published on 1 September an article on 'The Fall of Fiction'. Perhaps having learned from Stead's example that criticism of Haggard sold journals, Harris was both cruel and abusive. He attributed to Haggard sole responsibility for the contemporary decline in fiction and concluded: 'It is not that we grudge Mr Haggard his undeserved success, but that we grudge the comparative neglect of meritorious fiction. . . . He is a clever man, well able to take the measure of his own charlatanry. . . . He has accurately gauged the taste of a section of the reading public, which the triumph of his experiment proves to be a large section. But that taste — the taste for such an ill-compounded *mélange* of the sham-real and the sham-romantic — is a deplorable symptom. There is among the very poor in our large cities a class of persons who nightly resort to the gin-shop to purchase a mixture of every known liquor, the heterogeneous rinsings of a hundred glasses. . . . The taste for novels like Mr Rider Haggard's is quite as truly the craving for coarse and violent intoxicants because they coarsely and violently intoxicate.'[37]

Even the success of the dramatisation of *She* that opened at the Gaiety on 6 September,[38] did not alleviate the effects on Haggard of Harris's diatribe. Indeed as late as 1915 he was to describe Frank Harris as 'the malicious man who did me so much harm years ago'.[39]

As a defence against his attackers, Haggard wrote a special preface to *Mr Meeson's Will* which was to appear as a book in October. In this he is particularly concerned about 'the accusations of plagiarism which are now so freely brought against authors'. He concludes: 'Still, it is to be hoped that readers are left who hold that a book should be judged according to its merits and the skill with which its central ideas are handled, and not by the test of whether or no something can be raked from the literature of all times and countries that has a family resemblance to one or more of those ideas. If this hope is baseless novelists may throw aside their pens, and betake themselves to some more peaceful occupation.' Although such a possible reaction was clearly in Haggard's mind, he continued throughout the autumn of 1888 writing *Eric Brighteyes*.

Early in October, Andrew Lang wrote to say that he had found the missing manuscript of *The Song of the Bow*. He had apparently put it in a folio volume 'to keep it clean'. On 11 October, he wrote to Haggard: 'I only had time for a glance at the lost MS. Now I have read it . . . it isn't my idea how to do it (not that that matters). . . . I can't help regretting my veteran Odysseus — I don't think he would have been too "grey-eyed". If we really collaborated, as we proposed originally, I'd begin with him; bring him in your way to Egypt, introduce him to the old cove who'd tell him about Hatasu (as in yours) and then let things evolve, but keep all the English modern, except in highly-wrought passages, incantations, etc. I dare say it would make a funny mixture.'

Haggard, busy with his saga, obviously replied, asking Lang to do whatever rewriting he wished, because on 17 October Lang wrote: 'Having nothing to do this afternoon I did a lot of Ulysses. . . . If you can make it alive (it's as dead as mutton), the "local colour" is all right.' On 2 November, he wrote again: 'I have done a little more. Taken Od. into the darkness and given him a song, but I think he had been reading Swinburne when he wrote it.'

Lang tried to defend Haggard against Harris's attacks in an article written for the October number of *The Contemporary Review*. After dealing with each of the points made by Harris, Lang states: 'I own that many passages in *She* appeared to myself to show very extraordinary imagination.' Lang's words, rather than silencing Harris, provoked another attack. In November *The Fortnightly Review* published a letter 'Mr Haggard and his Henchman' which poured scorn on Lang's article, concluding: 'Mr Haggard's capacity for sweet victual must be enormous indeed if the praises he has already received have not yet glutted it. *Why* — to go no further — Mr Haggard could have little cause for complaint if he had even received no other tribute of admiration than the chant of laud resounding through all those journals which number among their contributors that unimpeachably impartial critic, his own friend and dedicatee, Mr Andrew Lang.'[40]

Another friend who helped Haggard at the time was W.J. Loftie who in March had designed Haggard's Egyptian bookplate and letter-heading which translated is 'H. Rider Haggard, the son of Ella, lady of the house, makes an oblation to Throth, the Lord of writing, who dwells in the moon.' Early in November, Haggard sent him the proofs of *Cleopatra*, which was to start its six-month serialisation in *The Illustrated London News* on 5 January, 1889. On 13 November, Loftie wrote: 'You will take it for granted that I am immensely interested in *Cleopatra* and if I may say so think it an advance in writing on anything else I have seen of yours.'[41] He worked on the proofs for several weeks, making corrections and suggesting alterations.

On 3 December, *Colonel Quaritch, V.C.* was published in three volumes, dedicated to Charles Longman. It was not well received by the critics. On 22 December, *The Scots Observer*, edited by W.E. Henley, declared: 'Mr Haggard must not only mix his colours with his brains, but, if he is to succeed as other men have succeeded, he must dip his pen in his blood. He is too successful, as the world measures success, to require to do this, and we fear that he has not the divine spark that will inspire him to do it without the force of that dire necessity which might have made him great in spite of himself. . . . Of *Colonel Quaritch* there is not much that need be said. . . . It is a great deal better than half the novels that are published, but is manifestly a pot-boiler; and, as the work of the author of *Jess*, it is unworthy of serious criticism.'[42]

Haggard finished writing *Eric Brighteyes* on Christmas Day, 1888, after working on it for almost four months. The novel is written in an archaic, almost Biblical, language that he had first used for Ayesha's speeches and then for much of *Cleopatra*. It is, however, an effective and original story in the saga style that experts on Icelandic literature have subsequently praised highly. Ralph Bergen Allen, for example, in *Old Icelandic Sources in the English Novel* states: '*Eric Brighteyes* is an essay in the saga style, Icelandic in theme, treatment, and details and spirit of writing.'[43]

The completed manuscript was sent immediately to Andrew Lang, and within days he was sending Haggard letters of praise. The first letter states: '*Eric* begins A1. . . . I think it is the best thing you have done, but of course I am saga-fain! I didn't think anyone could do it.' A few days later, Lang writes again: 'I have got Eric into Swanhild's toils, and I don't think I have come to a dull page yet. I don't want to flatter, but it literally surprises me that anyone should write such a story nowadays. . . . As literature I really think it is a masterpiece so far as I have gone. I'd almost as soon have expected more Homer as more saga.'

When he had finished the novel, Lang wrote: 'The more I consider *Eric*, the more I think that except *Cleopatra*, which you can't keep back, I'd publish no novel before *Eric*. It is so very much the best of the lot in all ways. Probably you don't agree, and the public probably won't stop to consider, but *it is*.' To this Haggard must have replied that he preferred *Cleopatra*, for Lang next writes: 'I wish it could appear tomorrow in a book. Comparisons are odious, and I understand your preferring *Cleopatra*. People inevitably prefer what gives them most serious labour. But it's a natural gift that really does the trick.'

While Lang was reading the manuscript of *Eric Brighteyes*, Haggard was finishing *The Song of the Bow* (*The World's Desire*). On 9 January, 1889, he completed it. For the previous eighteen months, apart from his trip to Iceland, he had been working on a book almost every day. In 1888 he had completed *Beatrice*, *Mr Meeson's Will*, *Eric Brighteyes* and most of *The World's Desire*. His income for the year from books alone again exceeded £10,000.

After finishing *The World's Desire*, Haggard took a few weeks' rest from writing. On 21 January he wrote to his mother, whose poor health increasingly concerned him, asking her to approve his dedication of *Cleopatra* to her.

To this his mother replied: 'I cannot object to your appreciatory dedication if you really think you inherit your literary tastes from me. Perhaps you do, *from me and mine*, for there was much intellectual power on my side of the family, but your inventive imagination has brought our obscure and unknown attempts to the surface. Circumstances, in my case, have always been steadfastly against me, a little disappointing I must confess, now in the evening of my life, when the shadows are closing and blotting out the bright but perhaps foolish gleams which brightened my youth.' The letter both moved and upset Haggard. It was clear that his mother's growing frailty and failing eyesight had forced her to accept that she would not live much longer to enjoy vicariously her son's literary successes.

Haggard's notebooks show that at this time he was also thinking of ideas for further novels. He must, therefore, have been very excited to read the comment Andrew Lang included in his article 'The Dreadful Trade' in *The Scots Observer* on 16 February: 'How delicious a novel *all* Zulu, without a white face in it, would be!'[44] Four months later he was to start just such a story, but before that, as he was all too aware, he had to write another pot-boiler for Spencer Blackett to complete the terms of his contract with them.

On 24 February, Haggard wrote to Aggie, who had moved to Brest where Jack had been appointed the Consul: 'I am going up to St Andrews for a week next Friday [to stay with Lang]. I expect it will be cold there. I have finished my Icelandic romance or Saga. The only person I have had any opinion of it is from Andrew Lang and he raves about it, which isn't much in his line, calls it a "masterpiece of literature" and says he as little expected to find more Saga as more Homer and that he never believed it could have been done. But of course he likes that kind of thing anyhow. I don't think it is bad in its way, though personally I prefer *Cleopatra*. But he don't.'[45] Having again been in contact with Aggie, Haggard decided that as soon as he had finished his next book he would travel to Brest and stay with her and Jack for a short holiday.

The following day, 25 February, he began to write *Allan's Wife* for Spencer Blackett and, despite his week's stay in St Andrews, the story was completed on 16 April. It is a splendidly told story of Allan Quatermain who, after his father's sudden death, went on his first elephant-hunting trip during which he met and married his second wife Stella. She dies immediately after giving birth to a boy, Harry, whose own death is recorded at the beginning of *Allan Quatermain*. The story is full of incident, including examples of African magic possibly inspired by David Leslie's *Among the Zulus* which Haggard had been lent by Lang.[46]

As *Allan's Wife* was not long enough to make a book, Haggard added the three Allan Quatermain stories that had been earlier published in magazines 'Hunter Quatermain's Story', 'A Tale of Three Lions', and 'Long Odds'. He also added a letter of dedication to the companion of his youth in Africa, Arthur Cochrane, who, having moved to London, was again in contact with Haggard. In the letter he states:

> For us too, Macumazahn, as for the land we loved, the mystery and promise of the morning are outworn; the mid-day sun burns overhead, and at times the way is weary. . . . But though we walk apart to-day, the past yet looks upon us with its unalterable eyes. Still we can remember many a boyish enterprise and adventure, lightly undertaken, which now would strike us as hazardous indeed.
>
> (From *Allan's Wife*)

These are not, as they might seem, the words of an old man. When Haggard wrote this dedication, steeped as it is in nostalgia and discontent with the present, he was only thirty-two. Yet, although Haggard has always been popularly regarded as a man of action, he had left Africa nearly eight years earlier. That period he had spent, apart from his holidays in Egypt and Iceland, almost unceasingly writing in his study or reading for the Bar. Few office workers could have had a less active or less adventurous life.

A few days after sending the completed manuscript of *Allan's Wife*, not to Andrew Lang, but direct to the publishers, Haggard must have been pleased to read W.E. Henley's balanced appraisal of his work that appeared in *The Scots Observer* on 27 April. In it Henley states: 'The popularity of Mr Haggard has been of unusually sudden growth. He is at the present moment, if the gossip of clubs and book-shops is to be believed, the most popular writer of fiction of the day. He is in his thirty-third year, and at that age neither Richardson nor Fielding, Miss Austen nor Scott, Marryat nor Thackeray, had begun the serious career of a novelist. . . . No author in our time has had an odder fate. Accepted with open arms by the great mass of readers — accepted, as numerous signs would seem to indicate, by the responsible leaders of his profession — Mr Haggard has been forced, to a degree scarcely paralleled of late, to run the gauntlet of petty newspaper criticism.'[47]

On 1 May, Haggard wrote to Aggie, informing her of the arrangements for his visit to her: 'My plan is to start by the night mail on Sunday 12th, travel through to Paris and come on to Brest by a day train. . . . I propose to return to Paris about 19th, spend a day or two there and then go to Ditchingham.' Four days later he wrote again to say that, although he was afflicted by gout, he would still arrive on 13 May. (This appears to have been the first attack of the disease from which he was to suffer at intervals throughout the rest of his life.) The reunion of Haggard and Aggie clearly went well. Whatever had caused the tension between them that existed after her marriage had ceased to be important. Haggard returned from his visit refreshed and ready to start work on what was to be the most original book he had written since *She*. First, however, he went to see his parents and was distressed to discover just how ill his mother had become. On 8 June he wrote to Aggie from Ditchingham: 'My billiard room isn't done yet. I don't believe it will be before August for they take their time here. On the other hand the new garden looks well. . . . I went over to Bradenham the other day. My Mother is I fear sinking slowly, but still sinking. On the day I was there her mind reminded me of a mirror after one has breathed on it — dulled. But she varies.'[48]

Haggard spent the next few weeks reading background material for the novel which, following Lang's suggestion, would be 'all Zulu, without a white face in it'. Inspired by his occasional reminiscences with Arthur Cochrane and stimulated by his visit to Aggie, Haggard thoroughly researched the early history of the Zulu race and Chaka, their king. Among the books that he studied were D. Leslie's *Among the Zulus and Amatongas* and F.B. Fynney's *Zululand and the Zulus*, both privately printed.

On 24 June *Cleopatra* was published in book-form with twenty-nine illustrations — several of them showing bare-breasted, Egyptian females — by R. Caton Woodville (the illustrator of the serialisation in *The Illustrated London News*) and M. Greiffenhagen, who was to become a friend of Haggard's. On 27 June, Haggard started work on his Zulu epic, *Nada the Lily*. The same day, Lang wrote to Haggard, after completing the corrections to the final part of the novel on which they were collaborating: 'I have been turning over *The World's Desire*, and the more I turn the more I dislike the idea of serial publication. It is emphatically a book for educated people only, and would lower your vogue with newspaper readers, if it were syndicated, to an extent beyond what the price the papers pay would make up for. I am about as sure as possible of this: it is a good deal my confounded *style*, which is more or less pretty, but infernally slow and trailing.' Haggard replied telling Lang he was wrong, and in time Watt sold the serial rights of the story to *New Review*, which had the 'educated' readership for which Lang thought the book was suitable.

Before the end of June, Haggard received letters from both his mother and father thanking him for their copy of *Cleopatra*. William Haggard wrote: 'This morning came a beautiful copy of *Cleopatra*, which your mother, with my assistance, opened herself and herself (for though it strained her eyes for the moment a bit, I would not help her in it, for I knew you and she would like her to do it best herself) read the dedication which gratified much her maternal heart — even unto tears.' On 29 June, his mother wrote: 'I have only a few minutes to write and thank you for your charming gift, but I must not let the week pass over without my doing so. I think it is got up as well as possible, and the Dedication is most successfully accomplished, which must be gratifying to you as to me.' It was an irony not lost on Haggard that, because of her failing eyesight, his mother was unlikely to read the book he had dedicated to her.

On 20 July, W.E. Henley wrote to Haggard from Edinburgh: 'I got a week at Windermere and took *Cleopatra* with me. I was alone, and I found her very good company. . . . The invention throughout is admirable — is good enough, indeed, to carry off the archaeology and the archaical style, though they are both large orders. . . . It has plenty of faults, but it has an abundance of promise and some excellent — some really excellent — achievement.' In his reply Haggard thanked Henley, but said that he anticipated that the critics would unite in their condemnation of the book. As he wrote, it must have been very much in his mind that it was Henley who had called Ayesha 'the heroic Barmaid — the Waitress in Apotheosis'.[49] On 26 July, Henley wrote again to Haggard: 'It is pleasant to know that I have paid a very little of my debt. I think the 'Romance and Farce' in the current *S.O.* will not displease you. . . . Meanwhile, you may put down the attacks partly to envy (for you can't deny that you've had a damn good innings) and partly to the inevitable reaction — for I don't know that your admirers have praised you in quite the right way. And you need bother yourself no more about them. Why should you? You are bound to win, and you need not care three straws for anything they say. You need only do your best, and leave the rest to time. That I believe to be the right philosophy of things. And so farewell.'

'Romance and Farce', a review of *Cleopatra* and *The Wrong Box* by Robert Louis Stevenson and Lloyd Osbourne, appeared in *The Scots Observer* on the same day that Henley wrote his letter. It declares: '*Cleopatra* is not likely to rival its author's earlier works in popularity. It is more ambitious, more serious, and more artistic. . . . The book is the highest of its author's achievements — the most artfully constructed, the most evenly sustained, the most passionate, impressive, and poetic. . . . It shows, moreover, how grotesquely unjust were the assertions that its author could only move his readers by the accumulation of extravagant horrors.'[50] The apparent finality of Henley's 'And so farewell' may well have been intentional for Haggard and Henley had little contact after this date. Perhaps this was due to Haggard's closeness to Andrew Lang, with whom Henley had quarrelled, declaring, 'I am completely sick of Andrew Lang and care not if I never hear from him again. I do not believe he wishes me well.'[51] Lang's last contribution to *The Scots Observer* had appeared on 4 May 1889.

Lang, however, continued to provide Haggard with considerable help and advice. After Haggard's return to London, Lang, for example, on 4 October wrote:

'Have you the proofs of *Beatrice* yet? I might as well read them over, if two pairs of peepers are better than one.' On 27 October Lang complained: 'They have sent me a lot of *Allan's Wife* I corrected before.'[52] From the large number of Lang's letters still extant it is apparent that during this period he was not only reading Haggard's proofs and manuscripts, but suggesting ideas and background reading.

Back in London, Haggard also made new friends during the autumn of 1889. One of these was John Gladwyn Jebb, an explorer of Mexico and managing director of the Santa Fé Copper Mines. He was introduced by a connection in the City who had interested Haggard in several Mexican investments through which he was subsequently to lose a considerable amount of money. Haggard quickly became very friendly with Jebb, who was a born teller of tales and had lived the adventurous life for which Haggard still pined. Later Haggard was to describe him as 'a brave and generous man who, as I firmly believe, never did, never even contemplated, a mean or doubtful act'.

Another teller of tales that Haggard met at this time was Rudyard Kipling who, in October 1889, arrived in London from India, aged twenty-three. Although almost unknown to the reading public, he was soon fêted by the major critics, including Lang who introduced him to the literary circle at the Savile. In an early letter Kipling complained: 'London is a vile place and Anstey and Haggard and Lang and Co. are pressing on me the wisdom of identifying myself with some set.'[53] On 18 November, John Addington Symonds wrote: 'Did I tell you of my making the acquaintance of Rudyard Kipling. . . . The Savile was all on the *qui vive* about him, when I lunched there once with Gosse. Rider Haggard appeared really aggrieved at a man with a double-barrelled name, older than his own, coming up. Literally.'[54] Yet, despite the obvious desire of London literary figures to fire a rivalry between the two men, they became good friends. Haggard invited Kipling to a dinner-party at 24 Redcliffe Square and, although Kipling arrived late because his hansom had collided with a van in Piccadilly, Haggard states in *The Days of My Life*: 'From that time forward we have always liked each other, perhaps because on many, though not on all, matters we find no point of difference.' Kipling too later recalled: 'I took to him at once, he being the stamp adored by children and trusted by men at sight; and he could tell tales, mainly about himself, that broke up the table.'[55]

Because of this fund of stories and his ability to make friends, Haggard was a welcome guest at dinner parties throughout London. Despite his sensibility to the attacks of critics, it was a time when he was anything but lonely. Among his many non-literary friends were Sir Redvers Buller (at whose house he met Lord Coleridge, the Chief Justice), Sir Henry Thompson (a distinguished doctor), Sir E. Wallis Budge (head of the Egyptian Department of the British Museum) and Sir William Richmond (the artist). His many dinner guests included Lord Goschen, Balfour, Lord Lytton, and Meredith Townsend.

Not only was his company sought, but he received letters of admiration from readers all over the world. On 30 October his brother William, who was First

Secretary at the British Embassy in Athens, wrote to him: 'It may interest you to hear that the Empress Frederick told me the other night that the last pleasure that her husband had on earth was reading your books, which he continued to do through his last days, and that he used to express the hope that he might live to make your acquaintance. . . . You will be glad to hear that the Prince of Wales and his family read *Cleopatra* on their way out here, and think it your best book.' On receiving this letter, Haggard decided both to visit William, leaving England on 13 December, and to dedicate *Eric Brighteyes* to H.I.M. Victoria, Empress Frederick of Germany. He soon heard from the Empress that she would be delighted to have the novel dedicated to her, and so on 3 December he sent her his draft dedications, adding: 'Should I be so fortunate as to win approval for [it], would it be too much to ask that one of the enclosed copies may be returned to me signed by your Majesty's hand, or that a *written* approval may be conveyed to me in some other way? I ask this in order to protect myself from any possible future charge of having presumed to write what I have written without full permission.' He also told her of his planned visit to Athens.

Yet, despite purchasing his tickets, hiring a Greek yacht, buying some hunting dogs and sending on ahead guns, stores and cartridges, Haggard did not make the trip. On Friday, 6 December, he was informed that his mother was seriously ill. In a letter to his brother Jack he chronicles the sad events of the next few days: 'I went down on the Friday night expecting to find her gone. She knew me then and spoke something about the children. On the Saturday morning she knew me also and laid her hand upon my head. That morning the doctor gave her but a few hours to live, yet she lived for two more days. She spoke for the last time on the Saturday night. (Ella thinks she once said Ella afterwards.) On that night we thought that she was dying, her breath turned icy cold and went down to nothing, but she opened her eyes and smiled very beautifully. My father read the prayer for the dying over her and then thanked her for her long life of love and duty as wife, mother and friend. To our surprise she said "Thankyou. Thankyou". On the Sunday morning she was again sensible and we bade her a last farewell. About midday, however, she sank into coma and I do not think she ever knew any more. About 8 on the Monday morning she opened her eyes and we knew that the last change was at hand. The breath grew ever fainter and at 20 minutes past 8 it ceased, the eyelids fluttered a while and all was done. There were present at her death — my father, Ella, Hocking, Miss Purnam and myself. Thus passed to her long home one of the best of women and mothers. We buried her on Thursday. She was carried on men's shoulders from the Hall to the Church — all the population followed and preceded her coffin.'[56]

Haggard was deeply upset by his mother's death. She was the first of his family to die and he never got over his deep, morose sense of loss. In his autobiography he states: 'Twenty-two years have passed since she left us, but I can say honestly that every one of those years has brought to me a deeper appreciation of her beautiful character. Indeed she seems to be much nearer to me now that she is dead than she was while she still lived. It is as though our intimacy and mutual understanding has grown in a way as real as it is mysterious. Someone says that the dead are never dead to us until they are forgotten, and if that be so, in my case my mother lives indeed. No night goes by that I do not think of her and pray that we may meet again to part no more. If our present positions were reversed, this would please me, could I know of it, and so I trust that this offering of a son's unalterable gratitude and affection may please her, for after all such things are the most fragrant flowers that we can lay upon the graves of our beloved. . . . I stood at her death-bed and received her last blessing. But of that long-drawn out and very sad scene, even after the lapse of two-and-twenty years, I cannot bear to write.'

At the time he seems not to have known how to react. He lashed out at William for leaving Athens, even though he was too late to attend the funeral. This unexpected return, Haggard claimed, meant that he would have to cancel his visit to Greece and would lose nearly a hundred pounds. In his letter to Jack he complains: 'I suppose the fact was that Will thought it a good chance of leave and now it can't be helped but I bet he will turn up presently and slate me for not going. I don't want to say anything against him — he may have good reason for what he has done, but I think he might have wired to ask what effect his contemplated change of plan would have upon my movements.'

And so Haggard stayed at home and worked on *Nada the Lily*, which he completed on 15 January 1890, after over six months' work. Distanced as he was from the years spent in Africa when night after night he had listened to the folk stories of the Zulu people and lived among some of the few white men to have studied Zulu history and traditions, Haggard in this book weaves his memories and recollections into a vivid and unique tribute to an African kingdom which, even when he wrote, had been overthrown and its people scattered. Some of the scenes are unforgettable, not least Galazi's description of the cave of wolves:

'Look now! There is a hole in the wall of the cave, where the firelight falls below the shadow of the roof, twice the height of a man from the floor. . . . There sat the bones of a man, and the black skin had withered on his bones, holding them together, and making him awful to see. His hands were open beside him, he leaned upon them, and in the right hand was a piece of hide from his moocha. It was half eaten, Umslopogaas; he had eaten it before he died. His eyes were also bound round with a band of leather, as though to hide something from their gaze, one foot was gone, one hung over the edge of the niche towards the floor, and beneath it on the floor, red with rust, lay the blade of a broken spear.

Now come hither Umslopogaas, place your hand upon the wall of the cave, just here; it is smooth, is it not? — smooth as the stones on which women grind their corn. "What made it so smooth?" you ask. I will tell you.

When I peered through the door of the cave I saw this: on the floor of the cave lay a she-wolf panting, as though she had galloped many a mile; she was great and fierce. Near to her was another wolf — he was a dog — old and black, bigger than any I have seen, a very father of wolves, and all his head and flanks were streaked with grey. But this wolf was on his feet. As I watched he drew back nearly to the mouth of the cave, then of a sudden he ran forward and bounded high into the air towards the withered foot of that which hung from the cleft of the rock. His pads struck upon the rock here where it is smooth, and there for a second he seemed to cling, while his great jaws closed with a clash but a spear's breadth beneath the dead man's foot. Then he fell back with a howl of rage, and drew slowly down the cave. Again he ran and leaped, again the great jaws closed, again he fell down howling. Then the she-wolf arose, and they sprang together, striving to pull him down who sat above. But it was all in vain; they could never come nearer than within a spear's breadth of the dead man's foot. And now, Umslopogaas, you know now why the rock is smooth and shines. From month to month and year to year the wolves had ravened there, seeking to devour the bones of him who sat above. Night upon night they had leaped thus against the wall of the cave, but never might their clashing jaws close upon his foot. One foot they had, indeed, but the other they could not come by.'

(From *Nada the Lily*)

This passage, with its familiar skeleton and severed foot, inspired Kipling to write the stories about Mowgli and the animals that became *The Jungle Book*, a debt he acknowledged in a letter to Haggard, dated 20 October, 1895: 'It was a chance sentence of yours in *Nada the Lily* that started me off on a track that ended in my writing a lot of wolf stories. You remember in your tale where the wolves leapt up at the foot of a man sitting on a rock? Somewhere on that page I got the notion.'[57]

But for Haggard *Nada the Lily* marked the end of an era. For seven years he had worked on one book after another, completing in that time fifteen novels, most of which were to be best-sellers widely read and widely loved throughout the world. Yet after *Nada the Lily* he did not start another book for sixteen months; in the next fourteen years he finished only nine novels; *Ayesha*, his sequel to *She* which he had already planned, was not written for fifteen years; his next Allan Quatermain story was not written until 1909, twenty years later; and none of the thirty-nine novels he was to write during the rest of his life would either delight or infuriate the critics. It is true that during the previous seven years Haggard had at times said that he would like to stop writing, but some deep, though ill-comprehended, need to write forced him to continue. It is true that in next few years his writing might well have been affected by other personal tragedies and new preoccupations. Yet it was when he had completed *Nada the Lily*, a few weeks after his mother's death, that Haggard lost the obsession to write that had all but become his *raison d'être*. He was at the height of his success and at an age when many writers have but just begun their careers.

This *volte-face* is a fact so significant that it would be remiss not to speculate upon its cause, which is, I think, not difficult to understand. In 'The Making of a Poem' Stephen Spender says, 'I suspect that every writer is secretly writing for *someone*, probably for a parent or teacher who did not believe in him in childhood.'[58] I am sure that this was true in Haggard's case and that the 'someone' was his mother to whom he dedicated *Cleopatra* because 'I thought it the best book I had written or was likely to write.' As soon as she died, he lost his deep desire to write. When she was alive, in trying to convince her of his worth, he often plumbed the depths of his soul, albeit unconsciously, to reveal the secrets of his passions and to portray his unsatisfying relationship with his wife. In the novels he wrote after his mother's death, he too often repeated familiar themes and revisited familiar places, for the 'white heat' and the originality had gone from his writing. When his mother died, so, to a large extent, did his creativity.

Nor was this the only effect of his mother's death. His interest in the dead that had obsessed him since his youth changed to the mawkish mourning so typical of his time. Driven by a desire to feel closer to her, he adopted much of her own simple religious faith with its emphasis on life after death. He began to read the Bible daily, later recording in his autobiography: 'I suppose that for the last fifteen or twenty years, except very occasionally through accident or a sense of unworthiness, scarcely a day has gone over my head on which I have not once (the last thing at night) and often more than once, read a portion of the Bible.' In his effort to rationalise the effects on him of his mother's death, Haggard also began to explore the idea of reincarnation, which provided a solution to his problem of wishing, either after death or in another life, to be reunited with both his mother (as a son) and with Lilith (as a lover):

Unless we have lived before, or the grotesque incongruities of life are to be explained in some way unknown to us, our present existence, to my mind, resembles . . . a great ball-room wherein a Puck-like Death acts as Master of Ceremonies. Here the highly born, the gifted and the successful are welcomed with shouts of praise, while the plain, the poorly dressed, the halt, are trodden underfoot; here partners, chosen at hazard, often enough seem to be dancing to a different time and step, till they are snatched asunder to meet no more; here one by one the revellers of all degrees are touched upon the shoulder by the Puck-like Death who calls the tune, and drop down, down into an impenetrable darkness, while others who knew them not are called to take their places.

But if we admit that every one of these has lived before and danced in other rooms, and will live again and dance in other rooms, then meaning informs the meaningless. Then those casual meetings and swift farewells, those loves and hatings, are not of chance; then those partners are *not* chosen at hazard after all.

(From *The Days of My Life*)

His acceptance of reincarnation brought with it, as an inescapable corollary, the belief that the nature of the next life was dependent upon one's performance in the present. Haggard from this time on, therefore, developed an acute awareness of his own past sins, both real and imaginary, and a feeling of anguished remorse that tortured his increasingly lonely, brooding life. And what were these sins? In a most important passage in his 'A Note on Religion' where he endeavours to show that the laws of Nature differ from the Law of God, Haggard reveals that his sins were sexual and hints that it was in Africa they were committed:

> If we go against the rules of the game as they are laid down for us by the creed we serve in that part of the world in which we have been born [*viz*. Great Britain], even when those rules seem not natural to us [*e.g.* when in Africa], we err. . . .
>
> Nature says to Everyman who is a man: 'See where She stands with longing arms and lips that murmur love. Hark to what She says who would be the mother of your child: "Seek! Seek for heaven hid in these dark eyes of mine and find all Earth's desire. Drink! Drink of the Mysteries from the cup of this rich heart of mine and learn what Life can be . . .'
>
> 'Touch not, taste not, handle not,' answers the cold stern Law. 'Pass on, she is not thine.'
>
> Often enough it is Nature that prevails and, having eaten of the apple that She, our Mother, gives us, we desire no other fruit. But always the end is the same: its sweetness turns to gravel in our mouth. Shame comes, sorrow comes; come death and separations. And, greater than all of these, remorse rises in the after years and stands over us at night, since, when our eyes are no longer clouded with the mists of passion, we see and bewail our wickedness.
>
> For sin has this quality. Like some bare, black peak in a plain of flowers it dominates all our landscape. However far we wander never can we escape the sight of it.
>
> (From *The Days of My Life*)

Perhaps it is not too fanciful to conclude that, because Haggard saw sin as being a 'bare, black peak', it was the black girl with whom he probably enjoyed his first sexual relationship who was the subject of the nightmares which disturbed even his waking days. It was the secret, haunting memory of her naked flesh that caused the remorse which encouraged him to believe that the tragedies he was to experience were a punishment not only for his sins but also for despoiling the purity of his love for Lilly. Those close to Haggard were to become well acquainted with his ever-present feeling of remorse, even if they were unaware of its cause. His nephew, Godfrey Haggard, comments: 'There is an undeniable note of sadness running through his Autobiography, not only for the ills of the world but also it would seem for some personal sorrow of his own. He speaks more than once of remorse. If he had reasons for remorse he would not be the kind of man to let himself forget it, though he would be the last to disclose what they were. It is only my guess, arrived at by putting one fact with another, that he attached to this feeling of contrition for something which had happened in the past, another non-rational belief (hinted at in his *Life* and easily to be gathered from his conversation) that he was dogged by evil luck — not directly evil to himself but to those he loved and whom he had befriended.'[59]

7

The Country Gentleman

Early in 1890 a member of Dr Johnson's Club called on John Murray and said, 'We had a most interesting discussion last night as to who were the greatest living masters of English prose — and it was finally decided that the following five stood pre-eminent: Froude, Ruskin, Newman, Matthew Arnold and Dean Church.'[1] A few days later Murray dined with Arnold and, after dinner, while smoking a cigar, he reported the conversation. Although pleased that his own name had been mentioned, Arnold said that he thought another should have been classed among them — Rider Haggard.

Most informed literary critics were inclined to believe that Haggard, despite his prodigiously successful career, had not written the masterpiece of which he was indubitably capable. Although his style was often flawed, he had by dint of unremitting toil begun to master the craft for which his formal education had left him woefully ill-prepared. His major weakness was his inability to understand that his strength lay in describing vast landscapes and chronicling the decline of civilisations. He was at his best in the lost kingdom of Kôr or the war camps of Chaka — worlds of his imagination; but he often felt the need in his fiction to inhabit the drawing-rooms of contemporary society — his real world from which he was using his writing to escape. To Haggard, a natural and experienced story-teller, one tale was as good as another and so, like the compulsive joke-teller, he lacked discrimination. Yet he won and retained a vast audience because the best of his stories have a touch of magic, that stuff of which his dreams were made. It was a world that the child in Haggard allowed him to believe in totally. When his mother died, it seems he lost that belief and writing fiction became a chore that was necessary only when money was required. In 1890, with an annual income from writing in excess of £10,000, Haggard did not need to undertake unnecessary chores.

Before the end of January, Haggard was delighted to receive the Empress Frederick's approval of his draft dedication, but by then he was engrossed in his one literary work of the year. As a tribute to his mother he was preparing for publication in a volume entitled *In Memoriam* her essay in verse 'Life and its Author'. On 5 February he wrote the introduction, in which he says: 'Of all women I have known she was certainly the most charming, and taken altogether she was the most brilliant. Beauty she did not possess to any remarkable degree, though the

139

gentle sweetness which characterized her face in youth, grew ever with her years, and may be said to have reached its most complete development upon her bed of death. . . . Her earnest religion had no bitterness in it; it was all charity, as her life was all love and self-sacrifice. Even to the end her thoughts were of others — of her husband, her children, her friends; even her desire to live on awhile sprang from a longing "to be of use" to those around her. But, when at length, after years of struggle, mortal sickness gained the victory, she faced death with that utter fearlessness which had characterised her through life; nor did her faith fail her.'[2]

Although he was not working on a book, Haggard, the most popular writer in the country, was still the object of critical abuse. In March *The Fortnightly Review* published 'King Plagiarism and His Court' by J. Runciman, who states that he wrote an article for the *Pall Mall Gazette* entitled 'How the Mail Steamer Went Down in Mid Atlantic' from which Haggard copied his ship collision in *Mr Meeson's Will*. Publicly Haggard ignored the article. He had learned that it was foolish to enter into a controversy with a journal or newspaper.

Meanwhile both publishers and most of the reading public enthusiastically received what Haggard had written. The serial of *Beatrice* was appearing (between January and May) in a variety of newspapers. On 7 March the serial rights of *The World's Desire* were purchased for £750 by *The New Review*, which published the first part in April. (Longmans had signed the contract for book publication on 12 December, 1889, giving the writers jointly a 20 per cent royalty.) On 25 March the first performance of the dramatisation of *Jess* was given at the Adelphi Theatre.[3] On 3 April *The Illustrated London News* purchased the serial rights of *Nada the Lily* for £1000. Immediately afterwards Lang was sent a typescript of the novel for correction and on 20 April he wrote: 'I read right through to Chaka's death. It is admirable, the epic of a dying people, but it wants relief. Massacre palls. . . . I have made a slight suggestion or so. I like *Eric* better, but this is perhaps more singular. How any white man can have such a natural gift of savagery, I don't know. The Wolves are astonishing.' A couple of days later, Lang wrote again: 'I've finished *Nada*. If all the reviewers in the world denied it, you can do the best sagas that have been done yet: except Njala perhaps. Poor Nada! I hope it will be done into Zulu.'

On 12 May, *Beatrice* was published in an edition of 10,000 copies and the following day Lang wrote thanking Haggard for a copy of the book: 'Many thanks for the book. You know exactly what I think of 'B.', but I like your *natural* novels better a long way than your modern ones at the best, which this probably is. Beatrice is all right when anything flares up, and all right when in the open air. . . . But, oh, how much I prefer Galazi and Skallagrim to these moderns!' Presumably because *Beatrice* was his first contemporary novel since *The Witch's Head*, Haggard also sent a copy of it to Cordy Jeaffreson who in his reply stated: 'It is a fine, stirring, effective story; but with all its power and dexterity it is not *the book* which will determine your eventual place in the annals of literature. You will write *that book* some ten years hence. . . . In a line, it is no small thing to have thrown off

Beatrice, but you will do something much greater when "you've come to forty year". The story strengthens my confidence in you, though it falls short of all I hoped for you. This is *not* damning with faint praise.' Haggard, somewhat peeved that his first literary mentor should be so unenthusiastic about *Beatrice*, sent Jeaffreson's letter to Lang, asking for his comments. Lang dutifully replied: 'I don't much agree with Jeaffreson. The book is a compromise, by its nature, and rather contains good things than is very good, to my taste, but it is only taste, not reason. Lord knows what you may write, or anybody read, in ten years. More than sufficient to the day is the evil thereof.'

About this time Charles Longman received the typescript of *Nada the Lily* (or *Nada the Lilly* as it was then called), which he read enthusiastically. On 14 May, he wrote: '*Nada* strikes me with wonder and awe. It is in some ways the greatest feat you have performed: I mean because you have constructed a story in which the *dramatis personae* are all savages and yet have kept the interest going throughout. There will of course be a terrible outcry about gore. I never read such a book. It is frightful, and the only justification for it is the fact that it is history, not imagination. Wherever it is possible I would tone down the effect rather than heighten it, so as to avoid the charge of wallowing or gloating as far as possible. The wolves and the wolf brethren are delightful; I wish you could have given us more of them. I was very glad to meet our old friend Umslopogaas as a boy. . . . Why do you spell Lily with two L's? It reminds me of Lilly and Skinner, the bootmakers.'

On 18 May, Mrs M. Loftie, the Egyptologist's wife and friend of the Haggards, in a letter about *Beatrice*, enclosed a suggested outline of another modern novel about a young woman: 'I have read *Beatrice* with great interest. . . . Did you ever think of taking as a heroine a young lady of birth in such a shop as Jago or Debenham or Freebody? I don't mean done in the Besant style, but from the little I know I fancy there is an amusing and unworked background for another Beatrice in one of those large shops. There is a lovely creature in Jago at present might inspire anyone and I believe a study of the life they live and their point of view from which they see life would at any rate make an excellent play. I send you a sketch I once made thinking I could work it up but I saw it was no use, it was deadly dull: but somehow I think the plot in other hands might be worked to advantage. I have no compunction in sending it to you to look at as half an hour will make for understanding what I mean and it is probably as useless to you as to me. Do not say anything about it please. I am ashamed of its vapidity. I only send it because the plot is not hackneyed.'[4] Four years later, Haggard was to use the idea of a shopgirl with a past in his novel *Joan Haste*.

At the time, however, Haggard had no interest in writing another book. He was completely involved in organising a revolutionary change in his way of life and that of his family. After his mother's death and his assumption of a more active religious life, he had become disillusioned with the social carousel of dinner-parties, club gatherings and literary junkets. He decided to give up the London house and, as his writing income was substantial, move permanently to Ditchingham where he anticipated being not just a landowner but a practising farmer. In this he was encouraged by recent developments, including the good harvests obtained for the previous five or six years, the establishment in 1889 of the Department of Agriculture with a Minister in charge, and recent reduction in rates and improvement grants awarded to farmers. More important, the tenancy of the Home Farm had been surrendered. Haggard relet twenty-six acres, but retained for his own use about a hundred and twenty acres of land in an appalling condition. 'The heart had been dragged out of it and very little put into it in return; for instance . . . the back lawn had been mown nine years in succession.' Ditchingham House too, having been occupied by tenants off and on for the previous ten years, was badly in need of renovation and redecoration. It was, therefore, advisable not to move to Ditchingham until the alterations had been done.

Haggard, however, decided upon a plan that would allow him to give up 24 Redcliffe Square and leave London while still postponing the family's move to Ditchingham. John Gladwyn Jebb, who with his wife had become a great friend of the Haggards, suggested that they should stay with him and his wife in Mexico where he had to return for a while to supervise his mining interests. Once there, Haggard could accompany him on his travels, inspecting the ruins of the Aztec civilisation and gathering material for a book on Montezuma. Jebb also told Haggard the story, as bizarre as any in Haggard's own romances, of how a certain Cuban called Don Anselmo had informed him of the secret hiding-place of Aztec treasure buried by Gautemoc, Montezuma's nephew. Haggard took little persuasion and soon he had worked out the detailed arrangements. The Jebbs would return to Mexico during the summer, which the Haggards would spend at Ditchingham initiating the alterations and generally preparing the house for their occupation. The Haggards would then return briefly to their house in London, the tenancy of which they would transfer at the end of the year to the Jebbs, who would take up residency there after returning from Mexico. At the beginning of January 1891, Haggard and his wife would sail for New York, from where they would travel by train to join the Jebbs in Mexico. After four or five months the two couples would together return to England, the Jebbs moving into 24 Redcliffe Square and the Haggards going to the refurbished Ditchingham House where they would be reunited with their children who meanwhile would have been staying with friends.

It seemed a perfect plan and on 3 June, soon after moving to Ditchingham, Haggard wrote to Aggie: 'This place is in the most beastly mess and I exist among the ruins — Louie being in Lowestoft. I think it will be nice when finished however.' On 24 June he wrote again to Aggie: 'We are very slowly getting straight here. The hall is done except the papering. That old oak I told you of has turned out the most beautiful stuff I ever saw. I did not know before how beautiful oak could be. It is brown as chocolate and striped and mottled in a wonderful way. Altogether the hall is a success. We went to see your mother on Sunday. She is fairly well, but I fear that hers is a solitary life.'

The summer passed with the Haggards busily putting their house and estate in order. For five months the members of the family were able to spend their days together because Haggard, almost for the first time since returning from Africa, had no writing commitments. Indeed the only article he wrote during 1890 was 'Golf for Duffers' about a sport in which his wife was particularly interested. It was, moreover, a warm sunny summer of idyllic days during which Haggard planned for his new life as a country gentleman. Sadly it was to be the last of the good summers for several years. In 1891 and 1892 it was extremely cold; in 1893 there was a drought; and in 1894 the harvest was exceptionally poor.

The Haggards planned to return to London on Thursday 30 October, but on the previous Sunday, while on their way to visit Aggie Barber's mother, they were informed that she had died. Stopping at a friend's house, Haggard wrote a letter to Aggie telling her the distressing news. An hour and a half later, having visited Glenwood where Mrs Barber had lived, he wrote a letter to Aggie's husband, his brother Jack: 'Louisa has seen Marjorie, but I have not. She is very mad with hysteria. . . . What is to become of Marjorie?'[5] Haggard was particularly concerned about Aggie's sister, Marjorie, because he had become very friendly with her, later recalling in his autobiography: 'She was a tall and pretty girl, very pleasant, very witty — I think one of the most amusing afternoons I ever had in my life I spent with her alone in the British Museum; it was our last meeting, I believe — and with all the eccentricity that so usually accompanies a touch of genius. At the time of her residence in Bungay she was under the sway of a Low Church mania, and used to appear dressed as a deaconess and with a large Bible pressed against her middle. Nor was she above laughing at herself when the ludicrous aspect of her get-up was pointed out to her.' After her mother's death she went to live with a lady doctor and her husband, eventually adopting their name.

Because of Mrs Barber's death and funeral, the Haggards delayed their return to London for a few days, but once they were there much work had to be done. Not only had preparations to be made for the trip to Mexico, but the contents of the Redcliffe Square house had to be packed. There was also much correspondence to be answered.

On 5 November, *The World's Desire* was published in an edition of 10,000 copies. Naturally the reviewers endeavoured to separate the contributions of Lang and Haggard. Most of them disliked the novel. Henley's *The National Observer* declared: 'Mr Lang we know and Mr Haggard we know: but of whom (or what?) is this "tortuous and ungodly" jumble of anarchy and culture? . . . This critic was moved to curse his literary gods and die at the thought of the most complete artistic suicide it has ever been his lot to chronicle.'[6] James Barrie in *The British Weekly* stated that 'the crowning misfortune of *The World's Desire* is that it is sometimes dull, a failing that we should not find in any book written by Mr Haggard or Mr Lang alone.'[7] Yet the reading public, perhaps encouraged by the controversy and a desire to solve a literary puzzle, liked the book and it sold well. Although somewhat irritated by much of the criticism, Haggard was too busy to be deeply perturbed. In a letter to Aggie on 26 November giving information about the planned visit to

Mexico, he writes uncomplainingly: 'I am sorry Jack found *The World's Desire* unreadable, but no doubt the archaic style is a little trying. Probably many will agree with him.'

A few days later Haggard, obviously delighted with the implied acceptance of his new role, relates in another letter to Aggie a brief anecdote: 'Last night at dinner party. Host: "Haggard, will you have some more wine?" Ancient member of the party on my left to whom I had been conversing about farming: "Pray, are you any relation to Rider Haggard?" "Yes. I am that person." "Indeed. Indeed. I thought he was an old man. Do you know I believed you were a farmer. You are modest, very modest. I thought you were a farmer." '[8]

Lang, however, was infuriated by the criticism of *The World's Desire*, especially the comments of Henley. Having simmered down, he wrote to Haggard on 17 December: 'I was an ass to vex myself about Henley: he seems to me to be possessed with a desire to insult everyone he knew in town: I can't imagine why, but he was more offensive when he was patronising. Also the laws of the game prevent me from having a shot at him, if ever there was an opportunity, and I think I could do it sweetly.'[9] Lang also wrote to tell Haggard about a letter he had received from Robert Louis Stevenson: 'He thinks much of it "too steep", bars Od [ysseus] killing so many enemies — exactly what Longinus says of Homer — and fears Meriamun is likely to play down Helen. He is kind enough to say "the style is all right".'

> 1.
> Awdawcious Odyshes,
> Your conduc' is vicious,
> Your tale is suspicious
>   An' queer.
> Ye ancient sea-roamer,
> Ye dour auld beach-comber,

Correspondence was, however, of little interest to Haggard. Disturbed as he was by the death of his mother and Mrs Barber, he became convinced, as the date of his departure approached, that he was himself doomed to die soon. So certain did he become that, although discussing his feeling with no one, he made careful preparations for his death, such as depositing all his important papers in a dispatch-box at Grindlay's Bank. He was, therefore, very distressed when the day came to say good-bye to his son Jock, who it had been arranged, was to stay with the Gosses. 'I bade him good-bye,' he later recalled, 'and tore myself away. I returned after some hours. A chance, I forget what, had prevented the servant, a tall dark woman whose name is lost to me, from starting with him to Delamere Crescent till later than was expected. He was still in my study — about to go. Once more I went through that agony of a separation which I knew to be the last. With a cheerful face I kissed him — I remember how he flung his arms about my neck — in a cheerful voice I blessed him and bade him farewell, promising to write. Then he went through the door and it was finished. I think I wept.'

Haggard and his wife sailed on the *Etruria* for New York, where they arrived on 10 January 1891. To his surprise Haggard was beseiged by reporters. *The New York Times* gave an account of his reception: 'In the parlor of the Victoria Hotel last night, from 7 to 7.30, a tall, lank, middle-aged man was fidgeting about in an alleged easy chair, tying his legs into bowknots and doing everything with his hands that the hands of a naturally awkward man ever did do when he was in a state of nervousness. . . . He was undergoing examination by eight or ten newspaper men. . . . "How did you enjoy your interview with the customs officer?" "How do you like New York?" "Where are you going when you leave here and what for?" "How old are you?" "What is your opinion about the elevated railroad?" "How do American reporters compare with the reporters in England?" These and scores of other questions were fired at the victim of newspaper enterprise. . . . Mr Haggard did not urge his torturers to remain after they showed their readiness to leave.'[10]

Having been lavishly entertained in New York, the Haggards travelled by train to New Orleans, where once again they were fêted as celebrities, before continuing their journey to the Jebbs' home in Mexico City.

Despite finding that Don Ariselmo had disappeared, Haggard and Jebb started to plan their treasure-hunt, intending to set off on Monday 9 February. The day before, as the two couples were getting ready for church, Mrs Jebb received a telegram. She called the Haggards into her bedroom:

'Something is wrong with one of your children,' she said brokenly.
'Which?' I asked, aware that this meant death, no less, and waited.
'Jock,' was the reply, and the dreadful telegram, our first intimation of his illness, was read. It said that he had 'passed away peacefully' some few hours before. There were no details or explanations.

Then in truth I descended into hell. Of the sufferings of the poor mother I will not speak. They belong to her alone.

I can see the room now. Jebb weeping by the unmade bed, the used basins — all, all. And in the midst of it myself — with a broken heart!

(From *The Days of My Life*)

Later that day, Haggard wrote to his father: 'We have within the last two hours received the awful news of the death of our most beloved son, and I have telegraphed you asking you to represent me at the funeral. As you will understand my dear wife and myself are utterly overwhelmed and can only say one thing — God's will be done. The boy has gone hence before sin and sorrow have touched him, leaving us to mourn his memory — to hope for reunion with him in God's own time. So it is — so it must be. With our feelings in this distant place, unable even to stand at his graveside — you and all your kin, will understand and sympathize. We were starting for Chiapas and Palenque in the morning, but shall not go now — still we may stop here awhile before undertaking the journey home — for, alas, we cannot arrive in time to be of any use. I have given directions that he should be buried near the Chancel door at Ditchingham — where I hope to lie at his side one day.'

The death of his only son seemed to prove to Haggard the veracity of his belief that those close to him were destined to suffer because of his own sins. That this was the tortuous conclusion of his disturbed mind his daughter confirms in *The Cloak That I Left*: 'The bitterness of his loss grew almost unbearable. Added to this there was undoubtedly the psychological obsession that his child's life had paid the price of the father's sin; that it was required in expiation of transgression, and being so required increased his guilt. That belief (to judge from chance remarks and pencilled passages in his well-worn Bible) he carried with him, an unhealed wound, until the day of his death.'[12] Haggard's mental state deteriorated rapidly. 'My nerves broke down entirely,' he later commented, 'and the rest of the Mexican visit, with its rough journeyings, is to me a kind of nightmare.'

Although it was clearly sensible to cancel the treasure hunt, Jebb, realising how disturbed his friend was, persuaded Haggard to accompany him on a journey to some Mexican mines. The two men rode for miles along winding tracks through the mountains to remote villages. At Queretaro, Haggard felt so ill that he became convinced that he was about to die, but a travelling American doctor who chanced to call assured him that he was suffering only from a severe nervous shock. Meanwhile Louie stayed behind in Mexico City with Mrs Jebb. She kept her intense grief to herself, for as her daughter records: 'She had an iron self-control, most unusual in a woman, a control so rigid that all her life those who were nearest to her seldom knew what her thoughts or feelings were. She said little, but spent hour after hour pacing up and down the wide flat roof, to the sad discomfort of her kind-hearted hostess.'[13]

Not only did Haggard's absence mean that both he and his wife were able in their disparate ways to brood upon their loss, but it ensured that they did not speak to each other about their feelings, allowing each to blame the other, at least in part, for their son's death. If one or other of them had stayed behind in England, they reasoned, Jock might still have been alive. And so the rift that had already developed in their relationship was deepened, and their lives came to assume an even more independent course. Never again were Haggard and his wife to make an overseas trip alone together.

While Haggard and Jebb travelled on through Chiapas, an area then rarely visited by Europeans, Louie and Mrs Jebb packed their mutual belongings and prepared to sail on a steamer to New York. The plan was that they would be joined by their husbands at Frontera, but unfortunately it misfired and the two women arrived in New York without them. Eventually after many adventures, including a narrow escape from brigands, Haggard and Jebb met up with their wives and together took a ship for Liverpool. Throughout the voyage, Haggard suffered from influenza. 'Needless to say,' he recalls in his autobiography, 'our homecoming was very sad. After, I think, only one night in London we came to Ditchingham, where I found my two little girls dressed in black and — a grave.'

In torment, Haggard listened to the distressing tale of Jock's fatal illness. While he was suffering from measles an unsuspected gastric ulcer perforated, peritonitis

146

resulted and within thirty-six hours the nine-year-old boy was dead. From then on, Haggard never spoke Jock's name, nor was anyone allowed to speak to him about the boy. All his toys, letters and books were locked in cupboards or stored in the attic. But Haggard's memories could not be so easily erased. Tormented by guilt he brooded on the past. He was especially upset by the sad irony that Allan Quatermain, which he had dedicated to Jock, prophetically began: 'I have just buried my boy, my poor handsome boy of whom I was so proud, and my heart is broken. It is very hard having only one son to lose him thus.' Haggard's overriding thought, however, was that his son's death had been his responsibility and on the cross over the grave he had carved 'I shall go to him'.

In the weeks that followed, Haggard's physical and mental condition did not improve. Long bouts of influenza caused digestive disturbances, violent headaches and acute depression. He found no solace in his family, friends or estate. Even the publication of *Eric Brighteyes* on 13 May can have but little interested him, although he did send a copy of the book to Rudyard Kipling, who replied: 'Very many thanks for Eric which the Club waiter man handed me only a day or two ago. Give me war anyway. . . . But it's all as strong as wire rope and 'twere impertinent of me to criticize.'[14]

The state of Haggard's health was such that it seems surprising that on 5 June he started writing his Mexican novel *Montezuma's Daughter*, on which he worked steadily for the next three months. It is a strange brooding story set in the sixteenth century that tells of the adventurous life of Thomas Wingfield, a native of Bungay, whose name (for there was a real Thomas Wingfield who died in 1593 and became one of the chief benefactors of Bungay) Haggard may well have seen on a tombstone while making one of his increasingly frequent walks round a churchyard. Subsequently Haggard denied having any foreknowledge of the name, claiming that it was an example of literary coincidence: 'Certainly I did think it strange when, subsequent to the writing of the book, I discovered from Mr Herbert Hartcup, the lawyer, who is a trustee of the Bungay Charities, that a man called Thomas Wingfield did live and die at that exact time.'

In *Montezuma's Daughter*, Wingfield falls in love with and becomes engaged to the daughter of the Ditchingham squire, who bitterly opposes the match; but shortly afterwards Wingfield's mother is killed by a Spaniard and so, seeking revenge, he travels to Spain where he amasses his fortune. Still in search of his mother's murderer he journeys to Mexico and in time is accepted as a god, marries Montezuma's daughter who bears him several children, and with Guatemoc hides the Aztec treasure so that it will not be plundered by the Spanish. Eventually, after the death of his wife and children, Wingfield returns to Ditchingham — some twenty years after he had left — where he meets and marries his childhood sweetheart.

Although, as his daughter states, the novel 'lacks a spirit which was there before', it reveals much about the nature of Haggard's thoughts as he was writing. The story is a nightmarish distortion of his own life, or rather his unbalanced recollection of it. Wingfield's mother is stabbed because her murderer, whom he had captured, escapes while he is proposing to the squire's daughter. He is, therefore, able to blame himself for his mother's death. Despite being in love with his betrothed, Wingfield (like Haggard) marries another. She is (perhaps like the woman with whom Haggard believed he had sullied the purity of his love) a beautiful native; but the marriage is cursed for all the children die, including the eldest, his favourite son:

> Ah! we think much of the sorrows of our youth, and should a sweetheart give us the go by we fill the world with moans and swear that it holds no comfort for us. But when we bend our heads before the shrouded shape of some lost child, then it is that for the first time we learn how terrible grief can be. Time, they tell us, will bring consolation, but it is false, for such sorrows time has no salves — I say it who am old — as they are so they shall be. There is no hope but faith, there is no comfort save in the truth that love which might have withered in the earth grows fastest in the tomb, to flower gloriously in heaven; that no love indeed can be perfect till God sanctifies and completes it with His seal of death.
>
> (From *Montezuma's Daughter*)

The treasure that Wingfield hides is the one that Haggard had set out for Mexico to find. Most interestingly, the woman whom Wingfield loves and to whom he returns after the end of his marriage and his many misfortunes is called Lily:

> Now I could see the woman's shape in the moonlight; it was tall and stately and clad in a white robe. Presently she lifted her head to watch the flitter of a bat and the moonlight lit upon her face. It was the face of Lily Bozard, my lost love, beautiful as of yore, though grown older and stamped with the seal of some great sorrow.
>
> (From *Montezuma's Daughter*)

The choice of name cannot have been a coincidence and it strongly suggests that in his confusion and torment Haggard returned for solace to his love for Lilly which, as was his wont with the things that mattered to him, he never for a moment forgot.

It appears that the writing of *Montezuma's Daughter*, which was completed on 3 September, was for Haggard a therapeutic act. Afterwards, although still isolated from his former close friends, he began to take an increasing active interest in his estate and home, which was so crammed with curios collected on his travels that it had begun to take on the appearance of a museum.

Haggard also took some interest in business arrangements connected with his writing and the world outside. On 13 September, he wrote his long, laudatory dedication of *Nada the Lily* to his former chief, Sir Theophilus Shepstone. A month later, obviously deciding to cut himself off from the critical bickering of the Savile, he asked Besant if he would put his name down for the Athenaeum. Besant replied: 'I am going to the club on Tuesday night. You ought to come in under Rule 3 most certainly and I don't think it is necessary for you to have your name down.'[15]

(Nothing came of it, however, and Haggard was not made a member of the Athenaeum until 1895.)

On 17 October, George Newnes Ltd. purchased for its magazine *Tit-Bits* the serial rights of an African romance to be called *The People of the Mist*. Although Haggard at the time had not yet worked out a plot, he received £1,000 for promising to deliver a story in not less than twenty parts by 1 November 1893. Two days later, on 19 October, *The Graphic* purchased the serial rights of *Montezuma's Daughter* for £800, to be paid in two instalments. It was agreed that the manuscript of not less than twenty parts of 100,000 words in total should be delivered on or before 1 May 1893, thus allowing Haggard plenty of time to revise the novel he had already written. He sent it immediately, as was his custom, to Andrew Lang, who on 6 December wrote to say the novel contained 'too much gore', adding that 'the murder of the children may stodge the reader'. Haggard never again sent his manuscripts to Lang for correction and the two men, now with different attitudes and objectives, began to drift apart.

No doubt prompted by Haggard's withdrawal from the London literary scene and his absence from the gossip columns of popular newspapers, *The Strand* sent Harry How to Ditchingham in December to collect information on Haggard for one of its series of 'Illustrated Interviews'. (It was published in January 1892.) How reported: 'There is positively little about Mr Haggard — whom, perhaps, one might describe as a country gentleman by profession and a novelist by accident — suggestive of the literary man. Literature! We talked of gardening and flowers over the dinner table; learnt how he had brought many of the ferns in his fernhouse 3,000 miles — carrying them on mules overland and in canoes down the rivers — from tropical Mexico.' How also noted that Haggard had ceased to read a review of any of his books 'unless it chances to appear in some paper which he takes in, because he says that, if the notice be favourable, it is apt to give an author too good an idea of himself; and, if the reverse, to worry and discourage him, and to disgust him with his work. Moreover, he is of opinion that the writer of a book knows a great deal more of its strong and weak points than any reviewer, however impartial, which all reviewers are not.'

Despite the considerable interest aroused by the appearance of *Nada the Lily* as a serial in *The Illustrated London News* (the first part appearing on 2 January 1892), Haggard had no wish to start another novel, and did not do so throughout 1892. Indeed at about this time he first had what was to become the recurring nightmare he describes in his autobiography:

Who does not know that order of dream wherein we seem to move among the dead and in their company, with eager yet trembling feet, to try the cold waters of the stream of Death?

Well, through the ivory gates of such a dream as this at times I seem to see my spiritual heritage spread large before me in a world of pictured silence. . . . I see a certain chamber, low and large, which overlooks the dreaming landscape . . .

standing in the recess doorway of this chamber, I see in its far corner, seated at a desk above the cupboard terrace, myself younger than I am now, wearing some sort of white garments and bending over the desk at work, with papers spread before me. At the sight a kind of terror seizes me lest this fair place should be but a scented purgatory, where, in payment for my sins, I am doomed to write fiction for ever and a day.

(From *The Days of my Life*)

He obviously had, however, intentions of restarting his writing career, for he continued to sell the rights of books that had not even been commenced. On 8 April, the serial rights of another Mexican novel (which he was to call *Heart of the World*) were sold to *Pearson's Weekly* for £1,000. It was to consist of twenty-six parts, each of 4,000 words. The delivery date was August Bank holiday, 1894. On 7 May, Tillotson's purchased the American serial rights of *Montezuma's Daughter* and *The People of the Mist* for £500 each. In his letter of acceptance to Watt, Haggard wrote: 'I think that we must accept the offer of the Tillotsons. My market has fallen a bit as was to be expected, also there are great difficulties about these American serial rights. At least the Tillotsons do not bother us about book rights which I much prefer should remain in the hands of the Longmans.'[16] He had, however, little cause for complaint, because he had earned £2,500 for the serial rights of two novels still to be written.

There is an obvious reason for Haggard's willingness to commit himself to future writing projects and his growing sense of wellbeing. Louie, in an effort to heal the rift between them and ease the mental torment of her husband, had revoked her decision not to have more children. Early in May, Haggard learned, to his immense delight, that she was pregnant. The possibility of another son gave his life new purpose. Having inherited his father's dynastic sense, he toiled to put in order his estate, his future son's inheritance.

Nada the Lily was published as a book on 9 May. Haggard's literary friends received it with warm praise. Gosse on 11 May wrote: 'Thank you for your kindness in sending me *Nada the Lily* which I value greatly. I think that in spite of the gloom of this story, and a sort of monotony inseparable from its nature, this will be regarded as one of the very best of your works. As a sustained piece of creation, of invention of a kind wholly outside our common knowledge, I am not sure that it is not your most extraordinary effort yet.'[17]

On 19 May Besant sent his thanks:' *Nada the Lily* is splendid — the best thing you have done since *She*. I read it all yesterday.'[18] Haggard also received from Lang a letter sent by Stevenson: 'If you see Haggard, tell him we have a great affection for his brother. Our home rejoices when we see him coming; and that Chaka mourning for his mother is great.' (Much to the distress of the whole Haggard family, Bazett, Haggard's elder brother, had deserted his wife and family. He obtained the post of British Land Commissioner in Samoa where he became a close friend of the Stevensons. Fanny, Stevenson's wife, described him as being 'gaily indiscreet'.)

Not all the critics thought as highly of the book as Haggard's friends. Many reviews expressed disgust at the cruelty and slaughter. Typical of these was *The Pall Mall Budget* which declared: 'What an odd dual existence must be that of Mr H. Ryder Haggard! In real life, no doubt, an inoffensive, estimable, God-fearing citizen — one of those "gentlemen and christians" whom he delights to describe — who would not hurt a fly save in the way of "sport", he is in imagination a very Attila or Tamburlaine, rejoicing in cruelty, revelling in carnage. During the composition of such a book as this *Nada the Lily* his mind must be a very shambles. He must wipe out an "impi" or two every morning before breakfast, devise new methods of massacre as he chips his egg, wade through gore to luncheon, and devote his hours of relaxation to the planning of single combats, hairs' breadth 'scapes, and murders by retail. . . . Take it all in all, *Nada the Lily* is probably the most sanguinary work of its size in existence. It is drenched, sodden, dripping with blood.'[19] As Haggard was not reading his reviews, he was able to ignore such comments. He was, however, delighted to receive Shepstone's acknowledgement of *Nada the Lily*: 'I need not say how gratifying to me that gift was; nor how deeply touching to me the kind words of the Dedication were. Indeed you give far more credit than I am entitled to. Your kindly expressions, however, vividly brought to mind a whole chapter of the pleasant past between us, the exact counterpart of which will, I suppose, never occur to any other two.'

As the exceptionally cold summer of 1892 passed, Haggard continued to adapt to his chosen life as a country gentleman. He was a regular church attender, often reading the lesson, though unable to pronounce some letters, causing him to say 'Vewy Forough Wogue', rather than 'Very Thorough Rogue'. Like his father, he became a Justice of the Peace, and spent many mornings with other Norfolk landowners sitting on the Magistrates' Bench at Loddon, passing judgement on cases of poaching, theft, and drunkenness.

Early in September, he was distressed to learn that a chill his father had caught, while waiting for the poll to be declared at an election, had turned to jaundice. On 7 September, he wrote to Aggie in Trieste:' I have been to see my father and am going again with Louie on Saturday. His appearance shocked me very much — brilliant yellow and much shrunken. His mind, however, is quite clear but at the best it is a complete breakup.'[20] In time William Haggard seemed to recover and again began to visit his friends and relatives, thus suppressing Haggard's natural inclination to anticipate his father's death.

Having received the typescript of *Montezuma's Daughter*, Haggard on 5 October wrote the book's dedication to Gladwyn Jebb: 'Strange as were the adventures and escapes of Thomas Wingfield, once of this parish, whereof these pages tell, your own can almost equal them in these latter days, and, since a fellow feeling makes us kind, you at least they may may move to a sight of sympathy. Among many a distant land you know that in which he loved and fought, following vengeance and his fate, and by your side, I saw its relics and its peoples, its volcanoes and its valleys. You know even where lies the treasure which, three centuries and more ago, he helped to bury, the countless treasure that an evil fortune held us back from seeking.' A few days later, on 12 October, the contract for the book's publication was signed with Longmans who agreed to pay a 20 per cent royalty.

The next few weeks for Haggard were ones of waiting and ever-growing expectations for the arrival of his son. At last, on 9 December 1892, exactly three years after the death of Haggard's mother, the child was born. Haggard was waiting in his study when the doctor came with the news that Louie had given birth to a healthy baby girl. The next day, Haggard wrote to Aggie: 'I dare say that you will have seen in the *Times* that the event has come off resulting in a girl, as a boy happened to be wanted. However she is a dear little baby and seems to be healthy and well developed which is a great thing, so it would be ungrateful to grumble. Indeed I am so fond of children that I would much rather have a girl than nothing at all. . . . Louie had what she calls a bad time but the doctor said few people can have a baby in five minutes all told. She felt it before dinner, began to be really ill about nine and the child was born at 20 to 1. They are both going on well.'[21] The daughter was called Lilias Rider Haggard.

Despite his disappointment that he did not have the son he had expected, the birth of his third daughter did much to restore his spirits, so much so that when a few days later he received by post a parcel containing the ashes of Dom D. de Castro which the sender thought would make a good foundation for a romance, Haggard saw the incident not as an ill omen but as a mildly humorous proof that cremation might have unfortunate repercussions. He wrote about the subject to *The Times* on 16 December — the first letter he had sent to the newspaper for over two years. It concludes: 'That our ashes or those of our friends may possibly be posted to the romance-writers of future generations in the hope of furnishing them with "copy" is a thought which gives no comfort even to an advocate of more sanitary methods of disposing of the dead.'[22]

A more significant sign of Haggard's improving spirits was his decision to start writing again. As he felt he could no longer endure continually stooping over a desk, he hired as a secretary Ida Hector, the eldest daughter of the Irish novelist Mrs Annie Hector who wrote under the pseudonym Mrs Alexander. She became, as earlier Aggie Barber had, a semi-permanent member of the Haggard household. In his autobiography, Haggard describes her as 'a very faithful friend and companion, to whose sound sense and literary judgment I am much indebted'. Miss Hector, as she was known to the family, was to work for Haggard throughout the rest of his life. After her arrival, Haggard never wrote another book by hand. Instead, as he paced up and down his study or sat slumped, smoking a pipe, in a comfortable armchair, he dictated to her his books, letters, and in later years many of his diary entries. 'Some people,' he afterwards declared, 'can dictate, and others cannot. Personally I have always found the method easy, provided the dictatee, if I may coin a word, is patient and does not go too fast. I imagine, for instance, that it would be impossible to dictate a novel to a shorthand-writer. Also, if the person who took down the words irritated one in any way, it would be still more impossible. Provided circumstances are congenial, however, the plan has merits, since to many the mere physical labour of writing clogs the mind.' Soon after Miss Hector had been engaged, Haggard purchased for her a typewriter with which, after receiving instruction, she was also able to produce the corrected typescript of much of Haggard's work. On occasions, however, Haggard also used the services of London-based typists.

The first piece of work Haggard produced in 1893 with Miss Hector's help seems to have been a long article, 'My First Book—*Dawn*' which had been commissioned by *The Idler* on 22 June 1892. (It appeared, the eleventh in a series, in April and Haggard received a payment of £30.) Immediately afterwards he started dictating *The People of the Mist*, his first novel for nearly eighteen months. He worked on it for a couple of hours both before and after dinner.

On 15 February, before the book was complete, Haggard's father wrote to say that he had again been taken ill. 'I have the jaundice as strong as before but I don't think I am so ill as before but of course I am a perfect invalid. . . . I must make arrangements to have somebody to come to see me for though I don't want to magnify things I must confess I don't think it would be desirable I should be here alone. . . . I thought of you, my dear Rider, and your wife 2 days ago — on which day 2 years ago I had to represent you at that sad event at Ditchingham Church.'[23]

When Haggard went to Bradenham at the end of February it was clear to him that his father might not have long to live. As he wandered alone through the surrounding countryside he knew and loved so well, Haggard was aware that his father's unsatisfactory financial position made it very possible that William, the eldest son, might have no alternative when he inherited Bradenham but to break the entail and sell the estate. The idea certainly crossed Haggard's mind that, if this should happen, he would like to purchase his family's home; but as Louie had made it clear that she would not have any more children he knew he would never have a son to whom he could leave it. His wife also disliked Bradenham, finding it lonely, and had no wish to leave her beloved Ditchingham. There was little point, therefore, in seriously contemplating the purchase of the Haggard estate. Depressed by the possibility that he was witnessing the end of an era, Haggard returned home after a few days. He was never again to see his father alive.

Shortly afterwards Haggard received the fragment of a letter, dated 2 March, written by Gladwyn Jebb, who had also been seriously ill for some time: 'I *may* make another rally but I confess my own working is the other way — as apart from the regular illness I am getting day by day awfully weak — so much so that I can't dress without help and can hardly keep out of bed longer than from 11 to 4 or something of that kind — '[24] Just over a fortnight later Jebb died at 24 Redcliffe Square, the Haggards' old home. On 22 March, Haggard wrote a note to be added to his dedication of *Montezuma's Daughter* to Jebb: 'Worn out prematurely by a life of hardship and extraordinary adventure, Mr Jebb passed away on March 18, 1893, taking with him the respect and affection of all who had the honour of his friendship. The author has learned with pleasure that the reading of this tale in proof and the fact of its dedication to himself afforded him some amusement and satisfaction in the intervals of his sufferings.' The incident naturally saddened Haggard, who saw it as ironic that Jebb, like his son, should die soon after a novel had been dedicated to him.

Haggard and his wife went up to stay with Mrs Jebb in London, expecting to be there for a month but, on 21 April, Haggard was informed — too late for him to reach Bradenham that day — that his father was dying. In the evening William Haggard told Hocking, the household maid, to give Rider his gold watch and chain. Just before he died, he said, 'God is everywhere. He is in this room, is He not?' The next day Haggard arrived and noted that: 'He looked fine and peaceful in death.' On 5 May, Haggard wrote to Jack about their father's death: 'He went very quickly at the last from internal haemorrhage but his mind remained clear till he sank into insensibility ten minutes before the end. The doctor stupidly enough neglected to warn us that the end was at hand with the result that no one was in the house except Aunt Fowler, Nitie* and the nurse whom we had sent from London that very day. He died at 9.40. . . . Will, Arthur and I are executors under a holograph will executed a few days before his death by which he leaves everything to William. The affairs are confused and I am doubtful if his personal estate is solvent, if it is not William will have to buy what he wants. . . . The worst of the business is the state of the trust affairs. The larger part, indeed nearly all my mother's fortune has been invested in land bought at an enormous price — as high as £60 an acre on which the loss will be at least 50% (I should say).[25]' On 23 June yet another person close to Haggard died. This was Sir Theophilus Shepstone, his old chief, to whom *Nada the Lily* had been dedicated.

On 26 June, *The Pall Mall Magazine* purchased for £1,500 the serial rights of a novel, at first called *The Way of the Transgressor*, which Haggard planned to write, based upon the idea of a shop-girl with a past that had been submitted to him nearly four years earlier by Mrs Loftie. When the offer was first made, Haggard asked Watt to urge Sir Douglas Straight, the co-editor, to increase the amount to £1,650, but this was rejected.

About this time, Haggard completed *The People of the Mist*, a long rambling tale, palely re-echoing his earlier successes and involving, as *Colonel Quaritch, V.C.* had done, the fortuitous rescue of a long-owned family estate. After the disgrace and suicide of Sir Thomas Outram, his estate is sold and his two sons, Leonard and Thomas, vow to recover it. Leonard, the younger son, is predictably semi-officially engaged to the beautiful Jane Beach who, after the brothers have gone to Africa, is pressurised by her family into marrying a rich man, the new owner of Outram Hall. When Tom dies, Leonard, searching for his fortune, finds Juanna Rodd (the daughter of an Englishman) who has been captured by the People of the Mist, a tribe in south-east Africa. To rescue her, Leonard goes through a form of marriage with a reluctant Juanna, who later, however, falls in love with him. After many

*William Haggard's second wife, Emily Hancox, whom he married in Brazil in 1886.

154

adventures they return to England where they discover that, after the death of both her husband and child, Jane — Leonard's never-to-be-forgotten-love — had also died, leaving Outram Hall and her considerable fortune to Leonard. Her letter of explanation concludes:

> Why is it that an affection like ours, which has never borne fruit even, should in the end prove stronger than any other earthly tie? Heaven knows, and Heaven alone, how passionately I loved and love my dead child; and yet, now that my own hour is at hand, it is of *you* that I think the most, you who are neither child nor husband. I suppose that I shall understand ere long, but, O Leonard, Leonard, Leonard, if, as I believe, my nature is immortal, I swear that such love as mine for you, however much it be dishonoured and betrayed, is still the most immortal part of it!
>
> (From *The People of the Mist*)

Perhaps the idea of Leonard's good fortune was prompted by Haggard's knowledge that his love, Lilly, lived in considerable opulence. Certainly the novel ends with successes for Leonard Outram that Haggard would have wished for himself:

> Ten years or so have gone by and Sir Leonard, now a member of Parliament and the Lord-Lieutenant of his county, comes out of church on the first Sunday in May accompanied by his wife, the stateliest matron in the country-side, and some three or four children, boys and girls together, as healthy as they are handsome.
>
> (From *The People of the Mist*)

During the summer, when Haggard was supervising the continuous improvements to his farm, he received two privately published volumes from Samoa. The first entitled *An Object of Pity: or, The Man Haggard* was compiled by Stevenson and some of his friends. The second, written by Bazett Haggard, was *Objects of Pity; or, Self and Company*. An accompanying letter from Stevenson stated: 'I send you herewith a couple of small (and, so to speak, indecent) volumes in which your brother and I have been indulging in the juvenile sport of shying bricks at each other. *Honi soit qui mal y pense*, say I.' Both books are full of now incomprehensible jests and gibes. Haggard himself said: 'I have studied them with zeal but am unable to make head or tail of them. Perhaps this is because I do not possess the key to the joke or understand the local allusions.' (When Stevenson died the following year, Bazett returned to England, broken in health and spirit.)

Prompted by Shepstone's death and the growing public interest in the area of Africa that was to become Rhodesia, Haggard wrote, in the autumn of 1893, several letters and articles on various aspects of the subject. For Andrew Lang's *The True Story Book*, published on 4 October, he wrote 'The Tale of Isandhlwana and Rorke's Drift'. Early in October he was interviewed by *The East Anglian Daily Press* on the causes of the Matabele War then raging. Two letters about Lobengula, the Chief of the Matabele, appeared in *The Times* on 12 and 19 October. An article 'The Matabele' was published in *The Pall Mall Gazette* on 23 October. Haggard's knowledge of the area provoked much interest and he was contacted by many public figures interested in African affairs. He was also asked to stand as the Conservative candidate for King's Lynn at the next General Election. Reluctantly he declined, knowing how difficult and expensive it would be for him to travel backwards and forwards between his home and the borough. There was also a strong possibility that he would be selected to contest his home constituency.

Refreshed by his renewed contact with public affairs, Haggard in November began work on the other novel he was contracted to write — the Mexican tale called *Heart of the World*, for which he had already prepared, as he was to do for almost all the other novels he was to write, a detailed plot of his story. About this time, in an interview he gave to Fred Dolman for *The Young Man*, Haggard spoke about his new method of writing: 'Most of my work is done in the winter, in the afternoon and evening. In the summer I like to enjoy the country, and every morning the farm claims my attention. Each of my recent books has occupied me for about six months. When I am at work on a book, I generally write three or four thousand words a day. . . . When once I have started on a new book, I am in a state of unrest until it is finished.'

Dolman also gives this interesting glimpse of life at Ditchingham House: 'Every morning before breakfast the whole household assembles in the hall for family prayers. Mrs Haggard and her two little girls, the half-dozen servants and any visitors who may be staying in the house, take their seats in the high-backed chairs, while Mr Haggard reads a chapter from the old family Bible which always stands on a large table, and afterwards offers a short prayer.'[26]

On 13 November, shortly after he had started dictating his new Mexican story to Miss Hector, *Montezuma's Daughter*, which had been running serially in *The Graphic* from 1 July, was published. A little later, on 23 December, the serialisation of *People of the Mist* began in *Tit-Bits Weekly*. It was not long before both books, which received little critical acclaim, caused some controversy.

James Britten, the Secretary of the Catholic Truth Society, had taken exception to an episode in *Montezuma's Daughter* that appeared in *The Graphic* on 29 July. In describing the walling up of a nun as a punishment for having had a baby, Haggard added a footnote:

Lest such cruelty should seem impossible and unprecedented, the writer may mention that in the museum of the city of Mexico he has seen the desiccated body of a young woman which was found immured in the walls of a religious building. With it is the body of an infant. Although the exact cause of her execution remains a matter of conjecture, there can be no doubt as to the manner of her death, for, in addition to other evidences, the marks of the rope with which her limbs were bound in life are still distinctly visible. Such in those days were the mercies of religion!

(From *Montezuma's Daughter*)

Britten asked for an explanation, also sending a pamphlet on 'The Immuring of

Nuns' that his society had published. In reply, Haggard sent a list of similar cases about which he had read, but he conceded that the immuring of nuns was a rarer occurrence than he had at first supposed. The matter seemed to have been dropped, but when the book was published including the offending footnote Britten, on 2 January 1894, wrote again: 'I observe with some surprise, and still more regret, that your reprint of *Montezuma's Daughter* contains unaltered the offensive and calumnious passages concerning convents, to which I called your attention some months since. I am writing to inform you that an article on 'Mr Rider Haggard and the Immuring of Nuns' appears in the *Month* for January, which will be immediately reprinted by our society in pamphlet form for general distribution.'

The following day Haggard acknowledged the letter, adding the postscript: 'I presume that you have printed my letter of the 8 August in your article. As you have carried our controversy into print I reserve to myself the liberty to do so.'[27] The sixteen-page article in the *Month* endeavoured to show that all the cases cited by Haggard had not taken place, concluding that there was no evidence to suppose that a nun had ever been walled up alive in a convent. On 17 January 1894, a long letter from Haggard on the subject, with copies of the correspondence between Britten and himself, was published in *The Pall Mall Gazette*. Haggard's letter concludes: 'I wonder if it has occurred to the members of the Catholic Truth Society that the raising of so much dust because of the introduction into a romance of an instance of cruelty supposed to have been perpetrated by priests more than three hundred years ago is nothing short of ridiculous? It is fortunately impossible to imagine any society representative of the Anglican branch of the Christian Church opening its heavy guns upon a novelist who wrote in an adverse spirit, say, of the persecution of the Jesuits in the eighteenth century, or the plundering of the religious houses by Henry VIII.' Further letters on the subject were published in *The Pall Mall Gazette* during the next couple of months and eventually Haggard announced that he was withdrawing the footnote from subsequent editions of the book.

No doubt because he was concerned about the sensation caused by *Montezuma's Daughter*, C.A. Pearson wrote to Haggard not only asking for more information about *Heart of the World*, but requesting that no material offensive to the readers should be included. On 17 February, Haggard replied: 'The actual date of the story *Heart of the World* which I am writing for you, is placed thirty or forty years ago. The tale, however, is of somewhat antique cast as it is told by an old Indian gentleman & its subject matter deals with his adventures & those of a white companion in the course of a visit to the fabled Golden City of the Indians, that the Spaniards were always searching for & could never find. The book ought to have been finished before now, but when it was nearly done I discovered what I had forgotten, that it was to be written in twenty-six instalments, & therefore am obliged to re-write it. . . . I have been careful in accordance with your request to avoid anything which could possibly give offence to the most susceptible of readers, not altogether an easy task, for strange people have strange manners.'[28]

Also on 17 February, an amusing letter appeared in *Tit-Bits* drawing the editor's attention to a mistake in the episode appearing that week of *The People of the Mist*. Haggard, having stated that the moon had set, describes the moon a few paragraphs later as being full. The letter, headed 'A Moan from the Moon', begins: 'I may be a cold, burnt-out old satellite, but I have my feelings all the same. Also, I have always acted as a well-conducted member of the Solar family, and have ever "pursued the even tenor of my way".'

Haggard, in his good-natured reply, states: 'How it came about that the Queen of the Night was made to misbehave herself so strangely in the pages of *The People of the Mist* I know not: but I incline to attribute her alleged conduct to the evil doings of the printers . . .'[29] (When the first edition of the book appeared, the reference to the full moon had been deleted. Haggard also made another change. Presumably because of the controversy concerning the walling-up alive of the nun in *Montezuma's Daughter*, he adds to a passage in which a priest gives his views on the dissolution of a marriage the footnote: 'The Editor does not hold himself responsible for Father Francisco's views on ecclesiastical marriage law.'

Towards the end of February, Haggard completed *Heart of the World*. This no doubt pleased him, for the knowledge of Africa he had revealed in his letters and articles had brought him new contacts and tempting offers. One of his new acquaintances was William Arthur Wills, an able and wealthy financier with considerable African interests, including part-ownership with Cameron Corlett Cannell of *The African Review*, in which a letter by Haggard on the possibility of South Africa declaring itself independent appeared on 3 February. Wills proposed to Haggard that he should assume the management of the literary section of *The African Review*, contributing regular articles, and that together they should exercise joint editorial control of the paper. In return Haggard would be given five hundred fully paid one-pound shares in the holding company Wills and Cannell Ltd. of which he would become a director at the annual salary of three hundred pounds. Much to the annoyance of his family, Haggard accepted the offer.

And so, some time in March, Haggard moved up to London and began his duties in a palatial City office that was at the centre of the African speculation boom. His articles and book reviews soon began appearing in *The African Review*. He was appointed the honorary president of the Anglo–African Writers' Club, which he described as 'a pleasant and useful dining society'. At the opening dinner on 23 April he was the guest of honour. On 26 April he was the guest speaker at the Zululand Mission Congress held at Church House, Westminster, where he made a speech explaining some merits of polygamy. Obviously relishing his new-found position as an acknowledged expert on affairs of great public interest, Haggard was fêted by influential people. He met Cecil Rhodes several times, on one occasion having breakfast with him at the Burlington Hotel. To his delight, many of those he met expressed the view that he should enter the House of Commons where he could represent African affairs. The idea fired him with enthusiasm, and so that he could finance the venture he decided to enter into a full partnership with Wills in his African investments. At home, according to his daughter, 'an anxious circle of family and friends watched his city career with awe and apprehension'. His brother Will wrote strongly advising him against entering into the partnership: 'You have said yourself, when Alfred suggested it,[30] that to start such a scheme without any chance of success was impossible — if this is not correct are you sure that Wills is the man to make the impossible possible? Think what his training has been in S. Africa. I would not hand myself over body and soul to a man of whom you know nothing, save that he is a more or less successful colonial journalistic adventurer, with your ignorance of business and distaste for business detail. You will have to consider also that if you give up writing novels others will spring up and take your place, and if your venture is a failure you might have to return to book-writing at a great disadvantage.'[31]

Although he did enter into a partnership with Wills, Haggard was unable, at least immediately, to give up writing fiction. Indeed, almost as soon as he arrived in London he began *The Way of the Transgressor*. When shortly afterwards the title of the forthcoming serial in *The Pall Mall Magazine* was announced, Haggard received several letters pointing out that a recent novel by Mrs E. Rentoul Esler had the almost identical title *The Way of Transgressors*. Haggard, therefore, decided to rename his story *Joan Haste*. Early in the summer of 1894 Haggard finished dictating the novel, which, like *Beatrice*, was an account of problems brought about by the indissolubility of marriage.

During the next few months, Haggard concentrated on his business affairs. Large sums of money were both made and lost, but it was not an enjoyable time for him. Later he recalled: 'It was all much too speculative and nerve-racking for me, while the burden of those companies weighed upon my mind heavily.' Suddenly Wills, a bachelor with a love of adventure, announced that he was going to Africa to fight in the Matabele War and might be away for a year or so, during which time Haggard would be left to conduct alone their intricate investment business. This was too much for Haggard. He asked Wills to dissolve the deed of partnership to which he was bound. Fortunately for Haggard, his partner agreed and signed a dissolution.

Somewhat distressed, but much to the relief of his family, Haggard — complete with his new-grown beard — returned to Ditchingham in the late autumn of 1894. He wrote his own epitaph on the less than successful incursion into commerce: 'My labours endured but for nine months — after which time I was delivered.' During his stay in London he had, however, made new friends and contacts which had made him even more determined to pursue a political career. Interestingly, *Joan Haste* (which began to appear, as a serial, in September) ends with the words of Henry's sister, whose husband also had political ambitions:

'And now, with your permission, Henry, I will order the carriage. I suppose that there will be policemen and reporters here presently, and you can understand

that just at this moment, with the elections coming on, Edward and I do not wish
to be mixed up in a most painful scandal.'

(From *Joan Haste*)

It was perhaps because he likewise feared any controversy which might damage his
own political prospects that Haggard reacted so strongly when he received two
letters from women claiming that men they knew had made advances to young
women after reading *Beatrice*. He asked Longman to suppress the novel, but was
informed that it was impossible. Longman, however, undertook to investigate the
stories. On 28 November, he wrote to Haggard: 'I will not write fully yet on the
subject, but I may say that the idea that the character of Beatrice could lead anyone
into vice is preposterous. Still less is the example of Bingham likely to throw an
unnatural glamour over seduction: in the first place, both he and Beatrice were
most unmercifully punished. Do not let this matter worry you. I assure you there is
nothing you need regret.' (Longman's confidence in Haggard's work was expressed in a practical way the next day when he signed the contracts to publish as
books *Joan Haste* and *Heart of the World*, agreeing to pay a royalty of 25 per cent in
the United Kingdom and 15 per cent in the United States.) Haggard was not,
however, reassured. He wrote a new preface for *Beatrice*, which he sent to Lang
asking him for his opinion. On 20 December, Lang replied: 'You confounded Ass.
The thing is Rot. Don't take it *au sérieux*. At least that is how it strikes *me*. If you
must say something, say what I leave in. The novel seems to me perfectly devoid of
moral harm.' The revised preface which Haggard sent to Longman and which was
included in all subsequent editions of the novel states:

It is humiliating to a novelist, after a long lapse of years, to be called upon to
emphasise the moral of his own book, especially when he has imagined that
moral to be writ large on every page of it. Yet this task falls to the lot of the
present writer, forced on him by the hysterical and anonymous or semi-
anonymous letter-writer. . . . Therefore he takes the opportunity to state,
amongst others too long to set out here, that this is the lesson he believed to be
illustrated by the tragic story of *Beatrice*, *to wit*:
Whatever the excuse or temptation, the man or woman who falls into undesirable relations with a married member of the other sex is both a sinner and a fool,
and, in this coin or in that, certainly will be called upon to pay the price of sin and
folly.

(From *Beatrice*)

On 25 December, Longman wrote: 'I like the Preface to *Beatrice* much better as
amended. Lang is quite right: your feelings in the matter did infinite credit to your
heart, but you disturbed yourself unnecessarily.' The whole incident, however,
deeply disturbed Haggard and he claimed that it 'more or less set me against the
writing of novels of modern life'.

Early in 1895 Haggard began an intensive campaign to enter Parliament at the
General Election likely to be called in the summer. The sitting member for East

Norfolk, Haggard's home constituency, was R.J. Price, a Liberal, who had no connections with the county. As there was every possibility of a national Conservative and Unionist victory at the election, the majority of 440 seemed vulnerable. As part of his effort to obtain selection as the prospective Unionist candidate, Haggard wrote three letters to *The Times* in January about the 'decrepit and even dangerous state of the farming interest in Eastern England'.

He did not ignore the business side of his writing, for even if he were to enter Parliament he would still need an income. One of the stories he planned to write for *The African Review* as part of his agreement with Wills was also sold to J.W. Arrowsmith on 15 January for £1,000, to be published in the firm's 1896 Christmas Annual. The agreement gave permission for the story of about 60,000 words to be published by another company in book form after 1 November 1898. Haggard, who must have been delighted at an arrangement that provided three separate British publications of the one story, had a plot in mind and gave as his possible titles *The Wizard*, *The Martyr* or *The Prophet*.

Haggard was also extremely pleased to be at last elected to the Athenaeum where he was able to continue collecting contacts and friends interested in African affairs. One such was Major F.R. Burnham, an American who after a most exciting life had joined Rhodes in Bulawayo. Haggard became very friendly with this lover of adventure, listening entranced to his many tales of dangerous escapades. Chief among these was the last stand of Major Wilson on the banks of the Shangani when Burnham escaped death only because he had been sent to bring help. Before Burnham left England for South Africa, Haggard asked him to write, in response to a list of questions, a detailed account of the incident.

On 11 February, Burnham replied: 'I shall take several days of the home voyage and write down all the details of the events you mention in your letter. 'Tis queer that you should so soon get a request of that nature from Longman and I am glad he has placed it in such able hands. Any point that you can take from the statements I send you, you are at liberty to use.'[32] On 4 March, Burnham wrote again from Johannesburg: 'The enclosed sheets are not entirely to my liking and I was on the point of destroying them entirely and perhaps should have done so. The sketch is only from memory of the country obtained on a very dark night mostly.'[33] Using Burnham's detailed notes, Haggard wrote the story of 'Wilson's Last Fight' which was included in Lang's *The Red True Story Book*, published in October.

At Norwich on 16 March, Haggard was unanimously adopted as the prospective Unionist and Agricultural candidate for the East Norfolk Division. In his adoption speech he made three main proposals: 'First I am of opinion that the £60,000 per annum at present raised by Land-tax in this country should be kept at home and should go to the relief of the Poor-rate in the districts in which it is collected. Secondly I would advocate that foreign barley coming into this country, unless it be crushed barley to be used as food for cattle, should be subjected to an import duty. . . . Every farthing of it should be devoted to a most truly democratic end, to the end of an Old Age Pension Scheme. . . . I suggest again that a bill should be passed to relieve pure beer of a proportion of the taxation upon it.'

Haggard's programme, a strange mixture of protectionism and radical reform, was not the official Conservative policy. Indeed in 1912 he was to declare: 'Now I understand that I never was a real Tory — that, in short, as a party man I am the most miserable failure. As a politician I should have been useless from any whip's point of view. He would — well, have struck me off his list as neither hot nor cold, as a dangerous and undesirable individual who, refusing to swallow the shibboleths of his tribe with shut eyes, actually dared to think for himself and to possess that hateful thing, "a cross-bench mind".'

Haggard's adoption speech and another made at North Walsham three days later were included in a broadside 'East Norfolk Representation' issued on 23 March. The same day *The Saturday Review* critically examined his election programme and concluded: 'The dissatisfied gentry, who cheered Mr Rider Haggard's childish panaceas for their ills, forget that if they make little or no money off their land, they possess compensations denied to other victims of the universal hard times. The very ownership of land in England gives them a social prestige not to be estimated by any measure of weight or coinage. Their names are in the county books; tugged forelocks and obsequious tradesmen's hats salute them at every turn; the village dogs gasp with admiration at their gaiters when they walk abroad. All these advantages, rooted in the placid natures of a kindly peasantry, Mr Haggard shares with his fellow squires. He has other advantages peculiar to himself, based upon the amiability of a vastly larger, though not less simple, popular constituency outside East Norfolk. He should content himself with these, and leave the weary task of politics to others. And if he will not, the Conservative party is clearly entitled to intervene, and make him leave politics alone, by the commonest rules of self-defence.'[34] The Conservative press made several such attacks on Haggard and the policies he advocated.

Undeterred, he enthusiastically mounted his campaign, aided by his old friend, Arthur Cochrane. In late April he began a round of speech-making, the local press reporting meetings at Sproston schoolroom on 18 April, the Tunns Inn in Thorpe St Andrews on 22 April, and the Aquarium Minor Hall in Yarmouth on 1 March. He also attended meetings in London, speaking at the annual meeting, chaired by the Prince of Wales, of the Printers' Pension, Almshouses and Orphan Asylum on 4 May, the annual meeting of the N.S.P.C.C. on 14 May, and at the Haggard Dinner given by the Authors' Club on 27 May. At the latter meeting he proposed, tongue-in-cheek, that a special tax should be imposed on newspaper paragraphists who made more money than novelists.

Also in May an article on 'Mr H. Rider Haggard at Ditchingham' by Alfred Wilcox appeared in *The Cable*. About his political views, Haggard states: 'Staunch Conservative though I am, I have told my supporters, and I may tell you also, that if I am returned to Parliament, and a Conservative Government comes into power and refuses to do justice to agriculturists, I shall vote against it. It is not enough that our wrongs should be listened to. We want active and vigorous measures for the alleviation of the distress.' Wilcox concludes his article: 'With a vivid sense of the needs of agriculturalists, he combines the power to compel attention to his views, and he has the faculty of exciting enthusiasm, which, joined to originality and eloquence, is irresistible, even in the House of Commons.'[35]

At the beginning of June, the election campaign proper began, and for six weeks Haggard travelled from one end of the constituency to the other either in a wherry through the Broads or by carriage. At meetings and smoking concerts Haggard spoke and Cochrane sang comic songs. The audiences were often hostile and then, Haggard reports, 'when the meeting was over my wife and I, with Cochrane and some other ladies, used to emerge and face the booing without, which sometimes was accompanied by hustling and stone-throwing'. His speech at Horsford St Faiths on 11 July was continually interrupted by an organised gang of youths, eventually breaking up in disorder. The next night, while passing through the village, Haggard was pelted with stones. A few days later a meeting at Colteshall was broken up, and Haggard and his party were pelted with rotten eggs. At Bacton it proved impossible to hold a meeting. On 17 July at North Walsham a group of his supporters was attacked. In addition many untruths were told about Haggard: the story was widely spread, for example, that he had murdered women and children in South Africa.

The worst incident of the election occurred on polling day, Friday 19 July. Haggard, his wife, Mr and Mrs Hartcup, and Cochrane made a tour of the district in a coach. Having been pelted with sand and stones at Sodham, they went on to Stalham where a mob set upon the coach. Haggard told a reporter from *The Pall Mall Gazette* what happened: 'All I know is that they swayed the coach backwards and forwards in their efforts to turn it over, and that when the three poor policemen attempted to protect us, and drew their truncheons, they were set upon in most cowardly fashion. I caught sight of one of them bleeding at the wrist and hands. We got our party safely into the Swan Hotel, despatched our telegrams to North Walsham and Yarmouth, and waited for three hours while the mob surged and raved in front of the house. . . . At last came the welcome message that a relief party from North Walsham and a force from Norwich, armed with cutlasses, were on the way to our relief. It was just about midnight that the North Walsham party appeared. I believe there was a slight fight at the outset, but almost directly our assailants fled with unanimity. I had to beg my friends not to retaliate, or they would have followed up the scoundrels, and there would have been a midnight fight with consequences not nice to contemplate.'[36]

Although at the time winning the seat seemed to Haggard 'about the most important thing in the whole world', he was defeated by 198 votes. The campaign had cost him a considerable amount — over £2,000 — and he had been disgusted by what he called 'indirect corruption', later commenting: 'From the moment a candidate appears on the field he is fair game, and every man's hand is in his pocket. Demands for "your patronage and support" fall on him, thick as leaves in Vallombrosa. I remember that I was even pestered to supply voters with wooden legs!'

More important, the attacks made on him left him mentally wounded and exceptionally bitter. He blamed the organised violence on Lord Wodehouse, the son of Lord Kimberley. In his notebook he wrote: 'Organised intimidation. Lord Woodhouse [*sic*] at bottom of it. His conduct. Why sh[ould] he continue to be on bench? Is there to be one law for lords & another for common men? How can L.W. sit on bench to try offences which he has himself inspired? This has won Norfolk for it reveals the forces behind Radicalism & the true objects of Radicalism.'[37] On 27 July, Balfour wrote to Haggard: 'I was shocked to see in the paper accounts of the violence with which some elections in the Eastern Counties, notably yours, were carried on. It is a scandal to the name of freedom, and I am puzzled to know why a contest carried on in the main with dignity and good nature in the rest of Britain, should have been soiled by the disgraceful scenes of which you and your friends were made the victims. . . . I am very sorry that, as the outcome of it all, you have failed to join the great Unionist Army which has been sent up to Westminster. You will have better luck, I am sure, next time.'[38] A summons was taken out against Lord Wodehouse and on 30 July he and a drover named Saul were fined for common assault.

The spectacle of Haggard striving desperately to right the wrongs he had suffered appeared unattractive to some commentators, including the London correspondent of *The New York Times*, who wrote: 'Rider Haggard's tempestuous boohooing about the way that the rustics chivvied him and his swell turnout in Norfolk lanes might have been funny if it had not been angering to see a grown man so little able to take a beating with decent grace.'[39] Always over-sensitive to any attack he considered unjust, Haggard withdrew to Ditchingham, prepared to turn his back on public life. He talked half-heartedly about starting a thoroughly good Conservative daily newspaper in Norwich, and was bombarded with letters from would-be employees. But nothing came of the idea, for he had returned to his own writing with a new enthusiasm. As he says: 'I found that the thorough change of thought seemed to have rested my mind, with the result that my imagination was fresher than it had been for some years before. Also the work itself was and has remained less irksome to me than during the years 1891 to 1895.' Having decided to write no more modern novels, he was restricted to African subjects, about which, because of his recent contact with those involved in African affairs, he had a renewed interest. He first wrote 'Black Heart and White Heart', a Zulu love-story set at the time of the Battle of Isandhlwana. It was first issued in the New Year's Number of *The African Review* in January, 1896.

Before the story appeared and before Haggard had started on another, an event occurred that involved him so deeply that he completely excludes it from his autobiography and other published writings. His daughter, Lilias, hints at what happened: 'It was during these years that Lilith [Lilly] came for a second time into Rider's life. Her marriage had ended in a disaster also involving her family, who were in consequence unable to help her. Rider, who half remained friends with them all, came to the rescue, took a small house where he installed her and the boys, and proceeded to do what he could to start them in life. A position which on the face of it was not a little difficult, and it was only owing to Louie's good faith and good sense that it worked as well as it did. She undertook all the arrangements, and was unwaveringly kind and sympathetic to Lilith, proving a warm-hearted friend both to her and her sons.'[40]

Lilly's husband, Francis Archer, was not only a stockbroker but the sole trustee of the Jackson fortune. Frederick Jackson, Lilly's only brother, took little interest in the family's finances and since the latter part of 1894 had been in Uganda as a First Class Assistant. To pay his gambling debts and other expenses incurred by a variety of pleasures, Archer had for several years been systematically embezzling the funds of both the trust and business clients. On 11 December 1895, at the instance of Colonel Thomas Davies Sewell, clerk to the Lorimers' Company, Archer was summonsed at the Guildhall 'for that, being instructed, as a broker, with a cheque for £493 11s with a direction in writing to apply the proceeds for a certain purpose, he unlawfully converted the same to his own use'.[41] When the officer of the Court went to serve the summons at the Archer's home in Somer's Place, he found that Archer was not there and so he served it on Lilly. The same day a warrant was issued for Archer's arrest; but by that time, with the help of friends, he had fled to Africa. On 25 December, Archer was adjudged bankrupt. Lilly and her family were left almost penniless and it appears that Haggard had to help not only her but also her sisters, none of whom had married. The new home found for the Jackson sisters was Red House, Aldeburgh, which in more recent times became the residence of Sir Benjamin Britten and Sir Peter Pears.

So Haggard's responsibilities and emotional strains were further increased. That his wife should apparently so readily accept his decision to provide for his love and her three sons is a sign not just of her practical, unemotional temperament, but that their lives had assumed a compatible independence that was untrammelled by either jealously or passion. In any case, Haggard had become and was to remain a source of financial support to all members of his own family when they were in difficulties. Increasingly Ditchingham House, sarcastically called 'The Lost Dogs' Home' by one brother, became a refuge for his many nephews and nieces. Haggard's family did not always, however, seem grateful. His daughter records: 'They bit the hand that fed them with the utmost regularity, they were jealous of him, abused him, and even insulted him in their astonishing letters, having no control over their pens and little over their tongues. They landed their children on him to look after, then basely sheltered behind their wives' skirts when domestic differences of opinion arose over doctors, health, education, and interfering grandmothers and mothers-in-law, or accused him of abusing their confidence.'[42]

On 29 December an event occurred that caused a public sensation and meant that Haggard was again called upon as an expert on African affairs. Dr L.S. Jameson, a colleague of Cecil Rhodes', led an armed force into the Transvaal Republic. The ill-timed and ill-advised Jameson Raid was easily defeated, but it encouraged the triumphant Boers to establish closer links with the Boers in the

Cape, thus encouraging the move towards a future conflict between the British and the Boers in South Africa. For much of the next two years Haggard was occupied writing the stories about Africa for which the public and publishers clamoured. His letter on such topics as the Transvaal crisis were published in *The Times* and he was frequently asked to give speeches on South Africa. There were also literary events in which he was involved. On 18 January 1896 he opened the Barrett–Browning Memorial Institute at Ledbury, in Shropshire, where his sister Ella lived. More important, he became in 1896 the Chairman of Committee of the Society of Authors, a post he held for two years.

In the early part of 1896, Haggard wrote *The Wizard*, the story of the struggle between Hokosa, the Wizard, and Thomas Owen, a missionary to the Children of Fire. Before it was complete, he sold for £1,000 to *The Graphic* the serial rights of a tale of the Great Trek of the Boers in 1836, which he was to call *Swallow*.

Events taking place in Africa were constantly being reported and, in a letter written on 31 May, Burnham informed Haggard of the death at Bulawayo of his daughter who had been called Nada after the Zulu heroine of *Nada the Lily*: 'Our Nada died in Laager of inflammation of the lungs caused by the draughty market buildings into which the women and children were huddled during the siege. Mrs Burnham arrived on first possible coach and had the consolation of being with her at the last. I on the day of her death was making a desperate ride through the Ingubo regiment and knew nothing until my arrival in Bula. . . . Like the Nada of your brain she bound all to her and leaves us all in deepest sorrow.'[43] Haggard, deeply upset by Nada's death, on 6 June wrote his dedication to *The Wizard*: 'To the memory of the child Nada Burnham who "bound all to her" and, while her father cut his way through the hordes of the Ingubu Regiment, perished of the hardships of war at Buluwayo on May 22nd, 1896, I dedicate this tale of Faith triumphant over savagery and death.'

After appearing serially in *The African Review*, *The Wizard* was published as *Arrowsmith's Christmas Annual for Boys* on 29 October. Before that date, Haggard had started *Swallow*, a tale told by the mother of Suzanne, the Swallow. She is a Boer, the wife of a Boer farmer. In the story Haggard gives a surprisingly sympathetic account of why the Boers hated and distrusted the British. After the book had been finished, Haggard on 14 December wrote to his sister Ella: 'It has been a somewhat trying year especially in the African market, but we have all of us much to be thankful for.'[44]

As 1897 began, Haggard had already started work on his fourth successive African tale, *Elissa; or The Doom of Zimbabwe*. In an attempt to show the city's Phoenician origins (then the accepted theory) Haggard tells how 'because of the fateful and predestined loves of Aziel the prince, and Elissa the priestess and daughter of Sakon, three thousand years and more ago, the ancient city of Zimboe fell at the hand of king Ithobal and his Tribes, so that to-day there remain of it nothing but a desolate grey tower of stone, and beneath, the crumbling bones of men.'

About this time Haggard, who since his new-found commitment to writing had managed to sustain a high if not increasing income, purchased Kessingland Grange on the east coast. This sprawling house, standing on the edge of a cliff, had originally been two coastguard cottages. There were sixteen bedrooms — each of which Haggard named after a British admiral — four reception rooms and two furnished halls. In the surrounding ten acres of land there was a croquet lawn and a tennis court. It was to be an ideal holiday home where Haggard could accommodate the ever-growing number of dependants, friends and relatives that had taken to descending upon Ditchingham in the summer.

One friend from whom Haggard had heard little for some time was Kipling, who after his marriage in January 1892 had crossed the Atlantic to live with his American wife. After their return in August 1896, they had lived near Torquay, but in June 1897 they had moved to Rottingdean. Early in July, Haggard received from Kipling a draft of the poem that he had promised the editor of *The Times* he would write in honour of Queen Victoria's Jubilee. Unfortunately Haggard's comments are lost, but Kipling wrote again on 10 July: 'Now, any nation save ourselves, with such a fleet as we have at present, would go out swiftly to trample the guts out of the rest of the world; and the fact that we do not seems to show that even if we aren't very civilized, we're about the one power with a glimmering of civilization in us. As you say, we've always had it somewhere in our composition. But my objection to that hymn is that it may be quoted as an excuse for lying down abjectly at all times and seasons and taking what any other country may think fit to give us. What I wanted to say was: "Don't gas but be ready to give people snuff" — and I only covered the first part of the notion.'[45] The poem or hymn, which Kipling completed six days later, was 'Recessional' — 'Lord God of Hosts be with us yet, lest we forget, lest we forget.'

In late August, Haggard went for a brief holiday to the Netherlands where he toured the white-washed churches, jotting in his notebook details of places visited and things seen which might provide background material for the story he had decided to write set in the time of William the Silent. On 14 December, *The Graphic* purchased for £900 the serial rights of the novel, provisionally called *The Secret of Sword Silence* but actually entitled *Lysbeth* when published. It was to have a maximum of 125,000 words and be delivered by September, 1899.

Haggard would have had difficulty in completing his novel about the Netherlands earlier, for he had agreed with Charles Longman to keep throughout 1898 a commonplace book, a daily diary in which he would record the events of *A Farmer's Year* which would be published serially in *Longman's Magazine* and then as a book. It was a new departure for him, and the result was to be a work of outstanding merit that has consistently been underrated.

Haggard is a superb diarist. Day after day he lovingly records the changes to the countryside with which he was so familiar. His entries are peopled by local characters and crammed with anecdotes. His observation and natural curiosity are given a free rein. The style is relaxed and Haggard's own changes of mood are as faithfully recorded as the subtle alterations in the hedgerow hues. For the first time he was not writing under pressure, and as he noted the cycle of the seasons he was writing not as a labour but for pleasure. It is sad that because Haggard has been stereotyped by the misinformed as a writer of adventure stories this literary gem has been all but ignored. It presents a vivid and detailed picture of Victorian, rural life that is charming, illuminating and totally absorbing:

April 20 As I chance to be one of the justices nominated to exercise the powers conferred by the Lunacy Acts, I am brought a good deal into contact with the insanity of this district, which, by the way, seems to be greatly on the increase and to occur chiefly among women. About breakfast-time on Sunday morning I was requested by an overseer to attend in a neighbouring village to satisfy myself by personal examination as to the madness of a certain pauper lunatic before she was removed to the asylum. This I promised to do, fixing the hour of two o'clock. In the middle of the service, however, on returning from the lectern after reading one of the Lessons, I found a young man by my pew with a note, on which was written, 'Lunatic waiting for you at church gate. Sir, please come and examine.'

Accordingly, as I judged the case must have become urgent, I went to investigate the condition of the poor woman's mind by means of a *tête-à-tête* with her in a fly at the gate of the churchyard. Having satisfied myself as to her insanity, I signed the orders necessary for her removal to the asylum, and reappeared in church before the conclusion of the Litany. It seems that it was not considered advisable that the patient should remain longer out of proper control; so, as she could not be removed without a magistrate's order, I was followed to the church.

August 6 In a greenhouse in this garden I have two tame toads, named Martha and Jane respectively. Also there is a tiny one called Babette, but she can hardly be counted, as she is so small and seldom on view. (Martha, there is reason to fear, has recently eaten Babette.)

These toads are strange and interesting creatures, differing much from each other in appearance and character. Martha is stout and dark coloured, a bold-natured toad of friendly habit; Jane, on the other hand, is pale and thin, with a depressed air which suggests resignation born of long experience of circumstances over which she has no control. Some of this depression may be due to the fact that once, entering the greenhouse in the twilight, I trod upon her accidentally, a shock from which she seems never to have recovered, although, owing to the adaptive powers of toads, beyond a slight flattening she took no physical harm from an adventure which must have been painful. Indeed, I am not sure that of the two of us I did not suffer most, for I know of few things more upsetting than the feel of a fat toad beneath one's foot. Anyhow, since that day Jane has looked reproachful and never quite trusted me.

(From *A Farmer's Year*)

On 20 July Haggard recorded in *A Farmer's Year*: 'I see in the paper to-day that the Government has given way suddenly on the Vaccination Bill, and that henceforth "conscientious objection" on the part of parents is to entitle them to disregard the law and neglect the vaccination of their children.' As his experiences in Mexico had made him aware of the ravages inflicted by a smallpox epidemic, the matter so upset him that he wrote *Dr Therne*, a propaganda novel in support of vaccination. As soon as it was finished, it was sent to Charles Longman, who on 14 September wrote: 'I sat up last night and read *Dr Therne*. It is dramatic all through and though the subject is painful and unpleasant there is nothing in the treatment that strikes a jarring note. The question of course is who will read it: you are of course going quite outside your regular clientele. . . . I think that 3/6 is the right price for it. As to the question of the serial I should recommend it, if you could get one just at the right time, as no doubt you would make more money that way. The only practicable time would be April–June 1899, so that the book should not be published within 3 months of *Swallow*. Failing that it should be published at once i.e. as soon as it can be got out.'[46]

Dr Therne was not, however, published as a serial: it came out as a book on 28 November. Among the people to whom Haggard sent a copy was Thomas Hardy. Considering how contentious the subject of vaccination was, it was courageous of Haggard to write a novel about it — a point noted by *The Lancet*: 'As a novelist and a politician alike it is evidently to his advantage to take no step that would be likely to alienate from him any large body of possible supporters. Yet he has risked losing many readers and creating a fanatical opposition to whatever he may do in a public or private capacity for the sake of telling the truth.' On 22 December, the executive committee of the Jenner Society, to whose members Haggard had dedicated the novel, passed a warm and unanimous resolution thanking him for his work.

Haggard spent almost all of 1898 — apart from a fortnight's visit in September to a friend, Colonel Lorne Stewart, the Laird of Coll in the Hebrides — at Ditchingham. Among the few visits he records is one from Frederick Jackson who, having returned from East Africa, arrived on 13 November. Haggard makes no mention, however, of Lilly, although certainly they kept in close touch. On 15 January 1899, Frederick Jackson, who had just been created a Companion of the Bath, wrote to his cousin, Arthur C. Hunter: 'I have been away, staying with Rider Haggard and Lilly since the 2nd and only returned last night. For 3 or 4 days I was laid up with bronchitis, the result of a rabbit shoot and bad weather combined.'[47] Shortly afterwards, Lilly's husband wrote asking her to join him in Africa. Against the advice of her friends, including Haggard, she agreed; and so, taking with her the youngest son, she left East Anglia and sailed away. When the ship neared Madeira, she wrote to Haggard: 'I received safely your kind note of farewell — also the photograph, which I indeed greatly value. I hope and trust we may meet again and in (for me) happier circumstances. For all your generous help in the time of need, for your friendship and never failing kindness I shall all my life feel the deepest gratitude.'[48] According to his daughter, Haggard wrote 'Finis!' under her name and filed away the letter. He was to see her again, but in even unhappier circumstances.

Haggard's brothers also caused problems. Bazett had returned from Samoa seriously ill and, ostracized by many of his family, was living at Parkstone. Andrew had left the army and, heavily indebted, fled to America — Haggard received letters from creditors demanding to know his whereabouts. There were too other worries. On 9 February 1899, Longman wrote: 'We have sold about 4,400 of the 3/6 edition of *Dr Therne* — it does not sell very fast now, but it does keep moving: 100 have gone in the last 10 days. We printed 10,000 so that we have over 5,000 left, and I fear that if a 6d edition were now published nearly all this stock would be rendered worthless.'[49]

Haggard also heard that Kipling who was staying at the Hotel Grenoble in New York with his family, had been taken seriously ill. He wrote, expressing his wish for a speedy recovery, but on 27 February, in a letter to his sister Ella, he states: 'I am much disturbed about Kipling. I do devoutly trust that he will pull through, poor chap. But he is a nervous, feverish man.'[50] Tragically, on 6 March, Josephine, the Kiplings' eldest daughter, died of fever. It was many months before Kipling recovered his physical and mental strength.

At this time Haggard was writing *Lysbeth* and he was doubtless encouraged by the complimentary reviews that appeared after the publication of *Swallow* on 1 March, five days after the American edition. Katherine Pearson Woods in an article 'The Evolution of an Artist' that appeared in the American *Bookman* stated: '*Swallow* is so immensely superior to everything else that he has ever done, that it seems to us to justify the title which we have given to this review. *Swallow*, indeed, is a veritable work of art.'[51]

Even greater attention, however, was paid to the serialisation of *A Farmer's Year* being published in *Longman's Magazine*. As a popular novelist, Haggard already received many letters: to these letters were added, with the appearance of *A Farmer's Year*, a great number more dealing with agricultural matters. Haggard was also increasingly invited to speak about rural problems, addressing, for example, the Norfolk Chamber of Commerce early in May and the Council of the Central and Associated Chambers of Agriculture on 30 May. As earlier he had been called upon as an expert on Africa, he was in 1899 given public recognition as an expert on the land.

Only the death of Bazett on 13 May marred the pleasure Haggard felt as once again he contemplated involvement in public affairs. Throughout the period that Lilly had been living near Ditchingham he had rarely strayed far away. Now that she had gone, he too felt the need to roam, and began planning another visit to Cyprus early in 1900. During the autumn, however, still very much aware of the departed Lilly, he wrote 'purely to please himself' *Stella Fregelius: A Tale of Three Destinies*, in which he describes how the spirit of a girl once known came between a man and his wife:

It was late, very late, and there, pale and haggard in the low light of the fire, once again Morris stood pleading with the radiant image which his heart revealed.

'Oh, speak! speak!' he moaned aloud . . . 'Become human. Speak. Let me touch your hand . . .'

Then a low and awful cry, and Morris turned to behold Mary his wife. At last she had seen and heard, and read his naked heart. At last she knew him — mad, and in his madness most unfaithful — a man who loved one dead and dragged her down to earth for company.

Look! there in his charmed and secret sight stood the spirit, and there, over against her, the mortal woman, and he — wavering — he lost between the two.

(From *Stella Fregelius*)

The mental torment Haggard was caused by his love for Lilly was sadly not cured by the writing of this novel in which his belief in the reuniting of true lovers after death is reaffirmed and, as he later wrote in his Author's Note: 'He treated the difficult theme, not indeed as he would have wished to do, but as best he could.'

On 2 October *A Farmer's Year* was published as a book, to almost total critical acclaim. *The Athenaeum* called it 'a most delightful and useful book . . . with a breadth of judgement and with a power of accurate observation which are unusual'[52]; *The Literary World* said it was 'of permanent value was portraying the agricultural life of the times'[53]; and *The New York Times* declared that 'the merits of it are unquestionable'[54]. In the ensuing weeks, Haggard, although still working on *Stella Fregelius*, was encouraged enough to plan further books including what he called 'The Cochrane Boer Story' and a sequel to *A Farmer's Year* entitled *A Flower Lover's Year*. On 11 October *The Queen* agreed to purchase twelve articles on Cyprus (each of about 3,000 words) at five guineas a thousand words.

The following day the governments of the Transvaal and Orange Free State declared war on British South Africa and the Boer War began. Although it had been eighteen years since he was last in Africa, Haggard was again called upon as an expert on a part of the world whose obvious problems were virtually incomprehensible to the British public. In a piece of blatant commercial exploitation, Kegan Paul, Trench, Trübner & Co. (the successors to Trübner & Co.) brought out on 20 October an abridged edition of Haggard's first book, *Cetywayo and His White Neighbours*, with a new introduction, renaming it *The Last Boer War*. (It was also issued in the United States as *A History of the Transvaal*.)

Despite the war in South Africa, Haggard continued to plan his trip to the Middle East. On 5 November he wrote to Aggie, who with Jack had moved to Florence: 'Thanks for Florence. Yes, all being well I propose to travel in the East this winter taking Arthur Green [his sister Ella's son] with me to do secretary and improve his mind. If I can manage it, I should like to return via Florence and perhaps meet Louie there. I want to go to Cyprus, Egypt and the Holy Land at any rate to the first and last, starting immediately after Xmas.'[55] As a result of Aggie's invitation, Haggard arranged to take Louie and their three children to stay in

Florence while he went on his travels with his nephew. On his return he planned to write his record of *A Flower Lover's Year*, the serial rights of which *The Queen* purchased on 16 November for £5 a thousand words, agreeing that publication should begin in May or June 1901.

The preparations for Haggard's overseas trip were almost complete when he received through Watt an invitation from Arthur Pearson to go to South Africa on the completion of the Boer War to write a series of articles for *The Daily Express*. Haggard was extremely interested in going to South Africa, where the Kiplings had taken to spending their winters. Negotiations, therefore, continued and, on 5 December, Haggard wrote again to Watt: 'Without speaking definitely or finally I incline to the opinion that some such arrangement as you suggest might be acceptable: 1. Mr Pearson to pay all expenses of myself and my family during our voyage to and from and sojourn at the Cape. . . . My family would have to live probably in some hired house in ordinary and decent comfort as they live at home. At the same time it must be remembered that travelling about South Africa with a secretary, and I should be obliged to take some gentleman in that capacity, costs a certain amount. Also to get the information I should require would possibly involve my having to do a little entertaining. It is necessary that I should be in a position to ask people to luncheon or dinner if advisable etc. 2. That all remuneration should be arranged upon a basis, as you suggest, of payment for universal serial rights at £20 per thousand words for matter to be supplied to the extent of about 150,000 words. I do not think that I could undertake to deal with so great a subject in a smaller space, though of course it might work out at less. . . . Still, if it were wished, the arrangement might be made thus: I to guarantee to supply a minimum of 100,000 words; Mr Pearson to guarantee conditionally upon my fulfilling my contract, to pay me a minimum of £2,500 up to a maximum of £3,000 according to the amount of matter supplied (or at the least a minimum of £2,000).'

Haggard further suggested that if the editor of *The Queen* 'should prove obdurate about the Flower Book, the only thing to do would be to pay damages. You see if the African business is to be done at all, it must be done next year, whereas the flowers grow up every year. . . . However, I have a suggestion to make. I have been engaged upon a story named *Stella Fregelius: A Tale of Three Destinies* of which I hope to be able to forward you the M.S. tomorrow. . . . This work by which I set some store is not of the romance order but would, I imagine, interest a good many readers. Would *The Queen* like to have the offer of it for serial publication?'[56] On 8 December, at Pearson's request, Haggard gave as examples of his possible expenses: passages to and from the Cape — £550; rent and family costs — £600; travelling expenses in South Africa — £500. On 20 December, Haggard signed the agreement which provided for all his requests.

And so, as the nineteenth century came to a close, Haggard prepared to leave England for an extended tour of the Middle East, assured in a new-found spirit of optimism that his future income and prospects were bright. His acceptance as an expert both on African and agricultural affairs made it possible that he would not have to write further adventure stories for money alone. Although his attempt to enter Parliament had failed, there was every possibility that he would be encouraged to commentate — in speeches and in his writing — on public affairs and matters of general concern. It seemed that, at forty-three, Haggard had ceased to be the precocious popular novelist constantly berated by critics and was set to become an establishment figure engendering respect from public and press alike.

8

Without the Gate

My opportunities have not been many, and for the most part I have made them for myself; the book writing, the agricultural research business, the public work for instance. Of course I might have done more in the last line by going into Parliament. But this really I have been never able to afford, since, except in the case of Labour members, it has designedly been made to suit the rich alone. . . . Therefore, such as I must remain mere hodman Peris, labouring and suffering without the Gate.
(From *The Private Diaries of Sir H. Rider Haggard*)

The prospect of leaving a cold and damp England in January 1900 delighted Haggard who more and more during the winters suffered from bronchitis. And so it was with relief that one foggy morning he departed from Charing Cross Station with his wife, three daughters, Arthur Green (his nephew), and Rose Hildyard (Louie's cousin); but, as had become customary for Haggard, the journey was full of unexpected and unwelcome incidents. On the way to Florence there was a gale in the Channel and all the children were sick; the St Gotthard tunnel was blocked by a derailed train; and a blinding snowstorm prevented the harassed travellers seeing much of the Alps. It is little wonder that Haggard described himself as 'a kind of railway Jonah'.

If I were asked to devise a place of punishment for sinners of what I may chance to consider the direst degree, a first-class continental hotel is the purgatorial spot to which I would commit them — for a century at a time. Yes, and thither they should travel once a month (with a family) in the *waggon-lit* of a *train de luxe* with all the steam-pipes turned on. . . . Rather would I dwell — for a life choice — in a cottage in the country on a pound a week than free in these foreign, gorgeous hostelries where every decoration strikes you like a blow, surrounded by hard servility on fire for unearned fees, fed with messes such as the soul loathes, and quailing beneath the advancing shadow of a monstrous bill.

(From *A Winter Pilgrimage*)

At last the party reached Florence, where Aggie lived in a vast house, full of long stone-floored corridors, with an overgrown garden that had once been a nuns' cemetery. It turned out to be the coldest winter Tuscany had experienced for years. There were fogs and piercing gales that reminded Haggard 'of winds I have felt blowing straight off the pack ice in northern latitudes'. Even worse, an influenza epidemic was raging. The three children fell ill. Frequently the bell of the chapel opposite Aggie's house tolled for the dead and in the street outside black-hooded figures carried the epidemic's victims to their burial. Distraught and helpless, Haggard moped around Florence, purchasing, as was his habit whenever abroad, any antique or curio that took his fancy.

At last, the children recovering, Haggard, feeling free to leave his family, set off on his travels with his less than competent secretary, Arthur Green. Their incident-filled train journeys took them to Naples, by way of Rome. After a visit to Pompeii, Haggard, suffering from an incessant cough, arrived at Brindisi ready to sail for Cyprus only to discover that, owing to an error made by Green, all the luggage had been sent on to Reggio.

Later, in his autobiography, Haggard recorded that Green 'proved the most erratic secretary with whom I have ever come in contact. I could never find him when I wanted him, and as for the heavy typewriter which we dragged about with us, all he did with it was to drop it on my toes out of the rack of a railway train. At last I got sick of the article, which alone clung to us after he had lost all the luggage . . . and sent it home [from Cyprus] packed in the remains of a mule-saddle, or something of the sort.' As a result, Haggard was unable to write the articles he had verbally agreed to send regularly to *The Times*. Even so, the stay in Cyprus, spent mainly with Jebb's daughter and her husband, proved enjoyable and relaxing; but it was to his first tour of the Holy Land that Haggard was particularly looking forward, and he was not disappointed. Despite the beggars, difficulties with the Turkish authorities, and having to travel on horse-back along dusty roads, he felt 'a sojourn in the Holy Land is one of the highest and most excellent of educations'.

Haggard had anticipated, while in the Holy Land, finding the inspiration for a romance. In fact he found material for two — *Pearl-Maiden; A Tale of The Fall of Jerusalem*, and *The Brethren*, a story of the Crusades which was inspired by his visit to the Hill of the Beatitudes, Karn Hattin, where Saladin crushed the Christian power in Palestine.

As spring awakened the countryside, Haggard returned to Ditchingham and his family with cases of souvenirs, although a portmanteau and many packages had to be sent on separately from Port Said, including a canvas-covered basket containing Capernaum, a tortoise Haggard had found basking beside the Lake of Galilee. More important, his notebooks were full of jottings on which he worked for the next few months to record his story of *A Winter Pilgrimage*.

On 29 May, Longmans published *Black Heart and White Heart and Other Stories* (i.e. 'Elissa' and 'The Wizard'). As the Boer War still raged there was much interest in these African stories, but Haggard, apart from one letter to *The Times*, remained uninvolved, unlike Kipling, in the campaign of enthusiastic support for the war effort. His acute awareness of the problems in South Africa and the informed sympathy for the Boers' case that he had demonstrated in *Swallow* made him unprepared to add his voice to the loud, jingoistic trumpetings then filling the newspapers. As it seemed clear that the war was likely to drag on for some time he was also aware that there was little possibility of his being able, as arranged, to visit South Africa that winter to report on the after-war situation.

He chose, therefore, to busy himself with other matters. In addition to his farming, there was the business of writing. On 13 June, Longmans paid an advance of £750 on a 25 per cent royalty for the book rights of *Lysbeth*, which was to appear as a serial in *The Graphic* between 1 September 1900 and 2 March 1901. On 6 July, Haggard wrote to Watt: 'I have now finished the book which I shall call *A Winter Pilgrimage*. It is an account, more or less interesting I trust, of my travels in Cyprus, the Holy Land etc. You will remember that there was some arrangement under which *The Queen* was to publish certain letters — 12 I think — giving an account of these travels. The difficulty is, however, that that number of letters would not take them half through the book, which is about 112,000 words. Under the circumstances, what is to be done? Would they like to run the whole thing, or the first part of it? Or must I agree to their cancelling the bargain? I am by no means certain that it would not answer for them to publish the book. It would be a change to the ordinary run of matter and anything connected with the Holy Land always excites interest and commands readers.'[1]

Watt approached Percy Cox, the editor of *The Queen*, who agreed to take the additional section of 45,000 words on the Holy Land, paying £2 a thousand (instead of £5 5. 0.) for the extra words. On 10 August, having already informed Watt of his intention to write both *Pearl-Maiden* and a romance about Jerusalem at the time of the Crusades, Haggard sent a letter to his agent dealing with his books not then placed: '*Stella Fregelius* — This book is not in any way suitable to *The Graphic* and I hope that you did not give them the copy. It might suit *Harpers*, or, as I suggested, some of these Ladies' Magazines, but the people who I should like to read it are Smith Elder. It is a book which ought to be published in monthly and not in weekly instalments. Please, however, do not hawk it about. Than that I would far rather that it were held over for a while. *Jerusalem Romance* — I do not know that it is any use going to the labour of making a synopsis of the plot unless *The Graphic* would care to consider it. If this should be the case perhaps you will kindly let me know. . . . *Pearl-Maiden* — I note that *The Graphic* want 125,000 words. I think that *Pearl-Maiden* will run to this.'[2]

Soon afterwards Haggard began dictating *Pearl-Maiden* and on 15 November the serial rights of it were purchased by *The Graphic* for £700. Despite the public interest in Africa created by the Boer War, he was unprepared to write another African romance. Indeed he was unable to do so throughout the two and a half years of the war. Instead he spent most of that period on what he later called 'the heaviest labour of all my laborious life' — a detailed study of rural England. He was able to do this because, when Pearson of *The Daily Express* asked him through Watt to cancel the agreement by which he should have gone to South Africa, Haggard agreed on the condition that in place of the planned articles he should conduct for the newspaper an investigation into the state of English agriculture — an idea that

Mary Elizabeth Archer, née Jackson; Haggard's Lilly. 'One of the three lovely women whom I have seen in my life.'

A family group outside Ditchingham House – called by one brother 'The Lost Dogs' Home' because it became a refuge for Haggard's many nephews and nieces

In Yarmouth during Haggard's election campaign, July 1895. On polling day they were attacked by a mob and had to retreat to the Swan Hotel. They were rescued by a relief party with cutlasses

Haggard at Ditchingham. 'His fancy,' Lilias Haggard recalled, 'ran to flowing capes and voluminous tweeds.'

25 February 1919: the day on which Haggard received his knighthood. His diary entry records: 'The crown and cross are pretty, with a figure of Britannia and "For God and Empire" engraved on red enamel, but I think they would be more effective if they were somewhat larger.'

Haggard: a portrait by William Strang, 1916. 'Yesterday I sat again to Strang
who finished the drawing of me. Of course it is good but too "pretty" I think. I
look older than that.'

(*Above*) A still from the 1925 version of *She*, filmed in mid-winter in an old unheated Zeppelin shed near Berlin. Betty Blythe, the scantily clad heroine, suffered much from the cold

(*Below*) A still from *Moon in Israel*, an Austrian film made in 1924

H. Rider Haggard, Esq.,
    Ditchingham House,
        N o r f o l k.

Dear Sir,

    We are publishing a series of brief notes by well known
writers, and should be greatly obliged if you would favour us
with a few lines on a Postcard (for reproduction in facsimile)
commenting on any recently published book that you can
recommend to the general reader.

    We should like to have the card during the week, and
shall be glad to pay a fee of One Guinea for it.

                Yours faithfully,

                The Editor

A request from the Editor of *The Reader* to Rider Haggard, and his reply

The book that has interested
me most of late is that
by Sir Oliver Lodge upon
his catechism. To me
it seems full of truth &
original thought & well
worth the attention of
readers who seek these
things.

Theda Bara in *Cleopatra*, filmed in 1917

came to him, he recalls, 'while I was taking my bath one morning — a domestic occasion on which, for some reason explained, I have observed that I am more open to new impressions than at any other time.'

In the early months of 1901, Haggard completed *Pearl-Maiden* and signed contracts with Longmans for the book-publication of both *A Winter Pilgrimage* (20 per cent of 12/6) and *Pearl-Maiden* (25 per cent of 6/- with a £750 advance). He also planned and made preparations for his survey of twenty-six English counties. In this he was helped by Arthur Cochrane, his ever-faithful friend, who readily agreed to act as his secretary and companion. In March the pair set off by rail to Salisbury, the first stopping-place in a tour which was to last eight months and during which daily they interviewed landowners, tenants and farm labourers. They visited farms, small-holdings, food-manufacturing industries, and labourers' cottages. As Haggard asked the questions, Cochrane meticulously recorded the conversations. At night in the inn, farmhouse or hotel where they were staying, while Cochrane wrote up his voluminous notes and dealt with the considerable correspondence, Haggard worked on the articles which appeared twice a week in *The Daily Express* and *The Yorkshire Post* from 17 April to 3 October. His daughter records that Haggard's letters home chronicled 'the continually lost luggage, the strange and astonishing establishments, the peculiar meals, the damp beds and chills and stomach-aches, the appalling discomfort of historic old houses, the surprising comfort of modest farms, and the unvarying kindness with which he and Cochrane were welcomed by all and sundry'.[3] It is clear that right from the start Haggard considered that the articles he was writing were of secondary importance to the more detailed book he intended subsequently to compile. On 5 April, from the Rougemont Hotel, Exeter, he wrote to Aggie: 'The book is the thing. It ought to make a book and a half also. The job is extraordinarily interesting, but very hard.'[4]

On 11 April, just before his articles began to appear and while the serialisation of *A Winter Pilgrimage* was running in *The Queen, Lysbeth* was published. Many reviewers sought desperately to connect the new historical romance with the events in Africa which were then the major topic of interest. Typically, *The Review of Reviews* declares: 'Mr Haggard, deserting South Africa, which he has so often drenched with blood in the fields of contemporary romance, has made a bold incursion into the past, and gives us a lurid picture of love, adventure, torture and crime located in the Netherlands during the time when the Dutch were making their great world-famous struggle against Alva and the Spaniards. Some future Mr Haggard will probably write a similar story up from, and find fitting incidents in, the present war of independence in South Africa. It is to be hoped, if he does, that he will not paint the English so uniformly black as he does the Spaniards.'[5]

Unconcerned by such criticism, Haggard enthusiastically pursued his investigations. During his journeys he met and spoke at length to all the more important agriculturalists in England, including the Earl of Leicester and Lord Walsingham. As he witnessed the depressed state of the country's agriculture and the evidence of rural depopulation stemming as much as anything from low wages, Haggard became convinced that only a major social revolution in the countryside would make the land profitable again. He saw that the feudal system of land-holding practised by such men as his father was no longer practical:

> Feudal systems and feudal ideas have had their reign and are outworn. . . . I maintain that what is necessary now is not so much to support 'the dignity and comfort' of the heads of a few country families, which, in the vast majority of instances, can be done only by providing them with extraneous wealth, but rather the dignity and comfort of the heads of hundreds or thousands of small country owners or occupiers.
>
> (From *Rural England*)

In reaching this conclusion, Haggard was perhaps reacting, albeit unconsciously, both to not having a son of his own to inherit Ditchingham and to the obvious absurdity of the primogenetural succession that had bequeathed the virtually bankrupt Bradenham estate to his eldest brother who did not have the resources to make it prosperous. Certainly he was aware that, although the financial rewards were small, he had obtained much pleasure from farming his own land. He also realised that if, instead of being but an interested observer, he had been a labourer tilling his own acreage, the pleasure and the income would have been greater. He concluded, therefore, that the division of large estates into small-holdings provided the solution to the depressed state of rural England.

His long journey complete and his conclusion reached, Haggard, on 5 November, addressed a meeting in the Adelphi of the Associated Chambers of Agriculture at which he advocated the creation of small holdings as the best method of arresting rural depopulation. His speech attracted much interest and on 7 November *The Times* included several points from it in a leading article. At the Athenaeum that morning, Haggard wrote to the newspaper reiterating the main point in his argument: 'Where small-holdings are fashionable my experience is that the population increases or at any rate does not dwindle. A man will do for himself what he will not do for another, and after all there are worse things than hard work in the open air.'[6] Immediately afterwards he had a long interview with General William Booth, the founder of the Salvation Army, who was then a most sprightly seventy-two. They spoke about the thriving agricultural colony Booth had established at Hadleigh in Essex, and the social evils created by the rural exodus to the city slums. Although they had not met before, the two men found that they had much in common. Booth, whom Haggard described as 'one of the few great men of our time', saw in Haggard a sympathetic and, therefore useful, ally at a time when attacks on the Salvation Army were still made in the popular press; but Haggard also learned much from Booth, including information about land cultivation in Denmark, a subject he was to pursue.

Haggard spent much of the next twelve months, when not delivering speeches on his findings, working on *Rural England: Being an Account of Agricultural and Social Researches Carried Out in the Years 1901 & 1902*. As he wrote, he knew that he wished to do much more than amplify his fifty or so articles. His concern at what he had seen made it obvious that he must present a reasoned case for reforms that could be accomplished only with Government aid on a vast scale. The more he considered the statistics, the more convinced he became that the alarming state of agriculture was likely to endanger the country's security in the event of a European war:

> We seem to lay out about £4 per head of the population on imported food, as against, to quote an example by way of contrast, about 7s. per head of its population paid by Germany. . . . To me, in face of the continued decrease in our agricultural output, these figures are simply terrifying, since, although the question is one into which I do not propose to enter here, I am convinced that the risk of the starvation which might strike our Country in the event of a European war, is no mere spectre of the alarmist. It should be remembered that fleets of battleships, even if they could keep the great seas as open as is cheerfully supposed, can never control the operations of the foreign, and indeed of the home, speculators in foodstuffs. Within a fortnight of the declaration of such a war — which we must expect some day — corn would, I believe, stand at or near 100s. a quarter.

> (From *Rural England*)

Haggard was, therefore, in agreement with the points made by Kipling in a poem 'The Islanders', published in *The Times*, which attributed the defeats in South Africa to inadequate military planning and training:

> Sons of the sheltered city — unmade, unhandled, unmeet —
> Ye pushed them raw to the battle as ye picked them raw from
> the street.

The poem created much controversy, but on 4 January 1902, Haggard wrote to Kipling, who was staying at Cecil Rhodes's home in Cape Town, stating that he agreed that Britain was unprepared for war not only militarily but agriculturally. On 28 January, Kipling replied: 'Your side of the attack — the question of Food supply — is as you say *the* vital one. You have the figures and facts and the influence: and for goodness sake keep on hammering at it. What makes me sick is what makes you sick — the way, to wit, in which the responsible politician admits the cold truth of one's contention and then explicitly says that he doesn't dare "go in advance of public opinion" and so on. Well here's luck! We need it.'[7] It appears that it was at this time that Haggard, accepting his friend's stance, became the outspoken advocate of conscription he was to remain throughout his life.

Because of his work on *Rural England*, Haggard had been unable to start the gardening record that he had contracted to write for *The Queen*. On 7 February, Watt agreed with the magazine's editor that the manuscript would be ready for publication in January, 1904. Haggard was, therefore, able to continue with his mammoth task.

There were, however, worries for him to face. On 23 June, the day after his birthday, he wrote from Ditchingham to Aggie: 'I can't say that at 46 my outlook in a professional sense is altogether promising. It has come to this. I must break with Longmans as I simply can't sell my serial rights while they hold the book rights. It is a painful job, but since one must live it must be done. . . . I am still struggling and likely to struggle till autumn with this gigantic *Rural England* . . . which I don't suppose anybody will read when it is finished'.[8]

Not having written a popular book since *Swallow*, five years earlier, Haggard was all too aware that his income was declining steadily each year and that, if he wished to continue with his agricultural campaign, he must shortly produce a money-making work of fiction. Also, as he points out in his letter to Aggie, publishers expected to purchase both the book and serial rights of a novel. It was, therefore, no longer easy to sell the serial rights to a magazine and then the book rights to Longmans. Because of this, in the summer of 1902, both the serial and book rights of *The Brethren*, the story of the Crusades he planned to write, were purchased by Cassell, the first book of his to be published by that company since *King Solomon's Mines*, seventeen years before. On 14 October, Watt managed to complete a dual agreement by which T.P. O'Connor purchased for £750 the serial rights of *Stella Fregelius* (which Haggard had written in 1899) and Longmans agreed to publish the book. It was the last of Haggard's novels that Longmans published in Great Britain.

At about this time, Haggard decided that he would at last write the sequel to *She* that he had been contemplating ever since the original was published. For this Watt was able to obtain the most profitable contract Haggard had been given for many years. On 29 November, Ward Lock & Co. purchased for £1,100 the serial rights of the story (which it was agreed would not be less than 100,000 words) for inclusion in *Windsor Magazine*, and agreed to pay an advance of £1,000 on publication of the book.

On the previous day, 28 November, Longmans published in an edition of 1,500 *Rural England*, which Haggard had dedicated to 'Arthur H.D. Cochrane, the companion of these journeyings as of many previous adventures, and to all throughout England who have assisted me in my undertaking'. The two volumes with a total of 1,207 pages cost 36/-.

To bring about the changes in land-holding he was advocating, Haggard called upon the Government to make important reforms including extending the provisions of the Housing of the Working Classes Act to enable money for the purchase of farm cottages to be borrowed at low rates of interest from the Treasury. Faced with this practical, but socialist, programme, presented by a man assumed to be a member of the traditional Tory squirearchy, press reviewers were somewhat confused. *The Quarterly Review*, while stating that 'his portly volumes take their place by the side of the works of Arthur Young, Cobbett, and Caird', concluded that 'his gospel of dependence on the government is a confession of failure'.[9] Similarly *The Spectator*, while admitting 'not only its literary charm, but the great interest of much of the information contained in these volumes', announces that 'the writer does not distinguish his conclusions from his preconceptions . . . his judgement seems constitutionally pessimistic'.[10] Some individuals, however, were more wholehearted in their praise. Joseph Chamberlain wrote: 'I judge from what you say that we are very much at one. I am, and always have been, in favour of Small Holdings.' In a letter dated 22 December, Kipling began: 'Dear Cobbett-Young-Haggard, For the last week or more the wife and I have been reading *Rural England*, with deep joy (I don't mean on account of the state of things revealed) and admiration. I bought it lawfully in market overt and it stands with your *Farmer's Year* between Young's *Agriculture of Sussex* and *Selborne*. I take off my hat to you deeply and profoundly because it's a magnum opus and altogether fascinating and warning and chock full of instruction.'[11]

The publication of *Rural England*, and his need to increase his income made 1903 an exceptionally busy year for Haggard. In January he not only started *A Gardener's Year*, his record of the garden at Ditchingham House, he simultaneously began writing *The Brethren*. His work was, however, soon interrupted by a strange incident. On 14 January, he saw an advertisement stating that a new story of his entitled *The Secret of Dead Man's Mount* was being published serially in *The Home Companion*. This he sent in a letter to Charles Longman: 'Do you know what the enclosed means? I presume that it alludes to *Colonel Quaritch* which can scarcely be called a "new story" even if it appears as *The Secret of Dead Man's Mount*. Moreover, I never wrote the screed beginning "Dear Edward" as may be seen by reference to page 29 of *Colonel Quaritch* six shilling edition. I really think these people ought to be dropped on. It is not right to change a title of a story and advertise it as new.'[12]

On 16 January, Longman replied: 'In September last when I was away, an application came from a penny periodical called *The Home Companion* for permission to run *Colonel Quaritch* as a serial. As the serial rights were all sold to Tillotson, the application was referred to them. The advertisement you enclose is the result. I send you the numbers of *The Home Companion* which I have procured, which further explain the matter. It appears that they have rewritten the letter on page 29 of *Colonel Quaritch* with the view of introducing a fresh cipher and the person who guesses this cipher is to get £100. I have not yet had time to examine their version closely, but I see at once that it is in part abridged and also here and there altered from your text. As you have sold all serial rights I presume that we cannot stop Messrs Tillotson from selling them again, but surely they would be bound to see that the complete and correct text is printed. Also they have clearly no right to announce it, as they do in the advertisement, as a new story and under another title.'

Before Mr Justice Darling on 30 January, the solicitors Revington & Son applied for an injunction to restrain *The Home Companion* from continuing to print the story. The action was stayed, however, when the defendants agreed to pay the plaintiff's case and publish the following paragraph: 'We are requested by Mr

Rider Haggard to state that this serial story is an abbreviated version of his original story *Colonel Quaritch, V.C.* written by him and published by Messrs Longmans in 1888. The serial rights in this novel belong to us and Mr Rider Haggard is in no way responsible for its present publication. The alteration of the title, the abbreviation and the necessary alteration in the plot so as to preserve the secret in the letter of Sir James de la Molle were made by us without Mr Rider Haggard's knowledge or approval.'[13]

There were other, more pleasant, interruptions to Haggard's writing. He was frequently invited to address meetings of such bodies as the Royal Institution and various chambers of agriculture on his proposals for rural reform, especially the desirability of introducing an agricultural post, resettling the urban unemployed on the land, and introducing preferential tariffs. He was, however, very aware that these activities did not produce the income he required. On 13 February, he wrote to Stanley Weyman, another landowner and popular writer: 'You will understand what labour all this [has meant] . . . and I have to write novels in the cracks. (For 2 years there have been *no* cracks.) A man with a family must think of his living and theirs and one does not make a fortune out of books like *Rural England* or *A Farmer's Year*.'[14]

Haggard did, however, continue his campaign, endeavouring to persuade the ruling Unionist Government that small-holdings should be encouraged, but when it became apparent that his opinions were unacceptable he turned his attention to the Liberals. On 19 March he wrote to Asquith: 'I have read your speech reported yesterday and in consequence I am venturing to ask your acceptance of the copy of my recently published work *Rural England* which I send herewith. I hope that you may find time to glance at the book, and especially at the chapter headed "Conclusions". Most thoroughly do I agree with what you say as to the possibility of a vastly increased output of home-grown food. But this you will never get until you have co-operation and the *cheap carriage* which, as you may have seen, I am doing my best to advocate — under the form of an increase in postal facilities.' It was among the Radical party, which by nature and upbringing Haggard so disliked, that his agricultural ideas were to be received most attentively.

In mid-May, Haggard went to London where he spent four weeks speaking at meetings, visiting flower shows and, as he records in *A Gardener's Year*, attending an orchid auction, for if gardening was his hobby orchids were his passion and the glory of his garden was his orchid houses, where in the warm dampness and among the strange flowers of the tropics he could regularly inhabit a world other than that of the Norfolk countryside.

His first book of the year complete, Haggard wrote on 30 June to Cassell's: 'I beg to enclose the completed M.S. of my Crusading romance *The Brethren* of which, if I remember right, the first half is due to be delivered tomorrow. I only hope that you will like it as well as on the whole, I confess, I like it myself. I have arranged the story in twenty-four chapters, so that you can, if you think fit, print two in each issue of your magazine, on the presumption that it is to run for a year.' Cassell's, about to publish a Haggard novel for the first time since 1885, thought it was opportune to bring out at the same time a new edition of *King Solomon's Mines*, the revised copy of which Haggard delivered on 25 July, requesting 'that all the corrections are checked by some experienced and competent person and that if any doubt arises as to the reading of a passage the matter should be referred to me.'[15]

In August Haggard corrected the proofs of *Stella Fregelius* and on the 25th of the month wrote a letter of dedication:

My dear John Berwick,
  When you read her history in MS. you thought well of *Stella Fregelius* and, whilst I hesitated, urged her introduction to the world. Therefore I ask you, my severe and accomplished critic, to accept the burden of a book for which you are to some extent responsible. Whatever its fate, at least it has pleased you and therefore has not been written quite in vain.
                                                    (From *Stella Fregelius*)

John Berwick was, as Scott points out in his bibliography, a nom-de-plume for Aggie, and so the dedication suggests that Haggard, perhaps concerned about its clear autobiographical account of Lilly's influence on him, took the manuscript of the novel with him to Florence the previous year so that he could obtain Aggie's encouragement and reassurance.

Shortly afterwards Haggard began what was to be his most important novel written for several years, his sequel to *She*. The time he was spending on writing and his need for an increased income were such that, at the end of September, he decided to give up the 104 acres of the estate at Bedingham that he had farmed for twenty years. On 12 October, after the farm had been let, his seven horses, twenty-four head of neat stock and the agricultural implements were sold at a public auction, realising a total of £460 8s. 0d.

In December, shortly after *The Brethren* began appearing as a serial in *Cassell's Magazine*, Haggard completed his novel about Ayesha. On 16 December he sent an additional seven sheets to form a further chapter of the manuscript he had already submitted to the publishers. Although Haggard had resurrected *She*, he had been unable to re-create the magic and sensuality of the original. The story is peopled with familiar names, but they are but poor shadows of Holly, Vincey, Ayesha and Atene. There are, it is true, many adventures and incidents, but they lack tension and conviction. Even when Haggard creates a promising image, it seems as if his imagination is restricted, perhaps in part by his over-sensitive fear of harsh criticism. So, having introduced the giant red death-hounds of the Khan hunting a prince on a white horse, he concludes:

What followed I will not describe, but never shall I forget the scene of those two heaps of worrying wolves, and of the maniac Khan, who yelled, in his fiendish joy, and cheered on his death-hounds to finish their red work.
                                                    (From *Ayesha*)

Haggard was obviously much more at home in his garden than in the temples of Ayesha, as he implies when, a few weeks after completing the sequel, he wrote the last page of *A Gardener's Year*:

> Still if the garden has been unprofitable from causes beyond our control, I have, I confess, found it as delightful as ever to work and wander in, and even to describe. Indeed, if a reader here and there receives as much pleasure from the perusal of this humble, daily record of my horticultural struggles and vicissitudes, as I have from the setting of them down, I shall count myself most fortunate. . . .
>
> Now in the first days of the new year — may it bring prosperity to all sweet gardens and those who own and tend them — I gather this morning a white Rosebud and a single flower of Anemone that is whiter yet. To me the one is a ghost from the grave of dead, forgotten Summer, and the other a spirit of the Spring, breathing that eternal promise which was from the ancient days and evermore shall be.
>
> (From *A Gardener's Year*)

It was the flowers, rather than the story of Ayesha's love, that in 1903 provided Haggard with 'that eternal promise'.

The year had, however, been a successful one as far as Haggard was concerned, for he had completed the three books he had contracted to write, and so, early in 1904, he made plans to spend several months in Egypt, returning home by way of Italy and Spain. In January he gave several speeches on agricultural matters and wrote an article on 'The Small Farmer in England' for *The Youth's Companion*. After arranging with *The Daily Mail* on 2 February that he would be paid £12 12s 0d. for each of six articles on 'Egypt To-Day', Haggard and his eldest daughter Angela sailed on the incident-packed maiden voyage of a P. & O. ship. They ran aground in the Thames, a sailor died and was buried at sea, a violent gale buffeted them in the Channel, the new engines overheated, the chief engineer went mad, a shipwreck was narrowly avoided off Crete, and a sandstorm covered the deck in mud. They were understandably relieved to arrive at Port Said. In Egypt they visited the temple of Abu Simbel, and, guided by Howard Carter, inspected the recently discovered tomb of Queen Nefertiti. Because, since his previous visit to Egypt, he had become fully convinced in his belief in reincarnation, Haggard was distressed by the wholescale robbing and desecration of the ancient tombs and felt certain that entombed remains should lie undisturbed until the Day of Resurrection. On the return journey, aboard R.M.S. *Mongolia*, he dedicated *The Brethren* to his eldest sister, Ella. After a brief visit to Naples, Haggard and Angela went on to the south of Spain, in which he had already planned to set another historical novel. He was there enthralled by the wonders of such buildings as the Alhambra in Granada, the mosque at Cordova, and Seville's vast cathedral.

After his return to England, Haggard, using the notes made during his Egyptian journey, began to write a novel which was 'the result of reflections which occurred to me among the Egyptian sands and the empty cells of long-departed anchorites'.

In June he was invited to the wedding of his niece Nellie, Ella's daughter and Arthur Green's sister; but the prospect of a family reunion somewhat disturbed him and on 26 June he wrote to Ella: 'I am in a quandary about Alfred. Certainly I don't wish to prevent his being asked to Nellie's wedding (would rather stay away myself) nor do I wish to meet his Lordship and spend the nuptial hours in wrangling with him over imaginary wrongs he suffered in 1895 and in proving to him that I am not a millionaire.'[16]

It appears that at this time Haggard was also concerned that, despite his genuine interest in agricultural matters and the considerable amount of serious writing he had undertaken, there were people who still dismissed him as 'a mere writer of romances and boys' books'. So, when Cassell's wrote asking what kind of illustrations he envisaged for *The Brethren*, he replied: 'The suggestion that I have to make is that, as in any case it is only proposed to insert eight pictures, it would be quite as well to publish the book entirely unillustrated. Personally, after a large experience I am quite doubtful, unless they happen to be super-excellent or forcibly to strike the public taste, of the advantage of illustrations in a novel. On the other hand, I am quite certain that a story is often judged by its illustrations, since it is so much easier to look at the pictures than to read the text. Now I hope that *The Brethren* may appeal to some readers who are not boys, as I fear that the illustrations will cause it at once to be classed among boys' books. I urge therefore that the best plan would be to have none at all.'[17]

On the night of the next day, Saturday 9 July, Haggard, after going to bed at about 12.30, had a nightmare: 'I was awakened by my wife's voice calling to me from her own bed upon the other side of the room. I dreamed that a black retriever dog, a most amiable and intelligent beast named Bob, which was the property of my eldest daughter, was lying on its side among brushwood, or rough growth of some sort, by water. In my vision the dog was trying to speak to me in words, and, failing, transmitted to my mind in an undefined fashion the knowledge that it was dying. Then everything vanished, and I woke to hear my wife asking me why on earth I was making those horrible and weird noises. I replied that I had had a nightmare about a fearful struggle, and that I had dreamed that old Bob was in a dreadful way, and was trying to talk to me and to tell me about it.'

On Sunday evening it was discovered that Bob was missing and on Thursday, 14 July, Haggard and Charles Debingfield, a servant, discovered the dog's body, floating against a weir in the River Waveney. Subsequent investigations revealed that Bob had been killed by a train a few hours before Haggard's nightmare. The incident, which was later fully reported in the *Journal of the Society of Psychical Research*, forced Haggard to conclude: 'There is a more intimate ghostly connection between all members of the animal world, including man, than has hitherto been believed, at any rate by Western peoples.' Because of this, although previously having derived much pleasure from shooting, he decided that he would never kill another living creature, with the exception of fish.

The Brethren was published on 30 September, as Haggard wished, without illustrations. He thought highly of the book, recording in his private diary on 28 December, 1920: 'I have been engaged in reperusing *The Brethren*. . . . It has interested me enormously and, "though I says it as shouldn't", if it is not a good romance of the poetical variety, I don't know what is! The trouble is to get the public to read historical stories from which they shy, being I think, afraid lest they should be learning something unawares — trapped into knowledge so to speak. Personally, however, I like all history and find it agreeable to absorb it in the form of a good novel. Also this one has been read by some, since I see by the title page, that this edition of fifty thousand copies is the eighteenth.'

While staying at Kessingland in October, Haggard had a considerable amount of correspondence about the title of his sequel to *She* with Ward Lock, who disliked *Hes*, his original suggestion. Various suggestions were made, but eventually Haggard agreed to the title *Ayesha — The Return of She*.[18] Under that title, the story began appearing in *The Windsor Magazine* in December.

Throughout the autumn, while he was writing the Egyptian novel that he had decided to call *Renunciation*, Haggard kept up his campaign of trying to persuade the Government to introduce some of the agricultural reforms he had proposed. On 13 November, Lord Onslow, the Minister of Agriculture, wrote: 'I have read with much interest not only your book on Rural England, but your speeches and letters to the Press on rural subjects; and I thoroughly appreciate how much you have done to educate public opinion on rural matters. I know, too, that in your opinion the Government have shown themselves supine in dealing with these questions. Difficulties there are which perhaps are not within your knowledge. . . . I am in accord with you in much that you hold, but it is only possible for the Board of Agriculture to act where neither legislation nor expenditure is necessary. I expect to be in London most of next week and the week after; and if you should chance to be coming to town, I should much like to discuss some of these subjects with you.'

In response to this invitation, Haggard went to see Lord Onslow and they discussed such matters as small-holdings. Haggard later ruefully recalled: 'In the end he asked me what I thought had best be done. I replied that it would be well to begin by making a thorough inquiry into the circumstances of the whole business. He agreed, and we parted; nor did I ever meet him again except once at a public dinner. Subsequently he appointed a committee to investigate small-holdings, on which he did *not* offer me a seat. Nor, to the best of my recollection, was I even asked to give evidence.'

Also in November, Haggard signed an agreement with Cassell's by which he undertook to deliver an African romance by 30 June 1905, and in return for both the book and serial rights he received £450, by far the lowest advance he had been paid since the publication of *She* in 1887. Haggard's income from writing had dropped to almost a third of what it had been at its peak between 1889 and 1894. The books that he had written since his mother's death had either been about agriculture, which appealed little to the general public, or were historical romances that failed to capture the wide readership which continued to purchase his early novels in the large number of cheap editions flooding the bookstalls but providing the author with a meagre royalty. In 1903, for example, W.T. Stead had launched his series of Penny Novels with *She*, which quickly sold half a million copies. At this time, however, Haggard had neither the interest nor the inspiration to create adventure stories that were of such originality that they would appeal to critics and the public alike. Increasingly he saw fiction merely as a way of providing an income that would subsidise his other activities such as farming and writing about those subjects he wished to explore.

The Way of the Spirit[19] was such a book, in which Haggard tells the story of Rupert Ullenshaw's 'great, and to all appearance successful, Platonic experiment', when, after an unhappy marriage, he arrives in Egypt where he falls in love with Mea but, because of his wedding vows, their relationship remains unconsummated:

> This, then, was their marriage, there amidst the desert sands and beneath the desert stars, which they felt even then were less eternal than the troth they plighted; as it proved, the strangest and yet the happiest and most blessed marriage that ever was celebrated between man and woman — or so they came to think.
>
> (From *The Way of the Spirit*)

Some seven years later, Edith, Ullenshaw's wife, arrives in Egypt and asks her husband to return with her. Before he can, however, he catches the plague and dies. Mea, who has nursed him, also contracts the disease and before her death she speaks to Edith:

> 'I greet you, lady,' she said to Edith. 'Well have I nursed our lord, but now he has passed from us — home, and I — I follow him,' and she pointed over the shattered temple and the wall of mountains upwards to the splendid sky.
>
> 'You follow him; you follow him!' gasped Edith. 'What do you mean?'
>
> By way of answer, Mea tore open her white wrappings and showed her bosom marked with those spots of plague that appear only just before the end.
>
> 'It was his last and best gift to me,' she cried in Arabic. 'Soon, very soon we two shall have done with separations and with griefs. Hearken you, his lady according to your law. He had determined that to-morrow he would have gone back with you whom he forgave, as I do. But we prayed, he and I — yes, knee by knee we prayed to our God, that He would save us from this sacrifice, and He has answered to our prayer . . .
>
> Then while they gazed and wondered, with slow steps Mea reeled to the couch upon which the corpse of Rupert lay; uttering one low cry of love and triumph, she cast herself beside him, and there she died.
>
> (From *The Way of the Spirit*)

It was almost certainly while he was writing *The Way of the Spirit*, his vivid renunciation of sexual love and the reaffirmation of his belief in eternal love, that

Haggard was informed that Archer, Lilly's husband, was dying in Africa of tertiary syphilis and that, it would not be long before Lilly returned home with her youngest son to join the other two boys for whose education Haggard had assumed financial responsibility. In the event it was to be a couple of years before Archer died and Lilly, already ravaged by the venereal disease, returned to East Anglia and Haggard's protection.

When *The Way of the Spirit* was complete, Haggard went to stay with the Kiplings at Batemans, the seventeenth-century house near Burwash in Sussex which they had purchased in 1902. On 22 November, Haggard wrote to his wife: 'I got down here all right and was whirled off by R.K.'s motor (which I find however he don't drive himself) to this place about 4 miles from the Station. This is a most charming house which K. has bought. The front part including hall in which I am writing about 1600, the rest older. All panelled, with old stone arched doorways, and he has furnished it according.'[20] The two men discussed *The Way of the Spirit*, and when Haggard departed he left the manuscript with Kipling who on 2 December wrote: 'I've been up in town or I should have written when I returned *Renunciation*. . . . I did as I have done with a many of your books – simply surrendered myself to the joy of reading and read on.' In Haggard's reply he pointed out that Cassell's were not interested in the novel, and, on 5 December, Kipling wrote again: 'I think if Time wasn't an object I'd let the book lie till I could get it taken serially. How would McClure do in America? It looks to me like a tale that serially would suit him. I don't know whether the *Bystander* in England goes in for serial stuff but I think Cassells was a fool not to take it. Anyhow I'd devote six months to investigations and then if it didn't do I'd sell outright as a book.'[21] Although a publisher was soon found for *The Way of the Spirit*, it neither appeared as a serial nor was it published in America.

1904 was not a happy year for Haggard. In addition to the tragic news about Lilly, his career both as a writer and as an agricultural expert seemed to be in decline. Thrown in again upon himself, he had changed his attitudes both to the collection of antiquities from Egyptian tombs and shooting. His life seemed to have lost purpose, and the ambitions with which he had once been fired seemed to have died. Then, as was so often the way in Haggard's life, things suddenly and dramatically changed. On 14 January 1905, the day after *A Gardener's Year* was published, Alfred Lyttelton, the Secretary of State for the Colonies, unexpectedly wrote: 'The Rhodes Trustees have agreed to give a sum of £300 (inclusive of all expenses) to defray the expense of sending a Commissioner to the United States to inspect and report upon the "Labour Colonies" established in the United States by the Salvation Army. . . . It is thought that if on inquiry this system is found to be financially sound and to be of real benefit to the poorer classes, it might prove a useful model for some analogous system of settlement from the United Kingdom to the Colonies. . . . It is the desire of the Rhodes Trustees that the Commissioner should be nominated by and report to the Secretary of State for the Colonies. I should be very glad if you would consent to do the work, for which your experience as an observer both of men and agricultural affairs so eminently qualifies you.'

Haggard accepted with alacrity and a few days later received his appointment as a Commissioner. His pleasure could not even be dampened by the letter which Longman sent him on 30 January: 'I am afraid that I cannot run *Renunciation* in the magazine. The fact is that no minor alterations would alter the fact that, for good reasons, Rupert renounces sexual relations except under marriage conditions. This is the basis of the book which cannot be put in the background, and it is this particular relation which I think it is better not to discuss in magazines. I have been a good deal tempted by the desire to have another of your stories in the magazine, but there it is — we all have our cranks, and that I suppose is mine. *A Gardener's Year* seems going steadily. We have now 451 left out of 1500 printed.'[22]

At first glance it might seem strange that Haggard was selected for such a mission, but whoever in the Government was responsible made a most astute decision. At a time when the ruling unionist coalition was under fire for its failure to take any decisive action to protect the declining agricultural industry, Haggard was more than an outspoken proponent of action; as an ex-Unionist Parliamentary candidate, an active party member, a figure popular with the masses, and a representative of the landowning class that was the bedrock of Conservatism, he was an embarrassment to the Party and Government he was so very willing to serve. The reforms he was proposing — which had already attracted popular support — were both expensive and unacceptably revolutionary to the establishment. The mission proposed by Lyttelton had the virtue of diverting Haggard and his many readers from the notion of establishing small holdings at home to the possibility of resettling the urban unemployment in the colonies. Yet, because the funds were provided by the Rhodes Trustees, Haggard would not be officially a Government representative (a Commissioner, not a *Royal* Commissioner) so that whatever recommendations he made could, if necessary, be ignored. Also the mission would give publicity to the Salvation Army which, while acceptable to the Government, might go some way to mollifying General Booth, whose constant revelations about the plight of the urban poor were even more damaging to the Cabinet than Haggard's writings. As the two men, so disparate in backgrounds, had already met and were acceptable to each other, the clever proponent of this scheme, whether Lyttelton, Onslow or Balfour, was able in what was to be a General Election year to redirect the critical fire of two powerful figures from the home front to those colonies across the seas that had but little effect on the British electorate.

Uninvolved in such political deviousness, Haggard enthusiastically made preparations for his visit to the United States. Deciding to take as his secretary his elder daughter, Angela — then twenty-two — Haggard booked passages for them both on the *Teutonic* and before its departure on 22 February he called on Lyttelton and Booth, arranged to spend a few days in the United States with his friend Burnham (then living at 625 Orange Grove Avenue, Pasadena, California) and, as a preliminary to his tour, visited the Hadleigh Colony of the Salvation Army in Essex.

Being aware that the mission would both be time-consuming and leave him out of pocket, Haggard had also to make some arrangements for the writing which produced his income. He delivered the synopsis of *Fair Margaret*, a historical novel set in Spain, to his agent who already had the completed manuscript of *The Way of the Spirit* to be placed. In addition Haggard was contracted to write an African romance for Cassell's to be delivered by 30 June. This he started and continued during the voyage to the United States.

On his arrival in New York, Haggard, as in 1891, was seized upon by reporters. At the Waldorf Hotel, a ringing telephone awakened Angela at two in the morning. Having answered, she ran into her father's adjoining room, where Haggard was also taking a call, and exclaimed: 'Oh, dad, *do* come here! There is a lunatic on the telephone who says he wants me to come out walking in the streets!' It emerged that a newspaper was distributing free food to the New York poor and thought that Haggard's presence would provide good publicity!

When being interviewed by the press, Haggard was most reluctant to talk about his writing. *The New York Herald*, for example, reported: 'Mr Haggard made interviewing difficult as long as the talk clung to literature. He answered a question briefly and courteously in a dozen words, and then relaxed into his pipe and waited for the next query. It was only when he got to the practical side of life that he began to warm up and talk without prodding. Then the coldness, the indifference, the reserve — whatever you wish to call the typical English manner with strangers — fell away from Mr Haggard like a mask. He grew earnest, enthusiastic, cogent; but always without self-praise or over-confidence.'[23]

After attending public receptions in New York and Philadelphia, Haggard went to Washington where on 9 March he met President Theodore Roosevelt. The two men established an immediate warm rapport and a few days later Haggard and Angela were entertained at a White House luncheon where, according to Haggard, Roosevelt said: 'It is an odd thing, Mr Haggard, that you and I, brought up in different countries and following such different pursuits, should have identical ideas and aims. I have been reading your book *Rural England*, and I tell you that what you think, I think, and what you want to do, I want to do.'

During his seven weeks in America, Haggard visited and reported on not only the Salvation Army Colonies at Fort Romie in California, Fort Amity in Colorado and Fort Herrick in Ohio, but also the Vacant Lot Cultivation Scene in Philadelphia, Mormon small-holdings at Salt Lake City, and the Government irrigation scheme at Yuma where, because of a 'wash-out' of the Colorado River, Haggard and his daughter were in danger of being drowned. In Canada, at Haggard's request, the Prime Minister, Wilfred Laurier, promised 240,000 acres of land to be used for a settlement scheme such as Haggard had inspected in the United States. As he had thereby accomplished everything he had set out to do, he was rightfully delighted; but for Haggard the mission was not only a success, it was a real turning-point.

Greeted and entertained by eminent public figures as an equal, travelling in private railcars accompanied by not just his daughter but a whole retinue of helpers provided by the Salvation Army, and listened to everywhere with respect, Haggard was convinced that in such public service he had found his true vocation. In a speech delivered to the Canadian Club in Russel House, Ottawa, he declared that he no longer found his real inspiration in writing: 'Of course, the time comes to every writer, I suppose, when he has an inspiration and does something which he knows to be better than he ever did before. . . . Then, perhaps, he begins to understand — it comes into his mind — that that was not his real inspiration . . . He turns and wonders where it is. And he turns, let us say, and looks at the dull masses of misery that pervade the globe, he looks and wonders, and he thinks: Is there nothing that I, humble as I am, can do to help alleviate that misery, to lift up those who are fallen, to lift them up for their own good and for the good of the world? And then, gentlemen, he knows that that, not the gaudy, exciting work is the real inspiration of his life.'

Having been given a platform, Haggard extended his simple programme of rural reform to a comprehensive recipe for the salvation of the Western world. Resettlement on the land, he argued, had the beneficial result of enabling the large families to be supported that were an impossibility in city slums. Such an increase in the population provided a necessary bastion against the expansionist threats of other races. So in his Canadian speech, Haggard continued: 'We must look at facts. With dwellers on the land self-interest comes in; on the land alone will the supply of children be available that is necessary to carrying on our white races.'

Convinced that labour settlements in the colonies would help solve the problem of urban poverty in Britain, Haggard urged the Canadians to accept large-scale immigration so that their sparsely inhabited country should be more fully utilised as farmland. Although his speech may now seem naïve and racialistic, Haggard saw himself as a protector of his race and culture. A nationalist he was, and a convinced imperialist whose major concern was to build strong Dominions, for he believed it was on them in the future that Britain must rely for the food that it could no longer grow for itself. He was not, however, an extremist urging the supremacy of a white or Anglo-Saxon master-race. His enthusiastic advocacy of settlement in the Dominions was derived not from notions of racial conquest but from his informed sympathy for the appalling conditions in which lived his country's urban poor.

Despite his public successes, Haggard had some personal upsets. He became very frightened when, on the last leg of their journey, Angela developed influenza. Also, his brother Andrew, whom he had discovered living in straitened circumstances in Maine, wrote angrily refusing Haggard's invitation to see him and Angela off at New York: 'As to coming down to New York to see you sailing home again after your rapid and triumphal progress — and leaving me behind, well, my dear Rider, it would be too absolutely distressing and I could not stand it. To be alone on the wharf in New York, with no friends, no glory, no excitement, no money, while seeing the smoke from your funnels disappearing. And then the headlines in the papers — "Departure of Rider Haggard" — "Distinguished Novelist Leaves for Europe" — "Americans are like his Brothers" — That sort of thing greeting me everywhere would be too much altogether.'[24]

While sailing back home on the *Majestic*, Haggard worked busily on his papers and wrote a brief account of his mission for Lyttelton, whom he went to see some weeks after his return when the lengthy report had been completed. During the very brief interview, Haggard asked the Colonial Secretary if he was satisfied with the document. 'Satisfied?' he replied. 'I think it is splendid. I wish the Prime Minister would take it up. But Arthur won't read it — you know Arthur won't read it.' Naturally Haggard was disappointed, contrasting such summary consideration with the attention lavished on him by Roosevelt. For a time he assumed that because he had accomplished his mission so successfully, he would be sent elsewhere for a similar purpose. Thus on 15 May he wrote to the Bishop of Salisbury turning down a speaking engagement on 5 October: 'By the date you name, for aught I know, I may be sent abroad again.'[25] He also tried to lobby support for an extension of his work, writing on 20 May to Lord Rosebery, the Chairman of the Rhodes Trust: 'I have ventured to suggest that a Commissioner should be sent to South Africa and especially to Rhodesia, to examine those Colonies and see what they are prepared to do to help. I have great hope that the tobacco industry in Rhodesia gives an opening to the small-holder. I think also that your Lordship will agree with me that a British population is desirable in that country.' He rapidly realised, however, that land settlement was something of a nuisance to the Government, which, having decided to do as little as possible, referred the matter to a Departmental Committee.

Meanwhile Haggard had to attend to his writing. While he had been away, Hutchinson's on 10 March had agreed to publish both *The Way of the Spirit* and *Fair Margaret*, paying an advance of £750 on each against a royalty of 25 per cent on the 6/- edition. On 29 May he agreed with Cassell's to write another African romance of 110,000 words, half to be delivered by 31 March 1907 and half in June 1907. For this Cassell's agreed to pay £900 for the serial rights on receipt of the manuscript and an advance of £750 on publication. Before he could work out the plot of this romance, however, Haggard had to complete the African tale for Cassell's that he had started writing earlier in the year and that was provisionally entitled *The Spirit of Bambatse*.

On 19 June, Haggard's official *Report on the Salvation Army Colonies in the United States and at Hadleigh, England, with Scheme of National Land Settlement* (a Blue Book) was published. Press reaction was most favourable, *The Times*, for example, declaring in a leading article: 'Mr Rider Haggard has completed with commendable despatch a work of great interest to all who have at heart the national welfare. . . . With the object which he had in view there will be general sympathy. The drift to the town; the severance from the land of people who become degraded physically and otherwise in great cities; the sight of vast tracts of fertile land lying uncultivated, while thousands annually move helplessly and blindly towards cities, there to mix in a population of waifs and driftwood; the "tendency to race-ruin, a product of our Western culture", due greatly to living in crowded quarters of great cities — all that is so grave an evil that any alleviation of it is to be prized. . . . Mr Rider Haggard will, it is to be hoped, be enabled to continue his inquiries, and tell us how his plan can be carried out in England, dear land, excessive rates and the rising demands of rural district Councils notwithstanding.'[26] The call for Haggard to be enabled to continue his work was taken up by many newspapers and journals, including the *Review of Reviews* which concluded an article on 'Commissioner H. Rider Haggard' by stating: 'The scheme is business-like, sound and ready. The agents are waiting. The appointment of Mr Rider Haggard as Superintendent of Land Settlements should be gazetted tomorrow.'[27]

While Haggard waited for Government action, he undertook a considerably increased amount of speech-making and letter-writing. He also prepared a popular version of his report, entitled *The Poor and the Land*, which was published on 15 August by Longmans. But it was all to no avail. The Department Committee finally reported: 'Though we fully recognise the zeal and ability Mr Rider Haggard has shown in making his investigations and preparing his Report, and trust that much good may be done indirectly by the ventilation of the suggestions that he has made, we regret to be obliged to say that we consider his scheme to be open to many objections that, even if we were prepared to advocate colonisation in principle, we could not recommend that this particular scheme should be adopted.'

And so, despite his efforts in other directions, Haggard was left to do nothing but continue writing fiction. Having completed his African romance, he sent it off to Cassell's, who objected to his title, *The Spirit of Bambatse*. On 31 July he wrote: 'I vote for *The Guardian and the Gold. An African Romance*. I don't think that *The Lady Aphrodite* or any fancy title of that sort would suit this kind of story; at least I should write a very different one, if I were commissioned to produce anything that could live up to it. The other thing is more or less descriptive of the tale, and the word "Gold" is always attractive in romance.'[28] Eventually it was settled that the romance would be published as *Benita*, because Cassell's preferred a short title for the publicity posters that in the event they never published.

About this time, Haggard asked Kipling if *The Way of the Spirit* could be dedicated to him. Kipling readily agreed and on 14 August, Haggard wrote for inclusion in the novel his letter of dedication: 'Both of us believe that there are higher aims in life than the weaving of stories well or ill, and according to our separate occasions strive to fulfil this faith. Still, when we talked together of the plan of this tale, and when you read the written book, your judgement thereof was such as all of us hope for from an honest and instructed friend — generally in vain. So, as you found interest in it, I offer it to you, in token of much I cannot write. But you will understand.'

Shortly afterwards, exhausted by his mission, during which he had travelled over six thousand miles by train, his speech-making and heavy writing commitment, Haggard fell ill and was taken into a London nursing home where he was operated on by Professor Rose, assisted by Dr Lyne Stivens, an old friend. He was still there several weeks later when on 6 October *Ayesha* was published. Lang, to whom it was dedicated, wrote immediately: 'You may think me a hound, but I only found out as I went to bed last night that *Ayesha* was in the drawing-room. Awfully good of you to make such a nice dedication, grammar right too. . . . I am almost afraid to read 'She', as at 61,00000 one has no longer the joyous credulity of forty, and even *your* imagination is out of the fifth form. However, plenty of boys are about, and I hope they will be victims of the enchantress.' A few days later, however, he sent a more reassuring note: 'It is all right: I am Thrilled: so much obliged. I thought I was too Old, but the Eternal Boy is still on the job.'

After leaving the nursing home, Haggard went to recuperate at the home of Dr Stivens. While there he visited the Kiplings for a couple of days. Together the two worked on a plot for the next African romance Haggard was to write for Cassell's, *The Ghost Kings*. On three sheets of foolscap they wrote alternately a detailed outline of a story about a girl and the boy she grows to love, both children of Natal colonists, who meet the Ghost People, a strange African tribe whose life-force is a tree. Clearly Kipling was doing all he could to encourage his friend's recovery. This he helped to accomplish and, early in November, Haggard was well enough to begin again a programme of public speaking and to start his novel *Fair Margaret*.

On 5 December, Balfour, accepting that his tottering Unionist coalition could no longer govern effectively, resigned the premiership and Campbell-Bannerman formed a Liberal ministry. Shortly after the Cabinet was announced, the *Review of Reviews* published in January 1906 a paragraph headed 'Where is Mr Rider Haggard?' that stated: 'The appointment of Lord Carrington as Minister of Agriculture, coupled with C-B.'s emphatic declaration in favour of land reform and the return of the people to the country, points to immediate action. Mr Rider Haggard ought to be despatched at once to report upon all that has been done in this direction in Denmark, Holland, Belgium, and Bavaria. . . . There is no more capable agricultural commissioner than Mr Rider Haggard, and he has quite recently done excellent work in his report on Canadian Colonisation. It is to be hoped that Lord Carrington will have despatched him to the Continent before Parliament assembles.'[29]

In the General Election, the Liberals inflicted a humiliating defeat on the Unionists, many of whose leaders, including Balfour and Lyttelton, found themselves temporarily without seats. Elected as they were largely by working-class voters, it seemed likely that the Liberals might make use of Haggard and his ideas and so, although still a committed if not convinced Tory, he waited expectantly. Towards the end of February he was asked to give evidence before a committee called by the Government to consider small-holdings. In his letter of reply, he states: 'I think that what the country needs is a settled agricultural policy which by its inherent incidence and effects would promote the growth of small-holdings. I believe that the model for that policy is to be found in Denmark, and that it would be exceedingly wise and useful to thoroughly re-investigate the conditions there (and in some other European countries, such as Holland and Belgium) with a view to ascertaining which of their laws and regulations could be adapted with advantage to the United Kingdom. This investigation I should be prepared to undertake if that were wished by the Government.'

In March, having temporarily moved up to London, Haggard presented his evidence, attended a lecture given by G.B. Shaw at a meeting of the Fabian Society, and addressed the Garden City Association. Also in March, *The Way of the Spirit* was published, a book which Watt described as 'perhaps one of your best and finest books'.[30]

He was not, however, called upon to undertake further investigations and so, back at Ditchingham, Haggard continued writing *Fair Margaret*, the serial rights of which had been purchased by *The Lady's Realm* for £900. Prepared for his work to be interrupted at any time, he also undertook to review the occasional book for *The Saturday Review* (at £2. 6s. 0d. each) and to write another article, 'Thebes of the Hundred Gates', for *The Youth's Companion* (for which he was to be paid $225).

On 12 June, Haggard was invited to present evidence to the Select Committee on the Housing of the Working Classes Amendment Bill. He appeared before the Committee on 25 June and his evidence was later included in the published Report. It was not the important work he hoped to perform, but it was something. Meanwhile, when he read that a Royal Commission on Coast Erosion was to be appointed, he wrote to Lloyd George, the President of the Board of Trade, explaining how he had prevented the sea eroding the cliffs in front of his Kessingland house by planting marram grass. Lloyd George asked to see him and in time Haggard was appointed a member of the Royal Commission, that was at first chaired by Lord Ashby St Ledgers, a young man whose early success in public life drove Haggard to comment: 'How strangely do the lots of men vary, especially in this old-established land! One toils all his life to attain in old age, or more probably not to attain at all, what another steps into from the beginning as a natural right and almost without effort on his part.'

With Haggard's appointment as a Royal Commissioner the die was cast and the pattern of his life established that was to endure almost until his death. With but brief interruptions he worked tirelessly for almost all the next nineteen years on Government and other official committees, travelling vast distances and giving his time and energy, receiving no pay for his services. Writing fiction became simply a chore to be fitted in when there was no other, more important, demand. It is then hardly surprising that, although he was still to write another twenty-six novels, few had much merit and his income from writing steadily continued to decline. Why then was he so keen to undertake arduous, unpaid work, largely on behalf of a ruling political party with which he was not really in sympathy? Certainly his desire to serve his country was genuine, and was, he later claimed, inspired by a desire to ensure that his name was remembered for something worthwhile. But behind this ambition, a driving force perhaps unsuspected even by Haggard, was a need both to expiate his youthful sins and to stop writing seriously. The ill-comprehended desire to write that had driven him until his mother's death had been replaced by a wish to dwell on those subjects dear to her — rural life, gardening, history and the

195

ancient culture of Egypt. Having exhausted these, Haggard could do little but recall themes already used and places he had with excitement once explored. Having long ago lost the inspiration for his invention, he had by this time also run out of subjects. There was very little left that he wanted to say in fiction. It is true that a ready market still existed for his regurgitations and that, if ever chastised for pandering to it, Haggard could salve his artistic conscience by dismissing his own writing as being of far less importance than the services he was performing for the State.

For the next five years, Haggard served on the Royal Commission which soon added Afforestation to its original subject of Coastal Erosion. He faithfully attended every meeting but one and from the start was Chairman of the Unemployed Labour and Reclamation Committee. He also chaired two of the tours that were made of the coasts of Great Britain and Ireland, leading him later to speculate, 'I wonder if there is a groin or an eroded beach on the shores of the United Kingdom that I have not seen and thoughtfully considered.'

His professional and private life continued in the intervals between his bouts of public service, which he found so much more preferable to the political life he had once contemplated. In an interview published in *The Christian Commonwealth* on 1 November 1906, when asked if he had given up the idea of entering Parliament, he replied: 'My time is fully occupied, and I am not a party man. Unless you can swallow holusbolus a given set of opinions it is not easy to mix in current politics. Personally, I have an unfortunate habit of trying to see what is good on both sides. So I do what I can as an outsider.'[31]

Haggard, now that he was truly in the public eye, had to deal with mountains of correspondence from all over the world. He was constantly being asked by newspapers and journals to give his opinions on almost any matter of public interest; organisations by the score requested subscriptions or messages of support; and there were many requests for interviews, information and short articles. In addition, Haggard had to earn his living. In the autumn of 1906 he began writing *The Ghost Kings*, but finding the plot worked out with Kipling not to his liking he relegated the idea to a small section at the end of the book which appears intrusive and is handled uncertainly. The major part becomes little more than a competent telling of how yet another white woman is welcomed as a goddess by an African tribe. While he was working on *The Ghost Kings*, Haggard agreed to write a third African romance for Cassell's. On 24 November, A.P. Watt wrote to Arthur Spurgeon of Cassell's quoting a letter from Haggard: 'If Mr Spurgeon wishes it, I will come to see him as regards the plot, but perhaps it will be enough if I tell him that it will be laid partly in England and partly in Africa and that it will involve sundry adventures of (I hope) a rather weird and original order, and that it will be called, probably, *The Yellow God*. Perhaps he will be content to leave the rest to me. . . . By the way please ask him to be careful not to let out the title lest we should have a whole Olympus full of "Yellow Gods".'[32] The agreement was signed on 27 November, Cassell's paying £450 for the serial rights and an advance of £750 on the book's publication.

Perhaps revealing an awareness in the decline of Haggard's invention, Charles Longman on 6 January 1907 wrote to his long-time friend about *Fair Margaret*, which had started appearing serially in *The Lady's Realm* two months earlier: 'I hanker after another King Solomon or Allan Quatermain. Hunting, adventure, some of the peculiar vein of humour of those early yarns, romance — all these I can do with, but no mystics, if you please. Now you know just the sort of book I want and there are lots of other thick heads who want just the same.'[33] There was little possibility, however, of Haggard's producing work similar to his early novels. During the next couple of years, his writing constantly interrupted, he was content to dictate from his previously worked-out plots romances that were merely accept-ably competent — *The Yellow God*, *The Lady of Blossholme* (in contracts signed on 11 July 1907 *The British Weekly* purchased the serial rights for £750 and Hodder & Stoughton agreed to pay on book publication an advance of £750, as they also did for the historical novel *Red Eve*), *Morning Star* (an Egyptian romance) and *Queen Sheba's Ring*.

Despite this almost frenetic activity, Haggard was all the time extremely aware of his own declining fortunes, and was constantly on the look-out for additional income. On 22 March 1907, he wrote to his friend, Burnham: 'Recently in London I met Mr John Wesley De Kay, president of the Mexican Packing Co., of which the headquarters are in Mexico City. Mr De Kay . . . made certain propositions to me. Included in these propositions is one that I have accepted, that I should travel to Mexico and there inspect some undefined block, or blocks of land, with a view to ascertaining their suitability for European settlement and also their agricultural possibilities. I hope to start from England upon this business about the middle of June. . . . I have been wondering if, could the matter be arranged as I think, I could venture to ask your assistance in this business.'[34]

Nothing, however, came of the scheme, and early in the summer Haggard decided that Kessingland must pay for its keep and so it was let, but in response to an inquiry from the estate agent department of Harrods, as to whether it was still available, he wrote on 16 July: 'I don't know whether you ever receive applications for the purchase of houses or land on the East Coast, but in case you do, I may mention that I might be willing to consider a proposal to buy Kessingland Grange, unfurnished of course. . . . The situation is admirably adapted to the purposes of an hotel.'

Although the house was not sold, his financial position was such that when in June he was approached by the South Norfolk Unionist Association to offer himself as the prospective candidate for the division, Haggard on 5 June replied: 'I thank your Executive Committee very much for the kind suggestion which you convey to me which might be attractive had I the time and money at disposal. This, however, is not the case.'[35] On 18 August, while on Commission business in Maidenhead, he wrote to his wife, saying that he had met some people who lived in Malaga and knew Jack, Aggie, and their two daughters well: 'They tell me that Joan is a charming girl, only rather too full of "character" and that she ought not to be sent back to Malaga. Phoebe, they say, never does a stroke of drawing or anything now. Aggie is very worn out and tired and "wants a rest". Jack, I gather, passing strange and has taken up bull-fighting as a scientific study — a rum crowd. Joan is coming to stay with us isn't she? I should like to see the child. I wish I were rich enough to look after the whole pack of them.'[36]

In September, after the publication of *Fair Margaret*, Haggard's eldest daughter, Angela, married her cousin, Bazett's second son, Tom. The two families had seen little of each other for many years, until the romance had blossomed the previous year; but Haggard did not oppose the match, thinking perhaps that, because his daughter would be retaining his name, there was some possibility that a son might be born who would inherit the Haggard name and estate.

About this time, Lilly, suffering from the tertiary syphilis that had killed her husband, returned to live with her sisters in Aldeburgh. Haggard's daughter records: 'For a year or two she lingered on, and as often as they could Rider and Louie went to see her — the ravaged shadow of the woman Rider had loved when they were both young.'[37]

Another friend with whom Haggard continued to have some contact was Andrew Lang who, towards the end of 1907, wrote suggesting a further collaboration for a story about a Scottish Covenanter, but Haggard did not like the idea, although he seems to have been momentarily tempted to try writing something likely to be of merit. On 28 December, he replied: 'I'd *like* to do another book with you before we skip — awfully. I think you were a bit discouraged about the *W. Desire* because a lot of *ignorant* fools slated it, but in my opinion you were wrong. That work I believe will last. . . . Well now: I don't care much for your Covenanter who would speak Scotch, etc. (*i.e.* at first sight). He would not have much of a public or enlist the heart. Can you not think of something 'big and beautiful', something that has an *idea* in it? . . . You see the thing must have a heart; mere adventures are not enough: I can turn *them* out by the peck.'

In 1908, Haggard kept busy enough with his Commission and writing to stave off the depression from which he might well otherwise have suffered. Convinced as he was, however, that those around him were at times called upon to pay the price of his own sins, he could not forget either Lilly's suffering or the apparently inevitable decline in his family's fortune. On 6 February, he heard from Watt that Cassell's might be interested in publishing the Egyptian story he was writing, providing 'it has a good love interest'. The following day, Haggard replied: 'I note what you say re Messrs Cassell and the romance of Old Egypt. This will have a 'good love interest' (a great deal more than in the case of *The Yellow God*), the tale being that of an Egyptian Queen who is wooed and, after many strange adventures which include a good deal of the ancient magic, won by a subject who has been her foster-brother, the descendant of a discarded dynasty. I propose to call the story

Morning Star, A Romance of Old Egypt and I think that it should prove something a little out of the common run.'[38]

Cassell's signed the agreement for book publication in March, agreeing to pay an advance against royalties of £450. Though now writing as much as he had ever done, he was getting less and less for each book. Despite large sales in numerous cheap editions, it had become rare for him to earn much more for his recently published books than the amount paid as an advance. His income from writing had fallen to less than a third of what once it had been. For the year ending 5 April 1908, it was only £3,356 13s 4d, still a high figure but less than adequate to live in any way lavishly. Nor did the demands on his income lessen. In addition to the help he was providing for Lilly and her children, he was constantly being called upon to support one member or other of his own extremely large family. About this time, for example, Andrew wrote acknowledging the receipt of money Haggard had sent: 'It has a great deal more significance than the actual gift, old fellow. It has taken me back to the days of our boyhood when we were all in all to each other. It has shown me that the love which still exists between us is the love that has always existed, that you want to help me, above all that you are not careless of my fate. The fact that it is done cheerfully, kindly, and with loving words has given me the most immense pleasure.'[39]

On 21 May, his brother Jack died in Malaga, and so Haggard's responsibilities were extended to helping Aggie and her children. With what seems to amount almost to a growing desperation, he sold on 23 May the book and serial rights of *Queen Sheba's Ring*, a novel to consist of 90,000 words for delivery to Eveleigh Nash by December 1908, for £375 on delivery of the manuscript and an advance of a further £375 to be paid six months later.

Haggard's life was now lived at a hectic pace. When not tramping around the shores of Britain or helping to complete the reports of the Royal Commission on Coastal Erosion, the first of which appeared in 1907, he kept to his routine at home of walking or cycling round the estate in the morning, attending to correspondence after lunch, and then dictating to Miss Hector or a typist his current romance. There was little time for any pleasure or recreation. Although only in his early fifties, Haggard increasingly stood aloof not only from his family but the people he met. Falling easily into the roles of public speaker and government inspector, he was greeted everywhere with respect bordering on awe. In appearance he was impressive. His nephew recalls: 'He was long and loose-limbed, with sparkling, rather piercing blue eyes, a big nose over a sensitive mouth and a small beard which had turned grey. His hair was untidy. He wore his tie knotted through a gold ring (which once had graced the hand of a Pharaoh) and he avoided a crease to his trousers. His clothes rather hung than sat upon him; I think he had them made what is called 'easy fitting'. He looked like somebody and people, when I walked with him in London, turned to stare at him.'[40] But increasingly, he was a lonely man who although having many acquaintances, had few friends. It was his misfortune that almost all the people to whom he had been close both in Africa when young and afterwards as a newly successful writer in London had been so much older than himself. Referring in 1911 to the literary circle at the Savile to which he had once belonged, Haggard sadly comments: 'Of this company the most are dead, though I believe Gosse still lunches there. He must feel himself to be a kind of monument erected over many graves. The last time that I visited the club there was not a soul in the place whom I knew. So feeling lonely and overpressed by sundry memories, I sent in my resignation of membership.'

Of Haggard's old literary friends, he remained close to only Kipling, whom he went to visit at the beginning of October, a week or so after the publication of *The Ghost Kings*, on the plot for a part of which they had worked together. Once again the two men spoke about a novel that Haggard was about to write, this time a historical romance to be called *Red Eve*. Set in the mid-fourteenth century, it was to be the story of the difficult love affair between Eve Clavering and Hugh de Cressi, both children of the Suffolk marshes. Kipling appears to have suggested the allegorical character Murgh, the Second Thing created, the Gateway of the Gods, for on a surviving piece of Batemans stationery he first selects the name from various possibilities and then provides a pencil sketch of Murgh.

On his return home, Haggard signed a contract with Cassell's once more for an African story, although this was to be the first in a new Allan Quatermain series. He agreed to deliver a minimum of 70,000 words by the end of 1909 and Cassell's agreed to pay £450 on delivery for the serial rights and a £750 advance on publication.

Then he began writing *Red Eve*, which was to be an unusual and at times disturbing story. Throughout the six months that he was working on it, he frequently visited Lilly, whom it was obvious was slowly being consumed by her then incurable ailment. As had not happened for many years, Haggard in his writing used both his experiences and, unconsciously, his nightmares. The novel begins in and around the marshes of Blytheburgh, an area Haggard passed through on the way to see Lilly in Aldeburgh. The story is more than a simple one of separated lovers. It tells of how the Black Death swept across Europe:

Such was the beginning of the awful plague, which travelled from the East to Venice and all Europe, and afterwards became known by the name of the Black Death. Day by day the number of its victims increased; the hundreds of yesterday were the thousands of tomorrow. Soon the graveyards were full, the plague-pits long and deep were full, and the dead were taken out to sea by shiploads and there cast into the ocean. At length even this could not be done, since none were forthcoming who would dare the task. For it became known that those who did so themselves would surely die.

So where folk fell, there they lay. In the houses were many of them; they cumbered and poisoned the streets and the very churches. Even the animals sickened and perished, until that great city turned into an open tomb. The reek of it tainted the air for miles around, so that even those who passed it in ships far out to sea turned faint and presently themselves sickened and died. But ere they died they bore on the fatal gift to other lands.

(From *Red Eve*)

While he was writing and waiting for Lilly's sad end, on 11 February 1909, Diana, his first grandchild, born to Angela and Tom Haggard less than seven months earlier, died. Lilias, Angela's sister, records: 'The baby . . . proved, as the years went by, the only child of her parents, in fact the only child born to Bazett's four sons. With the little urn of ashes laid away beneath the black marble slab in the chancel of Ditchingham Church (which Rider had designed intending it to be his own resting-place) was laid also the end of many hopes.'[41]

On 22 April, after much suffering, Lilly, aged fifty-five, at last died, as her death certificate records, of Tabes Dorsalis — the collapse of the nervous system due to syphilis. Haggard in his autobiography refers to the death of the woman with whom, some thirty-five years earlier, he had fallen in love: 'I was present at her death-bed — for happily I was able to be of service to her in her later life — and subsequently, with my wife, who had become her friend many years before, was one of the few mourners at her funeral. At the church where this took place it is the custom to carry out coffins through the big western door. As I followed hers the general aspect of the arch of this door reminded me of something, at the moment I could not remember what. Then it came back to me. It was exactly like that other arch through which I had followed her to her carriage on the night when first we met. Also, strangely different as were the surroundings, there were accessories, floral and other, that were similar in their general effect.' Mary Elizabeth Archer (*née* Jackson), Haggard's Lilly, was buried in Aldeburgh churchyard beneath a white marble tombstone carved with two strands of intertwined arum lilies.

Haggard, unable either to forget or not inwardly grieve, could but throw himself with even greater determination into public service and the business of writing by which he earned his living. For a while he went to stay in London, where on 11 May he arranged to see Lloyd George and strongly advocated that to handle the development grants for afforestation a permanent Royal Commission should be established on which he would like to serve. Although afterwards hopeful, Haggard realised, however, that nothing would be done in a hurry.

Meanwhile he continued to be concerned about his financial position. In the year ending 5 April 1909, his earnings from writing were £3,521 18s. 7d. Even after his property rents and dividends from investments were added his total income was under £4,200. On 22 May 1909 he wrote to Burnham, from whom he had just received a letter describing the explorations of John Hays Hammond's Yaqui Land and Water Company: 'Give Hays Hammond[42] my love and ask him if he would not like me to come and report upon it as a matter of business for the benefit of the British and American peoples. If so I am open to an offer (if it is good enough) or at least I think I am. It really depends upon my Government work which is gradually reducing me to financial ruin, for in our country Government don't pay. You do the work, they take the credit; that's the rule, and I can tell you I have done plenty during the last few years. . . . My second daughter, Dorothy, whom I daresay you remember, is engaged to be married to Major R.E. Cheyne of the Indian Cavalry. . . . He is at present head of a very good old Scotch family and a thoroughly reliable sort of man, but I wish there was a little money in the case. This, however, is lacking.'[43]

Haggard's offer to inspect the American property was not taken up, and back in Ditchingham he continued to write frantically. By the beginning of August he had completed *Child of Storm*, about another episode in Zulu history including the battle of the Tugela between Cetywayo and Umbelazi that Sir Melmoth Osborn had witnessed. Significantly, the heroine is a beautiful and extremely clever black girl, Mameena, and the real story is about her life and tragic end. It seems that after Lilly's death, Haggard's thoughts returned to the African girl of his memories and once more he re-created her in his fiction. Afterwards, he thought highly of *Child of Storm*, declaring in *The Days of My Life* that of all his books it is 'the most artistic'.

On 6 August, Haggard wrote to A.P. Watt: 'Mr Charles Longman has been staying here and on finding out that I was just completing a Zulu story told by Allan Quatermain said that he would very much like to see it. So I have given it to him to read. Of course he may not care for the story, but in case he does I have explained the situation to him very clearly. Briefly it is this: I was writing this story which is called *Child of the Storm* [sic] to be delivered to Cassell's next December. But I have another story written called *Red Eve* which might equally well be given to Cassell's . . . as I have not informed them of the subject of the tale. I have made it clear to Mr Longman that if he should wish for this *Child of the Storm* he would have to buy the serial rights straight away (no figures mentioned) and that we could not consent to him taking the story provisionally upon his succeeding in selling the serial rights.'

Ten days later, Haggard heard from Longman: 'I have read *Child of the Storm* and find it very much to my taste. I remember an advertisement of Heinemann's for a book of Hall Caine's some years ago in which in his 'puff' he said of the book 'The appeal is Elemental'. The phrase stuck in my mind and in the case of *The Child of the Storm* it seems to me that the appeal is 'elemental'. Love, hunting, fighting — these are the Elements and I own I like 'em. I have written to Watt to come and talk the matter over. I am afraid, however, that the serial issue may be insurmountable.'[44] Longman was right: he did not publish the book.

As he still felt that *Child of Storm* might be placed elsewhere, Haggard, to provide the novel required for Cassell's by the end of the year, began *Marie*, another Allan Quatermain story, this time set in the period when Dingaan murdered Retief and his Boer company. It was to be the third work of fiction he completed in 1909. Fortunately Haggard began to see some results of his hard work. In November, for the first time for many years, three of his novels were being serialised simultaneously (*Queen Sheba's Ring* in *Nash's Magazine*, *Morning Star* in *The Christian World News of the Week*, and *The Lady of Blossholme* in *The British Weekly*). As his name appeared in the press more often as a writer than as a political figure, a new interest seemed to be awakened in his earlier works. Writing to Watt in 1909, Haggard remarks: 'Thanks for the *King Solomon's Mines* accounts which I will return later. I observe that the receipts from that book have gone up considerably, perhaps because a new generation is coming along to read it.'[45]

His interest lay still, however, in public service, and so he was delighted to receive on Christmas Day 1909, a letter from Lord Ashby St Ledgers: 'I had a conversation yesterday with Lloyd George, and he intimated that he intended to offer you a post as Commissioner under the Development Board. I told him it was slave-driving not to offer you a salary with it, but he said that his limit of £3000 per annum had not enabled him yet to secure a permanent official, and that it would involve an amendment of the Act to provide anything for anyone else.'

Early in 1910 the Commission of the Development was appointed, but, much to his astonishment, Haggard was not included among its members. As the work of the Royal Commission on Coast Erosion was coming to an end, there was nothing left for Haggard but to write. On 21 March 1910, ten days after the publication of *Morning Star*, Haggard wrote to Doctor Wallis Budge, to whom the book had been dedicated: 'I am amusing myself dramatising *Morning Star*. . . . I should very much like to do some more old Egyptian stories, especially as so far as I can judge from such reviews as I have seen etc. people seem to like *Morning Star*! Have you any suggestions to make as to subjects that would be suitable to romance?'[46] By this time he had finished his story 'Smith and the Pharaohs', which was to appear serially in *The Strand Magazine*. Between 4 and 6 of April, Cassell's agreed to publish three more of his novels, agreeing to pay an advance of £750 each on receipt of the manuscripts of *Child of Storm* and two still to be written — *The Wanderer's Necklace* (a Viking romance) and *Love Eternal*. (None of the three novels, not even *Child of Storm*, was ever serialised.)

Towards the end of April, Haggard left home for the last tour of the Royal Commission — a study of the Irish coasts. He was chairman of the Committee travelling from Dublin to Wexford, Tramore and Dungarvan, the Shannon and the Fergus, and the coast of Clare. On 26 April, he wrote to his wife from the Sherbourne Hotel, Dublin: 'This seems a comfortable hotel only one ought to lock the bathroom. When I was there this morning — with nothing but a towel! — a young woman walked in. I said Hullo! She said Oh! and so the interview ended.'[47] On 12 May, after visiting the Abbey Theatre where he had been discussing his dramatisation of *Morning Star*, Haggard wrote again to his wife: 'I saw Miss O'Neill at the theatre this morning. She is wild to do the part of Ina if the thing can be fixed up and would I think do it extremely well. She has a great local reputation as an actress in Ireland. The company is coming to London so you will be able to see how she acts. Yeats, the poet, is the main spring of the Company, but he don't act. I did laugh at myself discussing plays. . . . I only wish I could make some money out of it. I have made up the plot of a patriotic Irish play.'[48] Haggard apparently left the manuscript of his dramatisation of *Morning Star* with W.B. Yeats, and later sent him his Irish play.

In the period after his return from Ireland, Haggard was again exceptionally busy. In an interval of attending to the final business of the Royal Commission, including helping with the last volume of the report, he watched the funeral procession of King Edward VII from the upper balcony of the Athenaeum, where he sat next to Thomas Hardy. He also met several important people, including General Booth, who asked him to write an account of the Salvation Army's social work in Great Britain, and Roosevelt, who was visiting Britain.

During June and July, Haggard, accompanied by D.R. Daniel, one of the secretaries of the Royal Commission, inspected much of the Salvation Army's social work, including hostels in London, Manchester and Glasgow. Afterwards he declared: 'I emerged from this work with a most whole-hearted admiration for the Salvation Army and its splendid, self-sacrificing labours among the lowest of the low.' Haggard's out-of-pocket expenses were paid by the Salvation Army, but he presented the organisation with the copyright of his report which he called *Regeneration*.

When this work and that with the Royal Commission had been completed, Haggard, confident that there was a greater possibility of being asked to undertake further public service if he meanwhile continued with his own investigations, decided to report on the farming conditions in Denmark. Before the arrangements were complete, he received a letter dated 8 September from W.B. Yeats: 'I have kept your plays too long for it to be right for me to keep them longer. Neither would be possible at the Abbey, as I feared when I saw you in London.'[49]

The possibility of achieving additional income from that source having been denied him, Haggard was delighted to receive a letter from the editor of *The Times* asking if he would be willing to write about his planned investigations into Danish agriculture. On 12 September, Haggard replied: 'I shall be pleased to make some arrangement with *The Times* as regards the serial use of what I may write about Danish agriculture. . . . The only agreement I have at present in connection with this proposed work is one with Messrs Longmans, who would like to publish the little book. I ought to state, however, that I cannot undertake to send you the copy direct from Denmark as I shall have no time there to prepare it. All that I could do would be to let you have it when it is completed after my return, and when that will be I cannot precisely say.'[50] Two days later, Watt arranged that *The Times* would pay Haggard £10 0s. 0d, per printed column for the actual amount of material used.

In mid-September, Haggard set off for Denmark with Lilias, his youngest daughter, and, as his secretary, Aggie. He toured farms and small-holdings, as always taking detailed notes, recording statistics, and interviewing a wide range of people concerned with agriculture. On 22 September, having visited Aagaard which he believed was the place from which the Haggard family had originated, he wrote to his wife: 'I confess I looked on the spot from whence, I believe, we all hailed with some emotion. An ancient manor house buried in trees with the remains of a moated castle alongside situated on a vast plain through which runs a little stream that gives the place its name — that's what it is like.'[51]

WITHOUT THE GATE

All too aware that for him, as for most other British farmers, 1910 had been a disastrous year with heavy rains ruining the crops, Haggard was even more impressed than he had anticipated by the successes and organisation of Danish agriculture. He saw that this, at least in part, was due to the active involvement of the Government in the railways, telephone system, and the purchase of land. The comparison between agricultural conditions in Denmark and in England depressed him, forcing him to conclude:

> Considered as a financial investment, the holding of landed property in many parts of England has become but an empty farce; from a business point of view our system seems a failure. The land, at any rate under the present methods of culture, carrying its present fixed burdens and at the present prices of produce, can rarely return three clear living profits — one to the owner, one to the farmer, and one to the labourer. I suggest that the first two of these might with advantage be amalgamated as they are in Denmark. The owner should be the farmer or the farmer the owner.
>
> (From *Rural Denmark*)

One morning, shortly after Haggard's return to England, the telephone rang at Ditchingham House and Miss Hector, who answered it, was asked by a representative of the Central News Agency in London if it were true that Haggard had died. She replied that to the best of her knowledge he was walking around the farm and was at least in an average state of health. Although the rumour was, therefore, denied, it was not quashed. On 24 October, Haggard received a telegram from the Authors' Club: 'Hope you are well. Rumours to contrary.' These rumours depressed Haggard. Not only had he no public duties to perform, but it appeared that, at the age of fifty-five, all his achievements lay behind him. He became convinced that the best years of his life had been lived and that he, at the same age as Lilly had been when she died, was entering old age. For a man who had always been active and ambitious, it was a chastening, unhappy time. Although he spent the remainder of the year completing his report on *Rural Denmark and Its Lessons*, he was bored, irritated by his own inactivity, and increasingly feeling both physically and mentally unwell. He records: 'I missed [the Royal] Commission very much, since its sittings took me to London from time to time, and gave me a change of mental occupation and interests. Indeed I do not remember ever being more consistently depressed than I was during the first part of the following winter. Here, as I no longer shoot, I had nothing to do. . . . Also bronchitis, which had threatened me for some years, troubled me much.'

On 10 December, six days before the official publication of *Regeneration*, Haggard received a letter from General Booth: 'I have just read *Regeneration*. It is admirable. You have not only seen into the character and purpose of the work we are trying to do, with the insight of a true genius, but with the sympathy of a big and generous soul. From my heart I thank you.' The book was extremely well received, but no offers of work from either the Government or any other source resulted.

205

Oppressed by his apparent imprisonment in the countryside which he loved but from which it had become his habit to escape at will, Haggard, in January 1911, after reading about a hare that had been pursued into the sea by hounds, began to write the strangest and least well known of all his books. It tells how a dreamer, Mahatma, is confronted by a hare travelling the Great White Road who tells how he has been shot at, chased by greyhounds, and finally hunted by a pack of hounds:

> Then pealed the question: 'Who hath suffered most? Let that one first taste of peace.'
> Now all the dim hosts surged forward since each outworn soul believed that it had suffered most and was in the bitterest need of peace. But the Helpers and the Guardians gently pressed them back, and again there pealed no question but a command.
> This was the command: 'DRAW NEAR, THOU HARE.'
>
> (From *The Mahatma and the Hare*)

On 31 March, Longmans agreed to publish Haggard's death-obsessed, anti-hunting nightmare.

A few weeks later, on 14 April, *Rural Denmark* was published, but although it was favourably reviewed it created no great stir. Disturbed that he seemed fated not to be able, as he wished, to spend his latter years in some worthwhile service, Haggard grew so depressed that he could not even contemplate writing another romance. It is true that there were occasional token acknowledgements of his existence. On 22 June, because of his services as a Royal Commissioner, he was able to purchase seats in a stand to view the Coronation Procession of George V, and on 27 July he was invited to give evidence before the Public Records commission; but, using a favourite expression of his, these were 'small beer'. He pined for greater, more important duties.

Still depressed, Haggard wrote on 8 August to Theodore Roosevelt, who had favourably reviewed *Regeneration* in *The Outlook*: 'I cannot tell you how greatly I appreciate the good opinion of a man like yourself, and, what is so very rare, the public expression of that opinion. As a private individual I find my task very hard: to drive into the intelligence of a blind and careless generation certain elementary facts which it cannot or will not understand is always difficult, especially if the wielder of the hammer is not rich. If I could afford it I would devote the rest of my life to this kind of educational work in my own land and others. But I fear I can't, and in this country no kind of help is forthcoming to make such efforts possible.' Roosevelt replied on 22 August: 'We must not permit ourselves to become soured by our own experiences, for being gloomy does not in the least help a man to reach others, and merely makes him less attractive to himself and all around him. Life is a campaign, and at best we are merely under officers or subalterns in it. We are bound to do our duty as efficiently and as fearlessly as we know how; but it is a good thing to remember that we must not be too much cast down even if things look wrong, because melancholy only tends to make us less and not more efficient, and buoyancy and good-humour and the ability to enjoy life all help instead of hindering a reformer.'

Before he had received this sound advice, Haggard had already started what he considered might well be his last major task. Surrounding himself with his notebooks, letters he had received and mementoes of the past, he began his autobiography on 11 August. First he wrote an introduction in which he examines the problem most disturbing him: 'The first question that I should ask myself and try to answer is, not to what extent I have achieved success, but by how much I have escaped failure in the world. . . . It has so come about that, although I have done other things, I must earn my living by the pen. Now of this I should not have complained had I been in a position to choose my own subject. But unhappily those subjects which attract me, such as agriculture and social research, are quite unremunerative. . . . As there is other work which I should have much preferred to do, I will not pretend that I have found, or find, the occupation [of writing fiction] altogether congenial, perhaps because at the bottom of my heart I share some of the British contempt for the craft of story-telling.' It was then with a feeling of failure and unfulfilment born of his boredom that Haggard began to write the story of his life. Intending it to be published only after his death, he was not writing for the public. Rather was it his opportunity to evaluate his achievements and justify his actions; but his pessimism led him to undervalue his successes and blame his disappointments on the perfidious hand of fate. The publication on 19 August of *Red Eve*, with its potent reminders of Lilly, did nothing to allay his depression.

Yet, in time, the writing of his autobiography did prove therapeutic. Already beginning to recover, he went on 30 September to stay for a few days with Kipling. In his notebook he records: 'I went through the plot of *The Mahatma and the Hare* with him. He thought it a fine thing but said that I should have carried it further. . . . I asked K. if his work was ever discussed in his own family. He said it was never mentioned, although he talked over things privately with his wife. His boy Jack had said to him the other day on his going to school at Wellington: "Thank heaven, Father. I hope that there I shall hear no more of 'Recessional'." I said it was the same in my own circle. He told me that his children showed no signs of imagination and that he was thankful for it. I said *ditto* — ditto.'[52]

The Mahatma and the Hare was published on 16 October and Haggard sent a copy to Andrew Lang, whom he had not seen for some time. Lang wrote on 18 October: 'Thanks for the Hare. . . . I bar chevying hares, but we are all hunted from birth to death by impecunious relations, disease, care, and every horror. The hare is not hunted half so much or half so endlessly.' In his reply, Haggard said: 'You are right: hunted we are, and by a large pack! Still I don't know that this justifies us in hunting other things. . . . As one grows old, I think the sadness of the world impresses one more and more. If there is nothing beyond it is indeed a tragedy. But, thank Heaven! I can't think that. I think it less and less. I am engaged on writing (for publication *AFTER* I have walked "the Great White Road") my reminiscences of my early life in Africa, etc. It is a sad job. There before me are the letters from those dear old friends of my youth, Shepstone, Osborn, Clarke and many others, and nearly every one of them is dead! But I don't believe that I shall never see them more; indeed I seem to grow nearer to them.'

A few weeks later, able at least to care about the problems of others, Haggard, at Longman's suggestion, wrote again to Lang hoping to alleviate his melancholia: 'I have come across a scheme we had (about a quarter of a century ago) for collaboration in a novel of Old Kôr. I think it has been in bottle long enough and should be decanted. What say you? Have you any ideas? I see stuff in it, but could not really tackle it just at present. It would be rather jolly to do another job with you, old fellow.' Lang, not impressed by this straw thrown into the wind, replied: 'Faire des objections c'est collaborer, but I don't think that I could do more. Had I any ideas of Kôr long ago? *She*, I think, is not easily to be raised again.' The idea of collaborating was not pursued, and the two men, friends for the best part of forty years, were never to meet again.

As the year drew to a close, Haggard, still suffering from bronchitis, remained absorbed by the self-torturing task of writing his autobiography. Surrounded in his study by reminders of past successes and disappointments, reliving his friendships and the doleful deaths of those whom he had loved, and becoming increasingly convinced that his life had been purposeless, he dwelt, conscious of his own old age, predominantly in the past. There seemed to be no future for him, forcing him to conclude that, 'It really seemed as if everything had come to an end.'

9

The Final Years

That Life is granted, not in Pleasure's round,
Or even Love's sweet dream, to lapse content:
Duty and Faith are words of solemn sound,
And to their echoes must thy soul be bent.

(From lines written for Haggard by his
mother when he first left home. July 1875)

I

Haggard's depression did not last, for before the end of 1911, as he records, 'of a sudden things changed, as they have a way of doing in life'. During the Christmas holidays, he received a letter from the Prime Minister announcing that the King had conferred a knighthood on him for his public service. Grateful for this recognition and believing that the title would improve his chances of being offered further Government work, Haggard readily accepted the honour that was promulgated in the New Year Honours List of 1912. Among the many who wrote to congratulate him was Kipling, who could not resist pointing out that the knighthood had been conferred by the Liberal Government he detested: 'The English papers are just in, with the New Year honours, and I made haste to send you all our heartiest congratulations on your Knighthood. It's the most sensible thing this alleged Government has ever done and if they had souls I might be tempted to believe that there was some good in 'em. You've done such good work for the State, for so long that in this case the State truly honours itself in honouring you. It's a banal phrase but you know what I mean and you will know too, that no one is more pleased than we are.'[1] His friend's approval must have been pleasing to Haggard for he was aware that Kipling had already twice refused to accept a knighthood.

Shortly afterwards, Haggard received another honour that he considered even more important. On 10 January 1912, Lewis Harcourt, the Colonial Secretary, wrote officially inviting Haggard to be one of the six British Royal Commissioners who with five others representing the Dominions were charged with visiting and reporting on Canada, Newfoundland, South Africa, Australia and New Zealand over a three-year period. In a subsequent personal letter, Harcourt urged acceptance, adding: 'I trust for the sake of the reading public that the Commission will not prevent you from pursuing a good deal of your usual avocations, and might even incidentally provide materials!' Even though he had been informed that 'there will be no remuneration for the Commissioners', Haggard was overjoyed. 'This,' he wrote, 'was recognition — with a vengeance.' Charles Longman, when Haggard told him the news, said: 'I would rather have heard this than that they had given you a peerage. Anyone can be a peer, but to be one of the six men chosen to represent the United Kingdom on a great Empire inquiry of this sort is a real honour.'

With this sentiment Haggard totally agreed. 'The compliment,' he wrote that year, 'seemed the more marked for the reason that it was paid to an individual who first became known to the public as a writer of romantic literature, an occupation that does not dispose the British nation to take those who follow it seriously. Now I saw that all my long years of toil in investigating and attempting to solve the grave problems which lie at the root of the welfare of our country had not been without effect upon the minds of its rulers, and I felt proportionately grateful and honoured.' He was able in his excitement to ignore the fact that none of the major recommendations made in either his Royal Commission or his own reports had actually been implemented.

His period of inactivity over, life for Haggard again became hectic. So that he could attend the Commission meetings at Scotland House, he took rooms at 5 Bryanston Street, off Oxford Street. Then when he realised that the first overseas tour would not commence until the end of the year, he decided to make a short visit to Egypt in the hope of shaking off his bronchitis. With Angela, his eldest daughter, as companion, he set off in mid-February. Already restored in spirits, Haggard, as he inspected the treasures discovered in recent excavations, also recovered from his ailment.

On his return, he had to face the problems that would arise because of his appointment as a Royal Commissioner. His writing income was still declining and the continuing depressed state of British agriculture meant that there were no profits to be made from his estate. He now needed to increase his income and, although he wished it was otherwise, he knew that he could only do this by writing popular romances. Yet, if he was to fulfil the responsibilities of his appointment, finding time to write would be even more difficult than it had been when he had been working on Coast Erosion and Afforestation. 'Of course,' he wrote, 'the acceptance of this Royal Commissionership involves serious sacrifices in my case, exclusive of that of long separation from my family. Thus it will necessitate the partial shutting down of my home here; and how I am to carry on my literary work in the intervals I do not know! I . . . feel that such considerations should not be allowed to interfere with the execution of what I look upon as a high and honourable duty.'

Before being appointed as a Royal Commissioner, Haggard had tentatively planned to spend the summer of 1912 compiling a report on the agriculture of Ireland. His need for an increased income forced him to abandon the plan, and so, even putting aside the autobiography, he decided to write another romance. He had signed contracts for the book publication of *Love Eternal* (a modern story) and *The Wanderer's Necklace* (a Viking tale), but it was unlikely that these would prove as profitable as *The Holy Flower*, an Allan Quatermain story for which both the serial and book rights had been purchased a few months earlier by Ward Lock for publication first in *The Windsor Magazine*. This book was intended to be the second in a new Allan Quatermain series, the first in which was *Marie* which had been well received when it appeared on 25 January, 1912.

The Holy Flower, which Haggard wrote between April and July, tells of a quest for a rare orchid that had been endowed with religious significance by an African tribe. (Collecting and growing orchids were passionate interests of Haggard's about which he had written at length in *A Gardener's Year*.) Less full of moralising than his books written in the previous few years, *The Holy Flower*, with its gorilla worshipped as a god by the tribe whose king it periodically kills, has many interesting ingredients; but Haggard, relying less and less on either his imagination or his own experiences, produces a light-weight story, any merit in which is undermined by an unexpected flippancy:

> And now the story shifts away to England. (Don't be afraid, my adventurous reader, if ever I have one, it is coming back to Africa again in a very few pages.)
>
> (From *The Holy Flower*)

Before *The Holy Flower* had been completed, Haggard again had resumed dictating his autobiography. This was almost certainly because, on 22 July, he read in the newspapers that Andrew Lang had died. That day he began a chapter paying tribute to his friend which follows somewhat incongruously after the one dealing with his son's death twenty-one years earlier — the point at which he almost certainly had earlier in his depression felt unable to continue. Although up to this point Haggard tells his story in some detail, he appears afterwards to be interested in little more than completing the work. He jumps from one event to another, quoting papers as they come to hand rather than in their chronological order. Much concerned to understand why he has given so much time and effort to writing fiction, a task he no longer enjoyed, he belittles his achievements, claiming incorrectly that his novels and romances had been dashed off and submitted to gullible publishers uncorrected. 'The method of romance-writing,' he proclaims, 'should, in my judgement, be swift, clear, and direct, with as little padding and as few trappings as possible. The story is the thing, and every word in the book should be a brick to build its edifice. Above all, no obscurity should be allowed. Let the characters be definite, even at the cost of a little crudeness, and so with the meaning of each sentence. Tricks of "style" and dark allusions may please the superior critic; they do not please the average reader, and — though this seems to be a fact that many forget, or only remember to deplore — a book is written that it may be read. The first duty of a story is to keep him who peruses it awake. . . . Such work should be written rapidly and, if possible, not rewritten, since wine of this character loses its bouquet when it is poured from glass to glass. . . . So it comes to this: the way to write a good romance is to sit down and write it almost without stopping.'

It is unfortunate that, after this belittling of his own art and achievement first appeared as part of the autobiography in 1926, it was taken as representing Haggard's consistent attitude to his writing rather than merely being, as it was, the thoughts expressed in 1912 when he had decided that writing was but the necessary way of financing his public service and he was seeking a justification for his newly adopted slipshod approach to his craft.

It is even possible that the attitude to romance-writing he expressed in his autobiography was not genuinely held in the summer of 1912 when it was written. Certainly he was then willing to rewrite sections of *Child of Storm*, which had been completed three years earlier, but was only just about to be printed. While in London during the summer he met Captain James Stuart, the assistant secretary of Native Affairs in South Africa, and from him obtained a considerable amount of additional information about the battle of Tuguela and Zulu customs. In a letter dated 16 August, Stuart sent Miss Hector further details, including the national anthem of the Zulus, in both vernacular and translation, adding: 'I do not remember ever having seen in print the great anthem above given. However that may be, the translation has not, for it was made today.'[2] The anthem, together with some of the other material supplied by Stuart, was included by Haggard in his revisions of *Child of Storm*.

At last, despite the time spent on other writing, Haggard succeeded in completing his autobiography on 25 September. On that day he wrote to Longman: 'I have just written the last word of *The Days of My Life*, and thankful I am to have done with that book.' The manuscript was sealed up and put into Longman's safe where it remained unopened till after Haggard's death. Next Haggard wrote two short stories: 'Barbara Who Came Back' for publication in *The Pall Mall Magazine* between March and April 1913, and 'Magepa the Buck' for *Pears' Christmas Annual* of 1912.

This work complete, Haggard was able to concentrate on making his arrangements for the first tour of the Dominions Royal Commission. On 30 October, he wrote to Lewis Harcourt: 'It occurs to me to ask whether, when I am in Australasia and elsewhere you would like me to send you some confidential letters, not, of course, on the affairs of the Dominions Royal Commission or, except indirectly perhaps, on anything with which it has to do, but on general topics.' Harcourt welcomed the suggestion and Haggard was prepared to make even more detailed notes during his tours than those he had been used to jotting down in his notebooks during his previous overseas trips. The routine of keeping what soon became a detailed daily diary was adhered to almost without a break until the end of his life.

Haggard decided that he would set off from England before the other Commissioners and visit his daughter Dorothy who was living in India with her husband Major Cheyne and their two children. To ensure that he saw as much as possible, he made arrangements that Salvation Army officers in both India and Ceylon would be available to show him something of the social work they were undertaking. He also, early in November, visited Rudyard Kipling to find out more about the country which had fascinated him for so long but which he had never before had the opportunity of visiting. Haggard took with him to Batemans the proofs of *Child of Storm*, from which he read long extracts to Kipling. Afterwards Haggard recorded: 'At the end, when my throat had given out, he said to the effect, There you see: what book is there of our day to which I could have listened like that all this time. He expressed himself of the work in very strong terms indeed, almost overpowering terms: "as terse and strong as a Greek play, not a word that could be improved or cut out," etc.' On 9 November, Kipling sent back to Ditchingham the proof with a letter in which he said: 'I've read it; re-read it and re-read it and I don't think you're wrong when you say it's the best you've done. *I* can't see where it needs anything being done to it. It marches straight off from the first and holds like a drug!'[3]

Delighted by his friend's praise and looking forward with great enthusiasm to participating in the important work of the Royal Commission, Haggard sailed for India on 29 November. He spent much of December and all of January, 1913, travelling through India and Ceylon, carefully noting his impressions and observations before joining other members of the Royal Commission on the *Medina* for the voyage to Melbourne.

When the ship docked on 17 February, Haggard was less than pleased when he was besieged by reporters wishing to talk to him about his novels. Feeling that such attention undermined the seriousness of the Royal Commission and might well be upsetting to the other members who were either Civil Servants or rich industrialists, he steadfastly refused to answer questions about his writing. The reporter of *The Age* (Melbourne) records: 'The last thing Sir Rider Haggard desires to talk about, apparently, is his own work as a novel writer. Statistics of immigration, the state of the rural population of the United Kingdom, the resources of the Commonwealth, these and similar matters are at present in the forefront of his horizon. "Everyone in Australia knows you by your books," was a remark made to the literary visitor yesterday. He waved the point aside — gracefully, but with the air of one who was not really responsible.'[4]

Shortly afterwards the Royal Commission sailed for New Zealand, where once again all the reporters, ignoring the other Royal Commissioners, wanted to talk only to the best-selling novelist, but Haggard would have none of it. On 1 March, *The Lyttelton Times*, under the headings 'Sir Rider Haggard — The Author of *King Solomon's Mines* — Not Interested in Romance', informed its readers: 'He does not look like a writer of fascinating romances, and does not talk like one. In appearance, in fact, he is a typical commonsense man of the world, observing things as they are, accumulating facts in his memory, and taking an interest in the commonplace affairs of daily life.'[5]

Because of his refusal to talk in public about his fiction and his obvious seriousness of purpose, Haggard was readily accepted as a colleague by the other Royal

Commissioners, especially the Chairman, Sir Edgar Vincent (later Lord D'Abernon), who became a close friend. With enthusiasm, Haggard accepted the responsibilities and the hard work, revelling in his position as a representative of the Imperial Government. Everywhere the Commission went, both in New Zealand and afterwards in Australia, he and the other members were given official receptions, lavishly entertained, and provided with any assistance requested. Throughout the tour, Haggard continued to be distressed if even passing reference was made to his writing. Thus in his diary he records: 'At Brisbane we were accorded another public reception at which speeches were made. One old gentleman who was called the father of the Local House of Commons instead of addressing himself to the Imperial matters in hand, dwelt chiefly upon my books while another dilated at length upon the character of Allan Quatermain. This on an official occasion was very trying to me.'[6]

Yet Haggard was all too aware that, however pleasurable his duties were, they were unpaid and his income had to be earned. Just after receiving copies of *Child of Storm*, which was published on 23 January, he attended a State Theatre Party in Melbourne put on for the Commission by the Government of Victoria. In his diary he records: 'The piece given by Mr Oscar Asche and his Company was *A Midsummer's Night's Dream*, a play for which I care but little, since it savours too much of pantomime. At the conclusion of the piece there was a gathering in the foyer of the theatre where I met many people. Among these were Mr and Mrs Oscar Asche, the former of whom said that he would much like to stage a Zulu play. So I promised to send him *Child of Storm* to read, which I did upon the morrow.'

The two men met again to discuss the project and, on 4 April, Haggard wrote to A.P. Watt: 'I have had several interviews here with Mr Oscar Asche . . . who has made up his mind to dramatize my book *Child of Storm* under the title of *Mameena* and to produce the same in London somewhere about Christmas time this year.' It having been decided that the dramatisation of the romance should be jointly written, Haggard, on 8 April while sailing to Cairns in north Queensland, wrote to Asche: 'I enclose a couple of rough sample scenes. Having no copy of *Child of Storm* with me, I have had to work from memory. I wish you would look through them and let me have your views. If you will get out a rough synopsis of your idea of what the various scenes and acts should be, I hope to be able to work on it on the way home.'

At intervals during his official business, Haggard continued to work on *Mameena*, very conscious that a long-running play produced in a West End theatre was likely to earn substantial sums. On 20 May, just before the Royal Commissioners left Australia, Asche wrote to Haggard from the Theatre Royal, Sydney: 'I am sending you herewith the script of *Mameena*. I wish you to understand that it is, with the exception of possibly the first two acts, in a rough state as, after all, I have not had very long to work on it; but I have indicated where it is necessary for the scenes to be written by you as you suggested. I have mapped out the play, I think, fairly well and have brought in all the essential points of the drama as far as the stage is understood by me.'[7]

By the time Haggard arrived home at the end of June, he had not only completed *Mameena* but written for Harcourt his confidential report on Australia and New Zealand in which he expressed disgust at the pleasure-loving population which with its low birth-rate and recurring labour troubles was, he felt, in grave danger of being seen as an easy conquest by the landless hordes of Japan and China.

As in a little over six months he would be leaving on the next Royal Commission tour (this time to South Africa), it was urgent that Haggard worked on ways of increasing his income. He was, therefore understandably delighted when Watt informed him that the fledgeling film industry was expressing considerable interest in his romances and that the sale of the rights might well produce considerable sums. In a letter, dated 5 July, in which he gives Watt permission to negotiate with the film companies, Haggard states: 'After our long association, as you may imagine, I have no wish to argue upon anything connected with money arrangements between us. . . . It is true that cinematograph rights were not known in those days (a quarter of a century ago!), but on the other hand, without the books there could be no cinematograph pictures. These are consequent upon the literary effort and depend upon the copyright.'[8]

Watt was also busy selling the rights of books Haggard was still to write. On 7 August, Cassell's agreed to publish *The Ivory Child*, undertaking to pay £500 on receipt of the manuscript for the serial rights and an advance of £750 on the book's publication. The following day, Cassell's, although not purchasing the serial rights, also agreed to pay an advance of £750 on the publication of *The Virgin of the Sun*, a Mexican romance, the plot for which Haggard had devised in 1891 as an alternative to the one he actually used for *Montezuma's Daughter*.

Haggard meanwhile had started writing *The Wanderer's Necklace*, his Viking romance, the idea for which had arisen during his visit to Aagard, his family's seat. It tells how Olaf the Northman opens a tumulus in which is buried the body of an ancestor called the Wanderer. When, in time, the romance was complete, Haggard showed the manuscript to Kipling, who declared: '*The Necklace* I like *immensely* — it all goes with a rush and a whirl and holds like all the others of yours.'[9] In November, Haggard dedicated *The Wanderer's Necklace* to his Chairman, Sir Edgar Vincent.

At the beginning of 1914, Haggard was looking forward to his return to South Africa. He decided that he would take with him Louie and Lilias and that on the way they would spend some time in Madeira. Before he left, he endeavoured to make final arrangements with Asche for the production of *Mameena*. Captain James Stuart had been hired, according to Asche 'with a bag of gold of considerable weight',[10] to collect artefacts, supervise the making of costumes, and teach the company Zulu customs. On 22 January 1914, Haggard wrote to Asche: 'I am leaving for South Africa on Saturday and do not expect to be in this country again until the end of May or beginning of June. I understand from Mr Stuart that you think of bringing out *Mameena* before that date. As I, therefore, shall not be available, perhaps you will kindly communicate with my secretary Miss Hector, 10 Warrington Gardens, Maida Hill, as to anything regarding the play'.[11]

On 24 January, five days before the publication of *The Wanderer's Necklace*, Haggard with his wife and youngest daughter sailed for Madeira, where for a week or two he amused himself wandering around the places he had described in *Dawn*. Then the Haggards joined members of the Royal Commission on the *Kinfauns Castle* and sailed for Cape Town where they arrived towards the end of February. As at sunrise he again saw Table Mountain, he remembered the time when, over thirty-two years earlier, he had watched the same scene as he had sailed away from South Africa: 'I have passed from youth to age since then but it was with pleasure mingled with a certain sadness that I saw the cloud-cap hanging like poured water down the kloofs and steep sides of Table Mountain.'

Haggard was soon busily at work, taking evidence and attending an apparently endless round of receptions — but among the numerous new faces and places he was occasionally to see a person or building he remembered. Such reminders of the past, Lilias reports, 'induced that strange mood which lasted all the months he was in Africa; a feeling as if he had come back from another life. Everything was so changed, towns unrecognizable, transport revolutionized by trains and motor where there had only been carts and ox wagons. . . . Then on a sudden, he would find some place unaltered, untouched by the years, smiling in the sunshine as it smiled in those high-hearted days of his youth. Some man or woman who, by those magic words "do you remember", recalled happy comradeship, dangers faced and shared, days of great adventure and endless promise, so that grey hairs and wrinkles were forgotten.'[12] Among the old friends Haggard met at the Cape was his old chief, Judge Kotzé, and together they nostalgically reminisced about the early frontier days.

From Cape Town the Commission went up country and in time the Haggards arrived at Newcastle where they visited Hilldrop, their first home. Lilias recalls that there her father glanced into the room where Jock was born more than thirty years ago, then turned away quickly'.[13] A few days later, the Haggards moved to Maritzburg where James Stuart met them. The next day, 27 March, Haggard was reunited with Mazooku, his old Zulu servant, who greeted him with the cry, 'Chief of old! Father! Here am I returned to serve you.' Haggard was both moved and delighted. From Mazooku and an old Zulu called Socwatsha, Haggard obtained much information that he was to use in *Finished*, the last of the trilogy (with *Marie* and *Child of Storm*) dealing with the history of the Zulus. In his diary, Haggard records: 'It was wonderful to watch old Socwatsha as he told his story of the battles, acting them as he spoke as only a Zulu can.'

During the remainder of the tour Haggard revisited many places that were full of memories for him, including Majuba, where the special train stopped so that the scene of the ill-fated battle could be inspected, and in Pretoria the house he and

216

Cochrane had built, 'the Palatial'. While Louie and Lilias travelled to Zululand, Haggard went up to Rhodesia. At Bulawayo he inspected the remnants of Lobengula's kraal, where his friends Patterson and Sergeaunt were received before their murder. Escorted by Richard Hall, he also visited the Zimbabwe ruins, where he was amused to discover that the local guide-book stated that he had used the ancient site as his model for the residence of She. In his diary, he noted: 'Mr Hall seemed somewhat aggrieved with me because he said I was responsible for various false ideas about Zimbabwe. . . . I had some difficulty in explaining to him that my sins were unintentional — that in fact Kôr was a land where the ruins were built by the Fairies of Imagination!'

From Rhodesia, Haggard travelled south to Durham where he said good-bye to Louie and Lilias who were returning home while he travelled around Zululand. Then, accompanied by Stuart and Mazooku he went first to Eshowe to visit the site of the kraal called Jazi, which means Finished, near where Cetywayo the last Zulu king had died. It was there that Haggard conceived the main idea for his story *Finished* which was to end with Cetywayo's death. Later he saw the site of Dingaan's kraal and the battlefield of Isandhlwana. Having enjoyed and been deeply moved by his journey through Zululand, travelling, as he put it, with 'men who are I suppose among the greatest living experts in Zulu history', Haggard said a sad farewell to Mazooku at Maritzburg and then returned to Durban where he wrote his private report for Lewis Harcourt. It concludes with an outspoken plea for a far more sympathetic treatment of the Zulus. In it Haggard reveals not only a genuine affection for the race among whom he had once lived but a humanity and foresight that are as impressive as at the time they were exceptional:

It is I am sure the greatest mistake to suppose that the native does not feel, or forgets, harsh treatment. On the contrary I believe that at the bottom of that secret mind of his, which so few of an alien race have the imagination and the sympathy to understand at all, he feels a great deal. Also his memory is very long. Listen to some old Zulu describing events which took place in the day of Chaka or Dingaan, when his nation was great and ruled the land. He quotes the very words that were said, the very deeds that were done. No syllable, no gesture is overlooked. It is all there written upon the book of his mind, and much else is there also, of which he does not speak to the white man — as yet. But a day may dawn when he, or his son, or his grandson will do so and then it will be found that no single blow or curse, or humiliation or act of robbery or injustice has been overlooked. Deaths in war he will take no account of, for he springs from a race of soldiers and is prepared to accept what he gives without complaint or malice. Death is, so to speak, the coin of his trade, as victory and defeat are its stakes, but with the rest it is otherwise. For these in some shape, probably one that is quite unforeseen, an hour of reckoning will surely strike. It is not possible in this or any other human affair, continually and with intent to sow the wind and always escape the reaping of the whirlwind.

(From *Letter to the Rt. Hon. Lewis Harcourt*)

When the letter was published in July 1914, it attracted little attention. There were about to arise far more pressing worries to agitate the British people than the distant possibility of racial conflict in South Africa.

As Haggard's ship steamed up the east coast of Africa towards Suez, he sat down in his cabin and wrote in his diary: 'So ends my visit to South Africa — on the whole it has been successful, if sad in some ways. I am truly grateful for the extreme kindness with which I have been welcomed everywhere, in fact I have experienced quite a little triumph. Affectionate as was my greeting I think really it was more to do with the fact I am a sort of curiosity, a survival from a past generation, than to my own individuality. . . . So to South Africa, farewell, which is the dominant word in my life. It is a fair land of which the charm still holds my heart and whose problems interest me more than ever. . . . It is impossible for me to avoid contrasting the feelings with which I leave it now that I have grown old, with those with which I bade good-bye to its shores in 1881 when I was young. Then life was before me, I had hopes and ambitions. Now life is practically behind me, with its many failures and its few successes.'

By the time that he had sailed through the Suez Canal, Haggard had lost the elation he had experienced in South Africa. The melancholia encouraged by the torment of frustrated ambitions and by the lonely inactivity of a long sea voyage led him to write, after completing his report: 'I dare say I shall never read it through and whether anyone else will who can say? Still it is done — but in truth I grow weary of journeying by land and sea.'

When he arrived back in England on 6 June, there were but six weeks before he was due to set off again on the Royal Commission's tour of Canada and Newfoundland. In this brief interval he attended to affairs on his farm, sat on the Commission's hearing considering Imperial communications, and discovered from Asche that the production of *Mameena* had been delayed until the late autumn. Then on 17 July, with his fellow British Commissioners (apart from the Chairman, Lord D'Abernon) he set off from Liverpool aboard the *Alsation*. Throughout almost all the voyage they steamed through dense fog. On 25 July, Haggard, in the first entry in the private diary that he was to keep regularly until just before his death, records: 'Except for a few hours at a time, we crept along through the dense, bewildering mist, doing two or three knots an hour [*sic*]. For two nights we lay motionless, screaming at the silent ice which was believed to be around us.'

Immediately after arriving in Newfoundland on 28 July, the Commissioners started their investigations, but that evening Sir Walter Davidson, the Governor, informed Haggard that 'somewhat serious trouble had arisen between Austria and Servia, which looked as if it might cause European complications'. The following day, Haggard wrote in his diary: 'Today we heard that there is grave peril of European war, news which racks us all with anxiety. It is strange how suddenly clouds spring up in what seemed to be a spotless international sky. . . . Poor England — without an adequate army! I am *very* anxious, and wonder whether Armageddon has come at last?' The Commissioners, under their acting Chairman

Sir Arthur Bateman, continued with their duties, but on the train travelling to Port au Basques a meeting was held to discuss what action should be taken by the Commission if Britain declared war. Haggard said that he would want to return home, living as he did on the East Coast, but that he would obey whatever orders he was given.

On 5 August, after arriving in Canada, he recorded: 'This morning we learned that England had declared war against Germany on the ground of the violation of the neutrality of Belgium by that Power. It is terrible, and of this business none can foresee the end. For years some of us have known that such a war must come, although millions at home have mocked at the idea. But always one hoped vaguely that it would not be in our day, knowing how ill we were prepared, owing to the madness of our nation, which has steadily refused to bear the burden of any form of National Service. Now the thing is on us in all its horror, and ready or unready, we must fight and win, or go under.'

While awaiting instruction from the British Government, the Commissioners continued to take evidence, but their minds were preoccupied by events at home. On 9 August, Haggard cabled Longman suggesting that he should write a History of the War, and with that end in view he began to include in his diary as much information about each day's events as he could gather. The next day a telegram was received from the British Government ordering the Commission to cease its work in a week's time after visiting the maritime provinces.

At a large public dinner in the Union Club, St John, on 12 August, Haggard was called upon to speak and, he wrote in his diary, 'everything that had been simmering in my mind for days seemed to rush to my lips, the difficulty being to know which thoughts to choose and in what words to clothe them.' His speech concluded: 'The Angel of Death appears in a dawn of blood: the Armageddon which has been so long foretold has at length fallen upon us. . . . We believe that with the aid of God we shall conquer, and that through us the world shall be free. If our belief is vain, goodnight to England and goodnight to all you who are of England. But it is not vain.'

A journalist who was present reports: 'Sir Rider Haggard was deadly pale and seemed nervous and highly strung and he spoke with a kind of repressed fervour that made the effect strange in the extreme. It was not so much the words that he spoke as the time and place and the circumstances in which he spoke that gave the utterance a meaning that left no doubt on the mind that the warnings had sunk deep and will sink deep into the minds of the Canadian nation to whom they seem to be addressed. After the speech there was a silence in which a pin could be heard dropping.'

On 21 August, Haggard sailed from Canada in the *Virginian* and, after 'a strange and depressing voyage, rushing through ice and reek in this dumb and shrouded ship', he reached Liverpool seven days later. In London he reported to Lord D'Abernon and Lewis Harcourt, who suggested that it was pointless writing the final report of the Commission until after the war. Haggard also visited Longman,

219

whom he found very depressed, and Watt, whom he asked to arrange for the postponement of *The Holy Flower*'s publication and the production of *Mameena*, neither of which Watt was able to do. Back home in Ditchingham, Haggard found evidence of the war even in rural Norfolk. Soldiers were camped on Bungay Common and on 4 September he spoke at a recruiting meeting in the town's drill hall. A few days later he had 10,000 copies of his speech, entitled *A Call to Arms* printed and distributed them to various press agencies and prominent people. His work with the Dominions Royal Commission having been brought to an abrupt halt, he was, with a growing desperation, looking for some service that he could perform. On 10 September, back again in London, he proposed to Harcourt that a Royal Commission to investigate allegations of German atrocities should be appointed, but he was informed that the Government had decided to take no such action at that time.

Haggard was himself soon affected by the tragedies of war. On 18 September, he was informed that his nephew Mark Haggard, Bazett's son, who was an officer in the Welch Regiment, had been killed while charging a German gun-emplacement. His death and his final cry 'Stick it, the Welch!' attracted much attention and were widely reported. Indeed the King telephoned Mark's widow to express personally his thanks, sorrow and sympathy.

At a time such as that Haggard could be hardly expected to enjoy the opening night of *Mameena*, a few weeks later. Yet it was a great success. Oscar Asche in his autobiography records: 'London had never before seen what appeared to be real Zulus in all their war rig-out. At the end of the wedding dance, in which over eighty dancers sang and danced till the curtain fell — and then was raised time after time — even the jaded first-nighters got up on their feet and sang the time and stamped their feet in rhythm. The critics were impressed, and we started off with a wonderful week's business.'[14]

Haggard in his diary on 4 October comments: 'The scenes are beautiful and the incidents interesting, but the drama as he conceives it is nowhere. However, it is of no use arguing with actor-managers. I should imagine that its career will be short.' And so it turned out to be, not because of Oscar Asche, who two years later was to write and produce one of the most successful of all shows, *Chu Chin Chow*, but because the Government introduced stringent street lighting restrictions that discouraged playgoers. *Mameena* was last performed on 14 January, 1915 when Asche's lease of the Globe expired. It was presented 113 times and lost at least £8,000.

Up to mid-November, Haggard was commuting regularly between his Commission meetings in London and Ditchingham, where he worked fitfully on a new romance, *The Ivory Child*, well aware of his need to fulfil his contractual obligations and to continue in the uncertain times to obtain an adequate income. The war and its effects were, however, uppermost in his mind. On 23 October, he heard that Freddie, Charles Longman's son, had been killed. Six of his own nephews and his son-in-law, Major Reginald Cheyne, were in the war. 'Old, gentle-born families like our own,' he wrote, 'bear a large share in the national defence. Would that I were not too old and full of ailments to take my share! I should like to carry a rifle again!'

It was decided on 11 November that the Dominions Royal Commission should be adjourned till the conclusion of the war and a farewell lunch was held for the members at the Cheshire Cheese, where they ate lark-pudding and toasted cheese. The following day Haggard, convinced that he would soon be called upon to serve his country in some way or other, moved with his wife into a flat near Hyde Park Corner. Although he continued to work on his romance, it was for Haggard a frustrating time. He was not actively involved in events, and the many newspapers he read contained too many rumours and far too little news.

By the end of the year he had completed *The Ivory Child*, a sequel to *The Holy Flower*, in which Allan Quatermain destroys Jana, the evil elephant god, and rescues Lady Ragnall who had been abducted during a visit to Egypt. Early in the story, Quatermain and Lady Ragnall smoke a hallucinatory herb called Taduki which enables them to see into the future. At the end of the story Lady Ragnall says, 'There is a time coming, some way off I think, when I and you — no one else, Mr Quatermain — will breathe that smoke again together and see strange things.' This Haggard used as the starting-point for his next romance, a continuation of *The Ivory Child* for which he had not at the time signed a contract. Despite, at the beginning of 1915, suffering from influenza, he started immediately on the story, called *The Ancient Allan*, which describes how, after smoking Taduki, Quatermain and the by now widowed Lady Ragnall dream about the past when in an earlier life he as Shabaka and she as Amada had lived and loved in ancient Egypt.

Still waiting to be called upon to do something more important than romance-writing, Haggard felt that the war, which for years he had been predicting when most had felt it was an impossibility, vindicated him as a writer who had encouraged patriotism and manly virtues. In his diary, on 16 January, he wrote: 'In some ways I think the war is doing good in England. It is bringing the people, or some of them, face to face with elementary facts which hitherto it has been the fashion to ignore and pretend are non-existent. To take one very humble example. How often have I been vituperated by rose-water critics because I have written of fighting and tried to inculcate certain elementary lessons, such as that it is a man's duty to defend his country, and that only those who are prepared for war can protect themselves and such as are dear to them. "Coarse! bloody! brutal! uncivilised!" such has been the talk. Well, and today have I done any harm by inoculating a certain number of the thousands who are at the front with these primary facts, even although my work has been held to be so infinitely inferior to that of Oscar Wilde, Bernard Shaw, and others?'

At last, Haggard was invited to undertake some public work. Early in February he was made the Chairman of the Belgian Agricultural Restoration Committee, but this work was not of the greatest importance and by the end of the month the committee had been absorbed into a similar one sponsored by the Royal Agricultural Society, to whose executive committee Haggard was appointed. By then, however, Haggard, still suffering from influenza and feeling unable to tolerate the London climate, had given up his flat and moved to the more bracing air of St Leonards on the south coast. In March, Haggard was asked to serve on another committee, which under the Chairmanship of Earl Grey, had been set up under the auspices of the Royal Commonwealth Society to consider land settlement at home and in the colonies after the war.

On 31 March, *The Holy Flower* was published. Writing to an anonymous reviewer who had praised the romance, Haggard stated: 'Personally I prefer to write fiction about old Egypt or historical subjects. . . . But what happens? My name, as you remark, is connected in the public idea with a certain stamp of African story and especially with one famous character. Therefore Editors and Publishers clamour for that kind of story reintroducing that famous character. If I write other things I am told they are "not so good", though I well know them to be much better. At the bottom of all this are the fashion-following critics themselves who absolutely resent any new departure, although often enough they also blame the author for sticking in his old *cliché*. . . . Oh, I grow weary of story-telling and could it be managed, would devote the days that remain to the problems of the Land, that greatest of all Causes, and to the service of my Country. But few of us can do exactly what we wish.'[15]

Haggard did not, of course, give in his letter the most important reason for his decision to keep resurrecting Allan Quatermain — his need for the greater income that the stories produced. He was, however, well aware of it, and when he eventually finished *The Ancient Allan* the last sentence opened the door for yet another sequel: 'But whatever Amada, I mean Lady Ragnall, said, there *was* plenty more Taduki, as I have good reason to know.'

After returning to Ditchingham on 16 April, Haggard continued working on his escapist romance. On 23 June, after it was complete, he received from Watt a letter sent by Cassell's to all its authors requesting that in fiction written for them all mention of the war should be avoided. Haggard commented: 'This is a curious little sign of the times, but what it means exactly I cannot pretend to say — that the public is "sick of the war" I suppose. If so I am not certain that this attitude is healthy, although personally the last thing I want to read or write fiction about is the war.'

During the summer, Haggard regularly attended the meetings of his two committees and took every opportunity he could to find ways in which he could serve his country. He wrote to *The Times* pressing for the appointment of a Minister of Food, but his letter was not published. On 25 June he wrote in his diary: 'I have received a polite letter from Lord Selborne explaining nebulously why he, or rather the permanent officials at the Board of Agriculture, find it impossible to make use of my services in any capacity. It would appear that men like myself who have life-long experience and much accumulated knowledge are practically of no value to the country. Yet foolishly enough perhaps, I feel sore, and not altogether for my own sake, since I know well enough that I could still do good work for the nation, if only I were given the chance. At present the only opportunity I have been offered — tentatively — is that of investigating the claims of soldiers' dependants to allowances!' Four days later, he recorded: 'I have heard from Curzon who tells me that if he can hear of any suitable public work for me to do, he will bear me in mind "since you are just the man who ought to be employed at such a time as this". But I don't suppose he will hear of anything.'

So desperate did Haggard's lack of involvement in the war make him that early in July, having purchased a Lee-Metford rifle, he joined the Ditchingham and Bungay Volunteer Defence Corps as a Commander. On 12 July, he drilled with the other volunteers on the common, and observed: 'The spectacle was distinctly funny — that of a lot of determined old gents stumping about and doing their best to execute manoeuvres which they did not understand.'

Fortunately for him, there were more important tasks to undertake. On 22 July, he took part in the Royal Colonial Institute 'After the War' Deputation to Bonar Law and Lord Selborne. In his speech on the settlement of soldiers and sailors in the Dominions after the war he said: 'I venture to submit that the business is one which ought to be followed up without any undue delay. There are these promises; they exist. But this is a mutable world. Governments change, conditions alter, troubles arise, enthusiasms evaporate, and if written bonds are left to rust for months or years, they may oxidise away. I submit, therefore, that the Home Government should appoint some machinery — some Board, on which the Dominions should perhaps he represented — to deal with these matters.' In his diary next day he noted: 'Sir John Taverner, the ex-Australian Agent General who also spoke, suggested that I should be sent round the Dominions to find out the minds of their governments on this and kindred matters, a remark at which Mr Bonar Law nodded his head. Whether anything will come of it, I neither know nor greatly care.' His last comment was less than the truth, and in the next few months he took any opportunity offered to win support for the idea. He also worked on *Finished*, the last of the trilogy concerning aspects of Zulu history, which begins with his own experiences at the Annexation of the Transvaal and ends with the death of Cetywayo at the Kraal Jazi, the site of which he had visited while in South Africa the previous year.

After taking a short fishing holiday with Lilias in Ireland, Haggard went to stay for a few days with his sister Ella in Ledbury. While there on 5 October he read in *The Yorkshire Post*: 'Mr Bonar Law has received from the Governments of the Dominions promises to cooperate in making provision for settling returned soldiers to the land. Mr Law has accordingly appointed a small Commission, of which Sir Rider Haggard is chairman, to visit the Dominions with a view to drawing up a scheme.'

In his diary he commented: 'I have heard nothing from Bonar Law or anyone else, except casual correspondents who wish to be connected with the Commission, as to the truth or falsity of this report. I have wired to Harding to ask for the facts. If there is anything in it, which personally I doubt, the business will be large and important and involve more world-wanderings.'

His excitement at the prospect that he might once again be involved in work of national importance was somewhat marred when two days later, after his return to Ditchingham, he was informed that John, Rudyard Kipling's son was reported 'wounded and missing'. Although he had not been in touch with his friend for some time, Haggard was well aware of what it meant to lose a son.

By the end of the month it was clear that the Government did not intend to authorise an investigation of post-war land-settlement in the Empire and at a committee meeting at the Royal Colonial Institute on 29 October it was suggested that Haggard should be sent to the Dominions by the Institute. Nothing was decided at that time, but, on 10 December, Sir Harry Wilson, the Secretary of the Royal Colonial Institute, telephoned to say that it would certainly be arranged for Haggard to visit Australasia, although nothing could be announced until sufficient subscriptions had been received to cover expenses.

Haggard's delight was intensified by the news he received from Watt that the film rights of several books had been sold. As the contracts have not survived it is impossible to give the exact terms, but certainly by the end of the following years H.L. Lucoque had purchased the rights to film six of Haggard's novels (*King Solomon's Mines*, *She*, *Allan Quatermain*, *Montezuma's Daughter*, *Queen Sheba's Ring*, and *Dawn*), apparently paying £1,500 on account of a royalty of 12½ per cent of the gross receipts, the rights being purchased for a seven-year period. By selling the film rights of books which, although still bought by the thousands in cheap editions, were bringing in but small royalties, Haggard received at least £9,000 between the beginning of 1915 and the end of 1916. This at first unexpected boon was to mean that for the rest of his life, although he continued writing, Haggard was to be provided with a large part of his income by the rapidly expanding film industry. The films that were made not only produced substantial sums, they also introduced the books on which they were based to a whole generation of new readers.

Although the Royal Colonial Institute received moneys to pay for Haggard's trip from many sources, an unexpected difficulty arose late in December. It was pointed out that as Haggard was still officially a Royal Commissioner, it would be necessary for the Government to approve his mission. In his diary on 22 December, Haggard noted: 'Somehow, I begin to doubt whether I shall ever get off to Australasia, nor do I really greatly care. I think it would be a good bit of Empire work which I should be very glad to put in as my offering, since I am too old to fight, but if the Government chooses to thwart it, as up to the present it has thwarted it in every way, notwithstanding all the representations that have been made to it from different quarters, well, I have nothing to say. Then I shall stop at home and attend to my own affairs.' The same day, he also records: 'I saw Kipling in town. He has heard nothing of John and evidently has practically lost hope. . . . Poor lad! He added that he was very fond of me and asked me what I had done to make his children so fond of me. I answered I didn't know except that young people like those who like them — a fact, I think, to which I owe the affection of so many of my nieces and nephews.' As a result of this meeting the two men began again to correspond and in the ensuing years before Haggard's death their friendship deepened.

As the Government raised no objections to his Dominion's mission, Haggard, on 3 January 1916, received from the Royal Colonial Institute his instructions to travel to South Africa, Australasia and Canada. In his diary he wrote: 'I can only hope that the mission will be fortunate and fruitful. At any rate it is my duty to take the risks, go ahead and do the work to the best of my ability. Here is my war offering!' It was an immense undertaking, especially for a man who, in his sixtieth year, suffered almost continually from chest ailments.

Yet Haggard was still able to think about other things. In a letter sent to Kipling about this time, he outlined an idea for a story he wished to write about a threat to destroy the world posed by Oro, a reborn super-human. In his reply, dated 7 January, 1916 (the day on which *The Ivory Child* was published), Kipling stated: 'Oro promises well. 'Gad what an undefeated and joyous imagination you have! I want fuller details, please, of what Oro did when he re-entered upon life on the earth. Can you send me a typed scenario.'[16] During his journey around the world, Haggard was to work on the details of the plot which he was eventually to use in the most original story he had written for many years, *When the World Shook*.

The next few weeks were hectic ones for Haggard as he made preparations for his long journey, helped by A.R. Uvedale Corbett, whom the Royal Colonial Institute appointed as his secretary. On 1 February a lunch given in Haggard's honour by the Institute at the Hotel Cecil was attended by about two hundred and fifty people. Lord Curzon took the chair, declaring that Haggard was 'a great Empire servant'. Although there were many other meetings to attend, letters to be written, and important people to be seen, Haggard also found time, on 7 February, to sign an agreement with Ward Lock for his recently completed romance *Finished* and to visit Lucoque's to see some films, including one taken of himself at Ditchingham ten days earlier.

Haggard, accompanied by Corbett and seen off by his wife and several friends, caught a train for Plymouth on 10 February. That evening, he wrote to his wife: 'I feel parting from you and the children very much indeed, my dear. But I have felt it to be my duty to undertake this long and arduous journey hoping (and indeed believing) that I shall emerge safe out of it at the end. So there is nothing more to be said.'[17] The next day he sailed on the *Kenilworth Castle* for South Africa, occupying himself during the voyage correcting the manuscripts of *The Ancient Allan* and *Finished*.

Haggard arrived at Cape Town on 27 February and the next day began his mission, which was to obtain from the government in each of the states and provinces he visited a written statement of the help that would be provided after the war for the settlement of soldiers and sailors. Although he did not expect to receive such a statement in South Africa, he did obtain from the Chartered Board of the British South Africa Co. the promise of a maximum of 500,000 acres in Rhodesia for approved overseas settlers.

Pleased with this success, Haggard set sail for Australia on 15 March. That day he started dictating to Corbett *The Empire and Its Land*, but after finishing two chapters on South Africa he abandoned the book. With little to do, he spent many hours watching the albatrosses flying about the ship. On 19 March, he recorded in his diary: 'I have evolved the plot of a new story to be called *The Fatal Albatross* of which the scene would be laid in some of the desolate islands we are passing, the Maori group perhaps. Or it might be called *Mary of Marion Isle*.' The same day he started writing a long letter to his wife. Once more lonely during a prolonged sea voyage, he had again become depressed: 'This kind of solitary confinement is not gay. All one's failures and failings rise before one in a melancholy procession till one is sick of contemplating them. In short it is a lonesome job and there is another fortnight of it ahead.' Three days later he added a note to the letter: 'On looking back I see I have been writing some melancholy stuff, which I would not have set down tonight. The truth is, my dear, that I have as many moods as a woman.'[18]

On 3 April, Haggard arrived in Tasmania. He spent the next ten weeks in Australia and New Zealand making speeches, attending meetings, and extracting, with some difficulty, the written statements he required. On 5 June, he received the news from home that the film of *She*, which had been given its first showing on 29 February, was doing well. (It had been produced for Lucoque by Will Barker, and starred Alice Delysia as Ayesha and Henry Vistor as Leo Vincey.) Ten days later, Haggard left Auckland in the *Niagara*, recording in his diary: 'So ends my visit to Australasia. Well on the whole it has been extraordinarily successful, much more so than I could have hoped. I trust that the results may prove enduring and for the good of the Empire.'

Once again, as he sailed across the Pacific, Haggard felt lonely and depressed. On 22 June, his birthday, he records: 'Today is my birthday; a very lonesome birthday amidst all this crowd of strangers in which I take no interest and who take no interest in me — except as a penny peep-show to some of them. Today I have definitely entered upon old age, for at sixty a man is old, especially when he begins young as I did. Let me look round: of my friends but two remain and one of these is broken-hearted. For me the world is largely peopled with the dead; I walk among ghosts, especially at night. Well ere long I must join their company; ten years more the Psalmist would give me, but with my weakened health I cannot expect as much, even should I escape accidents. My work, for the most part, lies behind me, rather poor stuff too — yet I will say this: I *have* worked. My talent may be of copper not of gold — how can I judge my own abilities? — but I have put it to the best use I could.' Well aware that it was enforced inactivity that permitted his depression, Haggard immediately started to write a long letter to Lilias, in which he gives the story outline of *When the World Shook*: 'I've been amusing myself on this ship compounding the plot of a really striking romance. Somebody very like cousin Rose and somebody say like John Scudamore [the Rector of Ditchingham] play important parts in it. Oh and lots of other things . . . the balance (or gyroscope) down in the bowels of the world on which the whole earth swings . . . It may sound unusual but I assure you it will make an excellent romance. Wait and see. But please don't give the gyroscope idea away; it is really priceless.'[19]

When he arrived at Victoria, British Columbia, on 28 June, his mood changed. Having been welcomed by his brother Andrew and many officials he was again in the thick of it and noted, 'Life is very real and earnest for me just now.' Everywhere he went he was given an enthusiastic welcome and on 8 July he was informed that a mountain and glacier in the Rockies were to be named after him. Travelling to Edmonton that day by train, he saw the Sir Rider Mountain and the Haggard Glacier, noting with pleasure: 'It is a wonderful and magnificent Alp, some ten thousand feet high and measuring many miles round its base. Snow lies on its summit even in summer and it has deep, ribbed glaciers and fir-clad ravines upon its flanks, while the crest has some resemblance to a lion.'

His journey across Canada having achieved satisfactory results, Haggard visited Theodore Roosevelt on 20 July. The two men talked for hours and later in his diary Haggard wrote: 'I wonder if we shall ever meet again. No, I do not wonder for I am sure that we shall *somewhere*. We have too much in common not to do so, though it may be perhaps in a state unknown.' The next day Haggard sailed from New York. The ship docked at Liverpool on 29 July and Haggard arrived home at Ditchingham two days later laden with curios collected throughout his journey. In the five months he had been away, he had circumnavigated the globe and successfully accomplished the mission he had been given. Single-handed and with conspicuous devotion he had acted as the unpaid emissary of a Government that disdainfully refused to admit publicly that his mission had even been given official sanction.

On 2 August he recorded in his diary that he saw his local doctor 'who prescribes rest and strychnine tonic and says I am not to travel again at present. That mission has taken it out of me.' The next night bombs were heard exploding and the occupants of Ditchingham House fled to the cellars where they were forced to spend nearly three hours. Zeppelins, it appeared, were flying over the area and one of the bombs they dropped fell about a hundred yards from the house. Not surprisingly, Haggard found it ironic that, having travelled the world in safety, he should return to be bombed in his own house.

Despite his ill-health, there was no rest for Haggard. Having finished his report to the Royal Colonial Institute, he had to attend to his own affairs. Longrigg, his farm steward, informed him that the local tribunal had been very rude when an appeal had been made against the military call-up of his milkmen, it being claimed that such a request was 'unpatriotic'. On 16 August, Haggard wrote: 'Well this occurrence settles my mind. I shall give up farming. I can no longer be exposed to all this pettiness for what brings me in nothing at all.' He gave notice of his intention to surrender the land he hired, and thus, after nearly thirty years, he ceased to be a practising farmer. During the next few weeks, he was frequently called upon to give speeches, attend meetings, and be interviewed by reporters. At the same time he was dictating to Miss Hector *Love Eternal*, a young man's story in which he included many autobiographical references such as experiences as Scoones and at spiritualist séances.

In mid-October the Haggards, again closing up Ditchingham House for the winter, moved to Thornsett, a furnished house in Budleigh Salterton, Devon. Early in November, having completed *Love Eternal*, Haggard began working on *When the World Shook* (at the time entitled *The Glittering Lady*). On the 8th, he visited Sir Norman Lockyer, a distinguished astronomer, to obtain for his story information about the changes that had taken place in the position of stars over a period of 250,000 years.

At a special dinner on 13 November, Haggard was made an honorary life fellow of the Royal Colonial Institute, but as the months since the completion of his mission passed, it became apparent that the Government did not intend to deal with post-war resettlement with any enthusiasm. Realising that his hard work might yet again have been wasted and growing increasingly alarmed at the effects the apparently unending war was having on the country, Haggard, suffering from another bronchial attack, felt increasingly ill at ease. On Boxing Day he wrote: 'Yesterday was Xmas Day, a sad, sad Xmas for many. I had not the heart to drink healths after dinner. That old custom reminds one of too much.'

For the next fortnight, Haggard was in London attending meetings of the Dominions Royal Commission which the Government had at last decided should prepare its final report. While there, on 12 January 1917, he saw the film of *Dawn* which had been made by Lucoque and starred Karina as Mildred Carr and Hubert Carter as Devil Caresfoot. 'It is not so bad,' he wrote, 'but as I have remarked before to an author these cinema performances of his books are full of woe and grief. The women as usual are better than the men!' Back in Budleigh Salterton he worked with Sir Edward Harding on the Commission's report. Much to his disappointment he was not made chairman of the Empire Emigration Committee that the Government established to consider the results of his mission, although on 31 January he was appointed as one of the large number of committee members. A pleasing acknowledgement of his services, however, was made by the Royal Colonial Institute which on 7 March elected him to be one of its Vice-Presidents.

Just before he left Budleigh Salterton, Haggard finished *When the World Shook*. On 10 March he recorded: 'I am rather proud of having been able to do this work in the midst of so many distractions and anxieties, especially as I think it good of its sort. However this may be, it has served to take my mind off all the troubles among which we live, at any rate for an hour or two each day.' In London he met Kipling and read to him sections from his new novel, including the gyroscope scene, in which the evil Oro determines to change the axis of the earth rotation by diverting onto another path the gyroscope that runs through the bowels of the earth:

> The distant humming grew to a roar, the roar to a hellish hurricane of sound which presently drowned all attempts at ordinary speech.

Then bellowing like ten millions of bulls, at length far away there appeared something terrible. I can only describe its appearance as that of an attenuated mountain on fire. When it drew nearer I perceived that it was more like a ballet-dancer whirling round and round upon her toes, or rather all the ballet-dancers in the world rolled into one and then multiplied a million times in size. No, it was like a mushroom with two stalks, one above and one below, or a huge top with a point on which it spun, a swelling belly and another point above. But what a top! It must have been two thousand feet high, if it was an inch, and its circumference who could measure?

On it came, dancing, swaying and spinning at a rate inconceivable, so that it looked like a gigantic wheel of fire. Yet it was not fire that clothed it but rather some phosphorescence, since from it came no heat. Yes, a phosphorescence arranged in bands of ghastly blue and lurid red, with streaks of other colours running up between, and a kind of waving fringe of purple.

The fire-mountain thundered on with a voice like to that of avalanches or of icebergs crashing from their parent glaciers to the sea.

(From *When the World Shook*)

The scene has some similarities to Ayesha's transformation in *She*, but the details and the interpretation are very different. When what at first appears to be a giant column of fire approaches, it is described in the imagery of eroticism: a herd of bulls, whirling dancers, a mushroom, a swelling belly — the whole appearing like a gigantic phallus with an enormous head moving along a subterranean channel. But then, as the gyroscope comes nearer, it is seen not to be bathed in flames. It gives off no heat and the images used to describe it are cold and inanimate — avalanches and icebergs. In the end, the balance of the world is not changed; Oro is foiled in his attempt to divert the gyroscope. In *She* the climax of Ayesha's sudden transformation describes the experience of satiated lust turning into guilt and disgust; in *When the World Shook* the gyroscope scene, with its frustrated threat to change the world describes the experience of impotence, when the mental flames of desire are followed by a coldness of physical response so that the opportunity is lost.

Haggard was at the time approaching his sixty-first birthday and the days of his passion were for ever gone. *When the World Shook* was his last important novel. It delighted Kipling, who on 30 March said that it was 'a remarkable work of imagination — really a new thing'.

By the spring of 1917, Haggard, who like Kipling had long advocated a military alliance with the United States of America, was convinced that without that country's aid the war could not be won.* In his diary on 27 March he wrote: 'I believe that the sovereignty of the world must ultimately pass to America, with her

*As early as 1898 Haggard had written: 'One day the rest of the world, or most of it, I suppose, will fling itself at the throats of America and ourselves. That will be the day of Armageddon, after which may come the long peace. But the British Empire and the United States will dictate the terms of that peace.' (*A Farmer's Year*, p. 380)

enormous wealth and natural resources. Perhaps it is as well that this should be so, especially as America is our child, but thank God I shall not live to see all these changes. At least Britain has played a gallant part in the history of the world.' On 7 April, when he heard that the United States had declared war upon Germany, he wrote: 'The event is of stupendous importance in the history of the world and to what it may lead none can say, possibly to an alliance of the English-speaking peoples and a league to enforce peace on the world. Let us hope so.' He was also extremely pleased when two days later he received a letter from Roosevelt saying that he would be delighted to have *Finished* dedicated to him. (The book was published on 10 August.)

After an absence of six months, Haggard returned to Ditchingham on 20 April, but he had no intention of spending all the summer there. Needing to be in London for the meetings of the Empire Settlement Committee, he purchased the lease of a flat in London at 26 Ashley Gardens, Victoria, into which he was able to move on 5 June. The previous day he was chagrined to discover that although D'Abernon and Harding were to be decorated for their services on the Dominions Royal Commission, the other members were to be unrewarded for their five-year-long labour. It was bad enough that the final report of the Commission had been virtually ignored. Haggard rightly felt that, when titles were all but openly on sale, the Commissioners' services to the State should be publicly recognised. On 11 July, the Empire Settlement Committee met for the last time and in his diary he wrote: 'So there is an end of my public work — at any rate for the present.'

Haggard, back in Ditchingham, was left to concentrate again on his writing. On 24 July, he accepted an offer made by John Murray for *Moon of Israel*, the Egyptian story on which he was working. In addition to paying £250 for the serial rights and an advance of £500 on publication, John Murray agreed to give Haggard a half-share in the copyright of *Jess* which had been acquired when the publishers purchased Smith, Elder & Co.'s business.

Once again, without public duties, Haggard began to feel oppressed. Having already decided to give up farming, he set about putting his other affairs in order. On 10 September, the Curator of the Norwich Castle Museum called to collect the bound manuscripts of all the fiction he had written up to 1892 (apart from *Allan Quatermain*, given to Charles Longman, and *Mr Meeson's Will*, given to A.P. Watt). Haggard had decided to present them to the Norwich Corporation, 'the gift of a Norfolk man to Norfolk', because: 'Otherwise, within a very short period of a man's decease, there would be no one left who would take the slightest interest in them, and probably in the end they would find their way, unless they were destroyed by accident, to the counter of a sale room.' A fortnight later, his notices to quit the land he rented being about to expire and the harvest having been gathered, the sale was held of all his farm stock, which realised almost eight thousand pounds.

Having almost completed *Moon of Israel*, Haggard moved to his London flat in October, while his wife sought suitable accommodation for the winter in St

Leonards. On 5 November, he heard that his nephew and godson Lance, Arthur Haggard's second son, an Acting Major in the Princess Patricia's Canadian Regiment, had been killed. Sadly he wrote: 'It is a terrible business. Oh, when will God lift this cloud of death and blood from the face of our tortured world?'

Although he saw no prospect of work other than writing, Haggard, well aware of the ever rising prices and severe shortages, found consolation in his continued survival as a writer. On 8 November, Cassell's accepted *The Ancient Allan* and *When the World Shook*, the two completed romances for which a publisher had not hitherto been found. For each book Haggard was to be paid £400 on receipt of the manuscript for the serial rights and an advance of £750 on publication. 'At any rate,' Haggard wrote, 'I find that I can still command a market even in this time of war and misery. This is something at my age, and after publishing books for so long, and I am thankful for it.'

By mid-November, Haggard was again suffering from bronchial catarrh, and was glad to escape from London and move into a flat at 28 Grand Parade, St Leonards, where the milder climate and bracing sea breezes he felt were beneficial to him. Because of this, he decided to purchase North Lodge, which had once been the pay-gate of the town and had a public road running under an upper room he intended to make his study. Many repairs had to be carried out, however, before the Haggards could move into it. When, in December, he moved up to a foggy London to spend the Christmas period with his family, he fell ill and was forced to return alone to St Leonards, where because no servants had been engaged for the flat he went to stay at the Greeba Hotel. There he corrected the proofs of *Moon of Israel*, the serialisation of which was to begin appearing in *The Cornhill Magazine* at the beginning of 1918.

On 2 January, 1918, Haggard unexpectedly received from Sir Henry Rew, the head of the Agricultural Wages Board, an invitation to act as an investigator in the West Country. Doubtful as to whether his health was good enough for him to undertake his duties in winter, Haggard asked if he could be accompanied by Arthur Cochrane. As this was accepted, the ever-ready Haggard and his friend began their work in Exeter on 29 January. It was a foolish undertaking for a sick man of over sixty. In Truro on 3 February he was examined by a doctor who announced: 'Sir Rider Haggard is running grave risk in going about the country in a motor-car and stopping at casual inns. I have told him definitely that in my opinion he ought to give up his investigations and stop at home at St Leonards.' Haggard was left with no alternative but to follow the doctor's instruction, leaving Cochrane to carry on with the investigation by himself.

The sudden end to his journey was more than a disappointment to Haggard; it forced him to acknowledge that it was most unlikely that he would ever again be able to undertake any such mission. He was too old and too liable to illness to travel extensively as he had done for much of the previous ten years. It was likely that the dictum his mother had given him forty-two years earlier to follow the paths of duty could in the future only be fulfilled by such tasks as serving on committees or as a local magistrate. Yet he would keep as busy as he could. Throughout his adult life he had worked obsessively, occupying as much time as he could in writing, farming, undertaking research, making speeches, analysing events, pleading causes, writing letters, and serving his country. Nor did one task exclude another: while writing *King Solomon's Mines* he was reading for the Bar; while touring the Dominions he was planning new romances. He was a public figure, but also an amateur archaeologist, a collector of antiquities, a beloved uncle and father, a gardener, and the centre of attention at any party. By his sustained, frenetic activity, he kept at bay the anguish of remorse by which, when he was alone and inactive, he was tormented.

Although Haggard had an obsessive need to work, as far as possible throughout his life he selected those tasks which were most likely to ensure that, even though he had no son to inherit the Ditchingham estate his name would be remembered after his death. The quest for a measure of immortality was inspired by his childhood experiences. Then he acquired the seared awareness of his own mortality which resulted in his permanent preoccupation with all death's aspects and the evolution of his belief in reincarnation. As a child too he inwardly reacted to his father's irritable dismissiveness and his elder brother's overbearing arrogance, so that as a man he was determined to prove not only his worth but his actual superiority.

In his character, however, there was always a reserve, a holding-back. Miss Hector described him as 'a lonely man' and others considered him to be aloof. With those around him he did not share his secret world that was inhabited only by those he had loved and lost — Lilly, his partner for eternity; Jock, his son, who 'haunted the house the more obtrusively because everyone there pretended they could not see him, and the poor schoolboy wraith seemed to be begging piteously for some notice, so that he might be laid to rest';[20] and his mother, to whom he always felt so close. His introspectiveness, combined with a natural restlessness, might have made it difficult for Haggard to have a satisfactory home life. Yet, despite his somewhat strange relationship with his wife, it was she who provided the continuity and the security that he seemed destined never to obtain. Because Louie was independent, she placed few demands on her husband; but because she was obviously devoted to him she ensured that their home provided a relaxed, comfortable solace to which Haggard, the inveterate wanderer, always happily returned. It is true that she gave him little passion or intellectual stimulus; but the stability of her relationship with Haggard was more important. When he married, his own passion was suppressed; and he lacked confidence in his own considerable abilities so that he was very vulnerable to criticism that often caused him to change the object of his ambition, although it always remained his overriding aim to produce during his lifetime his own impressive memorial.

In this he was successful. Between 1881 and 1889, when his ill-comprehended need to write was created by his unconscious desire to win his mother's acclaim, he wrote *King Solomon's Mines*, *She*, *Allan Quatermain*, and *Nada the Lily*. Between

1890 and 1902, when after his mother's death he concentrated on agriculture (an interest that, his mother had assured him, he alone of all her children had inherited from her), he not only produced the outstanding record *The Farmer's Year* but as a result of his investigations made recommendations that, although mostly unadopted in his lifetime, were later largely implemented, especially during the Second World War. Between 1902 and 1918, when as a development of his agricultural work and in obedience to his mother's instruction that he should put first duty and faith, he used his energies in the service of his country and furthered the cause of migration to the Dominions, living long enough to see the passing of the Empire Settlement Bill in 1922.

Of all his achievements, posterity remembers most his first romances. In the introduction to *The Days of My Life*, Haggard wrote: 'Although it may seem much to claim, my belief is that some of my tales *will* live. Possibly this belief is quite erroneous, in which case in years to come I may be laughed at for its expression. It is obvious also that a great deal of what I have written is doomed to swift oblivion, since, even if it were all equally good, in the crowded days that are to come, days even more crowded than our own, posterity will not need much of the work of any individual. If he is remembered at all it will be by but a few books.' He was right. Although there is much more of his writing that deserves to be remembered and although many of his achievements have been generally forgotten, *She* and *King Solomon's Mines* remain, substantial memorials that are still read and loved throughout the world.

II

1918 was not a happy year for Haggard. On 17 April he heard that his brother Will had sold the family estate. 'Bradenham Hall,' he wrote, 'for many years has been a haunted house, in which ever since I saw my beloved mother die there, I have not cared to stay. Yet it was her home for nearly fifty years, and there was spent most of my childhood.' After returning to Ditchingham on 23 May, he was often to hear 'the sickening thuds of the distant guns, firing, firing eternally at the front'. In his diary on 4 June he recorded: 'The strain of this long war tells upon one's nerves. When those bombs explode I confess that my heart jumps and flutters. Also one grows no younger and does grow a great deal *thinner*. My clothes almost slip off me now as do the rings off my fingers.' There were other problems — the summer was exceptionally cold, prices were rising continuously, and the shortage of paper meant that many of his books went out of print.

On 20 August he visited 'that abomination of desolation, an ancient home that is being broken up'. He wandered round the half-empty rooms at Bradenham where familiar furniture had been labelled ready for the public auction. Having visited the graves of his mother and father, Haggard left, vowing that he would never return there again. At the sale a week later, the effects produced enormous prices, the auctioneer assuring the bidders that in the future everything would become very valuable because of its association with Haggard's childhood. Although he had left bids on many items, Haggard managed to purchase very few, but they included the bed he had slept in as a child and his butterfly cabinet in which only one dilapidated moth remained.

He was slightly cheered when, on 12 September, Lord Curzon wrote giving permission for *When the World Shook* to be dedicated to him. Haggard's dedicatory letter thanked Curzon for defending him from the accusations of plagiarism over thirty years before, and concludes: 'Therefore in gratitude and memory I ask you to accept this romance, as I know that you do not disdain the study of romance in the intervals of your Imperial work. The application of its parable to our state and possibilities — beneath or beyond these glimpses of the moon — I leave to your discernment.'

About this time, Haggard thought of offering himself as the Unionist candidate for East Norfolk in the post-War election, but on 10 October he wrote to his wife from Ledbury, where he was staying for a few days: 'No, I'm not going to have anything to do with E. Norfolk or an invitation like that, and have written to say so. . . . Standing for Parliament isn't much of a catch anyway to an elderly gent with a continual cold.'[21]

On 21 October Haggard spent his first night in North Lodge, St Leonards, which was for the next few years to be his winter home. Ten days later, *Moon of Israel* was published, by which time he had already started writing *She and Allan*, a romance in which, trying to capitalise on his early successes, his two most famous characters were to meet; but he had little hope of its attracting much attention for he had begun to regard himself as 'the deadest of dead letters'.

Even the abdication of the Kaiser and the end of the War did not raise his spirits. In his diary on 11 November he wrote: 'The Germans will never forgive nor forget; neither money nor comfort will tell with them henceforth. They have been beaten by England and they will live and die to smash England — she will never have a more deadly enemy than the new Germany. My dread is that in future years the easy-going, self-centred English will forget that just across the sea there is a mighty, cold-hearted and remorseless people waiting to strike her through the heart. For strike they will one day, or so I believe.'

On the day of the General Election, 14 December, Louie travelled to Norfolk so that she could vote, but Haggard, fearful of a bronchial attack, stayed at St Leonards. 'I confess,' he wrote, 'that I feel somewhat out of it. It is galling when, whatever may be the case with the physical, one's mental qualities are as good or better than ever to feel that one is a dead letter of no account. Yet doubtless it is better so at my age and in my present state of health. If I could have gone into Parliament young, I dare say that I might have made a fine career there; but I was a Unionist, and from Unionists too much *money* is expected. Also how could I have done the public work and earned my living as well?'

On 17 December, he received a letter from the Home Secretary informing him that the King was to confer on him the rank of a Knight Commander of the Most Excellent Order of the British Empire. 'Of course I am grateful,' Haggard commented, 'though what I have always wished to become is a Privy Councillor, which however I suppose is now beyond my reach. . . . However, one must not look a gift-horse in the mouth, and it is a recognition of my work for the Empire. I hope sincerely too that it may lead to my being offered more honorary work to do before I grow too old for it, but this of course is doubtful. I suppose that I must owe this compliment to Curzon. Anyway it shows that my work is not altogether forgotten, as I feared was the case.' Any pleasure Haggard derived from the news was, however, short-lived. On 7 January 1919, he was deeply distressed to hear that Theodore Roosevelt, from whom he had received a letter ten days earlier, had died.

In the first few months of 1919 Haggard completed *She and Allan* and, a few days after *When the World Shook* was published on 20 March, he moved from St Leonards to spend a few extremely busy weeks staying at his London flat. On 11 April, Hutchinson's accepted *She and Allan*, agreeing to pay £900 for the serial rights and an advance of £1000 on publication, the largest sums he had received for many years. Deeply concerned about the Russian Revolution and its possible effects on Great Britain, he several times met Admiral Sir Reginald Hall, the founder of an anti-Bolshevist movement called National Propaganda. He also became, at Lord Curzon's suggestion, a member of the Birth Rate Commission. On 12 May, he attended the trade view of the film of *King Solomon's Mines*, that had been made for African Film Productions Ltd. by H. Lisle Lucoque.

There were, however, irritations to spoil such moderate successes. After his return to Ditchingham at the end of May, he was upset by the damage caused at Kessingland Grange by the occupying soldiers and felt that the compensation he was offered was inadequate. He was disappointed in July to learn that he was not to be asked to serve on the Royal Commission on Agriculture. On 23 September, while staying in London, he received a letter from Watt's stating that on future contracts the agent's commission would be raised from 5 per cent to 10 per cent.

Returning to St Leonards early in October for the winter, Haggard began writing *The Virgin of the Sun*. On 31 October he went up to town to see a private view of the film of *Allan Quatermain*, noting in his diary: 'It is not at all bad, but it might be a great deal better. I wonder if the cinema business will ever be adequately handled in this country. It has great possibilities but it ought to be in the hands of artists and strictly upright men.' Three days later he wrote to *The Times* asking: 'Cannot better arrangements be made as to the release of films? Is it really necessary that these should be kept in cold storage for a solid year, as I understand will happen in the case of *Allan Quatermain*?'

Suffering again from bronchitis, Haggard was ill at ease. He ended his diary for 1919: 'This is the last day of an unhappy and disappointing year. I hope that the next may be better and more prosperous, but I cannot see any reason to suppose that it will.' Increasingly he felt out of tune with his times and pessimistic about the country's future. He was, therefore, pleased when on 14 January 1920, Wickham Steed, the editor of *The Times*, asked him to call at his office so that the possibility of starting a new movement to combat Bolshevism could be discussed. Eventually, having been assured that the scheme had Lord Northcliffe's backing, Haggard agreed to become the Chairman of what he named the Liberty League, and on 3 March there appeared in *The Times* a letter announcing its foundation signed by, among others, Haggard, Kipling and Lord Sydenham. Donations, it was requested, should be sent to Lieutenant-Colonel Maitland Edwards at 17 Bruton Street, Mayfair. The movement was much mocked by the popular press, *The Daily Herald* on 4 March publishing this verse:

Two Hearts that Beat as One

'Every Bolsh is a blackguard,'
Said Kipling to Haggard.
'And given to tippling,'
Said Haggard to Kipling.

'And a blooming outsider,'
Said Rudyard to Rider.
'Their domain is a blood-yard,'
Said Rider to Rudyard.

'That's just what I say,'
Said the author of *They*.
'I agree; I agree.'
Said the author of *She*.[22]

For several weeks Haggard fully occupied himself with Liberty League business, but when he arrived at the offices on 21 April he was informed that Edwards had absconded with the funds. As a result, the members of the committee had to make good the missing money. Northcliffe washed his hands of the affair, but eventually the fiasco was concealed from the public by amalgamating the National Propaganda movement with the Liberty League.

With relief Haggard returned to Ditchingham in mid-May. The Liberty League was to be his last attempt to involve himself in public events. On 22 June, his birthday, he wrote: 'How the years go by and how quickly the world slips past us. However, I think we live long enough. I can imagine no fate more awful than that of She left alone like a hard, everlasting rock on a water-scoured plain. Already I begin to be left alone. Shakespeare talks of "troops of friends" as an accompaniment of age, but mine are nearly all gone and, if we live again, as I hope and indeed believe, how know we that those friends will still care for us yonder? They may have forgotten or new interests may have intervened! It was one of my mistakes in life to make friends with men older than myself, and now time has taken nearly all of them.'

Although he was irritated, as those entering old age often are, by unwelcome changes that affected him (including increases in income tax, difficulties in obtaining servants, and the lack of respect shown him by some young people), Haggard in the latter years of his life, as he ordered his affairs, accepted the inevitability of his death with a resignation that at times merged into contentment.

While his health permitted him, he continued to be extremely active. He still served on committees, such as those considering the National Birth Rate, Empire Settlement, and the Relief of Allies, until their work ended. When in the spring of 1924 he heard that the Colonial Office intended to appoint a committee to consider problems connected with East Africa, he wrote to Curzon stating that he would like to be a member. On 19 June he was appointed to the committee, although not long after the first meeting in October the worsening state of his health prevented him from taking an active part in the proceedings.

During these years Haggard was also often invited to be a guest at official functions. Once or twice each year he attended a Royal Garden Party at Buckingham Palace. In 1921 his portrait painted by Maurice Greiffenhagen was one of the most talked-about exhibits at the Royal Academy. On 27 June, 1921, he was the guest of honour at the Lyceum Club Authors' Dinner. In the spring of 1922 he was the chief judge of a children's essay competition organised by the Lord Roberts Memorial Fund, and he was one of the authors invited to write in a miniature book that was included in the library of a dolls'-house presented to the Queen.

He was also able to travel again for pleasure. In October, 1920, he inspected the battlefields and war cemeteries in Belgium and visited the grave of his nephew Lance. Three times in the next two years he spent a fishing holiday with Ronald Ross, the Nobel Prize winner for medicine, who, after they had first met in 1917, became a close friend. Such breaks from his labours became very desirable as his physical state noticeably deteriorated. In addition to the influenza and bronchitis with which he was afflicted each winter, his gout returned with increased severity. Although it had become the pattern of his life to spend the summers at Ditchingham and the winters in St Leonards (for he sold his London flat in 1920), his family felt late in 1923 that it would not be wise for him to spend another complete winter in England, and so, in January, 1924, Haggard and Lilias sailed to Egypt where, despite the hordes of tourists, he had a pleasant if reflective time.

Much of Haggard's latter days were spent, as they had almost always been, in writing. Between January 1921 and December 1924 he wrote seven romances. The first of these was *Wisdom's Daughter*. On 18 March, 1921, Haggard wrote to Watt's: 'I note that Hutchinson is prepared to buy the British serial and British & Colonial book rights in the story I am now writing, provisionally named *Wisdom's Daughter: Being the Autobiography of She-Who-Must-Be-Obeyed* on the same terms as he gave for *She and Allan*. I agree to this proposal with the proviso that the book is not to appear in volume form until 1923. . . . The tale will be a little shorter than *She and Allan*, but as it is unfinished I cannot yet tell you the exact length.'[23] (*Wisdom's Daughter*, after appearing as a serial in *Hutchinson's Magazine*, was published on 9 March, 1923.) On 22 September, 1921, Hutchinson's agreed to pay £800 for the serial rights and an advance on publication of £800 for *Heu-Heu, or The Monster*. When the manuscript was delivered in March, 1923, however, they did not like the story and so it appeared in *Hutchinson's Magazine*, and as a book on 29 June, 1924, in an abridged form. Despite this, Hutchinson's were still willing to accept Haggard's romances and between 29 June and 5 September, 1923, they agreed to publish the last five books he was to write. For each they undertook to pay £300 for the serial rights and an advance of £700 on publication. *Queen of the Dawn: A Love Tale of Old Egypt* (which Haggard had completed on 1 April, 1922, before writing *Heu-Heu*) was not, however, serialised, although it appeared as a book on 21 April, 1925.

The remaining books were all published posthumously, and only one was serialised. This was *The Treasure of the Lake* which was published in September, 1926, after first appearing in Hutchinson's *Adventure Story Magazine*. *Allan and the Ice-Gods* (another episode in the drug-induced reliving of adventures by Allan Quatermain and Lady Ragnall) appeared on 20 May, 1927.* *Mary of Marion Isle* (the plot of which Haggard had devised in 1916) was first published in an edition of only 3500 copies on 4 January, 1929. Hutchinson's refused to publish *Belshazzar*, paying £55 compensation to Watt's. The romance was eventually issued by Stanley Paul & Co. in an edition of 2500 copies on 26 September, 1930.

It would have been better for Haggard's reputation if the clutch of books he wrote for Hutchinson's had never been published. As the last of his books to appear and to be reviewed, they did much to create the impression, very prevalent in the first decades after Haggard's death, that he was and had always been a third-rate writer of repetitive adventure yarns. Sadly, in imitating his earlier original works, Haggard was compared adversely with his own more successful imitators.

Perhaps Haggard continued writing because he needed to be occupied; perhaps it was a habit he could not break. It may also be that he was distressed because, although his earlier books still sold in vast numbers, he received little from them in royalties. In his diary on 5 September, 1921, he wrote: 'I have just received a six months' royalty account of some books of mine which are published at 2/- out of which a royal of 1½d. a copy is my share! Of these books about 68,000 were sold during the six months, but when publishers and other agents have had their cut, all I — the author — get for this great circulation is £302, of which again nearly half will be taken by the Income Tax.' Among his papers deposited in the Norfolk Record Office is a list showing that in the six months to 31 March, 1922, 52,886 copies of his books were sold in cheap editions, from which he earned £258. 12s. 11d.

30th January, 1922 I have just returned from spending a most interesting day with the Kiplings at Batemans. . . . We hammered out the skeleton plot for a romance I propose to write under some such title as *Alan and the Ice Gods*, which is to deal with the terrible advance of the Ice Ages upon a little handful of the primitive inhabitants of the earth. He has a marvellously fertile mind and I never knew anyone quite so quick at seizing and developing an idea. We spent a most amusing two hours over this plot and I have brought home the results in several sheets of MS. written by him and myself. (*The Private Diaries of Sir Henry Rider Haggard*, p. 236)

Fortunately for Haggard's finances he earned large sums from the film industry in his final years. In 1920 Fox Film Co. of the United States, who had made a film of *Cleopatra* starring Theda Bara, paid Haggard £5,000 for what he called 'the shameless plagiarism' of his romance. The same year, he sold the British film rights of *Swallow* (to African Film Productions) and *Stella Fregelius* (to Master's Films for an advance of £250 against a 10 per cent royalty on the first £5,000 of gross receipts and a 15 per cent royalty of the remainder). On 18 April, 1921, *The Times* published a review of the film *Stella* which stated that the ending was a terrible anti-climax. This angered Haggard so much that he wrote to *The Times* protesting against the film-makers' insistence on the 'happy-ending convention'.

Two days later, he recorded in his diary: 'I have spent the last two days in seeing (privately) the Italian made film of *Beatrice*. It has good points (especially those of the heroine's eyes!), but for an author the experience as usual is somewhat heart-breaking.' (The film, made by Unione Cinematografica Italiana, was produced by Herbert Brenon and starred Marie Doro.)

In 1924 the film rights were sold of *Moon of Israel* (to Sasha Films) and *She* and *Mr Meeson's Will* (bopth to H.L. Lucoque). The film of *Moon of Israel* was made in Austria and starred Arlette Marshall, Adelqui Millar and Maria Corda.

Despite the boost given to his income by returns from films, Haggard during these years also considered what he hoped might be money-making schemes. On 26 February 1921, he wrote to General Smuts, the Prime Minister of South Africa, offering to visit the country so that he could investigate the possibility of settling there upper-class inhabitants of the United Kingdom. On 24 August 1921, he offered to undertake a study of potential settlements for the Zionist Organisation. On 8 May 1922, he received a letter from Major Burnham inquiring if he would be prepared to undertake some work in America for John Hays Hammond. The following day Haggard replied: 'Well, I must say at once that I am too old for exploration or other work involving physical hardships, and of late years have (thanks to our cursed climate) suffered much from bronchial troubles which force me to live at St Leonards in the winter. . . . My intelligence, however, is as good as ever. . . . What is it that Mr Hammond proposes and for how long? To be frank, is he prepared to offer sufficient remuneration in meal or malt as we say (i.e. of one sort or another) to make it worth while to undertake certain risks and respon-sibilities?'[24] Nothing, however, came of these schemes.

As the months passed Haggard found himself recording in his diary not so much his own activities as the deaths of friends and relatives. On 29 March 1921, he wrote: 'I have just heard by wire of the sudden death from heart failure of my dearest sister, Ella Maddison Green.' His brother Andrew died on 13 May 1923. The next day, Haggard wrote: 'Alas! my dear brother, Andrew, has gone. He died last night at St Leonards, worn out with years of bronchitis. On this day week I went there to see him and was sure that he could not live long. Now the end has come. When he arrived, I think it was in 1919, from Canada, I thought he was a dying man but he recovered wonderfully.' On 29 October, 1924, he recorded in his diary: 'My sister-in-law Nitie, the wife of my brother William, is suddenly dead of heart failure.'

On 1 November, Haggard attended Nitie's funeral at Hartlip in pouring rain. He then went to stay in London, where five days later he proposed a toast to 'The Publishing Trade' at a dinner given to celebrate the bicentenary of Longmans, Green & Co. Afterwards, as he was trying to find a taxi, he was seized with what he described as 'a most fearful attack of indigestion'. He managed to travel to St Leonards, where he stayed in bed for a week at the East Sussex Club. He then felt better, although he concluded, 'In future I must be an even smaller eater than I have been in the past.'

Haggard returned to London on 25 November to speak on 'The Good and the Bad of the Imagination' at a dinner given by the Delphian Coterie. Unfortunately he was 'seized with gout at the dinner with other delights'. The doctors diagnosed an infection of the bladder and on 27 December, after his return to Ditchingham, he wrote: 'Well, we must suffer what it pleases God to send us with such patience as we may, but I begin to think that my active career is at an end and that I must resign from all public work. I wished to begin a new romance, but I cannot face it.' He was not to write any more books. Indeed, for the first time since he had started keeping his private diary, he had to give up making regular entries.

During the early months of 1925, he fought against the pain that racked his body. A nurse was hired to look after him, but there was no cheer for him during the cold winter days. In January, his oldest remaining friend, Arthur Cochrane, died. To Miss Hector, Haggard dictated for inclusion in his diary his friend's obituary: 'The loss to me is great, for though of late decades his domestic circumstances tended to separate us to a certain extent, we always remained close in spirit, as his last brief letters to me testify and there are few whom I more earnestly hope to meet again in some future state. This, I know, was also his desire.' On 3 February he dictated his next entry for his diary in which he recorded the deaths of Arthur, his youngest brother, and William Carr of Ditchingham Hall, his neighbour.

Deeply distressed by Haggard's illness, Rudyard Kipling began on 15 February to write a series of cheery, weekly letters. To one of these, on 2 March, Haggard dictated a long reply, in which he stated: 'Lying in bed here day after day, one dissects oneself with thoroughness and alas — a somewhat miserable anatomy appears. Lack of sufficient principle, or so it seems to me, rashness, want of steady aim (except where the country was concerned of which at heart I have always been the servant) and of character, liability to be swept away by primary impulses, which you will observe never trouble heroes in really first-class novels, for these turn them on and off with a tap of which the spout is directed only towards the heroine — all these bones and others equally unseemly, such as little secret jealousies, are very large and prominent. . . . I am glad to say that I am somewhat better. I got up yesterday and sat in the old study next door for a little while.'[25]

Haggard's health did not improve. On 26 March, he dictated what was to be the last paragraph in his diary: 'It is a long while since I made an entry in this diary, for the good reason that I have been laid up very ill with a horrible disease of the bladder that has been threatening me for some months, and am indeed still laid up and suffering many unpleasant things on which I will not dwell. I do so now, however, to record the death of Lord Curzon who is buried today. . . . May this great servant of this country forever rest in honour and in peace.'

By mid-April his condition had so deteriorated that the doctors attending him decided that he should go to London for a further examination and possibly an operation. Lilias records: 'It is obvious that Rider knew the end had come. So in her heart did Louie. On the grey spring morning that the ambulance was coming to fetch him, she was in his room helping with the last-minute preparations. The nurse had dressed him and left him in a chair, but he looked down at his overcoat as if something was missing, then got up, walked to the table where there was a bowl of daffodils, and taking one out pulled it through his buttonhole — then turned with rather a sad little smile to his wife. How many hundred times had she seen him do that. The last action of the morning ritual in his dressing-room; for every day the gardener brought in a buttonhole, a rose or carnation in summer, an orchid in winter. Rider was never without a flower. The little incident broke her control. "Rider," she said, "do you really want to go, dear? You have only got to say if you don't and we will send the ambulance back — are you quite, quite sure?" '[26]

Haggard went to the nursing home and had an operation that the doctors declared was 'entirely successful'. For three days he lay quietly, speaking little. Then he lapsed into semi-consciousness. Major Cheyne, his son-in-law, spent the night of 13 May by his bedside. While he watched the apparently sleeping body, a large building nearby caught fire. The blaze was soon visible from the bedroom. Suddenly Haggard sat up and pointed silently at the flames. 'My God,' Cheyne thought, 'an old Pharaoh!'[27]

The following day, 14 May, at about mid-day, Haggard died. His wife was at his side. Afterwards his body was cremated and the ashes buried in the chancel of Ditchingham Church under a slab of black marble.

Notes

The sources are given of quotations other than those taken from the published works of Sir H. Rider Haggard, including his autobiography, *The Days of My Life*.

CHAPTER ONE

1 Lilias Rider Haggard, *The Cloak That I Left* (1951), p.27.
2 *Ibid*, p.26.
3 *Ibid*, p.28.
4 Suire de la Molle in *Colonel Quaritch, V.C.* is based on his father.
5 H. Rider Haggard, 'Books Which Have Influenced Me', *The British Weekly*, May 27, 1887.
6 H. Rider Haggard, 'On Going Back', *Longman's Magazine*, XI (November, 1887), pp.61–66.
7 Mr Graham was the basis for Mr Fraser, Angela's tutor in *Dawn*.
8 Quoted in L. Haggard, *Cloak*, p.22.
9 *Ibid*, p.28.
10 Rosamond E.M. Harding, *An Anatomy of Inspiration* (1967), p.1.
11 L. Haggard, *Cloak*, pp.31–32.

CHAPTER TWO

1 *The South African Diaries of Sir Garnet Wolseley* (1971), p.249.
2 Haggard, 'Books Which Have Influenced Me'.
3 'Sir Rider Haggard', *The Natal Mercury*, April 18, 1914.
4 H. Rider Haggard, 'The Transvaal', *Macmillan's Magazine*, XXXVI (May, 1877), pp.70–79.
5 Quoted in L. Haggard, *Cloak*, p.49.
6 H. Rider Haggard, 'A Visit to the Chief Secocoeni', *Gentleman's Magazine*, CCXLIII (September, 1877), pp.302–318.
7 Sir John Kotzé, *Biographical Memoirs and Reminiscences* (n.d.), p.465.
8 *Ibid*, pp.481–482.
9 Quoted in L. Haggard, *Cloak*, p.73.
10 Kotzé, *Memoirs*, p.451.
11 Haggard, 'The Real *King Solomon's Mines*', *Cassell's Magazine*, XLIV (July, 1907), pp.144–151.
12 L. Haggard, *Cloak*, p.128.
13 Kotzé, *Memoirs*, pp.487–488.
14 L. Haggard, *Cloak*, p.72.
15 Letter in the Bradfer Lawrence Collection, Norfolk Record Office.
16 L. Haggard, *Cloak*, p.85.

17 Kotzé, *Memoirs*, p.523.
18 Quoted in L. Haggard, *Cloak*, p.82.
19 Draft letter in the Columbia Collection, Columbia University Library.

CHAPTER THREE

1 Quoted in L. Haggard, *Cloak*, p.89.
2 Letter, dated 1 August, in the Columbia Collection.
3 In the Columbia Collection.
4 Letter in Norfolk Record Office (MS 4694/31/1).
5 Quoted in L. Haggard, *Cloak*, p.92.
6 *Ibid*, pp.92–93.
7 *Ibid*, p.93.
8 Letter and memorandum in the C.O. Clark Collection, quoted in Morton Cohen, *Rider Haggard — His Life and Works* (1960), p.55.
9 Quoted in L. Haggard, *Cloak*, p.94.
10 *Ibid*, pp.94–95.
11 *Ibid*, pp.96–97.
12 *Ibid*, p.97.
13 Clark Collection, quoted in Cohen, *Haggard*, pp.55-56.
14 Quoted in L. Haggard, *Cloak*, p.99.
15 *Ibid*, p.202.
16 Clark Collection, quoted in Cohen, *Haggard*, p.57.
17 Quoted in L. Haggard, *Cloak*, p.106.

CHAPTER FOUR

1 Letter to Miss Agnes Barber in the Columbia Collection.
2 Letter in Norfolk Record Office (MS 4694/31/2).
3 *Ibid*, (MS 4694/31/3).
4 Letter in the Columbia Collection.
5 Letter in Norfolk Record Office (MS 4694/31/4).
6 J.E. Scott in *A Bibliography of the Works of Sir Henry Rider Haggard* gives the date of first publication as June 22, 1882. Haggard's surviving correspondence would suggest *Cetywayo and His White Neighbours* was not published until July 5 or 6.
7 Letter in the Columbia Collection.
8 L. Haggard, *Cloak*, p.117.
9 Letter in the Columbia Collection.
10 *Ibid*.
11 Entry for February 16, 1916.
12 L. Haggard, *Cloak*, p.119.
13 Letter in the Columbia Collection.
14 Sir Frederick John Jackson, *Early Days in East Africa* (1969), p.1.
15 Letter in the Columbia Collection.
16 Letters in the Columbia Collection.
17 In Norfolk Record Office (MS 4694/2/2).
18 Jackson, *Early Days*, p.1.
19 L. Haggard, *Cloak*, p.16.
20 *Academy*, XXV (March 22, 1884), p.200.
21 Cohen, *Haggard*, p.137.
22 Letter in the Columbia Collection.
23 Jackson, *Early Days*, pp.2–3.

24 Letters in the Columbia Collection.
25 Letter in the Columbia Collection.
26 *Ibid.*

CHAPTER FIVE

1 *Pall Mall Budget*, XXXIII (January 16, 1885), p.29.
2 *The Saturday Review*, LIX (January 17, 1885), pp.84–85.
3 Brian Doyle, *The Who's Who of Children's Literature* (1968), p.252.
4 L. Haggard, *Cloak*, pp.121–122.
5 In Norfolk Record Office.
6 'H. Rider Haggard', *The Book Buyer* (New York), IV (1894), pp.156–157.
7 Entry for January 6, 1917.
8 Letter in the Columbia Collection.
9 Scott, *Bibliography*, p.36.
10 Letter, dated August 28, 1884, in the Columbia Collection.
11 Jackson, *Early Days*, pp.11–12.
12 'The Real *King Solomon's Mines*', p.146.
13 Norman Etherington, 'South African Origins of Rider Haggard's Early African Romances', *Notes and Queries*, (October, 1977), pp.436–438.
14 'The Real *King Solomon's Mines*', p.145.
15 Newman Flower, *Just As It Happened* (1950), p.76.
16 In the A.P. Watt Collection.
17 In Norfolk Record Office.
18 E.F. Knight, *The Cruise of the "Falcon"* (1884), pp.326–327.
19 Newman Flower, 'The Most Amazing Book Ever Written', *The Radio Times*, (June 29, 1956), p.6.
20 *The Saturday Review*, LX (October 10, 1885), p.485.
21 *The Spectator*, LVIII (November 7, 1885), p.1473.
22 *The Athenaeum*, XXXVI (October 30, 1885), p. 568.
23 *Vanity Fair*, XXXVI (November 6, 1885), p.271.
24 *Public Opinion*, XLVIII (October 30, 1885), p.551.
25 Quoted in John Marlowe, *Cecil Rhodes: The Anatomy of Empire* (1972), p.9.
26. Letter in the Huntington Collection (HM43408).
27 Copy of the letter in the Cassell Collection.
28 Draft of letter in the Huntington Collection (HM43538).
29 L. Haggard, *Cloak*, p.91.
30 *Ibid*, p.202.
31 *Ibid*, p.21.
32 Harry How, 'Illustrated Interviews. No. VII: Mr. H. Rider Haggard', *Strand Magazine*, III (January, 1892), pp.3–17.
33 Letter in the Lockwood Collection.
34 *Letters Addressed to A.P. Watt* (1894), pp.28–29.
35 Jackson, *Early Days*, pp.54–56.
36 C.J. Jung, 'On the Relation of Analytical Psychology to Poetry', *The Collected Works of C.J. Jung* (1966), XV, p.73.
37 C.J. Jung, 'The Relations Between the Ego and the Unconscious', *The Collected Works of C.J. Jung* (1966), VII, p.190.
38 Cohen, *Haggard*, p.106.
39 See 'Origin of *She* – Grosvenor Survivors', a letter from F. Steinacher', *The Natal Witness*, February 24, 1907; and 'A Memory of Sir Rider Haggard', a letter from J. Burton Twigg, *John O'London's Weekly*, June 27, 1925, p.433.

NOTES

40   Lord Lytton, *A Strange Story* (1862), Chapter LXXXVII.
41   Letter in the A.P. Watt Collection.
42   Letter from Haggard to A.P. Watt in the A.P. Watt Collection.
43   *The Athenaeum*, No. 3062 (July 3, 1886), p.17.
44   'Fact and Fiction', *The Athenaeum*, No. 3063 (July 10, 1886), p.50.
45   Letter, dated 18 August, 1887, in the Columbia Collection.
46   L. Haggard, *Cloak*, p.16.
47   Letter in Norfolk Record Office.
48   *The Spectator*, LX (January 22, 1887), p.110–111.
49   *The Athenaeum*, No. 3090 (January 15, 1887). p.93
50   *The Pall Mall Budget*, XXXV (January 6, 1887), p.28.
51   'A Letter from London', *The Literary World* (Boston), XVIII (March 5, 1887), p.72.
52   Malcolm Elwin, *Old Gods Falling* (1939), p.16.
53   Henry Miller, *The Books in My Life* (1952), p.81.
54   George Moore, *Vale*.
55   Samuel M. Clark, 'Mr Haggard's Romances', *The Dial*, VIII (May, 1887), pp.5–7.

CHAPTER SIX

1   James Hepburn, *The Author's Empty Purse* (1968), p.20.
2   Quoted in L. Haggard, *Cloak*, p.131.
3   Quoted in L. Haggard, *Cloak*, p.132.
4   *Ibid*, p.133.
5   'Who is "She" and Where Did "She" Come From?', *Pall Mall Gazette*, XLV (March 11, 1887), pp.102.
6   'The Song of *Jess* and Who Wrote It', *Pall Mall Gazette*, XLV (March 24, 1887).
7   'The Strange Cases of *She* and *Jess*', *Pall Mall Gazette*, XLV (March 26, 1887), p.3.
8   'Can Mr Rider Haggard Write?', *Court and Society*, IV (March 30, 1887), p.305.
9   'The Ethics of Plagiarism', *Pall Mall Gazette*, XLV (March 30, 1887).
10   'Mr Rider Haggard and the Song in *Jess*', *Whitehall Review* (March 31, 1887), p.7.
11   'Literary and Art Notes', *Pall Mall Gazette*, XLV (April 15, 1887), p.3.
12   'The Ethics of Plagiarism', *Pall Mall Gazette*, XLV (April 3, 1887), p.3.
13   'The Song of *Jess* and How She Came by It', *Pall Mall Gazette*, XLV (April 19, 1887), p.5.
14   In Norfolk Record Office (MS4692/38).
15   August M. Moore, 'Rider Haggard and "The New School of Romance"', *Time*, XVI (May, 1887), pp.513–524.
16   Letter in the Lockwood Collection, quoted in Cohen, *Haggard*, p.127.
17   *Ibid*, p.128.
18   Clark, 'Romances', p.5.
19   'Hee-Hee!', *Punch*, (February 26, 1887). Among the other parodies that appeared in *Punch* were 'A Proposition and a Rider' (April 2, 1887); 'Adam Slaughterman' (August 27, 1887); 'The Doom of She' (March 31, 1888); and 'She-That-Ought-Not-To-Be-Played' (22 September, 1888).
20   Letter, dated 10 May, 1887, in Norfolk Record Office (MS4694/31/4).
21   Letter in the A.P. Watt Collection.
22   'Literary Plagiarism', *The Contemporary Review*, VI (June, 1887), pp.831–840.
23   Quoted in J. Runciman, 'King Plagiarism and His Court', *The Fortnightly Review*, CCCXXVII (March, 1890). p.426.
24   Scott in his *Bibliography* wrongly states (p.42) that the verses were omitted from the second and all subsequent editions.
25   'Gavin Ogilvy', *The British Weekly*, II (August 5, 1887), p.218.

26 *The Theatre*, X (August 1, 1887), pp.100–101.
27 Letter, dated August 18, 1887, in the Columbia Collection.
28 *Ibid*.
29 Agreement in the A.P. Watt Collection.
30 *Ibid*.
31 George Saintsbury, 'The Present State of the Novel', *The Fortnightly Review*, XCII (1887), pp.410–416.
32 Jackson, *Early Days*, pp.124–125.
33 *Ibid*, p.123.
34 'The Culture of the Horrible: Mr Haggard's Stories', *The Church Quarterly Review*, XXV (January, 1888), pp.389–411.
35 *The Athenaeum*, No. 3552 (November 23, 1895), pp.709–710.
36 *The Private Diaries of Sir H. Rider Haggard*, p.26.
37 'The Fall of Fiction', *The Fortnightly Review*, L (September 1, 1888), pp.324–336.
38 The play, written by Wm. Sidney and Clo Graves, was produced by Sophie Eyre, who also played the title role.
39 *Private Diaries*, p.23.
40 'Mr Haggard and His Henchman', *The Fortnightly Review*, CCLXIII (November, 1888), pp.684–688.
41 Letter in the Huntington Collection (HM43634).
42 *The Scots Observer*, I (December 22, 1888), p.137.
43 Ralph Bergen Allen, *Old Icelandic Sources in the English Novel* (1933), p.81.
44 Andrew Lang, 'The Dreadful Trade', *The Scots Observer*, I (February 16, 1889), pp.356–357.
45 Letter in the Columbia Collection.
46 Lang asks for the book back in a letter dated June 12, – . (In the Columbia Collection.)
47 W.E. Henley, 'Modern Men', *The Scots Observer*, I (April 27, 1889), pp.631–632.
48 Letters in the Columbia Collection.
49 'London Letter', *The Critic*, VII (February 12, 1887), p.78.
50 'Romance and Farce', *The Scots Observer*, II (July 27, 1889), pp.275–276.
51 John Connell, *W.E. Henley* (1949), p.168.
52 Letters in the Lockwood Collection.
53 C.E. Carrington, *The Life of Rudyard Kipling* (1955), p.108.
54 Horatio F. Brown, ed., *Letters and Papers of John Addington Symonds* (1923), p.228.
55 Rudyard Kipling, *Something of Myself* (1937), p.85.
56 Letter in the Columbia Collection.
57 Morton Cohen, *Rudyard Kipling to Rider Haggard* (1965), pp.31–32.
58 Stephen Spender, 'The Making of a Poem', *Partisan Review*, XIII (1946), No. 3.
59 L. Haggard, *Cloak*, p.21.

CHAPTER SEVEN

1 Letter, dated August 21, 1903, in the Huntington Collection (HM43651).
2 Ella Haggard, *Life and Its Author* (1890). Haggard's preface, 'In Memoriam', is dated February 5, 1890.
3 The play was adapted by Eweretta Lawrence (who played Jess) and J.J. Bisgood.
4 Letter in the Columbia Collection.
5 Letters to Aggie in the Columbia Collection.
6 'Culture and Anarchy', *The National Observer*, V (December 13, 1890), pp.99–100.
7 *The British Weekly*, IX (November 20, 1890), p.54.
8 Letters in the Columbia Collection.
9 Letter in the Lockwood Collection, quoted in Cohen, *Haggard*, p.218.

NOTES

10 'Rider Haggard Here', *New York Times*, XL (January 11, 1891), p.8.
11 L. Haggard, *Cloak*, pp.154–155.
12 *Ibid*, p.156.
13 *Ibid*, p.155.
14 Cohen, *Kipling to Haggard*, p.30.
15 Letter, dated October 13, 1891, in the Huntington Collection.
16 Letter in the A.P. Watt Collection.
17 Letter in the Huntington Collection (HM43489).
18 Letter in the Huntington Collection.
19 Quoted in *The Critic*, XVIII (July 9, 1892), p.23.
20 Letter in the Columbia Collection.
21 *Ibid*.
22 'A New Argument Against Cremation!', *The Times*, (December 19, 1892).
23 Letter in the Norfolk Record Office (MC32/36).
24 Mrs John Gladwyn Jebb, *A Strange Career: Life and Adventures of John Gladwyn Jebb* (1895), p.xxiii.
25 Letter in the Columbia Collection.
26 Quoted in 'How Mr Rider Haggard Works', *Review of Reviews*, IX (January, 1894), p.31.
27 The letters are included in 'Mr. Rider Haggard and the Immuring of Nuns', *Pall Mall Gazette* (January 17, 1894), pp.102.
28 Letter in the Norfolk Record Office (MS4694/31/9).
29 Letters quoted in Scott, *Bibliography*, pp.71–72.
30 'Alfred conceived the plan of obtaining some great concession of land and minerals from Lobengula. He was, I recollect, angry with me because I would not enter into his scheme with enthusiasm.' *Days*, II, p.115.
31 L. Haggard, *Cloak*, pp.168–169.
32 Letter in the Huntington Collection (HM43449).
33 *Ibid*, (HM43450).
34 'Mr Rider Haggard as Politician', *The Saturday Review*, 79 (March 23, 1895), pp.372–373.
35 Alfred Wilcox, 'Mr H. Rider Haggard at Ditchingham', *The Cable*, (May 11, 1895), p.297.
36 'The Rioting in East Norfolk', *Pall Mall Gazette*, (July 25, 1895), p.3.
37 In the Norfolk Record Office (MS4694/2/22).
38 Letter in the Huntington Collection (HM43406).
39 'Tumble of Liberals', *New York Times*, XLIV (July 28, 1895), p.1.
40 L. Haggard, *Cloak*, p.190.
41 *The Times*, December 12, 1895.
42 L. Haggard, *Cloak*, pp.189—190.
43 Letter in the Huntington Collection (HM43453).
44 Letter in the Columbia Collection.
45 Cohen, *Kipling to Haggard*, pp.33–34.
46 Letter in the Columbia Collection.
47 Letter in the Jackson Collection at the Royal Commonwealth Society.
48 Quoted in L. Haggard, *Cloak*, p.191.
49 Letter in the Columbia Collection.
50 *Ibid*.
51 Katherine Pearson Woods, 'The Evolution of an Artist', *Bookman* (U.S.A.), (June, 1899,) pp.350–352.
52 *The Athenaeum*, LI (January 6, 1900), p.21.
53 *The Literary World*, LXI (March 23, 1900), pp.273–274.

54 *New York Times*, XLVIII (August 19, 1899), p.55.
55 Letter in the Columbia Collection.
56 Letters in the Huntington Collection.

CHAPTER EIGHT

1   Letter in the A.P. Watt Collection.
2   Letter in the Huntington Collection.
3   L. Haggard, *Cloak*, p.182.
4   Letter in the Columbia Collection.
5   *The Review of Reviews*, XXIII (May, 1901), p.504.
6   'Small Holdings', *The Times*, November 8, 1901.
7   Cohen, *Kipling to Haggard*, p.47.
8   Letter in the Columbia Collection.
9   'The Needs of Rural England', *The Quarterly Review*, CXCVII (April, 1903), pp.540–568.
10 'Mr Rider Haggard's "Rural England"', *The Spectator*, XC (February 14, 1903), pp.540–568.
11 Cohen, *Kipling to Haggard*, p.49.
12 Letter in the Huntington Collection.
13 Correspondence in the author's collection.
14 Letter in the Huntington Collection (HM43692).
15 Copies of letters in the Huntington Collection.
16 Letter in the Columbia Collection.
17 Copy of letter in the Huntington Collection.
18 Copies of correspondence in the Columbia Collection.
19 The original title was *Renunciation*, but this, according to Haggard, did not please Kipling.
20 Cohen, *Kipling to Haggard*, p.53.
21 *Ibid*, pp.55–57.
22 Letter in the Huntington Collection (HM43640).
23 'H. Rider Haggard Turned Colonizer', *The New York Herald*, (March 19, 1905), p.3.
24 L. Haggard, *Cloak*, pp.188–189.
25 Letter in the author's collection.
26 This review, with many others, is reprinted in *The Poor and the Land*.
27 'Character Sketch – Commissioner H. Rider Haggard', *Review of Reviews*, XXXII (July, 1905), pp.21–27.
28 Letter in the Huntington Collection.
29 'Where is Mr Haggard?', *Review of Reviews*, XXXIII (January, 1906), pp. 9–10.
30 L. Haggard, *Cloak*, p.185.
31 A.D., 'An Interview with Mr H. Rider Haggard', *The Christian Commonwealth*, (November 1, 1906), pp.75–76.
32 Letter in the A.P. Watt Collection.
33 Letter in the Huntington Collection (HM43641).
34 Letter in the Huntington Collection.
35 Letters in the author's collection.
36 Letter in the Norfolk Record Office (MC 32/39/3).
37 L. Haggard, *Cloak*, p.202.
38 Letters in the A.P. Watt Collection.
39 L. Haggard, *Cloak*, p.189.
40 *Ibid*, p.19.

NOTES

41 *Ibid*, p.199.
42 Haggard had met Hays Hammond, an explorer and mining-engineer, while travelling across America in 1905.
43 Letter in the Huntington Collection.
44 Letters in the Huntington Collection.
45 Letter in the A.P. Watt Collection.
46 Letter in the Huntington Collection.
47 Letter in the Norfolk Record Office (MC 32/39/10).
48 *Ibid*, (MC 32/39/20).
49 Letter in the Lockwood Collection.
50 Letters in the A.P. Watt Collection.
51 Letter in the Norfolk Record Office (MC 32/39/24).
52 *Ibid*, (MS 4694/2/17).

CHAPTER NINE

1   Cohen, *Kipling to Haggard*, p.74.
2   Letter in the Columbia Collection.
3   Cohen, *Kipling to Haggard*, pp.75–76.
4   'Sir Rider Haggard – Fiction Writing and Agriculture', *The Age* (Melbourne), (February 18, 1913).
5   'Sir Rider Haggard – The Author of "King Solomon's Mines" ', *The Lyttelton Times*, (March 1, 1913), p.13.
6   Original in the possession of Commander E.M. Cheyne.
7   Letters in the Huntington Collection.
8   Letter in the A.P. Watt Collection (written by Miss Hector and signed by Haggard).
9   Cohen, *Kipling to Haggard*, p.80.
10 Oscar Asche, *Oscar Asche – His Life* (n.d.), p.157.
11 Letter in the Huntington Collection.
12 L. Haggard, *Cloak*, p.220.
13 *Ibid*, p.222.
14 *Asche*, p.159.
15 Letter in the Berg Collection, quoted in Cohen, *Haggard*, pp.268-269.
16 Cohen, *Kipling to Haggard*, p.88.
17 Letter in the Norfolk Record Office (MC 32/39/29).
18 *Ibid*, (MC 32/39/36).
19 *Ibid*, (MC 32/39/54).
20 L. Haggard, *Cloak*, p.16.
21 Letter in the Norfolk Record Office (MC 32/39/52).
22 Quoted in L. Haggard, *Cloak*, p.256.
23 Letter in the A.P. Watt Collection.
24 Letter in the Huntington Collection.
25 Cohen, *Kipling to Haggard*, pp. 143–144.
26 L. Haggard, *Cloak*, p.279.
27 *Ibid*, p.21.

Bibliography

In this list are given all the most important works on Haggard, including all those cited in the text. For additional material see the bibliography by J.E. Scott.

Unpublished Material

Cassell Collection. Letters and other holograph material owned by Cassell Ltd., 35 Red Lion Square, London WC1R 4SG.

Cheyne Collection. Letters to Haggard in the possession of Commander E.M. Cheyne, Ditchingham House, Bungay, Suffolk.

Columbia Collection. Haggard correspondence in the Columbia University Library, 116th Street & Broadway, New York 10027.

Higgins Collection. Letters and Haggard memorabilia in the possession of the author.

Huntington Collection. Letters and other holograph material in the Henry E. Huntington Library, San Marino, California 91108.

Lockwood Collection. Letters to Haggard in the Lockwood Memorial Library, State University of New York at Buffalo, 3435 Main Street, Buffalo, New York 14214.

Norfolk Collection. A large quantity of material, including holograph manuscripts of the early novels, in the Norfolk Record Office.

Watt Collection. Letters and contracts owned by A.P. Watt & Son, 26/28 Bedford Row, London WC1R 4HL.

Published Material

A.D. 'An Interview with Mr H. Rider Haggard', The *Christian Commonwealth*, (November 1, 1906), pp. 75–76.

African Review, 'Mr Rudyard Kipling', (May 21, 1898), pp. 311–313.

Age (Melbourne), 'Sir Rider Haggard – Fiction Writing and Agriculture', (February 18, 1913), p.1.

ALLEN, Ralph Bergen: *Old Icelandic Sources in the English Novel*, University of Pennsylvania Press, 1933.

A.M.F.R. 'A Letter from London', *Literary World* (Boston), (March 5, 1887), p.72.

BIBLIOGRAPHY

Answers, 'Life Stories of Successful Men – Mr H. Rider Haggard', (June 15, 1895), p.67.

ASCHE, Oscar: *Oscar Asche, His Life*, Hurst & Blackett, n.d.

ASCHERSON, Neal: 'He', *The Spectator*, (August 26, 1968), p.314.

Athenaeum, 'Fact and Fiction', (July 10, 1886), p.50.

BESANT, Walter: 'Chronicle and Comment', *Bookman* (New York), (November, 1895), pp.179–180.

Black and White Illustrated Budget, 'Real Faces and Places in Fiction – Mr Rider Haggard's Umslopogaas', (December 19, 1903), p. 35–36.

BLACKMAN, Aylward M. 'The Nugent and Haggard Collections of Egyptian Antiquities', *Journal of Egyptian Archaeology*, (1917), pp.39–46.

Book Buyer (New York), 'H. Rider Haggard', (May, 1887), pp.156–157.

Book News (Philadelphia), 'H. Rider Haggard', (June, 1890), pp.344–345.

BOWKER, R.R. 'London as a Literary Centre', *Harper's New Monthly Magazine*, (June, 1888), pp.14–15.

BROUGHTON, Mrs G. 'R.K. and Rider Haggard', *The Kipling Journal*, (April, 1956), pp.8–10.

BROWN, Horatio F., ed. *Letters and Papers of John Addington Symonds*, John Murray, 1923.

BRYANT, A.T. *The Zulu People*, Shuter & Shooter (Pietermaritzburg), 1949.

BUCKLEY, Jerome Hamilton: *William Ernest Henley, A Study in 'Counter Decadence' of the 'Nineties*, Princeton University Press.

CALDER, Jenni: *Heroes – From Byron to Guevara*, Hamish Hamilton, 1977.

CARRINGTON, C.E. *The Life of Rudyard Kipling*, Doubleday & Co (New York), 1955.

Church Quarterly Review, 'The Culture of the Horrible: Mr Haggard's Stories', (January, 1888), pp.389–411.

CLARK, Samuel M. 'Mr Haggard's Romances', *Dial*, (May, 1887), pp.5–7.

COHEN, Morton: *Rider Haggard – His Life and Works*, Hutchinson, 1960.

COHEN, Morton: *Rudyard Kipling to Rider Haggard*, Hutchinson, 1965.

COLENSO, Frances E. & DURNFORD, E. *History of the Zulu War*, Chapman & Hall, 1880.

CONNELL, John: *W.E. Henley*, Constable, 1949.

Contemporary Review, 'Literary Plagiarism', (June, 1887), pp.831–840.

CONWAY, William Martin: *Episodes in a Varied Life*, Country Life Ltd., 1932.

Court and Society, 'Can Mr Rider Haggard Write?', (March 30, 1887), p.305.

Critic, 'London Letter', (February 12, 1887), p.78.

Critic, 'Rider the Ripper', (July 9, 1892), p.23.

DARTON, F.J. Harvey: *Children's Books in England*, Cambridge University Press, 1970.

DOLMAN, Frederick: 'Mr Rider Haggard at Home', *Black and White*, (August 11, 1894), pp.178–179.

DOYLE, Brian: *The Who's Who of Children's Literature*, Hugh Evelyn, 1968.

ELWIN, Malcolm: *Old God's Falling*, Hutchinson, 1939.

'ESSARTI': 'Interesting People – H. Rider Haggard', *Winter's Weekly*, (March 19, 1892), pp.337–338.

ETHERINGTON, Norman: 'South African Origins of Rider Haggard's Early African Romances', *Notes and Queries*, (October, 1977), pp.436–438.

FLETCHER, Ian: 'Can Haggard Ride Again?', *The Listener*, (July 29, 1971), pp.136–138.

FLOWER, Newman: *Just As It Happened*, Cassell, 1950.

FLOWER, Newman: 'The Most Amazing Book Ever Written', *Radio Times*, (June 29, 1956), p.6.

Fortnightly Review, 'The Fall of Fiction', (September 1, 1888), pp. 324–326.

Fortnightly Review, 'Mr Haggard and His Henchmen', (November, 1888), pp.684–688.

Forum (New York), 'The Profitable Reading of Fiction', (1888), p.65.

GAMBLE, Peter: 'The Two Rider Haggards', *John O'London's Weekly*, (May 18, 1945), p.6.

Gardener, 'Mr Rider Haggard and His Orchids', (September 23, 1899), p.653.

GISSING, Algernon & Ellen: *Letters of George Gissing*, Constable, 1937.

Graphic, 'A Chat with Mr Rider Haggard', (July 29, 1905), pp.124–125.

GREEN, Roger Lancelyn: *Tellers of Tales*, Edmund Ward, 1946.

GREENE, Graham: *The Lost Childhood and Other Essays*, Eyre & Spottiswoode, 1954.

GROSS, John, ed. *Rudyard Kipling — The Man, His Work and His World*, Weidenfeld & Nicolson, 1972.

HAGGARD, Lilias Rider: *The Cloak That I Left*, Hodder & Stoughton, 1951.

HAGGARD, Lilias Rider: 'The Real Rider Haggard', *Pearson's Magazine*, (January, 1935), pp. 29–33.

HAGGARD, Henry Rider: 'About Fiction', *Contemporary Review* (February, 1887), pp.172–180.

HAGGARD, Henry Rider: 'Books Which Have Influenced Me', *British Weekly Extra*, No. 1., n.d.

HAGGARD, Henry Rider: 'An English Garden', *Black and White*, (May 5, 1906), p.614.

HAGGARD, Henry Rider: 'In the Transvaal of 1877', *The Golden Penny*, (April 24, 1897), pp.396–397 & (May 1, 1897), pp.420–421.

HAGGARD, Henry Rider: 'A Journey Through Zululand', *Windsor Magazine*, (December, 1916), pp.85–90.

HAGGARD, Henry Rider: 'My First Book – Dawn', *The Idler*, (March, 1893), pp.279–291.

HAGGARD, Henry Rider: 'On Going Back', *Longman's Magazine*, (November, 1887), pp.61–66.

HAGGARD, Henry Rider: 'The Real *King Solomon's Mines*', *Cassell's Magazine*, (July, 1907), pp.144–151.

BIBLIOGRAPHY

HAGGARD, Henry Rider: 'A Remarkable Service', *The Christian*, (December 15, 1910), p.24.

HAGGARD, Henry Rider: 'The Transvaal', *Macmillan's Magazine*, (May, 1877), pp.71–79.

HAGGARD, Henry Rider: 'A Visit to the Chief Secoceoni', *Gentleman's Magazine*, (September, 1877), pp.302–318.

HAGGARD, Henry Rider: 'A Zulu War Dance', *Gentleman's Magazine*, (July, 1877), pp.94–97.

HAMILTON, Cosmo: *Unwritten History*, Little, Brown & Co. (Boston), 1924.

HENLEY, W.E. 'Modern Men', *The Scots Observer*, (April 27, 1889), pp.631–632.

HEPBURN, James: *The Author's Empty Purse and the Rise of the Literary Agent*, Oxford University Press, 1968.

HINZ, Evelyn J. 'Rider Haggard's *She*: An Archetypal "History of Adventure" ', *Studies in the Novel*, (1972), pp.416–431.

HOW, Harry: 'Illustrated Interviews No. VII – Mr H. Rider Haggard', *Strand*, (January, 1892), pp.3–17.

HUDDLESTON, Sisley: 'A Rider Haggard Boom in France – Has *She* Been Plagiarised?', *John O' London's Weekly*, (May 1, 1920), p.104.

HUTCHINSON, Horace G. 'Sir Rider Haggard's Autobiography', *Edinburgh Review*, (October, 1926), pp.343–355.

JACKSON, Frederick: *Early Days in East Africa*, Dawsons, 1969.

JEAFFRESON, John Cordy: *A Book of Recollections*, Hurst & Blackett, 1894.

JEBB, Mrs John Gladwyn: *A Strange Career; Life and Adventures of John Gladwyn Jebb*, William Blackwood & Sons, 1895.

JOSEPH, M. 'The Romance of Rider Haggard', *John O' London's Weekly* (March 5, 1921), p.572.

Journal of the Society for Psychical Research, 'Case L.1139 Dream', (October, 1904), pp.278–290.

KIPLING, Rudyard: *Something of Myself — For My Friends Known and Unknown*, Macmillan, 1937.

KOTZÉ, John: *Biographical Memoirs and Reminiscences*, Maskew Miller (Cape Town), m.d.

LANG, Andrew: 'The Dreadful Trade', *The Scots Observer*, (February 16, 1889), pp.356–357.

LANG, Andrew: 'Literary Plagiarism', *The Contemporary Review*, (June, 1887), pp.831–840.

Letters Addresses to A.P. Watt, A.P. Watt & Son, 1894.

LEYDS, E.J. *The First Annexation of the Transvaal*, T. Fisher Unwin, 1906.

Listener, 'A Born Story-Teller', (June 22, 1961), p.1078.

Literary World, 'Mr H Rider Haggard', (March 15, 1906), pp.121–122.

Literary World (Boston), ' "Squire" Rider Haggard at Home', (November 10, 1888), pp.393–394.

LONGMAN, Charles James: *The House of Longman (1724–1800)*, Longmans, Green & Co., 1936.

Lyttelton Times, 'Sir Rider Haggard – The Author of *King Solomon's Mines*', (March 1, 1913), p.13.

MACDONALD, Duff: *Africana; or, The Heart of Heathen Africa*, Simpkin Marshall & Co., 1882.

METHUEN, Henry H. *Life in the Wilderness: or Wanderings in South Africa*, Richard Bentley, 1846.

MICHAEL, Leo: *She, an Allegory of the Church*, Frank F. Lovell & Co. (New York), 1889.

MILLER, Henry: *The Books in My Life*, Peter Owen, 1952.

MOORE, Augustus M. 'Rider Haggard and "The New School of Romance" ', *Time*, (May, 1887), p.305.

MOSS, John G. 'Three Motifs in Haggard's *She*', *English Literature in Transition*, (1973), pp.27–34.

NASH, Eveleigh: *I Liked the Life I Lived*, John Murray, 1941.

Natal Mercury, 'Sir Rider Haggard – Talks of Old Durban', (April 18, 1914).

National Observer, 'Culture and Anarchy', (December 13, 1890), pp.99–100.

New York Herald, 'H. Rider Haggard Turned Colonizer', (March 19, 1905), p.3.

New York Times, 'Boers Are Loyal, Says Rider Haggard', (October 18, 1914), p.4.

New York Times, 'Rider Haggard Here', (January 11, 1891), p.8.

New York Times, 'Tumble of Liberals', (July 28, 1895), p.1.

NORTHROP, W.B. 'H. Rider Haggard: Story-Writer and Psychologist', *Cassell's Magazine*, (1908), pp.478-481.

NOWELL-SMITH, Simon: *The House of Cassell, 1848-1958*, Cassell & Co., 1958.

O'BRIEN, E.D. 'The Adventurous Life of a Great Storyteller', *Illustrated London News*, (May 26, 1951), p.857.

'OGILVY, Gavin' (J.M. Barrie): 'H. Rider Haggard', *The British Weekly*, (August 5, 1887), p.218.

Pall Mall Gazette, 'The Ethics of Plagiarism', (March 30, 1887), p.3.

Pall Mall Gazette, 'The Ethics of Plagiarism', (April 3, 1887), p.3.

Pall Mall Gazette, 'Literary and Art Notes', (April 15, 1887), p.3.

Pall Mall Gazette, 'Mr Rider Haggard and the Immuring of Nuns', (January 17, 1894), pp.1-2.

Pall Mall Gazette, 'The Rioting in East Norfolk', (July 25, 1895), p.3.

Pall Mall Gazette, 'The Song of *Jess* and How She Came By It', (April 19, 1887), p.5.

Pall Mall Gazette, 'The Strange Cases of *She* and *Jess*', (March 26, 1887), p.3.

Pall Mall Gazette, (Who is *She* and Where Did *She* Come From', (March 11, 1887), pp.1-2.

PARTINGTON, Wilfred: 'Champion of the British Farmer', *Farmers Weekly*, (September 11, 1936), p.25.

PEMBERTON, Max: *Sixty Years Ago and After*, Hutchinson & Co., 1936.

BIBLIOGRAPHY

Quarterly Review, 'The Needs of Rural England', (April, 1903), pp.540–568.

RANDELL, Wilfred L. 'Sir H. Rider Haggard and His Work', *The Bookman*, (August, 1922), pp.206–207.

Review of Reviews, 'Character Sketch – Commissioner H. Rider Haggard', (July, 1905), pp.21–27.

Review of Reviews, 'How Mr Rider Haggard Works', (January, 1894), p.31.

Review of Reviews, 'Where is Mr Haggard?', (January, 1906), pp.9–10.

RUNCIMAN, J. 'King Plagiarism and His Court', *The Fortnightly Review*, (March, 1890), p.426.

SAINTSBURY, George: 'The Present State of the Novel', *The Fortnightly Review*, (1887), pp.410-416.

SANDISON, Alan: *The Wheel of Empire*, Macmillan, 1967.

Saturday Review, 'The Modern Novel', (1882), pp.633-634.

Saturday Review, 'Mr Rider Haggard as Politician', (March 23, 1895), pp.372–373.

Scots Observer, 'Modern Men', (April 27, 1889), pp.631–632.

SCOTT, J.E. *A Bibliography of the Works of Sir Henry Rider Haggard, 1856—1925*, Elkin Mathews Ltd., 1947.

SCOTT, J.E. 'Hatchers-out of Tales', *New Colophon*, (1948), pp.348–356.

S.D. 'Ride On, Sir Knight, Ride ON!', *John O' London's Weekly*, (November 17, 1923), p.242.

SELOUS, Frederick Courteney: *A Hunter's Wanderings in Africa*, Richard Bentley & Son, 1894.

SHAND, Alex Innes: 'The Novelists and Their Patrons', *The Fortnightly Review*, (1886), pp.23–35.

SHANKS, Edward: 'Sir Rider Haggard and the Novel of Adventure', *The London Mercury*, (November, 1924), pp.71–79.

Spectator, 'Mr Rider Haggard's *Rural England*', (February 14, 1903), pp.540–568.

Spectator, 'Reality and Romance', (April 28, 1888), pp.569–571.

'THEOPHILUS': 'To the Author of *She*', *Month*, (September, 1888).

THURSTON, Herbert: 'Mr Rider Haggard and the Immuring of Nuns', (January, 1894), pp.14–29.

Times, 'Sir H. Rider Haggard, His Life and Career', (May 25, 1925), p.19.

TOWNSEND, John Rowe: *Written for Children*, Kestrel Books, (1974).

Transvaal Leader, 'S. Africa and the Empire – Sir Rider Haggard and Jess Cottage', (March 31, 1914), p.7.

TWIGG, J. Burton: 'A Memory of Sir Rider Haggard', *John O' London's Weekly*, (June 27, 1925), p.433.

United Empire, 'Empire Land Settlement', (1916), pp.784-797.

United Empire, 'Sir Rider Haggard's Great Tour – What It Means and What It Has Effected', (September 1916), pp.607–627.

WALPOLE, Hugh: 'Sir Henry Rider Haggard', *Dictionary of National Biography*, Oxford University Press, 1937.

WHEELER, Paul Mowbray: 'H. Rider Haggard', *Georgia Review*, (1966), pp.213–219.

WILCOX, Alfred: 'Mr H. Rider Haggard at Ditchingham', *The Cable*, (May 11, 1895), pp.372–373.

WILSON, Angus: *The Strange Ride of Rudyard Kipling – His Life and World*, Secker & Warburg, 1977.

WOODS, Katherine Pearson: 'The Evolution of an Artist', *Bookman* (U.S.A.), (June, 1899), pp.350–352.

ZWEIG, Paul: *The Adventurer*, J.M. Dent & Sons, 1974.

Index

Subheadings in the index are generally given in chronological order. Where this is impossible to determine, or irrelevant, they are given in alphabetical order.

Throughout the index Rider Haggard is referred to as HRH. His works are given as independent entries; works by other people are entered under the author's name.

INDEX

INDEX